Eating Disorders

Eating Disorders

Understanding Causes, Controversies, and Treatment

Volume 2: N–Z

JUSTINE J. REEL, EDITOR

An Imprint of ABC-CLIO, LLC

Santa Barbara, California • Denver, Colorado

Library of Congress Cataloging-in-Publication Data

Names: Reel, Justine J., editor.
Title: Eating disorders : understanding causes, controversies, and treatment
   / Justine J. Reel, editor.
Description: Santa Barbara, California : Greenwood, an imprint of ABC-CLIO,
   LLC, [2018] | Includes bibliographical references and index.
Identifiers: LCCN 2017046933 (print) | LCCN 2017048728 (ebook) | ISBN
   9781440853012 (eBook) | ISBN 9781440853005 (set : alk. paper) | ISBN
   9781440853029 (volume 1 : alk. paper) | ISBN 9781440853036 (volume 2 :
   alk. paper)
Subjects: LCSH: Eating disorders—Diagnosis. | Eating disorders—Treatment.
Classification: LCC RC552.E18 (ebook) | LCC RC552.E18 E293 2018 (print) | DDC
   616.85/26--dc23
LC record available at https://lccn.loc.gov/2017046933

ISBN: 978-1-4408-5300-5 (set)
       978-1-4408-5302-9 (vol. 1)
       978-1-4408-5303-6 (vol. 2)
       978-1-4408-5301-2 (ebook)

22 21 20 19 18   1 2 3 4 5

This book is also available as an eBook.

Greenwood
An Imprint of ABC-CLIO, LLC

ABC-CLIO, LLC
130 Cremona Drive, P.O. Box 1911
Santa Barbara, California 93116-1911
www.abc-clio.com

This book is printed on acid-free paper ∞

Manufactured in the United States of America

This book is dedicated to my mentor, friend and colleague, Dr. Carole Oglesby. Carole has been there for me personally and professionally every step of my journey. She has made a game changing impact on girls and women in sport as well as female faculty members and leaders. Carole, you helped me secure a faculty position at West Chester University and Temple University when no one was hiring recently graduated PhDs. Carole, we will always remember the symphony in Philadelphia and hiking in Yosemite with fondness. You are one in a million and we will always love you.

Contents

Acknowledgments   *xvii*

Introduction   *xix*

Chronology   *xxiii*

VOLUME 1

Academy for Eating Disorders   1

Acceptance and Commitment Therapy   2

Adolescent Development   4

Advocacy Groups   10

Aerobics   16

Aesthetic Sports   18

Aging and Body Image   22

Airbrushing   26

Alexithymia   27

Amenorrhea   28

Anorexia Athletica   30

Anorexia Nervosa   32

Anxiety Disorders   36

Art Therapy   38

Assertiveness Training   39

Assessment   40

ATHENA   47

Athletic Trainers   48

Avoidant/Restrictive Food Intake Disorder   50

Ballet   55

Bariatric Surgery   57

Bigorexia   58

Binge Eating Disorder   59

Binge Eating Disorder Association   63

Body Alienation   64

Body Avoidance   67

Body Checking   68

Body Distortion   70

Body Dysmorphic Disorder   72

Body Esteem   74

Body Image   76

Body Image Globally   81

Body Image in Males   92

Body Mass Index   98

Bodybuilding   100

BodyWorks   102

Books about Eating Disorders   104

Bulimia Nervosa   107

Carpenter, Karen   111

Causes   112

Celebrities and Eating Disorders   116

Cheerleading   122

Children and Adolescents   125

Coaches   129

Cognitive Behavioral Therapy   132

Cognitive Behavioral Therapy Guided Self-Help Treatment   135

Cognitive Dissonance Interventions   138

Comorbidity   141

Coping Skills   143

Cosmetic Surgery and Eating Disorders   146

Dancers   151

Dehydration   153

Dental Complications   155

Depression   157

Detox Diets and Cleanses   158

Diabetes   160

Diagnostic and Statistical Manual of Mental Disorders   164

Diagnostic Interview   166

Dialectical Behavior Therapy   168

Diet Pills   171

Dietary Restraint   173

Disordered Eating   175

Distance Running   176

Diuretics   177

Dolls   180

Dove Campaign for Real Beauty   181

Drill Team/Dance Team   183

Drive for Muscularity   184

Eating Disorder Not Otherwise Specified   191

Eating Disorders Anonymous   192

Edema   193

Electrocardiogram   195

Electrolyte Imbalance   197

Emotional Eating   200

Endurance Sports   201

Energy Availability   204

Equine Therapy   205

Exercise   206

Exercise Dependence   211

Exposure Therapy   214

Eye Movement Desensitization and Reprocessing   217

Fad Diets   221

Family Influences   222

Family Therapy   226

Fat Bias/Fat Discrimination   233

Female Athlete Triad   239

Femininity Ideals   244

Figural Rating Scales   247

Figure Skating   248

Fiji Study   251

Flight Attendants   253

Food Addiction   255

Food Allergies   257

Food Desert   259

Food Phobia   262

Food Security   263

Full of Ourselves   268

Gastrointestinal Complications Associated with Eating Disorders   271

Gender and Sex   274

Gymnastics   276

Hattou Shin Ideal   279

Health at Every Size Approach   280

Health Care Costs of Eating Disorders   282

History of Eating Disorders   285

Impulsivity   289

Infertility   290

Integrative Approaches   291

Intellectual Disabilities and Body Image   294

International Association of Eating Disorder Professionals   297

Internet and Eating Disorders   298

Intuitive Eating   301

Intuitive Exercise   305

Jockeys   311

Journaling   313

Ketoacidosis   315

Lanugo   317

Late Life and Late-Onset Eating Disorders   318

Laxative Abuse   319

Legislation on Eating Disorders   321

Leptin   325

Let's Move!   327

Levels of Care   328

Masculinity Ideals   331

Maudsley Family Therapy   333

Media   334

Medical and Health Consequences   337

Medications and Eating Disorders   349

Menopause   350

Military   352

Mindfulness   354

Models and Eating Disorders   356

Mortality Rates   361

Motivational Interviewing   363

Movies and Eating Disorders   365

Muscle Dysmorphia   369

Myth of the "Freshman 15"   374

VOLUME 2

National Eating Disorders Association   381

Neurofeedback   382

Nia   384

Night Eating Syndrome   385

Nutrition Treatment Approaches   387

Nutritional Deficiencies   395

Obesity   399

Objectification Theory   402

Obligatory Exercise   405

Obsessive-Compulsive Disorder   407

Off the C.U.F.F.   410

Oligomenorrhea   411

Operation Beautiful   413

Orthorexia Nervosa   414

Osteoporosis   415

Overeaters Anonymous   417

Paleo Diet   419

Parents   421

Personality Characteristics   427

Personality Disorders   431

Physical Self-Perceptions   433

Pica   437

Picky Eating   438

Planet Health   444

Plus-Size Models and Clothing   446

Post-Traumatic Stress Disorder   449

Pregnancy   452

Prevention   457

Pro-Ana   462

Prognosis   464

Protective Factors   465

Psychodrama   469

Psychodynamic Psychotherapy Approaches   472

Puberty   474

Purging   476

Recovery   479

Refeeding Syndrome   480

Referring Someone for Eating Disorder Treatment   483

Reflections   485

Relapse   486

Religion   490

Residential Treatment   492

Resiliency   495

Risk Factors   500

Rowing   502

Rumination Disorder   504

Selective Eating Disorder   509

Self-Care   510

Self-Help Interventions   511

Self-Injury   515

Self-Presentation Theory   517

Ski Jumping   520

Skin Tone   521

Social Comparison Theory   523

Social Contagion Theory   525

Social Media and Eating Disorders   528

Social Physique Anxiety   532

Somatic Experiencing   534

Sorority Women   536

Sports   537

Students Promoting Eating Disorder Awareness and Knowledge   542

Substance Abuse   543

Suicide   546

Swimming and Synchronized Swimming   548

Tanning Behaviors and Body Image   551

Team Sports   552

Teasing   555

Television Programs and Eating Disorders   557

Therapeutic Recreation   563

Trauma   564

Treatment   566

Twelve-Step Programs   576

Vegetarianism   579

Virtual Reality   580

Visceral Sensitivity   582

Wannarexia   587

Weight Class Sports   588

Weight Manipulation   589

Weight Pressures in Sport   592

Weight Stigma   598

Wrestling   603

Yoga   607

Zinc   611

Controversies and Debates   613

Case Illustrations   653

Glossary   669

Directory of Resources   671

About the Editor and Contributors   679

Index   683

Acknowledgments

Thank you to the contributors and to Maxine Taylor who has served as my developmental editor for the past five years. Your patience in the process as well as your tireless effort to make the work stronger are admirable. I appreciate the unwavering commitment of ABC-CLIO to publish relevant books that offer accessible language for parents, teens, and the general public. Finally, I am grateful to my friends and family members who serve as my biggest cheerleaders.

Introduction

My fascination with eating disorders and body image began in the 1980s after Karen Carpenter died from an eating disorder in 1983. As a teenager, I did recognize any drawbacks to being too thin or being overly disciplined with regard to one's diet. In fact, the term "anorexia nervosa" was new to me, as eating disorders were not discussed in health classes or in blogs. Pro-ana websites and social media did not exist. I understood the emotions and the psyche linked to striving for a different body and wanting to be smaller, blonder, and more attractive to the opposite sex.

As a master's student, my goal was to study weight pressures associated with high school and college cheerleaders that can contribute to body dissatisfaction and disordered eating behaviors. At the time of this publication, I have studied weight pressures among female and male athletes across sports and dance for the past 22 years as a researcher. I have also investigated the influences of age, race/ethnicity, and gender on body image and eating behaviors in a variety of populations. My current research focus has expanded to include the role of exercise in treatment of eating disorders.

As a licensed professional counselor in the states of Utah and North Carolina, I have observed eating disorders from the other side of the office working in residential, inpatient, and outpatient settings. I had the opportunity to help develop the first eating disorder residential treatment program in Salt Lake City and created an exercise education component as part of the treatment and recovery process to address exercise dependence. As a primary therapist, I observed clients who lost their jobs, lost their families, dropped out of school, and/or were hospitalized due to dangerously low potassium levels. I realized that the treatment process resembled a rollercoaster, with some clients improving in the residential setting and showing symptom reduction only to slip when they transitioned to an outpatient level of care. Other clients would begin to develop self-harming behaviors once their eating disorder behaviors subsided.

Being an eating disorder treatment provider is extremely rewarding; however, more recently, I have been focusing on prevention by integrating eating disorder and obesity prevention efforts in programming for adolescents and their parents. I started a student organization at the University of Utah in 2002 called Students Promoting Eating Disorder Awareness and Knowledge to increase awareness about eating disorders and to promote positive body image. Although societal awareness has improved exponentially since Karen Carpenter's death, over 10 million individuals suffer from eating disorders in the United States. Many cases go undiagnosed for years and many individuals are overlooked because they do not meet the traditional stereotype of having an eating disorder—being young, white, thin, and female. It is estimated that 10–25 percent of eating disorder cases are males who have severely deteriorated when they finally present for treatment.

Fortunately, treatment options have improved and now include eating disorder treatment facilities in most states. Treatment continues to be expensive and can run upward of $1,000/day and may not be covered by one's insurance. Families struggle to make decisions on what is affordable versus what is necessary for their daughter's or son's health and survival. Exceptions to this expensive treatment include Eating Disorder Anonymous, a few nonprofit treatment centers, and Overeaters Anonymous, which provide free support groups in communities across the country.

Eating disorders are often oversimplified and misunderstood as being only about eating and food. However, the tendency to develop disordered eating can be attributed to a complex set of factors including biological, genetic, psychological, and social components. A person can be predisposed to develop mental health concerns based on family history. Psychological influences may include the intense emotions underlying a dysfunctional relationship with food, exercise, and the self. Individuals with eating disorders express poor self-esteem, perfectionism, and intense body dissatisfaction. Social factors may include relationships with other people who model dieting behavior or the media, which promotes a message emphasizing the importance of being thin. These media messages can help guide an inner dialogue that focuses on appearance flaws and weight. Having a desire to change the way one looks coupled with exhibiting a strong fear of gaining weight can lead to behaviors such as restricting, purging (e.g., self-induced vomiting, laxatives), or binge eating episodes. The diagnostic categories of eating disorders (anorexia nervosa, bulimia nervosa, and binge eating disorder) seek to classify disorders by symptoms largely for insurance purposes. However, disordered eating behaviors exist along a spectrum, and it is important to recognize that the underlying psychological characteristics and emotions can be interconnected for binge eating and restricting behaviors. Therefore, programs that target the country's obesity epidemic should be careful to address underlying emotional eating; adequate emphasis should be placed on developing a more positive relationship with food and with one's body. In this volume you will read about a few prevention programs, such as Healthy Buddies and Full of Ourselves, which seek to promote health and prevent eating disorders.

Finally, the volume includes information about how to refer someone who is suspected of having an eating disorder. Being a friend or family member can be extremely difficult, so to help them eating disorder resources are provided as well as specific entries on treatment modalities (e.g., nutritional treatment approaches). Case studies and interviews are presented to illuminate the intricacies associated with various presentations of eating disorders. It should be noted that although patterns exist across individuals with eating disorder symptoms, each person is and should be treated as an individual and unique case.

In sum, as a voice of recovery, an eating disorder researcher, an eating disorder therapist, and the author/editor of this two-volume encyclopedia about the causes, treatment, and prevention of eating disorders, I hope that you will use this book for your own personal and professional needs. If you are writing a research paper you will find the necessary background information here. You will also be able to locate valuable resources and information about how best to support someone with an eating disorder. If you are struggling with an eating disorder you may even see yourself on these pages.

Justine J. Reel, PhD, LPC, CMPC

Chronology

1300s	A female saint, Catherine of Siena (1347–1380), is said to eat "only a handful of herbs each day," representing food refusal and prolonged fasting common among female and male saints from 1200 to 1500.
1686	First medically diagnosed case of anorexia nervosa, a 20-year-old female, is termed by Richard Morton as "nervous atrophy" and described as "a skeleton only clad with skin."
1865	Dunglison's dictionary defines anorexia as "absence of appetite."
1874	British Physician Sir William Gull formally uses the term "anorexia nervosa" (lack of desire to eat due to a mental condition).
1903	Psychiatrist Pierre Janet describes "mixed" eating disorder case of Nadja and emphasizes the obsession with thinness, refusal of food, and secret binges leading to the medical term "bulimia" (derived from Latin meaning "hunger of an ox").
1950s	Binge eating is observed and reported in obesity studies by Dr. Albert Stunkard of the University of Pennsylvania; clients referred to as "compulsive overeaters."
1952	Anorexia nervosa is included in the original *Diagnostic and Statistical Manual of Mental Disorders* as a "psychophysiological reaction."
January 1960	Overeaters Anonymous (OA) is founded by Rozanne S. and two women to provide a twelve-step group that addresses issues related to food.
1968	Anorexia nervosa is listed under special symptoms/feeding disturbances in the *Diagnostic and Statistical Manual of Mental Disorders*, second edition (*DSM-II*).
1978	Hilde Bruch publishes *The Golden Cage* to depict anorexia nervosa for lay audiences.
1980	First classification of eating disorders as a separate section; bulimia nervosa receives first mention as a psychiatric disorder in *Diagnostic and Statistical Manual of Mental Disorders*, third edition (*DSM-III*).
1981	First scientific journal for eating disorders, *International Journal of Eating Disorders,* publishes first volume.

February 1983   Karen Carpenter dies of heart failure associated with anorexia nervosa at age 32.

1985   The Renfrew Center, the first freestanding eating disorder treatment facility, opens its doors in Philadelphia, Pennsylvania.

1985   International Association of Eating Disorder Professionals (IAEDP) is formed to provide training to eating disorder providers.

1987   De Coverley Veale introduces the term "exercise dependence" to describe a negative mood state experienced in the absence of exercise.

1992   The term "binge eating disorder" is formally introduced in the scientific literature by Robert Spitzer in the *International Journal of Eating Disorders*.

1992   Christy Henrich, an Olympic gymnast, dies from complications due to an eating disorder.

1993   Professional organization Academy for Eating Disorders (AED) hosts its first meeting of 33 clinicians and researchers in Tulsa, Oklahoma.

1994   Binge eating disorder (BED) is included in the research criteria for the *Diagnostic and Statistical Manual of Mental Disorders*, fourth edition (*DSM-IV*).

1997   Heidi Guenther, a professional ballet dancer from the Boston Ballet Company, dies from an eating disorder.

2000   Eating Disorders Anonymous (EDA) is formed by Alcoholics Anonymous members in Phoenix, Arizona, to offer a twelve-step group for eating disorders.

2001   National Eating Disorder Association (NEDA), a nonprofit eating disorder organization, is formed to help families.

2002   Students Promoting Eating Disorder Awareness and Knowledge is founded at the University of Utah to conduct eating disorder research and outreach.

2013   The *Diagnostic and Statistical Manual of Mental Disorders*, fifth edition (*DSM-5*) is published with substantial changes to eating disorder and feeding disorder diagnoses. The diagnosis of eating disorder not otherwise specified is eliminated.

NATIONAL EATING DISORDERS ASSOCIATION

The National Eating Disorders Association (NEDA) is a nonprofit organization created to expand eating disorder prevention efforts and access to quality eating disorder treatment. The mission of NEDA is to support individuals and families affected by eating disorders and to stimulate initiatives to treat and prevent eating disorders. Every year, NEDA hosts an annual convention to bring in professional speakers who address treatment professionals, families, and individuals recovering from eating disorders. NEDA also offers research grants to young investigators who desire to advance the field and explore innovative topics related to eating disorders.

History of National Eating Disorders Association

NEDA was formed in 2001 when two existing organizations, Eating Disorders Awareness and Prevention (EDAP) and the American Anorexia Bulimia Association (AABA), merged into one. A national toll-free helpline has been provided since 1999 to help individuals find eating disorder treatment. The organization vision is: NEDA *envisions a world without eating disorders.*

National Eating Disorders Awareness Week

On an annual basis, NEDA promotes a nationwide Eating Disorders Awareness Week every February to raise awareness of eating disorders. Each year has a theme and includes activities to mark the event, including walks to represent the awareness week. Groups around the country at universities, high schools, and treatment centers organize local and regional events to honor the week. For example, the University of Utah hosts Love Your Body Week to promote positive body image and raise eating disorder awareness during the national eating disorders awareness week. Purple ribbons may be worn as a symbol of eating disorders awareness and memorials are held to honor persons lost to eating disorders. During this week, many individuals and families are able to identify there is a problem, seek support for struggles with eating disorders, and find appropriate treatment.

Compared to organizations like the Academy for Eating Disorders and the International Association of Eating Disorder Professionals, which are geared toward treatment professionals and researchers, NEDA helps individuals and families with eating disorders. NEDA has a distinct outreach focus as marked by a national effort to host an eating disorders awareness week and other prevention efforts.

Additionally, NEDA serves as a unique resource for families, friends, coaches, treatment professionals, and educators with articles, videos, and toolkits.

Justine J. Reel

See also: Academy for Eating Disorders; Advocacy Groups; Eating Disorders Anonymous; International Association of Eating Disorder Professionals; Legislation on Eating Disorders

Bibliography

"NEDA." National Eating Disorders Association. Accessed November 18, 2016. https://www.nationaleatingdisorders.org/.

NEUROFEEDBACK

Neurofeedback (NFB)—also called "EEG biofeedback," "neurotherapy," or "neuro-biofeedback"—is a method of biofeedback that uses real-time displays of electro-encephalography to show brain wave activity. The goal of neurofeedback is to train people to gain self-control over electrophysiological processes in the human brain. Neurofeedback uses sensors placed on the scalp to measure activity, with measurements displayed using video displays or sound. The trainee (person receiving the neurofeedback) uses the signals from the displays to obtain information about his or her brain wave activity. When brain wave activity changes in the direction desired by a trainer who is directing the session, a positive reward feedback is given to a trainee. If the change is in the opposite direction from what was intended, then either different feedback is given or the provision of otherwise attained positive feedback is inhibited or blocked. Rewards and reinforcements can be as simple as a change in the pitch of a tone or as complex as a certain type of movement of a character in a video game.

Before an individual begins neurofeedback, a diagnostic test, a quantitative electroencephalogram (QEEG), can be performed to measure and identify abnormal patterns of cortical activity because many neurological and medical disorders are accompanied by such abnormalities. Clinical training with EEG feedback can enable an individual to modify patterns, normalizing brain activity. Neurofeedback practice is growing rapidly with wide acceptance for application in a variety of medical, neurological, and emotional disorders.

History of Neurofeedback

In 1924, Hans Berger, a German psychiatrist, connected two small round disks of metal to a client's scalp and monitored a small current by using a ballistic galvanometer. From 1929 through 1938, Berger published several reports about his studies of EEGs. Much of the modern knowledge regarding neurofeedback is due to his research.

Berger analyzed EEGs through descriptive rather than numerical values. In 1932, Dr. G. Dietsch analyzed seven records of EEG and became the first researcher of quantitative (numerical analysis) EEG (QEEG), widely used today to measure abnormal brain patterns. In 1968, Dr. Joseph Kamiya published his groundbreaking alpha brain wave experiments in *Psychology Today*. Specifically, Kamiya found alpha brain states were related to relaxation, which meant that alpha brain wave training showed potential for alleviating stress and stress-related conditions.

During the late 1960s and early 1970s, Barbara Brown authored several books on biofeedback that increased public awareness about neurofeedback. Brown likened brain wave self-regulation to switching on an electric train. In the past 10 years, neurofeedback has emphasized the significance of deep-state, or alpha-theta, training (nonintellectual, nonverbal, and not available to analysis in one's wakened state). Alpha-theta (deep-state) training has been used in the treatment of various addictions and anxiety. This low frequency training involves accessing painful or repressed memories through an alpha-theta state by accessing nonverbal, nonintellectual material.

Complementary Therapy

Neurofeedback and biofeedback are attractive approaches for individuals seeking alternatives to traditional psychotherapy; they allow a client to have a more active role in his or her health care. Neurofeedback represents a holistic emphasis on body, mind, and spirit and is noninvasive. Finally, neurofeedback engages the body in healing by training the brain to send corrective messages. Therefore, neurofeedback can be useful to treat eating disorders and related concerns as an adjunct to traditional or alternative therapies. Mirasol Eating Disorder Treatment Center in Tucson, Arizona, employs individual neurofeedback sessions at least three times weekly as part of its holistic treatment protocol with a belief that changes in the mind and emotions affect the body, and changes in the body influence the mind and emotions. NFB emphasizes training individuals to self-regulate, gain awareness, increase control over their bodies, brains, and nervous systems, and improve flexibility in physiological response. The positive effects of feedback training enhance health, learning, and performance. In clinical settings, neurofeedback and biofeedback are often combined with adjunctive therapies, including relaxation training, visualization, behavior therapies, client education, and other strategies.

Neurofeedback in Practice

A typical neurofeedback therapy session may be as follows:

1. In a 90-minute intake, a client will complete a questionnaire to identify the complaints. In some cases, a full EEG will be performed and recorded.
2. If a full EEG is advised, the recording is usually conducted on 19–21 sites on the scalp, providing a brain map (QEEG). The brain map is compared to a database to establish areas of over- and underactivity based on brain map averages of individuals in the same age group and sex brackets. Several commercial providers construct the databases.

3. The neurofeedback session involves placing sensors on the head. Feedback may be a certain tone, light, or game that will move and play when particular brain activity is detected. For other brain activity, the tone, light, or game is taken away.
4. A usual course of sessions entails 20–40 visits. At the beginning of each session, a client reports complaints and other mental effects. On the basis of this report, the therapy may be adjusted. In some cases, a client takes a feedback machine home for self-administered sessions.

Professional Standards and Neurofeedback

Neurofeedback and biofeedback rely on well-developed professional guidelines and standards for competent practice. A national certification organization, the Biofeedback Certification Institute of America, lists necessary knowledge and skills and conducts examinations to qualify individuals for certification in general biofeedback and neurofeedback. For more information, please visit www.bcia.org.

Juliann Cook Jeppsen

See also: Integrative Approaches; Treatment

Bibliography

Evans, James, and Andrew Abarbanel. *Introduction to Quantitative EEG and Neurofeedback.* San Diego: Academic Press, 1999.

Freeman, Lyn. *Mosby's Complementary & Alternative Medicine: A Research-Based Approach.* Philadelphia: Elsevier Science, 2008.

"Holistic Eating Disorder Treatment." Mirasol. Accessed November 18, 2016. http://www .mirasol.net/blog/holistic-treatment.php.

Kaiser, David. "Basic Principles of Quantitative EEG." *Journal of Adult Development* 12 (2005): 2–3. https://doi.org/10.1007/s10804-005-7025-9.

Yucha, Carolyn, and Doil Montgomery. *Evidenced-Based Practice in Biofeedback and Neurofeedback.* Las Vegas: University of Nevada, 2008.

NIA

Neuromuscular Integrative Action (Nia) is an expressive movement created in 1983 by Debbie and Carlos Rosas. According to its Californian founders, Nia is promotes health using sensory-based movement The original principles of Nia promoted the ability of diverse individuals of all shapes and sizes to connect with the body, mind, emotions, and spirit. Nia instructors are trained to design classes for all age groups, individual needs, and abilities.

The movements of Nia are composed of 9 forms and 52 principles of the martial arts, dance arts, and healing arts. Each category delivers unique components of the original movements. From dance arts, participants experience components of jazz, modern, and Duncan dance. The movements from the healing arts incorporate yoga, Feldenkrais, and Alexander techniques. From the martial arts, participants learn elements of Tai Chi, Tae Kwon Do, and Aikido. Nia movements have been known to soothe and ease the 13 principal joints. The sensations from Nia also stimulate tendons, ligaments, and all 20 digits of the toes and fingers. Additionally,

Nia massages internal organs. Through practicing Nia, individuals improve overall balance and physical strength.

Nia and Eating Disorder Treatment

Nia has been widely adopted as an effective therapeutic tool in the comprehensive treatment of eating disorders. Nia gently provides body–mind awareness and an understanding of the whole body. Through Nia movements, clients are encouraged to observe their thoughts, emotions, and body. The purpose of Nia in eating disorder treatment is to provide a nonjudgmental world to evaluate sensations of pleasure, listen to body cues, and trust the function of body movements. Typically, Nia classes for eating disorder treatment need to be modified based on a client's medical conditions—blood pressure, electrolyte concentrations, EKG, body weight, and bone density. To provide a safe and enjoyable experience in eating disorder treatment, Nia instructors are highly encouraged to complete training in eating disorders.

Nia has been used as a form of fitness and movement for many populations. It has been shown to be beneficial for eating disorder clients, especially as a group therapy option in a structured residential setting. Nia can be modified and individualized for persons of all ages, body shapes and fitness levels, and even for people in different phases of treatment and recovery.

Maya Miyairi

See also: Exercise; Intuitive Exercise

Bibliography

Lowry, Anne. "Nia: The Fountain of Youth?" *New Life Journal* 8, no. 7 (2007): 20.

Mearder, Lori L. "The Nia Technique: Through Movement We Find Health." *The Psychotherapy and Training Collective of New York*. Last modified August 18, 2009. Accessed November 22, 2017. http://www.psychotherapistsnyc.com/20090818.asp.

Oberliesen, Elise. "Freshness Factor Breathes Life into Nia Routine." *American Fitness* 3 (2009): 38–39.

NIGHT EATING SYNDROME

Night eating syndrome (NES) refers to dysfunctional eating patterns that occur relative to the time of day and are linked to obesity in some studies. NES was first described by Stunkard in 1955 as an eating disorder characterized by consumption of foods with low caloric intake in the earlier part of the day (morning anorexia), night eating, evening hyperphagia, and sleep disturbances. The definition of NES has been expanded to include another characteristic—awakening from sleep to eat (nocturnal ingestions). Sleep disruptions and mood disturbances have both been associated with these disordered-eating behaviors. Although NES has not received a separate diagnosis like anorexia nervosa and bulimia nervosa in the eating disorder section of the *Diagnostic and Statistical Manual of Mental Disorders*, fifth edition, it was identified and defined as part of the other specified feeding or eating disorder category in *DSM-5*.

Proposed Diagnostic Criteria for NES

During the First International Night Eating Symposium (April 26, 2008) held in Minneapolis, doctors and other experts developed a set of provisional research diagnostic criteria for NES. As originally conceived, NES was characterized by significant food intake at night. This is measured using the following criteria: at least 25 percent of food intake should have been consumed after the evening meal; at least two episodes of nocturnal eating (awakening from sleep to eat) should have occurred per week; and awareness of the nocturnal eating episodes should be present. Also, at least three of the following features should be reported:

1. Low or no desire to eat in the morning, or no breakfast on four or more mornings per week;
2. Having a strong urge to eat between dinner and sleep onset and/or during the night;
3. Insomnia (difficulty getting to sleep or staying asleep) at least four nights per week;
4. Having the belief one must eat to return to sleep; and
5. Depressed mood or mood deterioration in the evening hours.

To meet the research diagnostic criteria for NES an individual must maintain these dysfunctional patterns of eating for at least three months, and report difficulty participating in daily life activities; moreover, an individual's behavior should not be attributable to other conditions (e.g., substance abuse, medications). It is the hope of these researchers that by having a set of clearly defined criteria, NES can receive recognition and be understood as an eating disorder separate from anorexia nervosa, bulimia nervosa, and binge eating disorder.

Prevalence of NES

The prevalence of NES in the general population appears lower (1.5 percent) than for obesity clinic patients (6–14 percent). In individuals undergoing bariatric surgery the prevalence of NES ranges from 8 to 42 percent. In examining prevalence data, trends have been found for (1) obesity status; (2) age; (3) sex; (4) ethnicity; and (5) day of the week. Although NES is more common in obese individuals, NES does occur in individuals who are not necessarily overweight or obese. Adolescents were most likely to meet NES criteria and the elderly were least likely to exhibit NES symptoms. NES was more common in males than females and black Americans were more likely to experience NES than other races. Interestingly, survey research determined night eating occurs more often on weekends than weekdays.

Assessing Night Eating Syndrome

The Night Eating Questionnaire (NEQ) is a 14-item survey to assess behavioral and psychological symptoms of NES using a five-point Likert scale with responses ranging from "not at all likely" to "very likely." Current items of NEQ measure presence of morning hunger, times when food is consumed, food cravings, and control over food consumption after dinner and throughout the night. Items also assess mood disturbances and night eating.

Night eating syndrome is a less well-known condition associated with eating disorders. Individuals with NES consume vastly different amounts of food from day to night. NES has been included in the *DSM-5* as an example of another specified feeding or eating disorder.

Justine J. Reel

See also: Assessment; *Diagnostic and Statistical Manual of Mental Disorders*

Bibliography

Allison, Kelly C., Scott J. Crow, Rebecca R. Reeves, Della Smith West, John P. Foreyt, Vicki G. DiLillo, Thomas A. Wadden, Robert W. Jeffery, Brent Van Dorsten, and Albert J. Stunkard. "Binge Eating Disorder and Night Eating Syndrome in Adults with Type 2 Diabetes." *Obesity* 15, no. 5 (2007): 1–12. https://doi.org/10.1038/oby.2007.150.

Allison, Kelly C., Jennifer D. Lundgren, John P. O'Reardon, Allan Geliebter, Marci E. Gluck, Piergiuseppe Vinai, James E. Mitchell, Carlos H. Schenck, Michael J. Howell, Scott J. Crow, Scott Engel, Yael Latzer, Orna Tzischinsky, Mark W. Mahowald, and Albert J. Stunkard. "Proposed Diagnostic Criteria for Night Eating Syndrome." *International Journal of Eating Disorders* 43 (2010): 241–247. https://doi.org/10.1002/eat.20693.

Allison, Kelly C., Jennifer D. Lundgren, John P. O'Reardon, Nicole S. Martino, David B. Sarwer, Thomas A. Wadden, Ross D. Crosby, Scott G. Engel, and Albert J. Stunkard. "The Night Eating Questionnaire (NEQ): Psychometric Properties of a Measure of Severity of the Night Eating Syndrome." *Eating Behaviors* 9 (2008): 62–72. http://dx.doi.org/10.1016/j.eatbeh.2007.03.007.

American Psychiatric Association. *Diagnostic and Statistical Manual of Mental Disorders*, 5th ed. (DSM-5). Washington, DC: American Psychiatric Association Publishing, 2013.

Grave, Riccardo Dalle, Simona Calugi, Antonella Ruocco, and Giulio Marchesini. "Night Eating Syndrome and Weight Loss Outcome in Obese Patients." *International Journal of Eating Disorders* 44 (2011): 150–156. https://doi.org/10https://doi.org/10.1002/eat.20786.

Striegel-Moore, Ruth H., Debra L. Franko, Douglas Thompson, Sandra Affenito, Alexis May, and Helena C. Kraemer. "Exploring the Typology of Night Eating Syndrome." *International Journal of Eating Disorders* 41 (2008): 411–418. https://doi.org/10https://doi.org/10.1002/eat.20514.

Townsend, Ann B. "Night Eating Syndrome." *Holistic Nursing Practice* 21, no. 5 (2007): 217–221. https://doi.org/10https://doi.org/10.1097/01.HNP.0000287984.09720.59.

NUTRITION TREATMENT APPROACHES

Nutrition therapy is provided to individuals with medical or mental health illnesses. Nutritional support and treatment is provided by various health care workers; however, a registered dietitian is uniquely trained to provide nutrition therapy and education for diverse populations. A registered dietitian conducts nutrition assessments, implements nutrition interventions, helps normalize eating behaviors, supports an individual through his or her concerns associated with food and weight-related behavioral change, and provides nutrition education.

Nutrition Approaches for Eating Disorder Treatment: An Interview with Kati Joyner

Kati Joyner is a registered dietitian nutritionist and a certified eating disorder registered dietitian who is passionate about helping individuals rebuild a healthy relationship with food and exercise through proper nutrition education and nutrition therapy. Using a nondiet approach, she creates a space where individuals can feel free of judgment and able to explore how their eating habits contribute to their overall health and wellness.

Kati's experience includes working with individuals who are struggling with eating disorders at various levels of care including inpatient, residential, partial hospitalization (PHP), intensive outpatient (IOP), and outpatient. Kati began her career in 2009 working at the Renfrew Center in Charlotte, North Carolina. She and her husband moved to Raleigh, North Carolina, in 2013 where she began working as a clinical dietitian at Veritas Collaborative. In 2016, Kati and her husband decided to move to Wilmington, where she continues to treat eating disorders in private practice.

How did you get into the field of nutrition and eating disorders?

My undergraduate degree was in Health Fitness/Exercise Science with a minor in Women's Studies. One semester I was enrolled in a behavior change class along with a nutrition class and something "clicked." I recognized that nutrition counseling was something that I wanted to do, so, I decided to get my master's degree in Nutrition. While attending graduate school, I began my search for possible careers where I could use my nutrition degree to truly help people on their personal journey to become more balanced, healthy individuals. One of my internship rotations was at an eating disorder treatment facility, and I realized this was a perfect place to provide nutrition education in a supportive and therapeutic role. This was the beginning of my passion for working with individuals who are struggling with eating disorders. Since that time my passion has continued to grow and has never stopped. Every day I feel honored that these strong individuals trust me to be a small part of their recovery process!

What is your role on the treatment team for an eating disorder client?

My role on the treatment team for an eating disorder client is to provide a safe place for that client to explore their relationship with nutrition and exercise. I provide my client with support through nutrition and exercise education, hands-on experience, and a listening ear. I help guide my client in finding ways to add structure, yet flexibility, in their eating and exercise patterns. I support them in moving away from disordered, rigid behaviors and thoughts that are hindering them from meeting a goal of being a balanced and healthy individual. Ways to do this look different for every client depending on individual needs. However, some common things I do are review a client's intake through food logs and provide feedback, support the client in meal planning, and provide food exposures in the office or at restaurants to help with fears of challenge foods and/or social eating. I also listen to beliefs the client has about certain foods or exercise and provide them with evidence-based knowledge. In addition, I keep open communication with the client's treatment team members to ensure we are all supporting the client in working toward the same common goals for recovery.

Please describe the types of issues you see around disordered eating and eating disorders.

Types of issues that I see around disordered eating and eating disorders include all kinds of issues surrounding food and exercise. I see people struggling to find balance, variety, and moderation due to holding themselves to standards that aren't realistic or possible to maintain long term. When trying to meet these standards, individuals go to extremes that are harmful for their body. Extreme measures can involve restricting intake, compulsive exercise, self-induced vomiting, laxative/diuretic use, binge eating, and other harmful behaviors. These extreme measures lead to harmful effects physically, mentally, and emotionally.

When someone sees you for an eating disorder, what are common goals for treatment? Do these goals change depending on the type of eating disorder?

My overall goal for treatment is to normalize eating and exercise patterns by adding variety, balance, and moderation. To accomplish this, I encourage a client to eliminate and neutralize terms relating to food and weight like "good," "bad," "healthy," "unhealthy," "clean," "unclean," etc. These terms are attached to many negative emotions that keep individuals trapped in their disordered thoughts and behaviors. Another goal is to allow the client's body weight to settle at its natural set point instead of trying to reach and maintain a certain "magic number." It's critical for each client to work to let go of any specific numbers they may be focused on and to learn to trust their body. These goals are common goals no matter what eating disorder is being tackled.

What are the treatment strategies you use for someone who has an eating disorder?

Treatment strategies include helping individuals struggling with eating disorders build their own "tool boxes" of coping skills that they can use when needed. From my experiences of working at different treatment facilities, I am able to pull in various therapy techniques during nutrition sessions that include: cognitive behavioral therapy, dialectical behavioral therapy, motivational interviewing, and family-based treatment. I also help clients gain personal confidence, not only through goal setting but through hands-on experiences that could include food exposures and restaurant outings. I think seeing their struggles firsthand, being there to support individuals through their struggles, and helping them process their experiences in the moment can be so critical in their progress. These experiences help them build confidence in their own abilities. In addition, it's so important to support them in building their own support groups outside of their treatment team that include friends, family, coworkers, etc.

How do nutritional needs vary for children versus adults that you treat? Do you use a different approach (e.g., family involvement) for clients based on their age?

Nutritional needs vary for every individual and are based on many factors including age, height, current weight, goal weight, as well as individual nutrition history and eating disorder history. Adolescents typically require increased nutritional needs since they are still growing and developing. It is important that you use the adolescent's individual growth curves to ensure you are returning them to their normal growth pattern. Family involvement is vital for any individual struggling with an eating disorder, however, even more so for adolescents since they strive when provided guidance and boundaries. Eating disorders breed in isolation so the more support that can be enlisted the better.

What suggestions do you give for parents who are concerned that their children are dieting or developing unhealthy eating behaviors?

I would recommend that parents model healthy and balanced eating and exercise behaviors. Children are so sensitive to the environment around them and can very easily pick up on beliefs and behaviors from others. It's so important for parents to openly talk to their children about what they are hearing at school and in the media. National Eating Disorders Association offers great resources for parents if they need help with how to best support their loved one. Early intervention is always best if parents suspect their child could be struggling with an eating disorder.

Nutrition and Eating Disorder Clients

A registered dietitian (RD) is naturally a key component of a comprehensive eating disorder treatment program. It is necessary for an RD to understand the medical and psychological aspects of eating disorders, as she or he is part of a collaborative multidisciplinary treatment team that typically include a psychologist and physician. The specific goals for nutrition therapy can vary depending on an individual and eating disorder, but the ultimate goals are to (1) resolve nutrition-related complications, (2) normalize eating behaviors, (3) decrease fears and anxieties associated with food, and (4) provide education to dispel inaccurate beliefs related to food and weight. Treating eating disorder clients involves conducting a nutritional assessment, setting nutritional goals, implementing meal planning, and providing support for a client's nutritional changes. In addition, an RD will also help identify and monitor a healthy target weight range with frequent weight checks. Although ideally a separate exercise expert (e.g., exercise therapist, physical therapist, personal trainer) would manage exercise behaviors as part of a comprehensive treatment team, an RD often performs this function.

Nutrition Assessment for Eating Disorder Clients

A comprehensive nutrition assessment includes a detailed medical, dietary, weight, and eating disorder history. Additionally, an RD should inquire about any prescription medication, dietary supplements, or other over-the-counter medications that may interfere with nutrition status. The assessment allows an RD to evaluate an individual's current dietary intake (including food preferences and allergies), assess nutritional status, determine a target weight goal for optimal health, and assess nutrition knowledge and beliefs. An RD uses the information gathered from the assessment to determine appropriate treatment for an individual.

Nutrition Goals Specific to Anorexia Nervosa

Because a primary characteristic of anorexia nervosa is a refusal to maintain one's body weight at a minimally normal weight for age and height, an initial step for treatment addresses acute medical complications and the reversal of weight loss. An individual in the early stages of refeeding process to be monitored for complications (e.g., arrhythmia) associated with refeeding syndrome.

There is a risk for refeeding syndrome during the early reintroduction of food, specifically carbohydrates, into the body of a significantly malnourished individual. Refeeding syndrome results from the body adjusting from a catabolic to an anabolic state. As carbohydrates are introduced, the pancreas releases insulin resulting in the cellular uptake of magnesium, potassium, and phosphorus. The sudden drop in the serum concentration of these electrolytes can lead to cardiac complications such as arrhythmias. It is essential individuals who are more than 30 percent below their ideal body weight or who have rapidly lost weight are closely monitored for symptoms of refeeding syndrome. The initial caloric intake for anorexia nervosa treatment may start as low as 30–40 calories/kilogram/day. Once medical stability is established, caloric intake can safely be increased, by gradual increments of 200–300 calories every 3–4 days, to promote a weight gain of 1–3 pounds per week.

Nutrition Goals Specific to Bulimia Nervosa

Bulimia nervosa is characterized by chaotic eating behaviors with episodes of binge eating followed by compensatory behaviors such as self-induced vomiting, excessive exercise, starvation, or use of laxatives/diuretics. Initially, nutrition treatment should focus on a meal plan to reduce episodes of binge eating and purging, balance intake of carbohydrates, proteins, and fats, and normalize biochemical abnormalities. Nutrition education is essential to help an individual with bulimia nervosa understand normal eating and nutritional requirements, as well as the physical and psychological consequences associated with binge eating and compensatory behaviors.

Nutrition Goals for Binge Eating Disorder

Binge eating disorder is characterized by repeated episodes of binge eating, without the compensatory behaviors seen in bulimia nervosa. As in the case of bulimia nervosa, nutrition treatment begins with reducing binge eating episodes as well as following a balanced diet. Chronic dieting is often documented in binge eaters, and, therefore, the negative aspects of chronic dieting need to be discussed. Any medical complications associated with binge eating disorder—such as obesity, heart disease, hypertension, type 2 diabetes, hyperlipidemia—must be addressed as part of treatment.

Meal Planning for Eating Disorder Clients

The early stages of nutrition therapy involve stabilizing acute medical complications, preventing further weight loss, and increasing food intake or decreasing binge eating and/or purging behaviors. Regardless of diagnosis, the purpose of meal planning remains to assist an individual to develop an ability to select a well-balanced diet, in a carefree manner, while incorporating a variety of foods. This may be anxiety-provoking for many individuals; a sense of lost control and fear of excessive weight gain is common. Meal planning is not a permanent solution, rather it provides a way to guide an individual away from disordered-eating behaviors.

Meal plans should be tailored to meet an individual's specific requirements as well as his or her food preferences. Meal plans should have a balance of carbohydrates, proteins, and fats as well as vitamins and minerals. Nutrition status, medical conditions, current dietary intake, growth, and physical activity need to be considered when determining one's overall nutritional needs.

Exchange List for Meal Planning

The exchange list for meal planning was initially developed to help individuals with diabetes mellitus manage intake of carbohydrates and fats. The exchange system organizes foods based on the proportions of carbohydrates, proteins, and fats they contain. Portion sizes allow for the food on each list to have similar energy values. Foods on the same list can be interchanged without affecting total calories and balance of carbohydrates, proteins, and fats.

The exchange list is a popular approach for the treatment of eating disorders; it is a way to encourage clients to eat a balanced meal. Specifically, a client is prescribed a meal plan indicating how many exchanges he or she needs from each food list. A client is allowed more flexibility in making food choices as compared to a rigid meal plan with preset foods; at the same time, adequate nutritional intake is ensured.

Food Guide Pyramid (MyPyramid)

The Food Guide Pyramid was developed to teach nutrition guidelines to the general population. Foods were categorized into six groups and recommendations for the number of servings from each food group were determined. The traditional Food Guide Pyramid was updated in 2005 to individualize the recommended caloric intake for an individual and include physical activity. In 2011, the Food Guide Pyramid/MyPyramid, was replaced with MyPlate. MyPlate is a visual depiction of the 2010 Dietary Guidelines for America and demonstrates how to incorporate all food groups into a meal using a visual of a plate to replace the pyramid. A meal plan constructed from emphasizing categories of food groups can be useful in the treatment of eating disorders and in recovery. Developing healthy meal patterns, while ensuring proper portions of essential nutrients, can support a sustained healthy lifestyle beyond an eating disorder.

Calorie Counting

Individuals with eating disorders often enter treatment compulsively tracking calorie, fat, or carbohydrate intake. Eating disorder clients are often resistant to relinquishing control over the precise nutrient breakdown in the foods they consume. Calorie counting as a nutritional treatment approach may need to be used initially, until an individual is willing to use another method, such as the exchange list, as a meal plan. The sole or continued use of calorie counting may lead to a poor distribution of nutrients in a diet and not address underlying emotional concerns with food. Therefore, other approaches (e.g., intuitive eating) should be the ultimate goal in nutrition therapy with eating-disordered individuals.

Intuitive Eating

Intuitive eating refers to a nutritional philosophy built on recognizing and listening to one's biological cues to make food choices. Intuitive eating allows an individual to rely on internal signals to make food selections without guilt or ethical dilemma. It is important to recognize intuitive eating is not likely to be successful during weight restoration and it may take several months for individuals with anorexia nervosa and bulimia nervosa to detect hunger and fullness cues. However, nutrition therapy allows these individuals to work through becoming comfortable with eating.

Nutrition therapy is not limited to increasing caloric intake and weight restoration. Eating-disordered individuals have a variety of disordered food beliefs and behaviors. It is essential individuals be challenged to evaluate their food rules and behaviors. Individuals will often use an eating disorder to avoid certain foods or food groups. Food challenges are used to allow an individual an opportunity to confront distorted thoughts associated with all foods.

Determining Target Weight Range

Numerous formulas and charts are available to determine an ideal body weight. To calculate an individual's target weight range, it is important for a treatment provider to consider weight history, body composition, genetics, growth state, and physiological state. The body mass index (BMI) is a simple calculation to assess adiposity based on height and weight. BMI has been criticized as a physical marker because it does not differentiate between fat mass and lean body mass and does not consider body frame. BMI is calculated by dividing weight (kg) by height (m^2). These standards consider an individual to be underweight at a BMI of less than 18.5 kg/m^2. In adults, a BMI of 17.5 kg/m^2 is generally accepted as 85 percent of ideal body weight.

The Hamwi equation, developed by Dr. George Hamwi, is another method to calculate an ideal body weight. Height and frame structure are accounted for in this measurement. The formula for men is 106 pounds for the first five feet plus six pounds for every inch over five feet. For women, 100 pounds for the first five feet plus five pounds for every inch over five feet. Ten percent is added or subtracted for a large and small frame, respectively.

The Metropolitan Life Insurance weight charts were developed to determine a desirable weight for a decreased risk of mortality. However, the purpose of these weight charts has shifted to identifying an ideal weight for height and frame size.

The height value is based on height with shoes (1-inch heels) and indoor clothing (5 pounds for men and 3 pounds for women).These weight charts not appropriate for use with children and adolescents.

Ideal weight charts, formulas, and absolute BMI values need to be used cautiously with children and adolescents. They go through periods of growth, resulting in changes in BMI. Target weight ranges need to be adjusted for growth. Pre-illness growth charts can be used as a guide to determine appropriate BMI and weight percentile goals. Target body weight ranges should not be determined using a single formula or chart. Multiple factors need to be considered including weight history, familial weight history, body composition, and physiological and cognitive functionality. Due to natural fluctuations in weight, it is best to recommend a target weight range, rather than an absolute weight.

Weight Restoration Techniques

Complete weight restoration to a healthy weight for one's frame is essential to treat an eating disorder. Maintaining a below-normal weight inhibits psychotherapy, prevents an individual from fully addressing body image concerns, and potentially increases the risk of adverse health effects. Due to the increased caloric requirement for weight restoration, it may be difficult for an individual to rely solely on solid foods. Although using solid foods is most ideal, liquid nutrition support may be necessary in conditions such as (1) persistent failure to gain weight despite oral intake; (2) life-threatening weight loss; (3) worsening psychological state; or (4) unwillingness to cooperate with oral feedings.

Liquid nutrition supplementation can be used orally or enterally (feeding tube). There are several liquid nutrition supplemental drinks that can be consumed orally in conjunction with solid foods. These drinks allow for a balanced source of carbohydrates, proteins, and fats in addition to vitamins and minerals. Oral liquid nutrition supplements should be used when an individual is unable to consume his or her caloric goal due to physical and/or psychological difficulties. Supplemental drinks should be weaned as intake of solid foods allows for weight gain and stabilization at target weight range. In some circumstances, enteral nutrition is necessary to complement oral feedings or provide 100 percent of nutritional needs. Enteral nutrition support allows for the delivery of liquid nutrition via a tube entering the body (through the nasal cavity or the stomach) into the gastrointestinal tract. Nutrition can be delivered to the body continuously through the day and/or night or via bolus feedings (infusion of a larger volume of liquid nutrition supplement— up to 500 mL—into the stomach in a time span of less than 30 minutes) several times during the day. Continuous feeds may inhibit appetite, which can undermine oral intake.

In extreme cases of malnutrition or gastrointestinal disturbances, parenteral nutrition (PN) may be used. PN allows for the delivery of nutrients intravenously rather than through the gastrointestinal tract. This method of feeding is more invasive and consequently leads to a greater risk of infection and complications. Therefore, PN should be reserved for cases in which oral or enteral feeds are not practical.

Exercise

Individuals with eating disorders commonly engage in physical activity that can undermine nutritional goals. Once an individual is medically cleared to participate in physical activity, an RD needs to ensure caloric recommendations are increased according to the level of activity. Nutrition therapy should include education on the importance of nutrition in activity performance. Nutrition rehabilitation is not limited to full weight restoration and appropriate caloric consumption. Ultimately the goal of nutrition therapy is to assist an individual the point where he or she can eat without following a meal plan or engaging in compensatory behaviors; all this while maintaining optimal medical and weight status.

Amelia McBride

See also: Body Mass Index; Exercise; Intuitive Eating; Treatment

Bibliography

Henry, Beverly W., and Amy D. Ozier. "Position of the American Dietetic Associate: Nutrition Intervention in the Treatment of Anorexia Nervosa, Bulimia Nervosa, and Other Eating Disorders." *Journal of American Dietetic Association* 106, no. 12 (2006): 2073–2082. http://dx.doi.org/10.1016/j.jada.2006.09.007.

Reiff, Dan W., and Kathleen Kim Lampson Reiff. *Eating Disorders: Nutrition Therapy in the Recovery Process*, 2nd ed. Mercer Island: Life Enterprises, 2007.

Reiter, Christina Scribner, and Leah Graves. "Nutrition Therapy for Eating Disorders." *Nutrition in Clinical Practice* 25, no. 2 (2010): 122–136. https://doi.org/10https://doi.org/10.1177/0884533610361606.

Setnick, Jessica. *The Eating Disorder Clinical Pocket Guide: Quick Reference for Health Care Providers*. Dallas, TX: Snack Time Press, 2005.

Tribole, Evelyn, and Elyse Resch. *Intuitive Eating: A Revolutionary Program That Works*. New York: St. Martin's Griffin, 2003.

Woolsey, Monika M. *Eating Disorders: A Clinical Guide to Counseling and Treatment*. Chicago, IL: American Dietetic Association, 2002.

NUTRITIONAL DEFICIENCIES

Vitamins and minerals are micronutrients the body requires to function correctly. Food choices and disordered-eating behaviors vary between individuals with eating disorders; therefore, their types of nutrient deficiencies vary. For example, persons who avoid dairy products may have inadequate calcium and vitamin D intake. In addition, many eating disorder clients restrict dietary fat intake that inhibits absorption of fat soluble vitamins A, D, E, and K, leading to vitamin deficiencies. Nutritional deficiencies also result from inadequate dietary intake or from increased losses via fluids (i.e., as a result of vomiting, laxative abuse, or diuretic abuse). Some of the most common nutrient deficiencies are summarized below.

Electrolytes

Electrolytes, such as sodium, potassium, chloride, magnesium, and phosphorus, are affected by many types of weight control methods, including laxative or diuretic abuse, vomiting, excessive exercise, and dietary restriction. Electrolytes must be balanced outside and inside of cells for muscles and nerves to function properly and to maintain acid–base balance. Electrolyte imbalances cause muscle weakness or cramping, fatigue, irregular heartbeat, dizziness, confusion, and even death, if not treated. Electrolyte levels are closely monitored and replenished when nutrition is reintroduced and gradually increased in a malnourished client to assess for refeeding syndrome, in which an influx of electrolytes into cells leads to dangerously low levels of potassium, phosphorus, or magnesium outside of the cells.

Thiamine

Thiamine (vitamin B1) is required to metabolize carbohydrates. Although thiamine is in a wide variety of foods, low overall energy intake may lead to deficiency of this nutrient. Because there is an increased demand for thiamine when nutrition is reintroduced to a malnourished client, nutrition support protocols generally recommend thiamine supplementation when initiating a refeeding regimen to avoid acute thiamine deficiency. Deficiency in thiamine can lead to a syndrome called Wernicke's encephalopathy, characterized by neurological symptoms such as, confusion, lack of muscle coordination, involuntary eye movements, and short-term memory loss. One study found 38 percent of anorexia nervosa clients had laboratory values indicative of thiamine deficiency, and there have been several case reports regarding the diagnosis of Wernicke's encephalopathy in anorexia nervosa clients.

Calcium and Vitamin D

Calcium is a mineral predominantly stored in the bones and teeth to support their function. When blood calcium levels are low, calcium is released from the bone to increase blood levels; therefore, an assessment of serum calcium levels may not accurately indicate calcium status. Because bones weaken when stored calcium is leached into the blood, bone mineral density may be a better marker of calcium deficiency over the long term; calcium intake analysis based on food records could be used for a short-term indication. It is recommended eating-disordered clients who are not consuming adequate calcium, and clients who have amenorrhea, consume 1,500 milligrams per day. Calcium supplementation is often required until dietary intake is sufficient.

Similarly, vitamin D also plays a role in bone health by promoting calcium absorption from the gut, reabsorption of calcium by the kidneys, and the maintenance of blood calcium levels. It also supports immune function and is currently studied for its role in decreasing the risk for autoimmune diseases (e.g., type 1 diabetes, multiple sclerosis, rheumatoid arthritis) and certain types of cancer. Sunlight is the main natural source of vitamin D as it activates vitamin D synthesis in the body. There are few natural food sources of vitamin D, but many dairy products are fortified with vitamin D. Individuals who avoid dairy products include very little fat in their diet and receive very little sunlight exposure are at high risk for vitamin D deficiency. Many calcium supplements also contain vitamin D, but additional supplementation should be provided if vitamin D laboratory values are low.

Zinc

Zinc is a mineral with numerous physiological functions, including growth and development, immunity, neurological function, taste perception and appetite, and reproduction. Symptoms of zinc deficiency are stunted growth, weight loss, increased infection risk, poor wound healing, menstrual dysfunction, poor appetite, altered taste, and mood disturbances. One study found 40 percent of bulimia nervosa clients and 54 percent of anorexia nervosa clients had poor zinc status. In addition, vegetarian clients with anorexia nervosa, which describes approximately half this population, have been found to have lower dietary intake of zinc than anorexia nervosa clients who are not vegetarian, as red meat and certain types of seafood are rich in this mineral. Zinc is also not absorbed as well from meatless sources, such as whole grains, nuts, vegetables, and legumes, due to the high fiber content; thus, zinc requirements may be higher for persons who do not consume meat products. The body can also lose significant zinc with high stool output and other fluid losses as described above. Some research has shown anorexia nervosa clients who receive zinc supplementation have a higher rate of weight gain than clients who do not receive supplementation.

Iron

Iron is in red blood cells, transports oxygen to parts of the body. Iron consumption may be absent in eating-disordered individuals who follow vegetarian or vegan diets, as iron from plant sources is not absorbed as well as iron from meat sources. However, vitamin C enhances iron absorption; thus, it is beneficial to eat iron-containing foods with foods or beverages with high vitamin C content. Iron deficiency can lead to fatigue, difficulty in concentration, and increased risk for illnesses or infections. It is unclear whether eating disorder clients are at a higher risk for iron deficiency as research results have varied and it has been suggested amenorrhea may protect against iron deficiency anemia due to reduced blood loss. During nutritional recovery, however, iron needs may increase as tissues are rebuilding and more red blood cells are produced.

Holly E. Doetsch

See also: Electrolyte Imbalance; Medical and Health Consequences; Refeeding Syndrome; Zinc

Bibliography

Bakan, Rita, Carl L. Birmingham, Laurel Aeberhardt, and Elliot M. Goldner. "Dietary Zinc Intake of Vegetarian and Nonvegetarian Patients with Anorexia Nervosa." *International Journal of Eating Disorders* 13, no. 2 (1993): 229–233. https://doi.org/10.1002/1098-108X(199303)13:2<229::AID-EAT2260130211>3.0.CO;2-1.

Birmingham, Carl L., Elliot M. Goldner, and Rita Bakan. "Controlled Trial of Zinc Supplementation in Anorexia Nervosa." *International Journal of Eating Disorders* 15, no. 3 (1994): 251–255. https://doi.org/10.1002/1098-108X(199404)15:3<251::AID-EAT2260150308>3.0.CO;2-#.

Humphries, Laurie, Beverly Vivian, Mary A. Stuart, and Craig J. McClain. "Zinc Deficiency and Eating Disorders." *Journal of Clinical Psychiatry* 50, no. 12 (1989): 456–459.

Kennedy, Andrew, Michael Kohn, Ahti Lammi, and Simon Clarke. "Iron Status and Haematological Changes in Adolescent Female Inpatients with Anorexia Nervosa." *Journal of Paediatrics and Child Health* 40, no. 8 (2004): 430–432. https://doi.org/10.1111/j.1440-1754.2004.00432.x.

Khan, Laeeq U. R., Jamil Ahmed, Shakeeb Khan, and John MacFie. "Refeeding Syndrome: A Literature Review." *Gastroenterology Research and Practice* 2011 (2011): 1–6. http://dx.doi.org/10.1155/2011/410971.

Misra, Madhusmita, Patrika Tsai, Ellen J. Anderson, Jane L. Hubbard, Katie Gallagher, Leslie A. Soyka, Karen K. Miller, David B. Herzog, and Anne Klibanski. "Nutrient Intake in Community-Dwelling Adolescent Girls with Anorexia Nervosa and in Healthy Controls." *American Journal of Clinical Nutrition* 84, no. 4 (2006): 698–706.

Nova, Esther, Irene Lopez-Vidriero, Pilar Varela, Olga Toro, Jose Casas, and Ascension Marcos. "Indicators of Nutritional Status in Restricting-Type Anorexia Nervosa Patients: A 1-Year Follow-Up Study." *Clinical Nutrition* 23 (2004): 1353–1359. http://doi.org/10.1016/j.clnu.2004.05.004.

Peters, Todd E., Matthew Parvin, Christopher Petersen, Vivian C. Faircloth, and Richard L. Levine. "A Case Report of Wernicke's Encephalopathy in a Pediatric Patient with Anorexia Nervosa—Restricting Type." *Journal of Adolescent Health* 40, no. 4 (2007): 376–383. http://doi.org/10.1016/j.jadohealth.2006.11.140.

Setnick, Jessica. "Micronutrient Deficiencies and Supplementation in Anorexia and Bulimia Nervosa: A Review of the Literature." *Nutrition in Clinical Practice* 25, no. 2 (2010): 137–142. https://doi.org/10.1177/0884533610361478.

Winston, Anthony P., C. P. Jamieson, Webster Madira, Nicholas M. Gatward, and Robert L. Palmer. "Prevalence of Thiamin Deficiency in Anorexia Nervosa." *International Journal of Eating Disorders* 28, no. 4 (2000): 451–454. https://doi.org/10.1002/1098-108X(200012)28:4<451::AID-EAT14>3.0.CO;2-I.

0

OBESITY

Obesity is a medical condition where a person has a body mass index (BMI) equal to or greater than 30, which puts him or her at risk for numerous health conditions including type 2 diabetes, cardiovascular disease, stroke, and some cancers. The prevalence of obesity in children, adolescents, and adults has increased rapidly over the past 30 years. In fact, some researchers predict this obesity epidemic will contribute to a decline in life expectancy among Americans in the 21st century.

Prevalence of Obesity

The obesity prevalence in adults doubled between 1980 and 2004 with recent reports showing that two-thirds of adults are overweight (i.e., have a BMI of 25.0–29.9) or obese. In the United States, 28 percent of men, 34 percent of women, and almost 50 percent of non-Hispanic black women are obese. Obesity trends affect all racial and ethnic groups, all states, and socioeconomic strata. However, the largest increases in obesity have been observed in children and minority populations. Approximately 2 million U.S. children are estimated to be obese, with a recent study suggesting 36 percent of the pediatric population is overweight or obese.

Causes of Obesity

The causes of obesity include genetic, biological, and lifestyle factors related to one's environment. Genetic factors, associated with a family history of particular body types and shapes, can be passed to future generations. Biological factors contribute to a body's ability to regulate hunger and fullness and digest food efficiently. Lifestyle factors, however, are modifiable. At the most basic level, weight gain that leads to obesity corresponds to an energy imbalance (i.e., more energy or food intake than what is required for energy expenditure needs). Furthermore, U.S. adults and children have been shown to eat fast and convenient foods high in fat, sugar, and caloric content while being relatively inactive. Both children and adults fail to meet recommended quantities of fruits and vegetables or levels of physical activity to have optimal health. Physical education classes have been eliminated nationally and this removed a structured opportunity for physical activity.

Screen time (i.e., time spent watching television and on other devices) has been blamed for increased inactivity in children and adults. For example, it has been reported children who have more than two hours of screen time per day consume less fruits and vegetables and more of high-energy drinks and energy-dense foods;

they also engage in more snacking behavior. An Australian study found use of electronic devices by parents, siblings, and friends led to increased sedentary behavior and more screen time.

Treatment of Obesity

Traditional treatment of obesity included weight management to change nutritional habits and reduce food intake while increasing activity levels with weight loss as the primary goal. However, obesity treatment professionals now recognize the need to provide family-based treatment interventions (e.g., BodyWorks) that involve shaping a family environment to encourage healthy habits and education in parents and siblings. Additionally, the importance of acknowledging the psychological relationship with food and emotional eating has been noted and is often incorporated into treatment programs. There have been divergent viewpoints related to whether obesity treatment should be based on weight management (i.e., monitoring weight loss and gain) or a Health at Every Size approach to address health and obesity.

Prevention of Obesity

Obesity prevention has been a major focus for local, state, and national efforts to reverse the trend the epidemic among youths and their parents. Prevention programs include school-based and community-based programs using a variety of approaches to improve nutritional habits and increase physical activity. School-based programs may include efforts to reinstate physical education classes or to implement after-school programming that includes movement rather than screen time. Nutritional changes may be addressed in a variety of ways including removing vending machines, changing nutrient contents of school lunches, and/or providing educational classes about healthy eating. Community-based programs to address nutrition and physical activity recommendations and may be implemented with children, adolescents, or adults in a community setting (e.g., Boys and Girls Club, recreation center, or Head-Start program). The then first lady of the United States Michelle Obama placed much attention on the need to address childhood obesity with her Let's Move! campaign. Additionally, community-based efforts may target community weight loss goals, neighborhood walkabouts, and trail building to improve environments for health.

Obesity and Eating Disorders

The focus on the rising obesity rates in children and adults has minimized the severity of the eating disorder problem in this country. In some cases, obesity prevention efforts have actively promoted weight loss while inadvertently pushing a dieting mentality. This dieting mentality has led to restricting, fear of weight gain, and fasting among adolescents and children and can contribute to disordered eating behaviors. Therefore, researchers realize the need to integrate obesity and eating disorder prevention efforts so that individuals develop healthier behaviors that result in a positive relationship with food, exercise, and body. The Planet Health program discussed in a separate entry shows promise for reducing both obesity and eating disorder outcomes.

It is thought that as many as one-third to one-half of overweight and obese individuals meet the criteria for binge eating disorder. Therefore, it is important that when obesity is addressed, emotional eating and disordered eating characteristics are recognized. For example, individuals can move along the spectrum of one eating disorder (e.g., binge eating disorder) and develop new disordered behaviors that lead to a different eating disorder (e.g., anorexia nervosa). It is critical underlying psychological and emotional problems be treated for individuals who are overweight and obese.

Justine J. Reel

See also: Binge Eating Disorder; Body Mass Index; BodyWorks; Food Addiction; Health at Every Size Approach; Let's Move!; Planet Health; Plus-Size Models and Clothing; Prevention; Teasing; Weight Stigma

Bibliography

Boutelle, Kerri N., Robyn W. Birkeland, Peter J. Hannan, Mary Story, and Dianne Neumark-Sztainer. "Associations between Maternal Concern for Healthful Eating and Maternal Eating Behaviors, Home Food Availability, and Adolescent Eating Behaviors." *Journal of Nutrition Education Behavior* 39 (2007): 248–256. https://doi.org/10/1016/j.jneb.2007.04.179.

Brown, Judith E., Dorothy H. Broom, Jan M. Nicholson, and Michael Bittman. "Do Working Mothers Raise Couch Potato Kids? Maternal Employment and Children's Lifestyle Behaviours and Weight in Early Childhood." *Social Science & Medicine* 70 (2010): 1816–1824. https://doi.org/10.1016/j.socscimed.2010.01.040.

"Chevese Turner Educates about Binge Eating Disorder and Obesity." YouTube.com. Last modified November 11, 2010. Accessed November 18, 2016. http://youtu.be/zrYANKK0p2A.

Granich, Joanna, Michael Rosenberg, Matthew Knuiman, and Anna Timperio. "Understanding Children's Sedentary Behaviour: A Qualitative Study of the Family Home Environment." *Health Education Research* 25, no. 2 (2010): 199–210. https://doi.org/10.1093/her/cyn025.

Isnard, Pascale, Gregory Michel, Marie Laure Frelut, Gilbert Vila, Bruno Falissard, Wadih Naja, Jean Navarro, and Marie Christine Mouren Simeoni. "Binge Eating and Psychopathology in Severely Obese Adolescents." *International Journal of Eating Disorders* 34 (2003): 235–243. https://doi.org/10.1542/peds.2008-3727.

Kalarchain, Melissa A., Michele D. Levine, Silva A. Arslanian, Linda J. Ewing, Patricia R. Houch, Yu Cheng, Rebecca M. Ringham, Carrie A. Sheets, and Marsha D. Marcus. "Family-Based Treatment of Severe Pediatric Obesity: Randomized, Controlled Trial." *Pediatrics* 124 (2009): 1060–1068. https://doi.org/10.1542/peds.2008-3727

Khan, Laura Kettel, Kathleen Sobush, Dana Keener, Kenneth Goodman, Amy Lowry, Jakub Kakietek, and Susan Zaro. "Recommended Community Strategies and Measurements to Prevent Obesity in the United States." *Morbidity and Mortality Weekly Reports* 58, no. 7 (2009): 1–29.

Mckee, M. Diane, Stacia Maber, Darwin Deen, and Arthur E. Blank. "Counseling to Prevent Obesity among Preschool Children: Acceptability of a Pilot Urban Primary Care Intervention." *Annals of Family Medicine* 8, no. 3 (2010): 249–255.

Neumark-Sztainer, Dianne, Jess Haines, Ramona Robinson O'Brien, Peter J. Hannan, Michael Robins, Bonnie Morris, and Christine A. Petrich. "Ready. Set. ACTION! A Theater-Based Obesity Prevention Program for Children: A Feasibility Study." *Health Education Research* 24, no. 3 (2009): 407–420. https://doi.org/10.1093/her/cyn036.

Pott, Wilfried, Ozgur Albayrak, Johannes Hebebrand, and Ursula Pauli-Pott. "Treating Childhood Obesity: Family Background Variables and the Child's Success in a Weight Control Intervention." *International Journal of Eating Disorders* 42 (2009): 284–289. https://doi.org/10.1002/eat.20655.

Zenzen, Wandy, and Suha Kridli. "Integrative Review of School-Based Childhood Obesity Prevention Programs." *Journal of Pediatric Health Care* 23, no. 4 (2009): 242–258. https://doi.org/10.1016/j.pedhc.2008.04.008.

OBJECTIFICATION THEORY

Objectification theory is a framework that uses a sociocultural context to examine the consequences of sexual objectification of the lived experiences and mental health of girls and women. Women and girls are often portrayed as sexual objects in American culture. Thus, Fredrickson and Roberts, in 1997, proposed the objectification theory to understand how women are socialized to be sexual objects. This theory explains why women and girls develop mental health problems (i.e., eating disorders, depression, and sexual dysfunction) from being objectified.

Objectification of the Body

Sexualization of the body is represented in different forms such as sexual violence and sexualized evaluation. A subtle way of sexualized evaluation of the body is through external gaze or visually inspecting the body. Sexual objectification occurs when a woman's body is considered separate from her person and treated merely as an object for the use and pleasure of others. This sexual objectification occurs in interpersonal and social situations (e.g., workplace, parties) and in media representations (e.g., television shows, magazines, advertisements, Internet) where women's bodies are depicted as sexual objects. Women report being sexually watched and evaluated more often than men.

Self-Objectification

According to the theory, sexual objectification socializes girls and women to treat themselves as objects and believe they are evaluated based on their physical appearance. This internalization of an observer's perspective is *self-objectification*. Self-objectification can lead to self-consciousness characterized by habitual monitoring of body appearance (i.e., body surveillance). Individuals could internalize the objectification at varying degrees ranging from daily gazes from passersby to a single occurrence while walking by a group of the opposite sex. Nonetheless, this internalization of an observer's perspective on the physical self could lead to psychological consequences (i.e., body shame, anxiety, internal bodily awareness, and flow experiences).

Media and Self-Objectification

Fredrickson and Roberts (1997) suggest the most common ways of sexually objectifying women is through the visual media, and viewing these sexualized bodies and images may increase self-objectification. The use of thin-idealized women in the media is ubiquitous; therefore, it is likely that women will experience self-objectification several times per day. Women who watched video clips of women playing sports that emphasized leanness had higher scores on self-objectification than women who did not watch these video clips. In a more recent study, women who viewed thin-idealized magazine advertisements of other women reported higher levels of self-objectification than women who only viewed magazine advertisements of products without people. As predicted by objectification theory, the constant viewing thin-idealized images can encourage a woman to think about her physical appearance as if she is looking at it as a critical observer, by adopting a third-person perspective. Increased exposure to these images will elevate the level of self-objectification, and, in turn, place women at risk of experiencing the psychological consequences of self-objectification.

Consequences of Self-Objectification

The psychological consequences of self-objectification are increased body shame and anxiety and a reduced awareness of internal bodily states and flow experiences. Body shame is the emotion a woman could feel when she compares herself to an internalized or cultural standard and perceives she fails to meet the standard. Anxiety occurs when a woman feels threatened or fearful about when and how her body will be evaluated. Awareness of internal bodily states is the ability to accurately detect and interpret physiological sensations, such as physiological sexual arousal. Peak motivational states or flow experiences, according to Csikszentmihalyi, are unique times when people believe they are "living uncontrolled" by others, able to live freely and be creative and joyful.

Objectification theory states the experience of sexual objectification promotes self-objectification and body surveillance, which in turn promote body shame and anxiety and reduce or disrupt the flow and awareness of internal bodily states. Increased body shame and anxiety, and decreased flow and awareness of internal bodily states, can lead women to develop depression, eating disorders, and sexual dysfunction.

Self-Objectification among Women

Studies reveal women with heightened self-objectification experience more body shame and anxiety than women who report lower self-objectification. In addition, women with higher levels of self-objectification are more likely to restrain from eating cookies and chocolates in ethnically diverse groups of women. Women with more body shame tend to want to change their bodies through weight loss or cosmetic surgery. In a longitudinal study, college women's levels of body surveillance and body shame persisted over time but the same did not hold true for middle-aged women, indicating body surveillance and body shame is stable for young women. In a different study, women smokers who monitored their bodies had higher body shame, body dissatisfaction, and eating disorder symptoms. Women with higher appearance anxiety had higher eating disorder symptoms among an ethnically diverse sample, but this was not the case among adolescents, adults, and college women who were white.

Self-Objectification among Men

Researchers have also examined the application of objectification theory to men and boys. In general, men and boys reported lower self-objectification, body surveillance, and body shame than women and girls. However, African American women and men do not differ in levels of body shame, and Asian American men reported higher self-objectification than Asian American women. Although there are sex differences in levels of self-objectification, there are sex similarities in self-objectification and mental health consequences. Similar to findings for females, males who have higher self-objectification, body surveillance, and body shame have lower body esteem, self-esteem, and health-promoting behaviors. Also, consistent with findings for females, body surveillance leads to body shame and appearance anxiety, and, in turn, leads to eating disorder symptoms.

Self-objectification is related to body shame in men, but the type of situation that enhances self-objectification may differ for women and men. Women exposed to beauty magazines internalize the cultural standards of attractiveness, which leads to body dissatisfaction and eating disorder symptoms. Men exposed to fitness magazines had higher internalization that lead to body dissatisfaction, than men not exposed to fitness magazines. While beauty and fashion magazines convey messages about cultural body ideals to women, fitness magazines can communicate standards of masculinity and body ideals to men. These types of standards may promote different ways of body surveillance and body shame—women worry about being thin; men worry about building muscles. For example, men who were bodybuilders reported higher self-objectification and eating disorder symptoms than nonbodybuilders.

Sonya SooHoo

See also: Body Image; Femininity Ideals; Media

Bibliography

Bartky, Sandra L. *Femininity and Domination: Studies in the Phenomenology of Oppression.* New York: Routledge, 1990.

Csikszentmihalyi, Mihaly. *Flow: The Psychology of Optimal Experience.* New York: Harper Perennial, 1990.

Fredrickson, Barbara L., and Tomi-Ann Roberts. "Objectification Theory: Toward Understanding Women's Lived Experiences and Mental Health Risks." *Psychology of Women Quarterly* 21 (1997): 173–206. https://doi.org/10.1111/j.1471-6402.1997.tb00108.x

Fredrickson, Barbara L., Tomi-Ann Roberts, Stephanie M. Noll, Diane M. Quinn, and Jean M. Twenge. "That Swimsuit Becomes You: Sex Differences in Self-Objectification, Retrained Eating, and Math Performance." *Journal of Personality and Social Psychology* 75, no. 5 (1998): 269 284. http://dx.doi.org/10.1037/h0090332.

Hallsworth, Lisa, Tracey Wade, and Marika Tiggemann. "Individual Differences in Male Body-Image: An Examination of Self-Objectification in Recreational Body Builders." *British Journal of Health Psychology* 10 (2005): 453–465. https://doi.org/10.1348/135910705X26966.

Harrell, Zaje A. T., Barbara L. Fredrickson, Cynthia S. Pomerleau, and Susan Nolen-Hoeksema. "The Role of Trait Self-Objectification in Smoking among College Women." *Sex Roles* 54 (2006): 735–743. https://doi.org/10.1007/s11199-006-9041-z.

McKinley, Nita M. "Longitudinal Gender Differences in Objectified Body Consciousness and Weight-Related Attitudes and Behaviors: Cultural and Developmental Contexts in the Transition from College." *Sex Roles* 54 (2006): 159–173. https://doi.org/10.1007/s11199-006-9335-1.

Moradi, B. "Addressing Gender and Cultural Diversity in Body Image: Objectification Theory as a Framework for Integrating Theories and Grounding Research." *Sex Roles* 63 (2010): 138–148. https://doi.org/10.1007/s11199-010-9824-0.

Moradi, Bonnie, and Yu-Ping Huang. "Objectification Theory and Psychology of Women: A Decade of Advances and Future Directions." *Psychology of Women Quarterly* 32, no. 4 (2008): 377–398. https://doi.org/10.1111/j.1471-6402.2008.00452.x.

Noll, Stephanie M., and Barbara L. Fredrickson. "Mediational Model Linking Self-Objectification, Body Shame, and Disordered Eating." *Psychology of Women Quarterly* 22, no. 4 (1998): 623–636. https://doi.org/10.1111/j.1471-6402.1998.tb00181.x.

OBLIGATORY EXERCISE

Obligatory exercise is a term that refers to the activity of individuals who continue to exercise despite pain, allow exercise to interfere with significant relationships or work, lack time for other leisure pursuits, obsess with the activity (exercise), or show other psychological problems. Characteristics of obligatory exercise include (1) maintaining a rigorous schedule of vigorous exercise; (2) resisting the urge to cut exercise routines; (3) guilt and anxiety when the practice plan is violated; (4) pushing oneself even when tired, ill, in pain, or injured; (5) mental obsession with exercise; (6) keeping accurate records on exercise; and (7) outrageous compensatory increase in exercise to make up for lapses.

Obligatory Exercise and Eating Disorders

Obligatory exercisers feel compelled to engage in intense exercise, past the point of enjoyment or what would be considered mentally or physically healthy. Their attitudes toward exercise can be harmful to their physical and psychological well-being. Previous studies have revealed obligatory exercise is associated with drive for thinness in obligatory weight-lifters and runners, eating and body image attitudes in appearance-motivated exercisers, and eating-disordered behaviors in a community sample. Moreover, many studies have shown significant associations between the characteristics of obligatory runners and women with eating disorders. Examples of overlapping characteristics between obligatory exercisers and women with eating disorders include family backgrounds, socioeconomic status, certain personality characteristics (e.g., anger, perfectionism, and high self-expectations), a tendency for social isolation, high tolerance of pain and physical discomfort, and a tendency for depression.

Characteristics of Obligatory Exercise

Distinguishable characteristics of obligatory exercise are elevated concerns over mistakes, the pursuit of high personal standards, and extreme doubts about the quality of actions. The motivational drive of obligatory exercise behavior tends to be a combination of outcome after striving for unrealistic goals for physical activity, a pervasive sense of anxiety about personal adequacy, and the consequences of failure to maintain desired standards. One explanation about the reason behind the drive in obligatory exercisers describes a culture that encourages people to strive toward the optimal body composition (lean body mass to body fat ratio). In this competitive society, obligatory exercise behaviors may be linked to the establishment of strict dietary guidelines. This explanation has been consistent with other studies in obligatory exercise.

Psychological Characteristics of Obligatory Exercisers

Much like individuals who suffer from eating disorders, obligatory exercisers use strenuous exercise sessions and routines to have a sense of control to cope with low self-esteem and related psychological issues. Similar to anorexia athletica or exercise dependence, obligatory exercise behaviors (also called *overtraining*) may serve to reassure individuals, especially athletes, by nurturing confidence and self-worth as athletes prepare for performance. Although the rigorous training sessions may be associated with performance enhancement in sports, they bear resemblance to the features of eating disorders. This comparison may foster additional correlation with other psychological traits such as negative body image, low self-esteem, anxiety, depression, and a preoccupation with weight as observed in certain eating disorders.

Maya Miyairi

See also: Exercise; Exercise Dependence; Intuitive Exercise

Bibliography

De Young, Kyle P., and Drew A. Anderson. "The Importance of the Function of Exercise in the Relationship between Obligatory Exercise and Eating and Body Image Concerns." *Eating Behaviors* 11 (2010): 62–64. http://dx.doi.org/10.1016/j.eatbeh.2009.09.001.

Hall, Howard K., Andrew P. Hill, Paul R. Appleton, and Stephen A. Kozub. "The Mediating Influence of Unconditional Self-Acceptance and Labile Self-Esteem on the Relationship between Multidimensional Perfectionism and Exercise Dependence." *Psychology of Sport and Exercise* 10 (2009): 35–44. http://dx.doi.org/10.1016/j.psychsport.2008.05.003.

Hall, Howard K., Alistair W. Kerr, Stephen A. Kozub, and Steven B. Finnie. "Motivational Antecedents of Obligatory Exercise: The Influence of Achievement Goals and Multidimensional Perfectionism." *Psychology of Sport and Exercise* 8 (2007): 297–316. http://dx.doi.org/10.1016/j.psychsport.2006.04.007.

Krejci, Richard C., Roger Sargent, Kenneth J. Forand, John R. Ureda, Ruth P. Saunders, and J. Larry Durstine. "Psychological and Behavioral Differences among Females Classified as Bulimic, Obligatory Exerciser and Normal Control." *Psychiatry* 55 (1992): 185–193.

Matheson, Hilary, and Anne Crawford-Wright. "An Examination of Eating Disorder Profiles in Student Obligatory and Non-Obligatory Exercisers." *Journal of Sport Behavior* 23, no. 1 (2000): 42–50.

Pasman, Larry, and J. Kevin Thompson. "Body Image and Eating Disturbance in Obligatory Runners, Obligatory Weightlifters, and Sedentary Individuals." *International Journal of Eating Disorders* 7, no. 6 (1988): 759–769. https://doi.org/10.1002/1098-108X(198811)7:6<759::AID-EAT2260070605>3.0.CO;2-G.

Reel, Justine J., and Katherine A. Beals, eds. *The Hidden Faces of Eating Disorders and Body Image.* Reston, VA: AAHPERD/NAGWS, 2009.

Steffen, John J., and Bonnie J. Brehm. "The Dimensions of Obligatory Exercise." *Eating Disorders* 7 (1999): 219–226. http://dx.doi.org/10.1080/10640269908249287.

Yates, Alayne, Kevin Leehey, and Catherine M. Shisslak. "Running—An Analogue of Anorexia." *The New England Journal of Medicine* 308 (1983): 251–255. https://doi.org/10.1056/NEJM198302033080504.

OBSESSIVE-COMPULSIVE DISORDER

Obsessive-compulsive disorder (OCD) is classified as obsessive-compulsive and related disorders by the fifth edition of the *Diagnostic and Statistical Manual of Mental Disorders (DSM-5)*. OCD is characterized by unwanted and repeated thoughts (obsessions) and/or repetitive behaviors that an individual is driven to perform (compulsions). Obsessions or compulsions are time consuming (i.e., more than one hour per day) and cause distress. Further, the obsessions or compulsions can lead to functional impairment in work or social life. Repetitive behaviors, such as hand washing, checking, or cleaning, are used in attempts to reduce anxiety by making the obsessions go away. Engaging in the behaviors, however, provides only temporary relief and attempting to reduce behaviors can cause increased anxiety.

Comorbidity of OCD and Eating Disorders

Research findings demonstrate a frequent co-occurrence of eating disorders and OCD. Although all types of anxiety disorders can co-occur with eating disorders, OCD has one of the highest comorbidities (along with social phobia) of all anxiety disorders. Studies show the lifetime prevalence of OCD in clients with anorexia nervosa is 10–15 percent and the lifetime prevalence of OCD in clients with bulimia nervosa is up to 43 percent. Individuals primarily diagnosed with OCD have shown a lifetime prevalence of eating disorders ranging from 5 percent to 17 percent.

The relationship between OCD and eating disorders is not straightforward; some researchers argue OCD is a risk factor for developing an eating disorder; other researchers argue eating disorders trigger OCD tendencies. Interestingly, some researchers and clinicians have claimed eating disorders are a form of OCD while most experts maintain OCD and eating disorders are two distinct conditions and should receive separate diagnoses. Experts have reported that for eating-disordered individuals diagnosed with OCD, OCD usually precedes eating disorder onset, suggesting OCD might be a risk factor for eating disorders. Conversely, Yaryura-Tobias argued eating disorders lead to OCD symptoms. In 1986, Rothenberg suggested eating disorders were a symptom of OCD. However, most eating disorder experts agree that while OCD and eating disorders share similar features, they are in fact different disorders and should receive separate classifications.

For eating-disordered individuals who suffer from OCD, the effect of OCD on treatment responses is inconclusive. It has been suggested co-occurring OCD has little effect on eating disorder treatment. In fact, one study argued eating disorder clients with co-occurring OCD in an inpatient setting seem to have the same treatment prognosis as clients who do not have the OCD diagnosis, if the co-occurring OCD is treated using evidence-based practices. However, another study found OCD symptoms were significantly associated with poor treatment outcomes in anorexia nervosa clients. A separate study indicated greater severity in OCD symptomology at discharge was linked to a higher probability of eating disorder relapse. Researchers have also found eating disorder clients diagnosed with OCD had significantly longer duration of eating disorders, suggesting OCD might be a factor in maintaining eating disorders. Interestingly, clients with both OCD and eating disorders have been reported to be more likely to refuse treatment than clients with only OCD.

Severity and Comorbidity

Researchers agree that eating-disordered clients diagnosed with comorbid OCD exhibit a greater severity in illness and an increase in other mental health diagnoses such as major depressive disorder, bipolar disorder, post-traumatic stress disorder, or generalized anxiety disorder, compared to eating-disordered clients without OCD. Clients with comorbid eating disorders and OCD tend to develop an eating disorder at an earlier age, have longer eating disorder durations, are admitted to treatment with a lower body mass index (BMI), and report more prior inpatient treatment episodes for eating disorders. Some researchers have found evidence these clients have a worse prognosis than eating disorder clients without OCD.

Similarities between Eating Disorders and OCD

Eating disorders and OCD have considerable overlap with shared neurological, genetic, and psychological elements. Shared characteristics between the disorders suggest an association. The disorders share psychopathological similarities, such as obsessions or compulsions related to food (i.e., eating foods in a particular order), or overeating or restricting food. People with eating disorders and OCD also share personality traits, such as perfectionism, rigidity, and preoccupations with cleanliness. Eating disorders and OCD have similar epidemiological data including their prevalence, age of onset, course of the illness, and genetic predisposition. Both disorders show similar responses to the same pharmacological and psychotherapeutic approaches.

Although the disorders share many features, it is important to recognize they are distinct illnesses and to separate obsessions and compulsions stemming from an eating disorder from those linked to a direct diagnosis of OCD. A client who reports obsessions and compulsions around food, weight, appearance, and/or exercise—such as obsessive calorie counting—should not be given a diagnosis of OCD. If, however, an individual reports additional obsessions and compulsions beyond obsessions and/or compulsions related to food, weight, appearance, or exercise—such as counting—he or she should receive a secondary OCD diagnosis.

Researchers have expressed concerns specifically about differentiating between obsessions and compulsions linked to eating disorders and obsessions and compulsions due to OCD, in the case of persons with anorexia nervosa. Malnutrition and starvation can create obsessive-compulsive symptoms. As a result, in the case of people with anorexia nervosa who display obsessive-compulsive symptoms, experts question whether the symptoms are a direct result of starvation as opposed to true OCD symptoms. Another key difference between the disorders is that OCD is an ego-dystonic disorder, whereas anorexia nervosa is an ego-syntonic disorder. In other words, obsessions and compulsions in a person diagnosed with OCD are seen by the person as inconsistent with her beliefs and personality while those of a person diagnosed with anorexia nervosa are viewed by the person as consistent with her beliefs and personality.

Jessica Guenther and Justine J. Reel

See also: Anxiety Disorders; Comorbidity; *Diagnostic and Statistical Manual of Mental Disorders*; Food Phobia

Bibliography

American Psychiatric Association. *Diagnostic and Statistical Manual of Mental Disorders*, 5th ed. (*DSM-5*). Washington, DC: American Psychiatric Association Publishing, 2013.

Carter, J. C., E. Blackmore, K. Sutandar-Pinnock, and D. B. Woodside. "Relapse in Anorexia Nervosa: A Survival Analysis." *Psychological Medicine* 34 (2004): 671–679. https://doi.org/10.1017/S0033291703001168.

Cumella, Edward J., Zina Kally, and A. David Wall. "Treatment Responses of Inpatient Eating Disorder Women with and without Co-occurring Obsessive-Compulsive Disorder." *Eating Disorders* 15, no. 2 (2007): 111–124. http://dx.doi.org/10.1080/10640260701190634.

Fahy, Thomas A., Autor Osacar, and Isaac Marks. "History of Eating Disorders in Female Patients with Obsessive-Compulsive Disorder." *International Journal of Eating Disorders* 14, no. 4 (1993): 439–443. https://doi.org/10.1002/1098-108X(199312)14:4<439::AID-EAT2260140407>3.0.CO;2-6.

Halmi, Katherine A., Federica Tozzi, Laura M. Thornton, Scott Crow, Manfred Fichter, Allan S. Kaplan, Pamela Keel, Kelly L. Klump, Lisa R. Lilenfield, James E. Mitchell, Katherine H. Plotnicov, Christine Pollice, Alessandro Rotondo, Michael Strober, D. Blake Woodside, Wade H. Berretini, Walter H. Kaye, and Cynthia M. Bulik. "The Relationship among Perfectionism, Obsessive-Compulsive Personality Disorder, and

Obsessive-Compulsive Disorder in Individuals with Eating Disorders." *International Journal of Eating Disorders* 38, no. 4 (2005): 371–374. https://doi.org/10.1002/eat .20190.

Hsu, L. K. George, Walter Kaye, and Theodore Weltzin. "Are the Eating Disorders Related to Obsessive Compulsive Disorder?" *International Journal of Eating Disorders* 14, no. 3 (1993): 305–318. https://doi.org/10.1002/1098-108X(199311)14:3<305::AID-EAT 2260140309>3.0.CO;2-L.

Kaye, Walter H., Cynthia M. Bulik, Laura Thornton, Nicole Barbarich, Kim Masters, and The Price Foundation Collaborative Group. "Co-morbidity of Anxiety Disorders with Anorexia and Bulimia Nervosa." *The American Journal of Psychiatry* 161, no. 12 (2004): 2215–2221. http://dx.doi.org/10.1176/appi.ajp.161.12.2215.

Milos, Gabriella, Anja Spindler, Giovanni Ruggiero, Richard Klaghofer, and Ulrich Schnyder. "Co-morbidity of Obsessive-Compulsive Disorders and Duration of Eating Disorders." *International Journal of Eating Disorders* 31, no. 3 (2002): 284–289. https://doi .org/10.1002/eat.10013.

Roncero, Maria, Conxa Perpina, and Gemma Garcia-Soriano. "Study of Obsessive Compulsive Beliefs: Relationship with Eating Disorders." *Behavioural and Cognitive Psychotherapy* 39, no. 4 (2011): 457–470. https://doi.org/10.1017/S1352465811000099.

Sallet, Paulo C., Pedro Gomes de Alvarenga, Ygor Ferrão, Maria Alice de Mathis, Albina R. Torres, Andrea Marques, Ana G. Hounie, Victor Fossaluza, Maria Conceição do Rosario, Leonardo F. Fontenelle, Katia Petribu, and Bacy Fleitlich-Bilyk. "Eating Disorders in Patients with Obsessive-Compulsive Disorder: Prevalence and Clinical Correlates." *International Journal of Eating Disorders* 43, no. 4 (2010): 315–325. https://doi .org/10.1002/eat.20697.

Yaryura-Tobias, Jose A., Fugen A. Neziroglu, and Steven Kaplan. "Self-Mutilation, Anorexia, and Dysmenorrhea in Obsessive Compulsive Disorder." *International Journal of Eating Disorders* 17, no. 1 (1995): 33–38.

OFF THE C.U.F.F.

Off the C.U.F.F. (Calm, Unwavering, Firm, and Funny) is a skills training program created for parents who have children with eating disorders. Off the C.U.F.F. was developed by Dr. Nancy Zucker at Duke University Medical Center. The program opens the lines of communication between parents and daughters with the goal of building a healthy relationship to allow an environment that nurtures treatment of and recovery from an eating disorder.

Description of the Program

Off the C.U.F.F. is implemented in group settings to build skills among parents. The impetus for the program's development came from the realization that insurance support for inpatient eating disorder treatment was inadequate to meet the enormous needs of adolescents with eating disorders. The program provides parents with knowledge, skills, and an opportunity to practice these skills, to extend support to adolescents who require weight restoration and positive eating disorder recovery in the home environment.

The Off the C.U.F.F. group uses a process-focused approach rather than an outcome-oriented approach. In contrast to other eating disorder support groups for parents, Off the C.U.F.F. provides a structured agenda for teaching parenting skills related to eating. Parents are taught to avoid power struggles and conflicts over food while remaining calm and patient.

The three barriers to successful meals, negative perfectionism, expressed negative emotion, and poor self-efficacy, are identified and addressed. Parents learn to foster a home environment to promote acceptance while working on their emotional regulation. For example, parent participants are assigned an eating disorder behavior to target as well as an adaptive coping skill for modeling purposes.

The group also provides emotional support for parents who experience extreme stress related to a daughter's eating disorders. Parents become more attuned to their own eating and commentary related to their body image. Ultimately, parents are encouraged to serve as healthy role models for their daughters.

Evaluation of Off the C.U.F.F.

Although more outreach research is needed to evaluate this program, preliminary findings demonstrated successful outcomes for parent satisfaction and client (daughter) improvement. Of parents who participated in Off the C.U.F.F., 91 percent strongly agreed that the group was essential for their children's improvement and 82 percent of parents believed that their children would not be doing well if they had not participated. All parents reported the program helped them be better parents and they would recommend the group. A majority of parents thought the group helped them reduce stress, take better care of themselves, better handle stressful situations, and be more confident in parenting skills. For eating disorder clients, scores on weight concerns, shape concerns, and restraint decreased after the program, while body mass index scores improved for underweight clients.

Justine J. Reel

See also: Assertiveness Training; Family Influences; Parents; Prevention; Recovery

Bibliography

Sullivan, Michele G. "Parents Enlisted to Fight Teens' Eating Disorders: Skills-Training Program Gives Families the Tools and the Support They Need to Address Behavior at Home." *Family Practice News* (2001): 39.

Sullivan, Michele G. "Parents of Eating Disorder Patients Join Forces: Group Training Program Aims to Give Families the Skills to Reinforce Positive Eating Habits in Adolescents." *Child/Adolescent Psychiatry* (2003): 42.

Zucker, Nancy. *Off the C.U.F.F.: A Parents Skills Book for the Management of Disordered Eating.* Durham, NC: Duke University Medical Center, 2004.

OLIGOMENORRHEA

Oligomenorrhea is a condition in which a female's menstrual cycles last longer than 35 days after the onset of menses, resulting in fewer than 10 menstrual periods per year. The average menstrual cycle is 25–35 days. The primary cause of oligomenorrhea in individuals with eating disorders is presumed to be low energy availability (energy availability is the amount of dietary energy remaining for other physiological functions after exercise). Oligomenorrhea can occur with many types of eating disturbances that result in energy deficiency, either from inadequate energy intake, too much exercise, or a combination of both.

Health Consequences

Infrequent menstrual periods are associated with decreased bone mineral density, increased frequency of stress fractures and other musculoskeletal injuries in athletes, longer interruption of sports training from injuries, and impaired dilation of blood vessels (i.e., premature cardiovascular disease). It is possible these adverse effects occur because of the severity of menstrual cycle disturbance. For example, individuals with oligomenorrhea have been found to have lower bone mineral density and more vascular dysfunction than regularly menstruating women; however, individuals with amenorrhea (i.e., lack of any menstrual periods) have been found to have lower bone mass and greater impairment of vascular function than oligomenorrheic women.

Management

Increasing energy intake and/or reducing exercise energy expenditure are recommended to meet the energy demands of the reproductive system and restore regular menstrual cycles. Improvements in nutritional status and hormone levels have been shown to have a positive effect on bone health as well as vascular function. Early intervention is indicated to prevent long-term health complications.

Holly E. Doetsch

See also: Amenorrhea; Female Athlete Triad; Medical and Health Consequences

Bibliography

Beckvid Henriksson, Gabriella, Cathy Schnell, and Angelica Linden Hirschberg. "Women Endurance Runners with Menstrual Dysfunction Have Prolonged Interruption of Training Due to Injury." *Gynecologic and Obstetric Investigation* 49 (2000): 41–46. https://doi.org/10.1159/000010211.

Bennell, Kim L., Susan A. Malcolm, Shane A. Thomas, Sally J. Reid, Peter D. Brukner, Peter R. Ebeling, and John D. Wark. "Risk Factors for Stress Fractures in Track and Field Athletes: A Twelve-Month Prospective Study." *American Journal of Sports Medicine* 24, no. 6 (1996): 810–818. https://doi.org/10.1177/036354659602400617.

Drinkwater, Barbara L., Barbara Bruemner, and Charles H. Chesnut III. "Menstrual History as a Determinant of Current Bone Density in Young Athletes." *Journal of the American Medical Association* 263 (1990): 545–548. https://doi.org/10.1001/jama.1990.03440040084033.

Nattiv, Aurelia, Anne B. Loucks, Melinda M. Manore, Charlotte F. Sanborn, Jorunn Sundgot-Borgen, and Michelle P. Warren. "American College of Sports Medicine Position Stand. The Female Athlete Triad." *Medicine and Science in Sports and Exercise* 39, no. 10 (2007): 1867–1882. https://doi.org/10.1097/00005768-199705000-00037.

Ouvang, Fengxiu, Xiaobin Wang, Lester Arguelles, Linda L. Rosul, Scott A. Venners, Changzhong Chen, Yi-Hsiang Hsu, Henry A. Terwedow, Di Wu, Genfu Tang, Jianhua Yang,

Houxun Xing, Tonghua Zang, Binyan Wang, and Xiping Xu. "Menstrual Cycle Lengths and Bone Mineral Density: A Cross-Sectional, Population-Based Study in Rural Chinese Women Ages 30–49 Years." *Osteoporosis International* 18, no. 2 (2007): 221–233. https://doi.org/10.1007/s00198-006-0210-2.

Rauh, Mitchell J., Jeanne F. Nichols, and Michelle T. Barrack. "Relationships among Injury and Disordered Eating, Menstrual Dysfunction, and Low Bone Mineral Density in High School Athletes: A Prospective Study." *Journal of Athletic Training* 45, no. 3 (2010): 243–252.

Rickenlund, Anette, Maria J. Eriksson, Karin Schenck-Gustafsson, and Angelica Linden Hirschberg. "Amenorrhea in Female Athletes Is Associated with Endothelial Dysfunction and Unfavorable Lipid Profile." *Journal of Clinical Endocrinology and Metabolism* 90, no. 3 (2005): 1354–1359. http://dx.doi.org/10.1210/jc.2004-1286.

Tomten, S. E., J. A. Falch, K. I. Birkeland, P. Hemmersbach, and A. T. Høstmark. "Bone Mineral Density and Menstrual Irregularities. A Comparative Study on Cortical and Trabecular Bone Structures in Runners with Alleged Normal Eating Behavior." *International Journal of Sports Medicine* 19, no. 2 (1998): 92–97. https://doi.org/10.1055/s-2007-971888.

OPERATION BEAUTIFUL

Operation Beautiful promotes self-acceptance by using Post-it notes to spread positive, uplifting messages. The mission of Operation Beautiful is to make the statement "You are beautiful just the way you are." Operation Beautiful has combated fat talk (negative thoughts and criticisms about weight and size) by sticking Post-it notes on scales in public places that read, "You have no hold on my mood, my day or my life. I am MORE than just a number"

Operation Beautiful started in 2009 as a spontaneous act by a community college student, Caitlin Boyle who had been using positive self-affirmations in her life to fight perfectionist tendencies and negative self-talk. On a particularly stressful day, Boyle decided to make a strong statement by writing "You are beautiful" on a scrap sheet of paper and sticking it to a public bathroom mirror. She realized that she felt better because of looking at the positive message on the note. She took a photograph of the note and posted it on her blog to start a mission she called Operation Beautiful. Boyle urged other females to participate by posting positive notes in public places (e.g., mirrors, magazines, gym scales). Her appeal went viral almost immediately and Boyle's inbox was filled with e-mails from women around the world.

What started as a simple act in a private moment has spread to Post-it note campaigns around the world. Many universities (e.g., Michigan State University, University of Utah) have incorporated Post-it note campaigns into national eating disorder awareness week events. Other women and men have been motivated to spontaneously post positive messages in retail stores, schools, and in their homes. An unexpected benefit of Operation Beautiful has been the response from individuals who find the Post-it notes and are uplifted as a result.

Justine J. Reel

See also: Body Image; Full of Ourselves; Prevention

Bibliography

Boyle, Caitlin. "Operation Beautiful." Operation Beautiful. Last modified May 4, 2016. Accessed November 22, 2017. www.operationbeautiful.com.

Boyle, Caitlin. *Operation Beautiful: Transforming the Way You See Yourself One Post-it Note at a Time.* New York: Gotham Books, 2010

"'Operation Beautiful': Just Say No to Fat Talk!" *Today Show.* Last modified August 5, 2010. Accessed November 18, 2016. http://www.today.com/id/38560934/ns/today-today _books/t/operation-beautiful-just-say-no-fat-talk/#.WC8w49UrLIU.

ORTHOREXIA NERVOSA

Orthorexia nervosa describes an eating behavior characterized by a pathological obsession for biologically pure foods free of herbicides, pesticides, and other artificial substances. Although orthorexia nervosa is not a separate eating disorder diagnostic category, there are overlaps between orthorexia nervosa and other disordered-eating behaviors. Although consuming natural and organic foods is not pathological in itself, orthorexia nervosa is marked by an excessive preoccupation or concern associated with consuming healthy foods.

History of Orthorexia

The term *orthorexia* was coined by Steven Bratman in 1997 to describe eating-disordered behaviors related to excessive worry about the techniques and materials used in food preparation, and it was created from Greek, *orthos*, which means accurate or correct. The Greek word, *orexis*, means hunger and *orthorexia* translates to obsession of healthy and proper nutrition. Individuals with orthorexia nervosa have been found to experience obsessive thoughts about foods, loss of social relationships, and mood swings.

Differences between Orthorexia and Other Eating Disorders

Orthorexia nervosa is not a separate diagnosis in the current edition of the *Diagnostic and Statistical Manual of Mental Disorders (DSM-5)*. However, it is important to distinguish between orthorexia nervosa and other eating disorders (i.e., anorexia nervosa, bulimia nervosa, binge eating disorder). Although individuals with orthorexia nervosa exhibit features like anorexic individuals, such as being careful, detailed, and preoccupied with food, they have no fear associated of weight gain or body shape change. Individuals with orthorexia nervosa are concerned with certain foods being impure or toxic, but they are not motivated by weight loss. Orthorexia nervosa may lead to strict diets with a shortage of essential nutrients that result in a modification of social behaviors (e.g., eating out) related to food consumption.

Prevalence of Orthorexia

Although orthorexia nervosa has not been recognized as a disorder for as long as other eating disorders, several researchers have examined its prevalence. Certain groups are more at risk for orthorexia nervosa, including women, adolescents, athletes, physicians, and medical students. In one study, 43.6 percent of medical students in Erzurum, Turkey, met criteria for orthorexia nervosa, and male students who were younger showed a stronger orthorexic tendency. A separate study with dietitians found that although 52.3 percent did not exhibit orthorexia nervosa, 34.9 percent of dietitians demonstrated some orthorexic behavior and 12.8 percent exhibited orthorexia. These dietitians had some behaviors associated with orthorexia nervosa including avoidance of eating away from home for fear of unhealthy food, bringing one's food when eating away from home, and guilt or self-loathing when straying from one's eating plan.

Justine J. Reel

See also: Disordered Eating; Food Allergies; Intuitive Eating

Bibliography

American Psychiatric Association. *Diagnostic and Statistical Manual of Mental Disorders*, 5th ed. (*DSM-5*). Washington, DC: American Psychiatric Association Publishing, 2013.

Bosi, A. Tulay Bagci, Derya Camur, and Cagatay Guler. "Prevalence of Orthorexia Nervosa in Resident Medical Doctors in the Faculty of Medicine (Ankara, Turkey)." *Appetite* 49 (2007): 661–666. https://doi.org/10.1016/j.appet.2007.04.007.

Eriksson, L., A. Baigi, B. Marklund, and E. C. Lindgren. "Social Physique Anxiety and Sociocultural Attitudes toward Appearance Impact on Orthorexia Test in Fitness Participants." *Scandinavian Journal of Medicine & Science in Sports* 18 (2008): 389–394. https://doi.org/10.1111/j.1600-0838.2007.00723.x.

Fidan, Tulin, Vildan Ertekin, Sedat Isikay, and Ismet Kirpinar. "Prevalence of Orthorexia among Medical Students in Erzurum, Turkey." *Comprehensive Psychiatry* 51 (2010): 49–54. https://doi.org/10.1016/j.comppsych.2009.03.001.

Kimmer, A., M. V. Dias, and A. L. Teixeira. "On the Concept of Orthorexia Nervosa." *Scandinavian Journal of Medicine & Science in Sports* 18 (2008): 395–396. https://doi.org/10.1111/j.1600-0838.2008.00809.x.

Kinzi, Johann F., Katharina Hauer, Christian Traweger, and Ingrid Kiefer. "Orthorexia Nervosa in Dieticians." *Psychotherapy and Psychosomatics* 75 (2006): 395–396. https://doi.org/10.1159/000095447.

Korinth, Anne, Sonja Schiess, and Joachim Westenhoefer. "Eating Behavior and Eating Disorders in Students of Nutrition Sciences." *Public Health Nutrition* 13, no. 1 (2009): 32–37. https://doi.org/10.1017/S1368980009005709.

Vandereycken, Walter. "Media Hype, Diagnostic Fad or Genuine Disorder? Professionals' Opinions about Night Eating Syndrome, Orthrexia, Muscle Dysmorpia and Emetophobia." *Eating Disorders: Journal of Treatment and Prevention* 19 (2011): 145–155. https://doi.org/10.1080/10640266.2011.551634.

OSTEOPOROSIS

Osteoporosis is a bone disease associated with low bone mineral density and is represented by bone density loss of more than 2.5 standard deviations from what is normal for one's age. Osteoporosis and low bone density have been associated with advanced age, amenorrhea, and anorexia nervosa. Males and females with eating disorders have been found to experience bone density loss at higher rates than the general population. Therefore, bone density loss (previously osteoporosis) has been identified as a component of the female athlete triad intersecting with menstrual disturbance and energy availability.

Prevalence of Osteoporosis in Eating-Disordered Individuals

Bone density has been found to be reduced at either the spine or the hip by more than 2.5 standard deviations (i.e., osteoporosis) in almost 40 percent of eating-disordered clients. Alarmingly, 92 percent of eating-disordered clients had bone density reduced by more than one standard deviation showing the presence of osteopenia.

Although adolescents with anorexia nervosa typically experience a shorter duration of illness than older clients, one study found 41 percent of adolescents with anorexia nervosa had osteopenia and 11 percent met the criteria for osteoporosis. Because optimization of bone growth and achievement of peak bone mass occurs in adolescence, anorexia nervosa contributes to a long-term risk of stress fractures and irreversible skeletal damage.

Treatment Implications and Bone Health

Because of the risk of osteopenia and osteoporosis among in with anorexia nervosa, it is important to address bone health as part of comprehensive eating disorder treatment.

Hormonal Therapy

Once individuals have been assessed for bone health, it is common for physicians to prescribe supplemental estrogen as a form of hormonal replacement therapy or as an oral contraceptive for clients with anorexia nervosa to minimize osteopenia or osteoporosis. However, although 75–80 percent of physicians may use hormonal therapy to address bone health concerns, results have been mixed regarding the efficacy of estrogens in reversing bone loss.

Weight Restoration

Weight restoration is another common treatment method for clients with anorexia nervosa. Although weight restoration is important to restore bodily functions and avoid further medical complications, the direct effect of weight gain on bone health is unknown. As with hormonal therapy, conflicting results have been found in relation to the benefits of weight restoration in preventing bone density loss associated with anorexia nervosa.

Calcium Supplementation

Calcium may also be prescribed for individuals with anorexia nervosa. The American Academy of Pediatrics recommends adolescents consume 1,200 to 1,500 mg of calcium daily to meet bone health requirements. Although calcium supplementation is often encouraged in eating-disordered populations, calcium alone may be insufficient to prevent osteopenia and osteoporosis in individuals with anorexia nervosa.

Exercise

Weight-bearing exercise has been used to prevent osteoporosis and improve bone health in the general population. Exercise as an adjunct treatment may be beneficial for individuals with eating disorders if menstruation has been restored. However, eating-disordered individuals will not be medically cleared to exercise until they have experienced adequate weight restoration and are no longer medically compromised. It is critical once individuals can exercise, they gradually incorporate light physical activity to avoid the potential for stress fractures. Individuals must monitor the potential to abuse exercise that can lead to overtraining injuries and mental fatigue.

Justine J. Reel

See also: Amenorrhea; Female Athlete Triad; Medical and Health Consequences; Oligomenorrhea

Bibliography

Drinkwater, Barbara L., Barbara Bruemner, and Charles H. Chesnut III. "Menstrual History as a Determinant of Current Bone Density in Young Athletes." *Journal of the American Medical Association* 263, no. 4 (1990): 545–548. https://doi.org/10.1001/jama.1990.03440040084033.

Mehler, Philip S. "Osteoporosis in Anorexia Nervosa: Prevention and Treatment." *International Journal of Eating Disorders* 33, no. 2 (2003): 113–126. https://doi.org/10.1002/eat.10119.

Mehler, Philip S., and Thomas D. MacKenzie. "Treatment of Osteopenia and Osteoporosis in Anorexia Nervosa: A Systematic Review of the Literature." *International Journal of Eating Disorders* 42, no. 3 (2009): 195–201. https://doi.org/10.1002/eat.20593.

Nichols, David L., Charlotte F. Sanborn, and Eve V. Essery. "Bone Density and Young Athletic Women." *Sports Medicine* 37, no. 11 (2007): 1001–1014. https://doi.org/10.2165/00007256-200737110-00006.

Rauh, Mitchell J., Jeanne F. Nichols, and Michelle T. Barrack. "Relationships among Injury and Disordered Eating, Menstrual Dysfunction, and Low Bone Mineral Density in High School Athletes: A Prospective Study." *Journal of Athletic Training* 45, no. 3 (2010): 243–252.

OVEREATERS ANONYMOUS

Overeaters Anonymous (OA) refers to a twelve-step program for people who struggle with a dysfunctional relationship with food. Members include individuals who have been diagnosed with anorexia nervosa, bulimia nervosa, and binge eating disorder, as well as others who are compulsive eaters or who have a problem with food. OA hosts meetings around the world that offer a "fellowship of experience, strength and hope."

OA is funded by member contributions and does not charge fees or dues. Although OA is not a religious organization, like other twelve-step groups, OA promotes gaining strength from a higher power. OA provides emotional support to members and does not recommend any specific diet or meal plan. On its website, OA provides tools including a daily meditation for visitors.

History of OA

OA was founded in 1960 by three women to address compulsive overeating as a form of addiction. The chief founder conceived the idea of OA after attending a Gamblers Anonymous meeting with a friend two years earlier. Today, OA headquarters are in Rio Rancho, New Mexico, and membership is estimated to be over 54,000 people and 6,500 groups in 75 countries. OA has modified program materials from Alcoholics Anonymous to apply the twelve-step tradition to compulsive overeating to help individuals to admit their powerlessness over food and to begin physical, emotional, and spiritual healing.

Justine J. Reel

See also: Eating Disorders Anonymous; Recovery; Treatment; Twelve-Step Programs

Bibliography

"Overeaters Anonymous." OA.org. Accessed November 18, 2016. www.oa.org.

Stefano, S. C., J. Bacaltchuk, S. L. Blay, and P. Hay. "Self-Help Treatments for Disorders in Recurrent Binge Eating: A Systematic Review." *Acta Psychiatrica Scandinavica* 113 (2006): 452–459. https://doi.org/10.1111/j.1600-0447.2005.00735.x.

Wasson, Diane H., and Mary Jackson. "An Analysis of the Role of Overeaters Anonymous in Women's Recovery from Bulimia Nervosa." *Eating Disorders: Journal of Treatment and Prevention* 12 (2004): 337–356. https://doi.org/10.1080/10640260490521442.

P

PALEO DIET

Diet fads come and go just like fashion fads, beauty fads, and all others. One example of a fad diet, the Paleo diet, often referred to as the "caveman's diet" is based on the concept of eating like Paleolithic ancestors. Given that this popular diet is reported to get back to the roots of the ways human beings ate 10,000 years ago, it is often touted as a more natural meal plan than what an average American consumes. Specifically, the typical American diet includes many processed foods that evolved from the need to preserve food, due to convenience, and result in a high sodium and fat diet.

The Paleo diet does not allow processed foods and encourages followers to eliminate grains, dairy products, refined sugar, carbohydrates such as potatoes, and salts. The consumption of lean animals is encouraged with a preference shown for wild, free range, or grass-fed animals. Other acceptable food items for this diet are eggs and honey, fish and seafood, fresh fruits and vegetables, raw nuts and seeds, and oils such as olive, walnut, flaxseed, macadamia, avocado, and coconut oils. The rationale for this prescribed diet is partially supported by consuming *clean* calories that do not represent foods heavy in carbohydrates or fats.

A shift away from the typical American diet consisting of processed foods, often high in saturated fat, refined sugar, sodium, and total calories, toward a whole foods diet, is generally considered a healthy option by many nutrition experts. Moreover, another argument is that people on a Paleo diet may face reduced risk for anemia due to consuming increased amounts of red meat. The Paleo diet food choices are typically higher in fat, protein, and fiber; all of which increase satiety, the feeling of fullness, so overeating during a meal is less likely and a sense of fullness will last longer.

Proponents of the Paleo diet claim that this way of eating is healthier and leads to a variety of positive health outcomes including a decrease in caloric intake and lower body weight. Excess body weight has been linked to chronic disease risk so maintaining a healthy body weight is important. The Paleo diet has been associated with a decrease in harmful cholesterol (i.e., low-density lipoprotein cholesterol or LDLs) and an increase in good cholesterol (high-density lipoprotein cholesterol or HDLs). Having high levels of bad cholesterol (i.e., LDL) has been linked to increased risk of cardiovascular disease and stroke. Therefore, the Paleo diet is argued to be a healthy alternative to the American diet. It is unknown whether this dietary trend will be just another fad or whether this lifestyle is here to stay.

Justine J. Reel

See also: Detox Diets and Cleanses; Fad Diets

Bibliography

Caballero, Benamin. "The Global Epidemic of Obesity: An Overview." *Epidemiologic Reviews* 29 (2007): 1–5. https://doi.org/10.1093/epirev/mxm012.

Cordain, Loren. "A Brief History of the Contemporary Paleo Diet Movement." The Paleo Diet. Last modified July 24, 2015. Accessed November 22, 2017. http://thepaleodiet.com/a-brief-history-of-the-contemporary-paleo-diet-movement/.

Eaton, Stanley B., Loren Cordain, and Staffan Lindeberg. "Evolutionary Health Promotion: A Consideration of Common Counterarguments." *Preventive Medicine* 34 (2002): 119–123. https://doi.org/10.1006/pmed.2001.0966.

Eaton, Stanley B., and Stanley B. Eaton III. "Paleolithic vs. Modern Diets—Selected Pathophysiological Implications." *European Journal of Nutrition* 39, no. 2 (2000): 67–70. https://evolutionmedicine.files.wordpress.com/2009/11/eaton-2000.pdf.

Forman, John P., Meir J. Stampfer, and Gary C. Curhan. "Diet and Lifestyle Risk Factors Associated with Incident Hypertension in Women." *Journal of the American Medical Association* 302, no. 4 (2009): 401–411. https://doi.org/10.1001/jama.2009.1060.

Frassetto, Linda A., Monique Schloetter, Michele Mietus-Snyder, R. Curtis Morris Jr., and Anthony Sebastian. "Metabolic and Physiologic Improvements from Consuming a Paleolithic, Hunter-Gatherer Type Diet." *European Journal of Clinical Nutrition* 63, no. 8 (2009): 947–955. https://doi.org/10.1038/ejcn.2009.4.

Guthrie, Joanne F., Bing-Hwan Lin, and Elizabeth Frazao. "Role of Food Prepared Away from Home in the American Diet, 1977–78 versus 1994–96: Changes and Consequences." *Journal of Nutrition Education and Behavior* 34, no. 3 (2002): 140–150. https://doi.org/10.1016/S1499-4046(06)60083-3.

James, W. Philip T. "WHO Recognition of the Global Obesity Epidemic." *International Journal of Obesity* 32, suppl. 7 (2008): S120–S126. https://doi.org/10.1038/ijo.2008.247.

Leis, Harry P., Jr. "The Relationship of Diet to Cancer, Cardiovascular Disease and Longevity." *International Journal of Surgery* 76, no. 1 (1991): 1–5.

Lindeberg, Staffan. "Paleolithic Diets as a Model for Prevention and Treatment of Western Disease." *American Journal of Human Biology* 24, no. 2 (2012): 110–115. https://doi.org/10.1002/ajhb.22218.

Lindeberg, Staffan, Tommy Jonsson, Yvonne Granfeldt, E. Borgstrand, J. Soffman, Karin Sjöström, and Bo Ahrén. "A Palaeolithic Diet Improves Glucose Tolerance More Than a Mediterranean-Like Diet in Individuals with Ischaemic Heart Disease." *Diabetologia* 50, no. 9 (2007): 1795–1807. https://doi.org/10.1007/s00125-007-0716-y.

Masharani, Umesh, Prativa Sherchan, Monique C. Schloetter, Suzanne Stratford, Ai-Jiao Xiao, Anthony Sebastian, Nolte Kennedy, and Lynda A Frassetto. "Metabolic and Physiologic Effects from Consuming a Hunter-Gatherer (Paleolithic)-Type Diet in Type 2 Diabetes." *European Journal of Clinical Nutrition* 69, no. 8 (2015): 944–948. https://doi.org/10.1038/ejcn.2015.39.

Prentice, Andrew M. "The Emerging Epidemic of Obesity in Developing Countries." *International Journal of Epidemiology* 35, no. 1 (2006): 93–99. https://doi.org/10.1093/ije/dyi272.

van Dam, Rob M., Eric B. Rimm, Walter C. Willett, Meir J. Stampfer, and Frank B. Hu. "Dietary Patterns and Risk for Type 2 Diabetes Mellitus in U.S. Men." *Annals of Internal Medicine* 136, no. 3 (2002): 201–209. https://doi.org/10.7326/0003-4819-136-3-200202050-00008.

PARENTS

Parental eating behaviors and body image have been linked to the tendency for disordered eating practices, dietary restraint, and negative body image in young children and adolescents. For example, mothers who display symptoms of pathological eating behaviors were found to be more intrusive and controlling of their children's mealtimes and reported using more restrictive feeding practices. Fathers' eating attitudes and behaviors were also important determinants of children's eating attitudes and behaviors. Similarly, parents who express dissatisfaction with their bodies can model body shame and disgust, which is often internalized by younger children. This entry will discuss research related to eating disorder symptoms and parental styles, weight-related talk, and how parents can receive education about promoting healthy approaches to nutrition and physical activity to build positive body esteem and self-perceptions in children and adolescents.

Eating Disorder Symptoms and Parenting Styles

Mothers with eating disorder symptoms have a higher tendency to control children's feeding practices, characteristic of an authoritative parenting style. These mothers may also withdraw from conflict arising from stressful eating interactions with their children. This withdrawal may be associated with a more permissive or neglectful parenting style. In one study of 105 mothers with young children, higher levels of eating disorder symptoms in mothers were associated with authoritarian and permissive parenting styles.

Once children or adolescents display pathological eating behaviors, it is common for parents to oversee meals and encourage food consumption with a *finish your plate* mentality. Unfortunately, this type of encouragement around meals has not been found to be successful in curbing disordered eating behaviors. In fact, many treatment professionals caution parents to avoid being the food police, so that meals do not become a control issue. One exception is the Maudsley treatment approach that encourages parents to take an active role in the treatment team for eating disorders.

Influence of Mother Weight Talk and Dieting

Studies have found that parents' comments about weight and encouragement of dieting behaviors have adverse effects on the health of adolescents. For example, parental weight talk and weight-teasing were linked to decreased body satisfaction and led to eating disorder behaviors (e.g., fasting, restricting, skipping meals, purging).

Interestingly, one study found two-thirds of adolescent girls reported their mothers dieted or talked about their weight, and nearly half of the girls reported their mothers encouraged them to diet. In this same study, maternal dieting was associated with greater use of unhealthy and extreme weight control behaviors in the adolescent females. Mothers who talked about their weight, predicted weight

Parent of an Adult Daughter with an Eating Disorder:
An interview with "Sarah"

"Sarah" (pseudonym used to protect anonymity) is a parent of three children including a daughter who suffered with an eating disorder for a number of years. Sarah works as an executive assistant at a midsized university in the Southeastern United States. She expresses the perspective of a parent who actively works to support a daughter undergoing treatment for an eating disorder.

What age was your daughter when you realized she had a problem? What were the telltale signs that indicated she had an eating disorder?
Our daughter was a junior in college when we first suspected she had a problem. She was living in an apartment with four roommates in town. She would visit often. She was also dealing with a previous athletic injury postconcussion problem that we attributed any symptom or sign to, rather than the eating disorder. When we suspected she may have an eating disorder we asked her why she would always run upstairs to the bathroom immediately after eating and asked what she was doing or if she had a problem; she completely denied it. We were afraid to keep mentioning an eating disorder because we did not want to put the idea into her head. I mention this because our initial instincts were correct, but as a parent we tend to want to believe our children rather than trust our instincts.

Looking back, I missed so many telltale signs, always going into the bathroom right after eating, avoiding certain foods, distancing herself from friends, missing social events, avoiding going out to dinner, binge drinking, isolation, and becoming defiant. She also had cuts, sores, and redness around the corners of her mouth as well as dental problems. After graduation she moved to another state to live on her own and continued to isolate herself. When she was 23 we got a call from her therapist that she was bulimic and needed immediate medical attention.

What type of treatment did she receive (e.g., types of treatment providers and levels of care)? What seemed to work and what were the barriers for your daughter to overcoming her eating disorder?
She was immediately admitted to an intensive inpatient care facility that specialized in eating disorders while there she was also hospitalized as well to stabilize her electrolytes. The three week stay did not prove to be successful because of the constant conflict over the length of treatment needed, insurance issues, and her reluctance to address the eating disorder as a problem. While in treatment she also picked up other habits that she did not have before, stealing, hiding, and continuing to control her bulimia. She was unable to attend follow-up outpatient treatment therapy because the nearest care was over 100 miles away, which would have required her to stay in a hotel unsupervised to attend daily outpatient therapy. Because we could not afford this option as well as her uncooperative attitude, her therapist refused to continue treatment as well. This left her without any follow-up or treatment at all.

At this time her biggest barrier for her overcoming her eating disorder was herself, because she did not think this was a problem, or that she could die. Insurance also played a part, and I feel the center was more interested in the money rather than the patient, which took the focus away from the care of our daughter.

About a year later she finally admitted she had a problem and asked for help. We took her to an eating disorder treatment facility in our state. She received intensive inpatient care as well as hospitalization for her electrolytes. Her nine-week stay was successful because she was ready and receptive to treatment. It was not forced upon her. We were able to visit regularly, participate, and encourage her to heal and see the program through.

The biggest barrier for her overcoming her eating disorder was knowing she could not hide anymore and admitting she has a problem.

Did you engage in family therapy and how did you find that experience?

At the first eating disorder facility, we tried to have family therapy over the telephone, and the conversation was completely dominated about what would happen if the insurance would not continue to cover her stay. I cannot say we really focused on anything but insurance and also that she did not want to be in treatment.

We participated in family therapy at a facility in our state and it went very well. I think that we able to set the record straight (talk honestly and open and not let her tell half-truths) so the therapist could get a clear picture and our daughter could no longer lie or hide from problems this made a big difference.

We also participated in weekly drop in groups that were open to the current, and former patients and family. I found these sessions most helpful. It gave me the tools I need to talk to my daughter and to be able to tell if she is struggling. I was not alone.

What were the emotions you experienced being a parent of someone with an eating disorder?

There are so many emotions you experience as a parent. Scared, frightened that your child will die, always afraid of what's next. You are consumed with worry. You question everything you have done as a parent. You blame yourself. You are sad because you wonder if your child will ever be happy again. You are disappointed in your child for doing this to themselves and then you are disappointed in yourself for feeling this way about your child. You are angry because this is not what you wanted for your child. You feel lost and all alone. You are high strung and frustrated with the system and the fact that you can't concentrate on helping your child because you have to deal the logistics of finding the right care. You start to isolate yourself from friends and family yet you want to talk about it but are afraid of being judged, because of the stigma that goes with eating disorders. You feel guilty all the time because you also have other members of the family and responsibilities.

What would you tell other parents who just now realize their daughter or son has a problem? Any advice?

Looking back, I would tell other parents—trust your instincts. Don't be afraid to ask, and educate yourself on the signs. Look into the best care and the right fit for your daughter—you may need to get the best medical care at first, then find the best eating disorder facility. I would also tell them to talk to other parents or other girls that have been through this experience. It helps to know you are not alone. Also I learned little phrases and signs about struggling or relapsing that have helped me talk to my daughter. Be prepared to make some changes in your life as well. Do not police your child or force them to eat. It makes things worse, try to understand this is like any other disease and put yourself in their shoes. Offer encouragement as much as possible. This is a long, hard journey for everyone in the family. Tell your child you love her each and every day. Don't be a helicopter parent. Don't make them feel bad about themselves. You will find the right people and treatment for your child. Reach out to other parents who have and are experiencing what you are going through.

Do you believe it is possible for a person to be recovered from an eating disorder? Why or why not?
I do believe you can recover from an eating disorder, but like any other disease or addiction it will be a work in progress daily. In life there will be triggers and emotions that will set you back and hopefully with the right support system and inner strength you can fully recover.

What else would you like to add from the perspective of a parent who had a daughter with an eating disorder?
Dealing with a child with an eating disorder is one of the hardest challenges for a parent. I feel selfish when I say it has been one of the hardest times in my life because I do not have this disease, I don't have the body issues. When I reflect about my daughter, I think about all the changes and challenges she has been through; I am happy and thankful that I can see her enjoying life happy and healthy once again. Hang in there. You are not in this alone, we are learning more and more about eating disorders every day.

control behaviors and binge eating behaviors in daughters. Over a quarter (26 percent) of girls encouraged to diet by their mothers used extreme weight control behaviors, which was much higher than girls whose mothers did not encourage dieting behavior.

Influence of Father Dieting and Weight Talk

Forty percent of adolescent girls reported their father was on a diet, talked about his weight, or encouraged them to diet. Interestingly, father dieting was less associated with the negative outcomes that were observed for mother dieting. However, 22.2 percent of girls who reported their fathers talked about his weight admitted using extreme weight control behaviors, which was higher than for girls whose fathers did not discuss weight. Furthermore, girls' use of unhealthy weight control behaviors was associated with encouragement by their fathers to go on a diet.

Family Weight-Teasing

Alarmingly, one study found 60 percent of girls reported weight-related teasing by family members over the past year. Weight-related teasing by family members was associated with higher body mass index, body dissatisfaction, unhealthy weight control methods, and binge eating behaviors. The higher the frequency of weight-related teasing, the stronger the tendency to use more extreme weight control methods. Most researchers concur family members innocently tease adolescent children about weight and more education is needed about the influence this behavior can have triggering disordered eating and eating disorders.

Impact of Eating Disorders on Caregivers

Regardless of treatment approach used, it is important parents receive support and education during eating disorder treatment and recovery. Having a daughter, son, or loved one with an eating disorder can contribute to stress, guilt, and shame. One study found 27 percent of caregivers suffered from anxiety while 10.3 percent of caregivers reported depressive symptoms. Some of the significant stressors reported for mothers of eating-disordered individuals included the financial burden of treatment, inadequate health insurance (100 percent), family dynamics (70 percent), finding and navigating treatment (50 percent), and personal sacrifice (50 percent).

Identifying financial concerns related to treatment is not surprising, given the expense of eating disorder care. For instance, some residential eating disorder facilities charge $1,500 or more per day of treatment despite the need for more than 90 days of minimum treatment before discharge. Because it is unlikely an insurance company will pay for the recommended length of treatment, the family must often pay out of pocket to bridge the gap. Families reported using retirement funds or mortgaging a house to cover the costs in the desperation to save a son or daughter from an eating disorder.

Family dynamics are affected by the eating disorder and undergoing treatment. When a child is struggling with disordered eating, many family members report walking on egg shells. Once the problem is addressed, the family faces a long road of treatment and recovery. Parents note the effect this has on siblings, who may receive less attention and who may need to sacrifice their activities for time or finances required for eating disorder treatment. The dynamics of a family are often scrutinized in the treatment setting and certain family members may think they have been put under a microscope. Once contributing factors are identified, parents may be asked to change attitudes, communication patterns, and behaviors.

Unfortunately, parents express frustration that there is no clear path for eating disorder treatment. Because no single option was provided to treat a daughter or son, parents think they did not receive adequate guidance from treatment professionals (e.g., physicians). In some cases, options for specialized eating disorder treatment are scarce in a city or state, and providing care could require sending a son or daughter to another state with no guarantee of recovery. Some parents have also reported negative experiences with treatment providers or a lack of support upon discharge from an eating disorder–specific program into an outpatient setting.

Personal sacrifices are also cited by parents as a necessary outgrowth of providing treatment to a daughter or son with an eating disorder. Both parents reported the need to miss work to provide transportation or to attend appointments; they also reported financial sacrifices associated with the cost of treatment. Parents have expressed frustration over having routines disrupted by treatments (e.g., meal plans) that may require careful planning for family grocery shopping and meal preparation.

Parent Education

Although many factors contribute to disordered eating and eating disorders, parent dieting, talk about weight, and weight-related teasing all influence eating behaviors of children and adolescents. Therefore, it is necessary to provide parent education surrounding nutrition, physical activity, and body image. The BodyWorks program addresses the question of how to promote healthy eating and increased activity in the home." Another program, Off the C.U.F.F., teaches healthy communication skills that set the stage for stronger relationships between parents and adolescents. Ultimately, it is important parents receive support while their children receive treatment for eating disorders. Parents may find comfort by meeting with a therapist or attending a support group for parents of individuals with eating disorders.

Justine J. Reel

See also: BodyWorks; Children and Adolescents; Family Influences; Family Therapy; Off the C.U.F.F.

Bibliography

Blissett, Jackie, and Emma Haycraft. "Parental Eating Disorder Symptoms and Observations of Mealtime Interactions with Children." *Journal of Psychosomatic Research* 70 (2011): 368–371. https://doi.org/10.1016/j.jpsychores.2010.07.006.

Haycraft, Emma, and Jackie Blissett. "Eating Disorder Symptoms and Parenting Styles." *Appetite* 54 (2010): 221–224. https://doi.org/10/1016/j.appet.2009.11.009.

Keitel, Merle A., Melinda Parisi, Jessica L. Whitney, and Lauren F. Stack. "Salient Stressors for Mothers of Children and Adolescents with Anorexia Nervosa." *Eating Disorders: The Journal of Treatment and Prevention* 18 (2010): 435–444. https://doi.org/10.1080/10640266.2010. 511937.

Lock, James, and Daniel Le Grange. *Help Your Teenager Beat an Eating Disorder.* New York: Guilford Press, 2005.

Martin, Josune, Angel Padierna, Urko Aguirre, Jose M. Quintana, Carlota Las Hayas, and Pedro Munoz. "Quality of Life among Caregivers of Patients with Eating Disorders." *Quality of Life Research* 20, no. 9 (2011): 1359–1369. https://doi.org/10/1007/s11136-011-9873-z.

Neumark-Sztainer, Dianne, Katherine W. Bauer, Sarah Friend, Peter J. Hannan, Mary Story, and Jerica M. Berge. "Family Weight Talk and Dieting: How Much Do They Matter for Body Dissatisfaction and Disordered Eating Behaviors in Adolescent Girls." *Journal of Adolescent Health* 47 (2010): 270–276. https://doi.org/10.1016/j.jadohealth.2010.02.001.

Reba-Harreleson, Lauren, Ann Von Holle, Robert M. Hamer, Leila Torgersen, Ted Richborn-Kjennerud, and Cynthia M. Bulik. "Patterns of Maternal Feeding and Child Eating Associated with Eating Disorders in the Norwegian Mother and Child Cohort Study (MoBa)." *Eating Behaviors* 11, no. 1 (2010): 54–61. https://doi.org/10.1016/j.eatbeh.2009.09.004.

Rortveit, Kristine, Sture Astrom, and Elisabeth Sevrinsson. "The Meaning of Guilt and Shame: A Qualitative Study of Mothers Who Suffer from Eating Difficulties." *International Journal of Mental Health Nursing* 19 (2010): 231–239. https://doi.org/10.1111/j.1447-0349.2010.00672.x.

PERSONALITY CHARACTERISTICS

Eating disorders are caused by biological, psychological, and environmental factors. Psychological factors refer to personality characteristics commonly observed in individuals with eating disorders. Personality characteristics associated with eating disorders include, but are not limited to, perfectionism, impulsivity, being achievement-oriented, and exhibiting dichotomous thinking.

Perfectionism

Perfectionism is a personality trait characterized by high personal standards, self-criticism, intolerance of mistakes, and extreme organization and need for order. Perfectionism as a personality characteristic involves a tendency to place excessive emphasis on precision that involves overly critical evaluation of one's self if goals are not reached. This overconcern about mistakes often results in procrastination and the inability to complete tasks. One could imagine everyone experiences varying degrees of perfectionism during chance encounters on a daily basis. In the world of eating disorders, having high standards for self and a need for order are similar to the traits of other individuals without eating disorder diagnosis. On the other hand, perfectionism that results in a preoccupation with mistakes and performance anxiety has been shown to be higher in individuals diagnosed with eating disorders. Individuals with eating disorders also tend to set unrealistic personal standards and believe they are evaluated harshly by others. Additionally, research has indicated perfectionism does not operate differently by sex in individuals with eating disorders and is predictive of eating disorders 5–10 years down the road.

Research indicates perfectionism is strongly related to eating-disordered behaviors and highly perfectionistic individuals exhibit greater body dissatisfaction, dietary restraint, and purging behaviors. In one study, 17.6 percent of individuals with anorexia nervosa or bulimia nervosa demonstrated high self-oriented perfectionism and 10.2 percent of participants with clinically diagnosed eating disorders had high socially prescribed perfectionism. Statistically, the percentage of individuals with either type of perfectionism was significantly different from participants who were not eating-disordered. Of the two types of perfectionism, self-oriented perfectionism predicted eating disorders. Another study found 93 percent of the variance in body dissatisfaction, dietary restraint, and purging behaviors in women aged 18–31 years was explained by perfectionism. It has been suggested that perfectionism may be related to other personality characteristics that increase the risk of eating-disordered behaviors (e.g., perfectionism is related to low self-esteem), exacerbating the influence of either characteristic alone.

Impulsivity

Impulsiveness is a lack of forethought; it involves doing things with little regard for risks and consequences. Impulsiveness is linked to substance abuse and to bulimic symptoms. What is surprising is impulsiveness is more strongly related to purging behavior than binge eating behavior. It is unknown whether impulsiveness as a personality trait precedes bulimic symptomology or if the erratic mood changes result from dietary inconsistencies and emotional instability associated with bulimia nervosa. Additionally, individuals who exhibit more disordered-eating behaviors tend to demonstrate more sensation-seeking tendencies (e.g., outdoor activities that involve speed or danger, or trying novel experiences for the sake of experiencing new things). Sensation-seeking individuals are often more willing to take risks and ignore physical or social consequences of new and exciting experiences and sensations.

Interoceptive Awareness

Interoceptive awareness refers to clearly identifying one's emotions and accepting them. Individuals with eating disorders typically display poor interoceptive awareness. That is, they are often unclear about the type of physical or emotional response they are experiencing (e.g., knotted stomach) and tend to experience fear or guilt as a result of an experience. The second component, how one appraises or accepts physical or emotional experience, has been shown to be more predictive of dietary restraint in individuals with eating disorders. The nonacceptance of emotional/physical experience explained 27 percent of the variance in dietary restraint in a sample of 50 women with eating disorders in an outpatient treatment program. In another sample of 49 adolescents with eating disorders four years after an inpatient treatment program, interoceptive awareness was moderately negatively related to bulimic tendencies ($r = -.62, p < .01$). If one conceptualizes eating disorders on a continuum ranging from normal, asymptomatic eating behavior to eating-disordered behavior, individuals with low emotional awareness tend to be placed toward the symptomatic and eating-disordered end of the continuum.

Maturity Fears

Maturity fears represent the desire to return to preadolescent years when faced with the responsibilities of adulthood. A four-year longitudinal study of eating-disordered females demonstrated that maturity fears predicted poor outcomes in patients with anorexia. Among participants, maturity fears explained 62 percent of the variance in individuals with anorexia nervosa, restrictive type. With adults, maturity fears were revealed in 88.3 percent of individuals with anorexia nervosa.

Achievement Orientation

Achievement orientation is the need to succeed in comparison to others. That is, whereas some individuals may be motivated to improve their personal ability

PERSONALITY CHARACTERISTICS   **429**

beyond its previous measurement (e.g., marathon split times), individuals who are highly achievement-oriented are motivated to achieve in comparison to competition (e.g., placing first in the marathon). According to researchers, individuals with unresolved body image issues (i.e., overestimation of body shape and weight) tended to excessively control their diet and exercise habits to minimize body dissatisfaction. Additionally, hypercompetitiveness, or the need to be successful at all costs, has been documented in college students with eating disorders. As appearance is one domain of competition, it has been theorized that hypercompetitiveness is used by eating-disordered individuals to gain or regain control or to offset low self-esteem temporarily by being better than someone else. It is related to other personality traits common in individuals with eating disorders such as neuroticism and low self-esteem. As a result, hypercompetitiveness and the motivation to achieve in the domain of appearance (demonstrating achievement orientation) predicted disordered-eating behaviors in female college students.

Dichotomous Thinking

Dichotomous thinking refers to a need to see things as one way or another, black or white, right or wrong. Individuals who think in such extreme terms have more disordered-eating behaviors than individuals without eating-disordered symptoms and individuals who exhibit fewer disordered-eating behaviors. Although some research indicates dichotomous thinking does not increase at the same rate that disordered-eating behaviors increase, individuals who have disordered-eating behaviors report more dichotomous thinking than individuals who do not.

Neuroticism

Heightened levels of neuroticism, a propensity toward negative emotions like worry, anxiety, hypersensitivity, depression, guilt, fear, and disgust, are observed in individuals with disordered-eating behaviors. Individuals who exhibit more neurotic tendencies can have intense mood swings. This may interact with other personality traits present in individuals with disordered-eating behaviors. Neuroticism has been more evident in individuals with binge tendencies. It may be these individuals exhibit more neurotic tendencies because they tend to be more obsessive. That is, individuals with higher binge tendencies are more likely to express worry, anxiety, depression, guilt, and fear than clients with anorexia nervosa.

Approval from Others (Low Self-Esteem)

Although most individuals seek approval from others, research indicates the need to gain approval from others is higher in individuals with eating disorders. This need to obtain others' approval to be happy and impress others tends to increase as disordered eating symptomology intensifies. As some researchers suggest, gaining approval from others is based upon perceived worth (i.e., self-esteem) in the form of attractiveness. Therefore, if an individual requires approval from others to be happy, that individual must be viewed as attractive. This may be exacerbated in individuals who are preoccupied with physical appearance, may be more sensitive to interpersonal relationships, or have fragile self-esteem (i.e., narcissistic tendencies). Additionally, because individuals with eating-disordered symptomology often think in terms of black and white, they may believe the only way to gain approval is to lose weight and be perceived as attractive.

Researchers have found 20.8 percent of females in Spain in the age group of 12–21 years who exhibited higher scores on the EAT-40 had low self-esteem. As one might imagine, self-esteem is directly related to body dissatisfaction such that individuals with lower self-esteem also have greater body dissatisfaction. Moreover, individuals with lower self-esteem and greater body dissatisfaction tend to exhibit more disordered-eating behaviors. It seems low self-esteem, paired with high levels of perfectionism, may be a predisposing factor to eating disorder pathology.

Ashley M. Coker-Cranney and Justine J. Reel

See also: Causes; Personality Disorders; Protective Factors; Risk Factors

Bibliography

Borda Mas, Mercedes, Maria Luisa Avargues Navarro, Ana Maria Lopez Jimenez, Inmaculada Torres Perez, Carmen del Rio Sanchez, and Maria Angeles Perez San Gregorio. "Personality Traits and Eating Disorders: Mediating Effects of Self-Esteem and Perfectionism." *International Journal of Clinical and Health Psychology* 11 (2011): 205–227.

Burckle, Michelle A., Richard M. Ryckman, Joel A. Gold, Bill Thorton, and Roberta J. Audesse. "Forms of Competitive Attitude and Achievement Orientation in Relation to Disordered Eating." *Sex Roles* 40, no. 11 (1999): 853–870. https://doi.org/10.1023/A:1018873005147.

Cassin, Stephanie E., and Kristin M. von Ranson. "Personality and Eating Disorders: A Decade in Review." *Clinical Psychology Review* 25, no. 7 (2005): 895–916. http://dx.doi.org/10.1016/j.cpr.2005.04.012.

Castro-Fornieles, Josefina, Pilar Gual, Fransisca Lahortiga, Araceli Gila, Vanesa Casula, Cynthia Fuhrmann, Milagros Imirizaldu, Begona Saura, Esteve Martinez, and Josep Toro. "Self-Oriented Perfectionism in Eating Disorders." *International Journal of Eating Disorders* 40, no. 6 (2007): 562–568. https://doi.org/10.1002/eat.20393.

Cohen, Diane L., and Trent A. Petrie. "An Examination of Psychological Correlates of Disordered Eating among Undergraduate Women." *Sex Roles* 52, no. 1 (2005): 29–42. https://doi.org/10.1007/s11199-005-1191-x.

Garner, David M., Marion P. Olmsted, and Janet Polivy. "Development and Validation of a Multidimensional Eating Disorder Inventory for Anorexia Nervosa and Bulimia." *International Journal of Eating Disorders* 2 (1983): 15–34.

Merwin, Rhonda M., Nancy L. Zucker, Jennie L. Lacy, and Camden A. Elliott. "Interoceptive Awareness in Eating Disorders: Distinguishing Lack of Clarity from Non-acceptance of Internal Experience." *Cognition and Emotion* 24, no. 5 (2010): 892–902. http://dx.doi.org/10.1080/02699930902985845.

Peck, Lisa D., and Owen Richard Lightsey Jr. "The Eating Disorders Continuum, Self-Esteem, and Perfectionism." *Journal of Counseling and Development* 86, no. 2 (2008): 184–192. https://doi.org/10.1002/j.1556-6678.2008.tb00496.x.

Podar, Iris, Aave Hannus, and Juri Allik. "Personality and Affectivity Characteristics Associated with Eating Disorders: A Comparison of Eating Disordered, Weight-Preoccupied, and Normal Samples." *Journal of Personality Assessment* 73, no. 1 (1999): 133–147. http://dx.doi.org/10.1207/S15327752JPA730109.

Rossier, Valerie, Monique Bolognini, Bernard Plancherel, and Olivier Halfon. "Sensation Seeking: A Personality Trait Characteristic of Adolescent Girls and Young Women with Eating Disorders?" *European Eating Disorders Review* 8, no. 3 (2000): 245–252.

Stice, Eric. "Risk and Maintenance Factors for Eating Pathology: A Meta-Analytic Review." *Psychological Bulletin* 128, no. 5 (2002): 825–848. http://dx.doi.org/10.1037/0033 -2909.128.5.825.

van der Ham, T., D. C. van Stien, and H. van Engeland. "Personality Characteristics Predict Outcome of Eating Disorders in Adolescents: A 4-year Prospective Study." *European Child & Adolescent Psychiatry* 7, no. 2 (1998): 79–84. https://doi.org/10.1007 /s007870050051.

von Ransen, Kristin M. "Personality and Eating Disorders." In *Annual Review of Eating Disorders Part 2—2008,* edited by Stephen Wonderlich, James E. Mitchell, Martina de Zwaan, and Howard Steiger, 84–96. New York: Radcliffe Publishing, 2008.

PERSONALITY DISORDERS

Personality disorders represent a category of mental health diagnoses from the fifth edition of the *Diagnostic and Statistical Manual of Mental Disorders (DSM-5)* that covers a pattern of inflexible and maladaptive personality traits Certain enduring personality traits are displayed across social and personal contexts. An individual with a personality disorder often experiences subjective distress, problems with impulse control, and difficulty with interpersonal issues. Although personality disorders typically begin in adolescence or early adulthood, characteristics often endure and are tied to long-term concerns. When personality disorders are coupled with other mental disorders (e.g., eating disorders), the prognosis is generally poorer than if there was a sole diagnosis. Therefore, it is important that assessment for comorbid conditions (e.g., personality disorders) occur early in treatment with eating-disorder clients.

Types of Personality Disorders

The specific personality disorders identified in the *DSM-5* are paranoid personality disorder, schizoid personality disorder, schizotypal personality disorder, antisocial personality disorder, borderline personality disorder, histrionic personality disorder, narcissistic personality disorder, avoidant personality disorder, dependent personality disorder, obsessive-compulsive personality disorder, personality change due to another medical condition and other specified personality disorder, and unspecified personality disorder. Although all personality disorder diagnoses have been identified among eating-disordered clients, according to some studies the most common comorbid personality disorders with eating disorders are borderline personality disorder and obsessive-compulsive disorder. Borderline personality disorder is characterized by a pervasive pattern of instability in interpersonal relationships, self-image, and mood. Impulsivity is often observed by early adulthood and is present across contexts. Individuals with borderline personality disorder experience intense feelings of abandonment and have a pattern of intense and unstable relationships. It is common for these individuals to report love–hate relationships with others in their lives. Borderline personality disorder is the most commonly diagnosed personality disorder among individuals with an eating disorder diagnosis. In fact, borderline personality occurs in 28 percent of individuals with bulimia nervosa and in 25 percent of individuals who have anorexia nervosa with purging symptoms.

Obsessive-compulsive personality disorder was the second most common personality disorder in individuals with eating disorders. Obsessive-compulsive personality disorder, a separate diagnosis from obsessive-compulsive disorder (OCD), is characterized by a preoccupation with orderliness, perfectionism, and mental and interpersonal control. Individuals with obsessive-compulsive personality disorder struggle with flexibility, openness, and efficiency. Behaviors such as painstaking attention to rules, trivial details, lists, and schedules appear in early adulthood. Individuals with anorexia nervosa (restricting type) show a 22 percent prevalence rate of obsessive-compulsive personality disorder. These rates of personality disorders were higher than the estimated rates of 5–10 percent within the general population.

Treatment Implications of Personality Disorders and Eating Disorders

It is important to address rigid personality patterns and impulse control in treatment to prevent relapse in eating disorder clients who have personality disorders. Therefore, dialectical behavior therapy (DBT), originally developed for individuals with personality disorders, is commonly used as part of a comprehensive treatment program in individual and group settings. Individuals are challenged to be mindful and notice when they are experiencing emotional dysregulation so they can use effective and adaptive coping skills, rather than revert to eating-disordered behaviors. Unfortunately, personality disorders have often been associated with a lower recovery rate and higher rates of relapse in residential and inpatient populations. Therefore, clinicians with strong boundaries who are trained in DBT are most ideal for addressing the complexity of comorbid eating disorder and personality disorders.

Justine J. Reel

See also: Anxiety Disorders; Assessment; Comorbidity; Depression; Personality Characteristics; Treatment

Bibliography

American Psychiatric Association. *Diagnostic and Statistical Manual of Mental Disorders*, 5th ed. (*DSM-5*). Washington, DC: American Psychiatric Association Publishing, 2013.

American Psychiatric Association. *Diagnostic and Statistical Manual of Mental Disorders*, 4th ed., text rev. Washington, DC: American Psychiatric Association Publishing, 2000.

Chen, Eunice Yu, Milton Zebediah Brown, Melanie Susanna Harned, and Marsha Marie Linehan. "A Comparison of Borderline Personality Disorder with and without Eating Disorders." *Psychiatry Research* 170, no. 1 (2009): 86–90. https://doi.org/10.1016/j.psychres. 2009.03.006.

Chen, Eunice Yu, Michael Sean McCloskey, Sara Michelson, Kathryn Hope Gordon, and Emil Coccaro. "Characterizing Eating Disorders in a Personality Disorders Sample." *Psychiatry Research* 185 (2011): 427–432. https://doi.org/10.1016/j.psychres.2010.07.002.

Courbasson, Christine, and Jacqueline M. Brunshaw. "The Relationship between Concurrent Substance Use Disorders and Eating Disorders with Personality Disorders." *International Journal of Environmental Research and Public Health* 6 (2009): 2076–2089. https://doi.org/10.3390/ijerph6072076.

De Bolle, Marleen, Barbara De Clercq, Alexandra Pham-Scottez, Saskia Meis, Jean-Pierre Rolland, Julien Daniel Guelfi, Caroline Braet, and Filip De Fruyt. "Personality Pathology Comorbidity in Adult Females with Eating Disorders." *Journal of Health Psychology* 16 (2011): 303–313. https://doi.org/10.1177/1359105310374780.

Diaz-Marsa, Marina, Jose L. Carrasco, Laura de Anta, Rosa Molina, Jeronimo Saiz, Jesus Cesar, and Juan J. Lopez-Ibor. "Psychobiology of Borderline Personality Traits Related to Subtypes of Eating Disorders: A Study of Platelet MAO Activity." *Psychiatry Research* 190, no. 2–3 (2011): 287–290. https://doi.org/10.1016/j.psychres.2011.04.035.

Lilenfeld, Lisa Rachelle Riso, Carli Heather Jacobs, Amanda Michelle Woods, and Angela Katherine Picot. "A Prospective Study of Obsessive-Compulsive and Borderline Personality Traits, Race and Disordered Eating." *European Eating Disorders Review* 16 (2008): 124–132. https://doi.org/10.1002/erv.842.

Rowe, Sarah L., Jenny Jordan, Virginia V. W. Mcintosh, Frances A. Carter, Chris Frampton, Cynthia M. Bulik, and Peter R. Joyce. "Complex Personality Disorder in Bulimia Nervosa." *Comprehensive Psychiatry* 51 (2010): 592–598. https://doi.org/10.1016/j.comppsych.2010.02.012.

Sansone, Randy A., Jamie W. Chu, and Michael W. Wiederman. "Body Image and Borderline Personality Disorder among Psychiatric Inpatients." *Comprehensive Psychiatry* 51 (2010): 579–584. https://doi.org/10.1016/j.comppsych.2010.04.001.

Sansone, Randy A., and Lori A. Sansone. "Personality Pathology and Its Influence on Eating Disorders." *Innovations in Clinical Neuroscience* 8, no. 3 (2011): 14–17.

PHYSICAL SELF-PERCEPTIONS

Physical self-perceptions, part of an individual's overall self-concept, are specifically associated with how a person perceives his or her physical appearance, attractiveness, condition, strength, and competence. In other words, physical self-perceptions include an individual's evaluation of his or her physical appearance as well as physical abilities. Physical self-perceptions are strongly related to general self-concept and self-esteem.

Perceived Physical Attractiveness

Perceptions of physical appearance seem to have particular influence on how individuals see themselves overall. This is not surprising given the social influences of mass media and the value placed upon an attractive and sexually appealing physique. In cultures where physical beauty is desired and socially and economically rewarded, it is logical that appearance would play a central role in how individuals evaluate themselves. Physical self-perceptions appear to have a strong effect on girls and women, who generally rate their perceived appearance and attractiveness lower than boys and men. Strong cultural pressure to attain and maintain a socially and sexually desirable physique, directed toward females, probably contributes to this sex-related pattern.

Perceived Physical Competence

Perceived physical competence is another important aspect of physical self-concept and is moderately related to overall self-esteem. Individuals who believe they have strong physical skills and abilities are likely to have positive perceptions about themselves in general. Men and boys, compared to women and girls, tend to have more positive evaluations of physical skills and competence. Males are socialized to participate in sports and athletics from a young age, which may influence perceptions of athletic and physical ability and skills. Early experiences and social reinforcement send clear and consistent messages to boys that excelling in sports is a sign of masculinity, which is highly valued in society. Although it is now more socially acceptable for girls and women to participate in sports and be competent athletes, the expectation is still stronger for boys and men. Thus, sex differences in perceptions of physical and athletic competence remain.

Physical Self-Perceptions and Physique Control and Eating Behaviors

Positive perceptions of one's physical self are associated with a number of healthy physical behaviors and psychological characteristics. Individuals who think well of their bodies, in terms of both appearance and competence, are more likely to be physically active and engage in healthful eating. Similarly, positive psychological characteristics such as confidence and assertiveness are generally higher in individuals with positive self-evaluations of their bodies. Unfortunately, negative perceptions of one's physical self are related to unhealthy behaviors and psychological characteristics. Specifically, individuals with negative views of their bodies are more likely to engage in damaging body control and eating behaviors.

Some individuals, unhappy with physical appearance and competence, engage in behaviors intended to move their bodies toward what they perceive as a more desirable and attractive shape. Whereas girls and women often desire a thinner, leaner body shape, boys and men often want a more muscular and defined physique. Thus, the types of common body control behaviors vary. Both males and females report restricting eating and increasing physical activity. However, males are more likely to restrict eating to high-protein foods and to increase strength training with the goal of developing musculature and losing body fat. Females are more likely to restrict caloric intake and to increase aerobic activity to lose weight and attain a thinner physique. More extreme physique and weight and body control behaviors are self-induced vomiting and use of diuretics and laxatives. Such behaviors can be dangerous and damaging to one's physical health.

Negative perceptions of one's appearance and attractiveness also are associated with disordered eating attitudes and behaviors. Individuals who are unhappy and dissatisfied with their bodies are anxious about how others perceive and evaluate their physiques (e.g., social physique anxiety) and have higher tendencies to develop disordered-eating behaviors. For example, negative perceptions of physical attractiveness are related to binge eating and bulimic symptoms, body dissatisfaction, and a strong desire to be thin. Additionally, individuals diagnosed with eating disorders report more negative physical appearance perceptions compared to individuals without eating disorders. It may be the case that dissatisfaction with one's body promotes unhealthy eating behaviors; thus poor physical self-concept can be an early sign of potentially problematic eating.

Assessment of Physical Self-Perceptions

One of the most commonly used assessments of physical self-perception is the Physical Self-Perception Profile (PSPP), developed by Fox and Corbin in 1989. The PSPP includes five 6-item subscales: perceived sport competence, body attractiveness, physical conditioning, physical strength, and general self-worth. Items are presented in a structured alternative format; that is, individuals select one of two options presented (e.g., "Some people are fit" but "Other people are not fit") and then identify how true a statement is for them (e.g., "Very like me" or "Somewhat like me"). Items are scored and summed for each subscale for a subscale score, and all items are summed for a total test score. Low scores indicate poor self-perceptions, and high scores indicate positive self-perceptions. The PSPP is appropriate for adults and has demonstrated evidence of cross-cultural validity (i.e., the measurement is appropriate for use even with individuals outside of the United States). Additionally, there is a separate version of the PSPP that is appropriate for use with children and adolescents.

Strategies for Enhancing Physical Self-Perceptions

Although some individuals engage in excessive exercise or obligatory exercise to cope with negative physical self-perceptions associated with disordered eating, in general, physical activity improves perceived physical self-concept. In a review of research studies that implemented an exercise intervention, Fox found 78 percent of the studies demonstrated improved physical self-perceptions. There are several explanations for these findings. Actual improvements in physical fitness and changes in one's physique resulting from exercise may result in improved self-perceptions. As individuals engage in physical activity, their bodies may start to approximate socially idealized bodies, which, in turn, may lead to positive evaluations of appearance and attractiveness. Additionally, individuals may experience enhanced self-confidence and perceptions of competence associated with physical activity. Improvements in mood and reductions in negative affect from exercise may also contribute to the psychological benefit of physical activity and exercise, which may have positive effects on how individuals evaluate themselves and their bodies.

There seems to be a reciprocal relationship between physical self-concept and physical activity; physical self-concept influences physical activity and physical activity influences physical self-concept. In other words, (1) interventions targeting improved physical self-concept may be effective in increasing physical activity, and (2) interventions targeting increased physical activity may increase positive perceptions of the physical self. Thus, health professionals have multiple options for effectively intervening to improve the psychological and physical health of individuals.

Christy Greenleaf

See also: Body Esteem; Body Image; Figural Rating Scales; Prevention; Skin Tone

Bibliography

Bardone-Cone, Anna M., Lauren M. Schaefer, Christine R. Maldonado, Ellen E. Fitzsimmons, Megan B. Harney, Melissa A. Lawson, D. Paul Robinson, Aneesh Tosh, and Roma Smith. "Aspects of Self-Concept and Eating Disorder Recovery: What Does the Sense of Self Look Like When an Individual Recovers from an Eating Disorder?" *Journal of Social and Clinical Psychology* 29 (2010): 821–846.

Fox, Kenneth R. "The Effects of Exercise on Self-Perceptions and Self-Esteem." In *Physical Activity and Psychological Well-Being,* edited by Stuart J. H. Biddle, Kenneth R. Fox, and Steve H. Boutcher, 88–117. London: Routledge, 2000.

Fox, Kenneth R., and Charles B. Corbin. "The Physical Self-Perception Profile: Development and Preliminary Validation." *Journal of Sport & Exercise Psychology* 11 (1989): 408–430.

Gentile, Brittany, Shelly Grabe, Brenda Dolan-Pascoe, Jean M. Twenge, and Brooke E. Wells. "Gender Differences in Domain-Specific Self-Esteem: A Meta-Analysis." *Review of General Psychology* 13, no. 1 (2009): 34–45. http://dx.doi.org/10.1037/a0013689.

Hagger, Martin S., Stuart J. H. Biddle, Edward W. Chow, Natalia Stambulova, and Maria Kavussanu. "Physical Self-Perceptions in Adolescence: Generalizability of a Hierarchical Multidimensional Model across Three Cultures." *Journal of Cross-Cultural Psychology* 34, no. 6 (2003): 611–628. https://doi.org/10.1177/0022022103255437.

Hagger, Martin S., and Andy Stevenson. "Social Physique Anxiety and Physical Self-Esteem: Gender and Age Effects." *Psychology and Health* 25 (2010): 89–110. http://dx.doi.org/10.1080/08870440903160990.

Kerremans, Anneleen, Laurence Claes, and Patricia Bijttebier. "Disordered Eating in Adolescent Males and Females: Associations with Temperament, Emotional and Behavioral Problems and Perceived Self-Competence." *Personality and Individual Differences* 49, no. 8 (2010): 955–960. http://dx.doi.org/10.1016/j.paid.2010.08.003.

Marsh, Herbert W., Athanasious Papaioannou, and Yannis Theodorakis. "Causal Ordering of Physical Self-Concept and Exercise Behavior: Reciprocal Effects Model and the Influence of Physical Education Teachers." *Health Psychology* 25, no. 3 (2006): 316–328. http://dx.doi.org/10.1037/0278-6133.25.3.316.

Mehlenbeck, Robyn S., Elissa Jelalian, Elizabeth E. Lloyd-Richardson, and Chantelle N. Hart. "Effects of Behavioral Weight Control Intervention on Binge Eating Symptoms of Overweight Adolescents." *Psychology in the Schools* 46, no. 8 (2009): 776–786. https://doi.org/10.1002/pits.20416.

Taylor, Adrian E., and Ken R. Fox. "Effectiveness of a Primary Care Exercise Referral Intervention for Changing Physical Self-Perceptions over 9 Months." *Health Psychology* 24 (2005): 11–21. http://dx.doi.org/10.1037/0278-6133.24.1.11.

Welk, Gregory J., and Bob Eklund. "Validation of the Children and Youth Physical Self-Perceptions Profile for Young Children." *Psychology of Sport & Exercise* 6 (2005): 51–65. http://dx.doi.org/10.1016/j.psychsport.2003.10.006.

PICA

Pica is in the feeding and eating disorder section of the *Diagnostic and Statistical Manual of Mental Disorders*, fifth edition (*DSM-5*). Pica is the persistent eating of nonnutritive substances for at least one month, when this behavior is developmentally inappropriate (i.e., older than 18 to 24 months). The type of substance ingested varies by age with infants and younger children eating paint, plaster, string, hair, or cloth. Older children with pica have been observed eating animal droppings, sand, insects, leaves, or pebbles. Adolescents and adults with pica often consume clay or soil. Other nonfood substances ingested by individuals with pica include laundry starch, vinyl gloves, plastic, pencil erasers, ice, fingernails, coal, chalk, light bulbs, needles, cigarette butts, and burnt matches. In contrast to eating disorders like anorexia nervosa and bulimia nervosa, pica does not represent a food aversion, fear of gaining weight, or body image disturbance.

Frequency of Pica

The exact prevalence of pica is unknown because the disorder is often unrecognized and underreported. Pica is observed more commonly during the second and third years of life. Pica occurs in 25–33 percent of young children and in 20 percent of children seen in mental health clinics. Children who are developmentally delayed (i.e., intellectual disabilities) or suffering from autism are affected more often than children without intellectual disabilities. The risk for the development of pica and the severity of pica increases with increasing severity of the intellectual disability. In fact, pica represents the most prevalent type of eating-related diagnosis in individuals who have an intellectual disability. In one study, pica was observed in 25.8 percent of persons with intellectual disabilities in a mental health institution.

It is rare for an adult to have pica unless he or she has an intellectual disability, with a few exceptions cited for pregnant women. In terms of sex, pica typically occurs in equal numbers among boys and girls. It is considered rare for pica to occur in adolescent males of average intelligence who live in developed countries. Risk factors for pica include poverty, neglect, lack of parental supervision, and developmental delay.

Treatment for Pica

Treatment is indicated for persons with pica and has typically involved behavioral approaches using reinforcers and punishers to shape behaviors. Although behavioral approaches have shown moderate improvement, social interaction has been found to lower rates of pica. When an individual had the opportunity to have social contact, the more pica-related behaviors were reduced or went away. Treatment has often involved introducing a new task to replace pica behavior. Because pica can include ingesting toxic substances, it has been found to be more deadly than other forms of self-injurious behavior.

Justine J. Reel

See also: Avoidant/Restrictive Food Intake Disorder; *Diagnostic and Statistical Manual of Mental Disorders*; Intellectual Disabilities and Body Image; Nutritional Deficiencies; Orthorexia Nervosa; Picky Eating; Rumination Disorder

Bibliography

American Psychiatric Association. *Diagnostic and Statistical Manual of Mental Disorders*, 5th ed. (*DSM-5*). Washington, DC: American Psychiatric Association Publishing, 2013.

Ammaniti, Massimo, Loredana Lucarelli, Silvia Cimino, Francesca D'Olimpio, and Irene Chatoor. "Feeding Disorders of Infancy: A Longitudinal Study to Middle Childhood." *International Journal of Eating Disorders* 4 (2011): 1–9. https://doi.org/10.1002/eat.20925.

Fotoulaki, Maria, Paraskevi Panagopoulou, Ioannis Efstration, and Sanda Nousia-Arvanitakis. "Pitfalls in the Approach to Pica." *European Journal of Pediatrics* 166 (2007): 623–624. https://doi.org/10.1007/s00431-006-0282-1.

Maslinski, Pantcho G., and Jeffrey A. Loeb. "Pica-Associated Cerebral Edema in an Adult." *Journal of the Neurological Sciences* 225 (2004): 149–151. https://doi.org/10.1016/j.jns.2004.07.016.

Piazza, Cathleen C., Wayne W. Fisher, Gregory P. Hanley, Linda A. LeBlanc, April S. Worsdell, Steven E. Lindauer, and Kris M. Keeney. "Treatment of Pica through Multiple Analyses of Its Reinforcing Functions." *Journal of Applied Behavior Analysis* 31, no. 2 (1998): 165–189. https://doi.org/10.1901/jaba.1998.31-165.

Wasano, Lauren C., John C. Borrero, and Carolynn S. Kohn. "Brief Report: A Comparison of Indirect Versus Experimental Strategies for the Assessment of Pica." *Journal of Autism Developmental Disorders* 39 (2009): 1582–1586. https://doi.org/10.1007/s10803-009-0766-8.

PICKY EATING

When people hear the phrase "picky eater," images of young children who only eat French fries and chicken nuggets and who refuse to touch a vegetable might come to mind. Indeed, research has shown that roughly 25 percent of young children are picky eaters. Although most of research on this topic focuses primarily on children, there is accumulating evidence suggesting adults suffer from picky eating as well.

Picky eating is defined as a reluctance to try new foods, and a highly restricted diet. These highly restricted diets usually consist of highly palatable foods high in sugar and fats, such as French fries and chicken nuggets. In a range of populations and ages, picky eating has been associated with poor nutrition and an elevated risk for subsequent mental illness, particularly internalizing disorders such as depression and anxiety. In the most recent *Diagnostic and Statistical Manual of Mental Disorders* (*DSM-5*), a new diagnostic category was added under eating disorders to capture picky eating. This new category, referred to as avoidant/restrictive food intake disorder (ARFID), highlights the recent interest and emerging research on this topic.

Although typically seen as a problem affecting children, picky eating in adulthood is a rapidly growing area of interest. Children with picky eating appear to suffer from poorer nutritional quality and increased behavioral problems than non-picky eaters; however, picky eating can be a phase children eventually outgrow.

Children with Eating/Feeding Disorders:
An Interview with Hannah Hopkins

Hannah Hopkins is currently a master's student at the University of North Carolina at Wilmington in the school of social work. She is specializing in substance abuse and hopes to work in the addictions field. Prior to beginning her master's studies, Hannah received her bachelor's of science degree in psychology from Duke University. During her undergraduate career, Hannah got involved in the Duke Center for Eating Disorders through research, and this sparked her passion for research in this field. Following graduation from Duke, Hannah remained at the Center for Eating Disorders for a year where she worked on a clinical trial testing a new treatment for childhood picky eating and anxiety. She was responsible for recruiting children and their families for this study, as well as leading them through much of the research protocol over the course of several months. She also had the opportunity to be involved in several side projects, including a study investigating friendships in anorexia nervosa.

What tells you that a child is struggling with an eating or feeding disorder and may need treatment?
Children who have eating or feeding disorders typically show other signs of psychological distress. They may be anxious, withdrawn, or have temper outbursts. Obsessive-compulsive behaviors and depression are also common correlates of eating disorders in childhood. Complaining of chronic tummy pain is also common in children with an eating/feeding disorder; they may be too young to identify feelings of hunger, satiety, or even emotional experiences (e.g., nervous butterflies) that accompany eating disorders.

For parents, be on the lookout for children who put themselves on a diet, particularly if they seem "too young" to diet. Although this is certainly not a 100 percent guarantee that your child is suffering from an eating disorder, it does indicate that your child has identified a way in which they can control their bodies. Additionally, children who come from families where family members have a history of mental illness are at higher risk for eating disorders (as well as many other mental illnesses). A history of sexual or physical abuse can also put a child at higher risk for developing an eating disorder.

Teachers should be aware of children who exhibit anxiety at eating in front of others or who consistently complain of stomachaches. Chronic abdominal pain is one of the most frequent physical complaints in school-aged children, but it can put a child at greater risk for developing an eating disorder as they grow older. Children who come from chaotic or dysfunctional home environments may also be at greater risk for eating disorders.

It can often be very difficult for parents and caregivers to get resolution for their concerns when speaking with primary care providers (PCPs). The general benchmark used to assess children's health is whether they are meeting their anticipated growth markers. If the child appears to be on a developmentally healthy trajectory and does not manifest any extreme outward distress, it can be very difficult for family physicians and PCPs to identify feeding/eating disorders. If you suspect that your child may be struggling with a feeding/eating disorder, one of the best courses of action is to take your child to a specialist, such as a clinical psychologist or psychiatrist, with some experience in pediatric eating disorders.

How do difficulties with eating/feeding look different as children grow older?
In infants and babies (birth–24 months), eating and feeding disorders correlate directly with the child's development. Infants who fail to latch onto the breast/bottle, do not ingest an appropriate amount of food, or seem unmotivated to eat are considered to have a feeding disorder. As babies grow older, difficulties with weaning and the transition to solid foods become more important.

In early childhood (about 2–6 years), picky eating is the most common difficulty. Children who regularly refuse foods or who can eat only a very limited number of items may be at higher risk for eating disorder behaviors in adolescence or young adulthood. Oftentimes, these children are so particular in their food preferences that their parents/caregivers are forced to prepare special meals for them. In some cases, these children may be so limited in their choices that it makes it difficult to take the child to restaurants.

As children get older and enter school, serious eating difficulties may begin to manifest in other ways. For example, children who are at higher risk for eating disorders later in life may be unable to eat in front of others at lunchtime. School-aged children (6–12 years) may also begin to complain of chronic tummy pains or exhibit anxiety in anticipation of mealtimes. This may also be the age when children begin to say they're "on a diet."

Once children enter puberty around the age of 12, they are at a much higher risk for the onset of eating disorders. Teens who are struggling with eating disorders may withdraw socially, begin to wear baggy clothing, overexercise, or experiment with drugs, alcohol, or risky sexual behaviors. They may also suffer from depression, anxiety, and other mental illness. This is typically the age at which eating disorders like anorexia and bulimia first get diagnosed.

What does treatment for eating/feeding difficulties in children look like?
Treating eating and feeding disorders in childhood almost always involves the entire family. Parents and caregivers are active in the treatment process. Additionally, developmentally appropriate interventions are important for children (i.e., the language and content of therapy or counseling sessions needs to be tailored to the child's age and developmental status). This can present an extra challenge for therapists or medical professionals who are trying to connect with a child. Oftentimes, working with children calls for a more interactive and task-driven approach to therapy than would be used with adults. Interdisciplinary treatment is also important. Nutritionists, psychiatrists, therapists, teachers, guidance counselors, and parents may all be involved in the development and administration of therapy for these children.

Many researchers and medical professionals have cautioned that picky eating in childhood is not uncommon and may not be a cause for concern. What signs tell you when a child is experiencing eating difficulties that are beyond the scope of "normal"?
It is important to acknowledge that picky or fussy eating is quite common in children and is often a stage that children grow out of. However, in some cases, picky or fussy eating can be an indication of something more serious. Distinguishing between those cases is something that researchers and medical professionals are still trying to get a firm handle on. Currently, there is no hard and fast rule that has scientific evidence to support it. Unfortunately, this is often a very dissatisfactory and frightening answer for parents and caregivers who are concerned about

their child. Some warning signs that your child's picky eating is more serious may include the following:

- Your child's eating behaviors make it difficult to take them out to restaurants
- You must prepare special meals for your child
- Your child's eating preferences pose a risk for your child's health (e.g., no vegetable intake, will only eat junk food)

In general, children who are at higher risk for developing eating disorders may show signs of other mental illness, including anxiety, obsessive-compulsive behaviors, depression, and oppositional defiant disorder. Children who say they are dieting or frequently discuss their bodies in a negative or degrading way are also more likely to meet criteria for an eating disorder. Additionally, complaints of chronic unexplained tummy pains may also be a clue that your child is experiencing eating difficulties that warrant some additional attention.

What advice or recommendations would you give to a parent who is concerned about their child's eating behaviors?
Keeping a food diary is one of the best ways to collect information about your child's eating. Try to be as specific as possible in your diary, and try recording information about your child's mood and the environment as well. Food diaries help parents to identify patterns in their child's eating behaviors, and it also serves as a great resource for medical professionals if ever needed.

For parents who are struggling with trying to broaden their child's food choices, implementing a reward system is another great tool. The reward can be anything that the child finds enjoyable, like having a sleepover or getting extra TV time. Depending on what your goals are for the child, rewards can be earned for all sorts of behaviors, including trying new foods or finishing their vegetables. The reward system can be as simple or as complex as you wish, but try to keep the rewards attainable for the child.

If your concern persists, speak with others that your child has regular contact with, such as teachers or coaches. These individuals may be able to give you a more detailed picture of what your child's eating looks like in different contexts. Additionally, these people may be able to provide consistency in enforcing expectations for your child's mealtime/eating behavior.

Last, reach out to your family practitioner, PCP, or a specialist. Keep in mind that many family doctors are not trained in diagnosing or treating pediatric eating disorders, so seeking the opinion of a specialist may be an important step. Prepare for your appointment with a list of specific concerns and questions you would like to get answered. Bringing in a food diary or any sort of detailed record of the problem(s) is also helpful.

Adults with picky eating suffer from both the detrimental health effects of a limited diet and the negative effects associated with identifying as different from friends and family. Limited research has suggested that behavioral training, exposure therapy, and cognitive behavioral therapy are the most effective treatments for picky eating, but more research is needed to test treatments in adults as well as in children for whom picky eating is more than just a phase.

Picky Eating in Children

Roughly a quarter of all children between the ages of 1.5 years and 12 years old are picky eaters. For many children, this behavior is treated as a normal stage of development that tends to pass with maturity. For a few children, however, the problem persists longer, is more severe, and can be predictive of future health outcomes. Children who continue to be picky eaters (i.e., children for whom picky eating is more than just a phase) are more likely to exhibit generalized behavior problems (e.g., temper tantrums) and internalizing psychopathology (e.g., depression, anxiety) than nonpicky counterparts. Picky eating has been shown to significantly reduce the nutritional content of a child's diet and put a child at risk for being underweight throughout development. Additionally, having a persistent picky eater in a family has been shown to contribute to more family conflicts surrounding food, particularly between parents and child. Persistent picky eating in childhood has been associated with a higher risk of various mental disorders later in life, namely anorexia nervosa, anxiety disorders, and overall lower quality of life.

Several early life factors are implicated in the development of persistent picky eating in childhood. One study found that abnormal breastfeeding behaviors (fewer sucks per feeding) during the first month of life significantly predicted picky eating behaviors in young childhood. Children with difficult temperaments early in life were more likely to develop picky eating later in childhood. Other studies have found evidence suggesting a mother's attitudes toward eating and body image have important effects on children with picky eating; mothers who report being focused on their own weight and shape were significantly more likely to have a child who exhibited picky eating symptoms. Additionally, mothers who identified as being more emotional and who have greater negative affect were more likely to raise picky eaters.

Picky Eating in Adults

The majority of the literature investigating picky eating has focused on children and young adolescents, but a growing body of research is examining picky eating in adults. Adult picky eating is defined similarly to picky eating in children, with new food avoidance and a highly restricted diet being central to the definition. However, the definition of adult picky eating is often expanded to include sensory sensitivities (e.g., aversion to textures, tastes, and smells).

Although picky eating can sometimes be considered a normal stage of development in childhood, it is more complicated in the adult population. Adult picky eating is generally a long-standing behavioral pattern, and it is intertwined with individual's identities, family structure, and daily functioning. A recently published study investigated how adults with picky eating viewed themselves and their eating habits. Generally, these picky eaters were keenly aware of how their eating behaviors marked them as different from their friends and family, and many of them expressed sadness, shame, and embarrassment over the effect their pickiness had on social functioning. Additionally, many of the adult picky eaters viewed themselves as powerless over their diets.

Several factors characterize adult picky eaters and distinguish them from both nonpicky adults and adults with other eating disorders. One study surveyed over 6,500 adults and found picky eaters were significantly less likely to have four-year college degrees, exhibited higher obsessive-compulsive disorder symptoms, and reported poorer quality of interpersonal relationships compared to a healthy control group as well as an eating-disordered group. Other research has shown adult picky eaters consider themselves less healthy than others, are more rigid and ritualistic in their eating behaviors (e.g., food needs to be prepared a special way), and have higher levels of depression.

Treatment Approaches for Picky Eating

Interestingly, a significant amount of the research investigating treatment options for picky eaters has been conducted with children who have autism, a population for whom picky eating is extremely common and usually much more disruptive. Among the most popular and widely studied treatment approaches for young picky eaters are variants on behavioral training. Behavioral training uses goals to motivate change and monitor progress. For example, a behavioral training program for a five-year-old picky eater may set a minimum number of chews, swallows, and/or bites of food that need to be achieved per meal. Following successful completion of these goals, the child would get rewarded with something pleasurable, such as time to watch television along with praise for reaching the goal. This treatment option strengthens the association in a child's mind between achieving meal-related goals and the pleasurable activity or reward. Goals can be adjusted regularly and gradually to incorporate positive behaviors (e.g., add one new vegetable to try per week or add five chews per meal).

Another treatment option receiving attention in the literature is exposure therapy. Exposure therapy gradually introduces a noxious stimuli (i.e., something feared or unwanted by an individual) and uses elements of cognitive behavioral therapy to coach someone through these levels of exposure. For example, an exposure therapy program for the same five-year-old may focus on incorporating peas (a rejected food) into the child's diet. The first level of exposure to peas would be having a child smell peas. Next, the child would be asked to hold peas, then put one pea on the lips, then the tongue, then chew, etc., and gradually work up to a child tasting, chewing, and swallowing an entire serving of peas. With this treatment approach, food preparation plays an important role. For example, if a child refuses to eat carrots based on their texture (e.g., too crunchy), levels of exposure may include introducing carrots prepared differently (such as boiled, minced, shredded) to a child or pureeing the carrots and mixing them with other foods, such as applesauce or mashed potatoes. Typically, this approach works best with older individuals who are highly motivated to achieve a goal.

Generally, the incorporation of positive reinforcement and consistency in treatment approach is important in successful treatment of picky eating, regardless of which approach is used. With younger populations, parents and caregivers are often on the front lines of treatment. Parents are encouraged to consult with pediatricians, dieticians, and psychologists before, during, and after the treatment process to ensure treatment administration is maximized for effectiveness. When working with adult populations, it is important to factor in an individual's goals for eating, whether it be to incorporate more salads into a diet or be able to go to a restaurant and order an item from a menu without altering it in any way. Cognitive behavioral techniques have had the most promising results with older adolescents and may pose benefits for adults; currently, the research on treating picky eating in adults is too scarce to draw any conclusions.

Hannah J. Hopkins

See also: Children and Adolescents; Exposure Therapy; Food Phobia; Selective Eating Disorder

Bibliography

Cardona Cano, Sebastian, Henning Tiemeier, Daphne Van Hoeken, Anne Tharner, Vincent W. V. Jaddoe, Albert Hofman, Frank C. Verhulst, and Hans W. Hoek. "Trajectories of Picky Eating during Childhood: A General Population Study." *International Journal of Eating Disorders* 48, no. 6 (2015): 570–579. https://doi.org/10.1002/eat.22384.

Gentry, Joseph A., and James K. Luiselli. "Treating a Child's Selective Eating through Parent Implemented Feeding Intervention in the Home Setting." *Journal of Developmental and Physical Disabilities* 20, no. 1 (2008): 63–70. https://doi.org/10.1007/s10882-007-9080-6.

Hafstad, Gertrud Sofie, Dawit Shawel Abebe, Leila Torgersen, and Tilmann von Soest. "Picky Eating in Preschool Children: The Predictive Role of the Child's Temperament and Mother's Negative Affectivity." *Eating Behaviors* 14, no. 3 (2013): 274–277. https://doi.org/10.1016/j.eatbeh.2013.04.001.

Jacobi, Corinna, Gabriele Schmitz, and W. Stewart Agras. "Is Picky Eating an Eating Disorder?" *International Journal of Eating Disorders* 41, no. 7 (2008): 626–634. https://doi.org/10.1002/eat.20545.

Kauer, Jane, Marcia L. Pelchat, Paul Rozin, and Hana F. Zickgraf. "Adult Picky Eating. Phenomenology, Taste Sensitivity, and Psychological Correlates." *Appetite* 90 (2015): 219–228. https://doi.org/10.1016/j.appet.2015.03.001.

Thompson, Claire, Steven Cummins, Tim Brown, and Rosemary Kyle. "What Does It Mean to Be a 'Picky Eater'? A Qualitative Study of Food Related Identities and Practices." *Appetite* 84 (2015): 235–239. https://doi.org/10.1016/j.appet.2014.09.028.

Valdimarsdóttir, Hildur, Lilja Ýr Halldórsdóttir, and Zuilma Gabriela SigurÐardóttir. "Increasing the Variety of Foods Consumed by a Picky Eater: Generalization of Effects across Caregivers and Settings." Edited by Gregory P. Hanley. *Journal of Applied Behavior Analysis* 43, no. 1 (2010): 101–105. https://doi.org/10.1901/jaba.2010.43-101.

Wildes, Jennifer E., Nancy L. Zucker, and Marsha D. Marcus. "Picky Eating in Adults: Results of a Web-Based Survey." *International Journal of Eating Disorders* 45, no. 4 (2012): 575–582. https://doi.org/10.1002/eat.20975.

PLANET HEALTH

Planet Health is an interdisciplinary middle school health curriculum to address low activity levels that contribute to obesity and diabetes. The goal of Planet Health is to improve the fitness level and nutritional habits of students by providing classroom and physical education activities across school curricula for existing math, science, social studies, language arts, health, and physical education classes.

History of Planet Health

The Planet Health curriculum was developed and refined over seven years with the first edition of the program published in 2001. A team of researchers developed the Planet Health program and its accompanying microunits with funding from the National Institutes of Health. The curriculum was tested by more than 100 teachers with 2,000 students in four Boston-area school districts. During the two-year field testing, teachers helped to revise the curriculum and develop the final program. The second edition updated materials to incorporate new lessons, including decreasing consumption of sugar-sweetened beverages, and provide CD-ROM materials to teachers.

Evaluation of Planet Health

The effectiveness of Planet Health was evaluated using 10 schools with half assigned to receive the curriculum and half used as a control group. Planet Health was found to reduce obesity in female participants over two years with a noteworthy decrease in screen time. This decrease in screen time was found for both male and female participants. Additionally, an increase in knowledge about nutrition and physical activity and improved consumption of fruits and vegetables was reported for participants in Planet Health.

An unintended consequence of the program was a decrease in pathological eating behaviors observed in teen girls. To assess the effect of Planet Health on disordered-eating behaviors of middle school students, 480 girls in the age group of 10–14 years were assigned to either an intervention or a control condition. After the intervention, girls in the group that received Planet Health were less than half as likely to report purging or using diet pills at follow-up compared with girls in control groups.

Justine J. Reel

See also: Diabetes; Exercise; Full of Ourselves; Intuitive Eating; Intuitive Exercise; Obesity; Prevention

Bibliography

Austin, S. Bryn, Alison E. Field, Jean L. Wiecha, Karen E. Peterson, and Steven L. Gortmaker. "The Impact of a School-Based Obesity Prevention Trial on Disordered Weight-Control Behaviors in Early Adolescent Girls." *Archives of Pediatric Adolescent Medicine* 159, no. 3 (2005): 225–230. https://doi.org/10.1001/archpedi.159.3.225.

Carter, Jill, Jean L. Wiecha, Karen E. Peterson, Suzanne Nobrega, and Steven L. Gortmaker. *Planet Health: an Interdisciplinary Curriculum for Teaching Middle School Nutrition and Physical Activity*, 2nd ed. Champaign, IL: Human Kinetics, 2007.

Gortmaker, Steven L., Karen E. Peterson, Jean L. Wiecha, Arthur M. Sobol, Sujata Dixit, Mary K. Fox, and Nan Laird. "Reducing Obesity via a School-Based Interdisciplinary Intervention among Youth: Planet Health." *Archives of Pediatric Adolescent Medicine* 153, no. 4 (1999): 409–418. https://doi.org/10.1001/archpedi.153.4.409.

PLUS-SIZE MODELS AND CLOTHING

According to recent statistics, the average American woman wears size 16–18 in clothing. In the fashion world, any size above a size 6 is considered plus size or full figured. Many consumers as well as fashion models, designers, photographers, and critics of the fashion industry have highlighted the discrepancy between a preference for smaller models in commercial advertising/modeling and the size of the average U.S. adult. Recently, the fashion industry has shifted toward inclusivity, with many plus-size fashion models taking a more front-and-center position in the world of modeling. Women such as Tess Holliday, Ashley Graham, and Erica Schenk—who wear a size 16 or larger—have become pioneers in mainstreaming fuller figures in high fashion. Although the popular media has made great strides toward representation of diverse body types, many activists still argue that certain practices in the field of plus-size modeling represent remnants of *thin privilege,* or the preference shown for thinner bodies prevalent in the field as well as in Western societies more broadly.

Sizing in the Fashion Industry

The idea of defining a specific size for the average American woman began with a project undertaken by the U.S. government in the 1930s, continuing through the 1950s. Statisticians were sent out to measure a sample of U.S. women to standardize clothing sizes across garment types, manufacturers, and materials. Waist, bust, hip, and abdominal measurements were all collected. When the standardized size guidelines were released in the mid-1950s, it quickly became clear the guidelines were hopelessly incorrect. Nonwhite women were excluded, and other variables such as height were not properly included. Despite complaints from customers and manufacturers alike, the fashion and apparel industry continued to incorporate these standardized sizes into garments. By the 1970s, when the government released updated guidelines, the idea of clothing sizes had become intrinsic to the industry.

Clothing manufacturers quickly realized sizes could be arbitrarily altered to flatter consumers into thinking they wear a smaller size. For example, the hip, waist, and bust measurements of a size 6 in 2011 were identical to the measurements of a size 12 in 1958. As the use of sizes became more common in the fashion industry, so did the categorization of plus sizes. This term has its origins in the 1920s, where any garment designed for a body other than the straight, boyish figure popular in the flapper fashions of the Roaring Twenties were designated as "stout." Following the government's release of the standard size in the mid-1950s, clothing pieces larger than this standard size became known as plus-sized garments. This quickly shifted from referring specifically to the garments to describing the bodies for which these clothes were made. Although there is no formal definition of a plus size, most fashion designers and models agree anything above a size 6 or 8 today is considered plus sized.

Redefining the Term "Plus Size"

Consumers have long clamored for greater representation of fuller-figured women in fashion editorials, advertising campaigns, and runway shows. This is not surprising, given most U.S. adult women are decidedly plus sized. A study using data collected by the Centers for Disease Control and Prevention and U.S. census estimates the average U.S. woman wears a size 16 or size 18, a full 2 to 4 sizes larger than the long-held average of size 14. Additionally, this study suggests the average size has been higher than previously thought for multiple years, but a lack of scientific inquiry into the subject has left size 14 as the unchallenged average for two decades. Although this may seem like an unnecessary distinction or even an unwelcome one (given that it suggests that Americans are getting bigger), researchers argue that it serves to hold the fashion industry accountable for representing the variety of body types of consumers.

The past several years have seen an uptick in the frequency of plus-sized models featured in famous campaigns and brands. Many consumers are rebelling against the plus-size label, preferring alternative and more empowering words such as curvy and full figured, or doing away with a special name for larger sizes altogether. Models such as Erica Schenk, Ashley Graham, Robyn Lawley, Tess Holiday, and Candice Huffine have become trailblazers for succeeding in the fashion and modeling industry despite being curvy, which has been heavily stigmatized. Numerous brands and campaigns have been instrumental in challenging the industry's preference for thin bodies, notably Dove's Real Beauty campaign and the undergarment brand Aerie, which has pledged to never retouch photos of its models.

The Connection with Eating Disorders

Although the association between exposure to images of thin bodies and eating disorders is well established by a plethora of research studies, the effect exposure to plus-size bodies may have on disordered-eating behaviors is far less studied yet still of interest to many in the field. Research on this topic has been mixed. Some authors suggest exposing women to images of models with curvier frames has detrimental effects on mood and increases dietary restraint. Conversely, other researchers have found exposure to images of fuller-figured women boost mood and body satisfaction. Researchers have struggled to find a pattern to explain these polarized results. One study found the degree to which women identify with plus-size bodies affects their mood after being exposed to plus-size images. Women who identified more strongly with plus-size bodies reported more positive self-evaluations and less body dissatisfaction than women who did not identify as strongly. Additionally, the degree of restrained eating also effected the emotional reaction to plus-size images, with women who scored higher on measures of restrained eating reporting more negative reactions to viewing plus-size models.

The recent attention plus-sized models and pro-curvy campaigns have received in popular media coincides with the "healthy at every size"(sometimes referred to as "fat acceptance") movement. This movement centers on the idea that a wider variety of body types, shapes, and weights deserve equal representation and celebration as traditional thin beauty ideals. Although many think this movement champions acceptance, equality, and the much-needed redefinition of female beauty standards, others argue that this movement is detrimental to public health, particularly when viewed through the eating disorder lens. Researchers who study obesity and eating disorders have cautioned the public that, although the dangers of focusing on an unrealistic thin body are well recognized, there are dangers to becoming too accepting of heavier bodies as well. Higher body mass index and obesity status has been linked with of health concerns, including respiratory problems and heart disease. Animal studies have suggested humans may have a relatively short window of opportunity during which they can lose excess body weight before those extra pounds become hardwired in a body's weight regulation processes. By promoting acceptance of plus-sized bodies, some of which meet the medical definition of obese, individuals may become unmotivated to shed extra pounds or make the effort to maintain an active lifestyle, nutritious diet, and healthy body mass index.

Hannah J. Hopkins

See also: Health at Every Size Approach; Models and Eating Disorders; Obesity; Weight Stigma

Bibliography

Anschutz, Doeschka J., Rutger C. M. E. Engels, Eni S. Becker, and Tatjana Van Strien. "The Effects of TV Commercials Using Less Thin Models on Young Women's Mood, Body Image and Actual Food Intake." *Body Image* 6, no. 4 (2009): 270–276. https://doi.org/10.1016/j.bodyim.2009.07.007.

Aran, Isha. "Where Did 'Plus Sized' Come From, Anyway?" *Fusion.* Last modified March 27, 2015. Accessed November 22, 2017. http://fusion.net/story/110890/where-did-plus-sized-come-from-anyway/.

Christel, Deborah A., and Susan C. Dunn. "Average American Women's Clothing Size: Comparing National Health and Nutritional Examination Surveys (1988–2010) to ASTM International Misses & Women's Plus Size Clothing." *International Journal of Fashion Design, Technology and Education* (2016): 1–8. Accessed February 2, 2017. https://doi.org/10.1080/17543266.2016.1214291.

Czerniawski, Amanda M. "Beauty beyond a Size 16." *Contexts* 15, no. 2 (2016): 70–73. https://doi.org/10.1177/1536504216648157.

Ingraham, Christopher. "The Absurdity of Women's Clothing Sizes, in One Chart." *Washington Post.* Wonkblog. Last modified August 11, 2015. Accessed November 22, 2017. https://www.washingtonpost.com/news/wonk/wp/2015/08/11/the-absurdity-of-womens-clothing-sizes-in-one-chart/.

McCluskey, Megan. "Size 14 Model Iskra Lawrence Joins Aerie's Unretouched Campaign." *Time.* Last modified February 10, 2016. Accessed November 22, 2017. http://time.com/4215404/size-14-model-iskra-lawrence-newest-aerie-model/.

"More Plus-Size Models Could Change Women's Obsession with Thin Bodies." *Mental Health Weekly Digest* (2012): 92.

Papies, Esther K., and Kim A. H. Nicolaije. "Inspiration or Deflation? Feeling Similar or Dissimilar to Slim and Plus-Size Models Affects Self-Evaluation of Restrained Eaters." *Body Image* 9, no. 1 (2012): 76–85. https://doi.org/10.1016/j.bodyim.2011.08.004.

Sainsbury, Amanda, and Phillipa Hay. "Call for an Urgent Rethink of the 'Health at Every Size' Concept." *Journal of Eating Disorders* 2, no. 8 (2014): 1–4. https://doi.org/10.1186/2050-2974-2-8.

POST-TRAUMATIC STRESS DISORDER

Post-traumatic stress disorder (PTSD) is a mental illness that affects individuals who have experienced trauma. Symptoms include intrusive flashbacks of the trauma, avoidance of situations in which someone expects to have a flashback, and increased arousal (e.g., heart racing, hypervigilance). PTSD was first widely discussed in the context of combat veterans returning from deployments; but it has received wider attention for its applicability to other forms of trauma, including car accidents, sexual assaults, violent crimes, and terrorism. Given the frequency with which trauma precedes the development of an eating disorder, the overlap between eating disorders and PTSD is of particular interest to researchers and mental health providers. Understanding the connection between these disorders may lend insight into treating them, both individually and when they occur together.

Understanding Post-traumatic Stress Disorder

PTSD was first recognized as a mental disorder in the 1980s but has been a long-understood phenomenon, particularly in the context of warfare. Reaching back to the 16th century, individuals recounted stories of soldiers returning from war in various stages of what has been called shell shock, battle fatigue, nostalgia, neurosis, and many other things. In the United States, awareness of PTSD and its severity was catalyzed by particularly vicious conflicts in the 20th century, including the Korean and Vietnam Wars and Operation Desert Storm. PTSD received newfound attention in the wake of the September 11, 2001, terrorist attacks; many citizens not directly involved in the attack reported symptoms associated with a stress-response to acute trauma.

PTSD is now widely recognized around the world and has been applied to populations beyond combat veterans. Survivors of sexual assault, car crashes, and violent crimes have also exhibit PTSD symptoms. Witnessing trauma, such as children who see a parent being abused, can also prompt the onset of this disorder, as can vicarious trauma (trauma experienced by many mental health workers after hearing clients' stories of firsthand trauma). PTSD is characterized primarily by intrusive and overwhelming flashbacks to the traumatic event, often prompted by some triggering reminder of the trauma. A classic example is found in stories from survivors of concentration camps during World War II: after the war, they reported being unable to hear a train whistle without reliving their time as prisoners. These flashbacks often prompt individuals to avoid certain situations, such as driving a car after a horrific accident. The avoidance of certain situations or triggers can cause significant distress in a person's life. The flashbacks in PTSD are also accompanied by physiological symptoms, including increased heart rate, the fight-or-flight response, sweating, trembling, shaking, vomiting, and others.

Comorbidity of PTSD, Trauma, and Eating Disorders

Some authors have estimated as many as 35 percent of individuals with an eating disorder also meet criteria for a diagnosis of PTSD. Additionally, the severity of disordered eating increased with a diagnosis of PTSD. Individuals with PTSD and individuals with eating disorders share certain personality features, including alexithymia (difficulty recognizing and experiencing emotions), dissociation, impulsivity, and emotion dysregulation. This evidence suggests the same types of people are prone to these two different disorders. The overlap between PTSD and eating disorders is particularly strong for people with bulimia nervosa (BN) and binge eating disorder (BED), but is not as strong for anorexia nervosa. Researchers think the bingeing episodes in both BN and BED (and the subsequent purging in BN) are a dysfunctional emotional coping skill. In other words, the act of bingeing becomes a soothing experience that individuals with BN and BED use to cope with overwhelming emotions. In some cases, those emotions may be associated with a traumatic experience.

Trauma is one of the biggest predictors of an eating disorder that has thus far been identified. Most people who suffer from eating disorders report a history of sexual assault, emotional or physical abuse, being teased or bullied, losing a parent/loved one unexpectedly or at a young age, or witnessing parental separation/marital discord. This appears to be true equally in males and females, and childhood trauma is particularly critical in the development of disordered eating. Childhood trauma is particularly important for the development of impulsivity-related disordered-eating behaviors (e.g., bingeing) but less important in symptoms related to body concern, such as body dissatisfaction or weight preoccupation. This association is consistent with the pattern of overlap seen between PTSD and BN/BED. Therefore, it seems trauma predisposes individuals to develop impulsive personality characteristics, associated with bulimia and binge eating disorders but not anorexia.

Populations of Concern

Some populations are at greater risk of exposure to trauma based on lifestyle, occupation, or experiences. Military personnel have received significant attention in the PTSD literature, and as the number of women in the Armed Services grows, the awareness of eating disorders in the military grows. For combat veterans, the co-occurrence of PTSD and an eating disorder are potentially more likely given the high incidence of traumatic events that occur in combat. Additionally, women who serve in the military and who experience military sexual trauma (assault or harassment in a military context) are at high risk for developing PTSD and an eating disorder. Similarly, individuals in potentially traumatic occupations, such as firefighters, police officers, and EMTs, are also at higher risk for developing PTSD, an eating disorder, or both.

Another population of concern are individuals suffering from a substance use disorder. In certain cases, depending on drug of choice, socioeconomic status, geography, living situation, substance use predisposes an individual to a higher exposure to trauma. For example, women addicted to drugs are three times more likely than nonaddicted women to experience intimate partner violence. Additionally, these women may experience violence from drug dealers, strangers, sex trade clients, and law enforcement officers. Given the association between substance use and eating disorders and the higher rate substance users are exposed to trauma, the substance use population—particularly women—are at much higher risk of developing PTSD and/or an eating disorder.

Treatment

Identification of both PTSD and an eating disorder is critically important to develop an effective treatment plan. Treating one disorder without knowledge or acknowledgment of the other has been ineffectual given that these disorders are often mutually reinforcing. Therefore, mental health providers need to be sensitive to populations at higher risk for these two disorders and implement effective screening measures to test for both at the same time.

Once both PTSD and an eating disorder have been identified and diagnosed, the severity of each needs to be carefully evaluated and weighed against one another. Generally, the more severe disorder that causes more direct impairment will receive initial treatment attention. Little research around treating the co-occurrence of PTSD and an eating disorder make identifying specific treatment models almost impossible. However, it is recommended trauma therapy be initiated as soon as possible, given that an individual is maintaining a healthy BMI and purging no more than a few times per week. Trauma therapy has been shown to improve symptom severity of both PTSD and eating disorders in a few weeks. Once these symptoms are stabilized, a counselor and client can decide about which disorder—PTSD or the eating disorder—requires immediate treatment.

Hannah J. Hopkins

See also: Military; Substance Abuse; Trauma

Bibliography

Bisson, Jonathan I. "Post-Traumatic Stress Disorder." *Occupational Medicine* 57, no. 6 (2007): 399–403. https://doi.org/10.1093/occmed/kqm069.

Brewerton, Timothy D. "Eating Disorders, Trauma, and Comorbidity: Focus on PTSD." *Eating Disorders* 15, no. 4 (2007): 285–304. https://doi.org/10.1080/10640260701454311.

Fouladi, Farnaz, James E. Mitchell, Ross D. Crosby, Scott G. Engel, Scott Crow, Laura Hill, Daniel Le Grange, Pauline Powers, and Kristine J. Steffen. "Prevalence of Alcohol and Other Substance Use in Patients with Eating Disorders." *European Eating Disorders Review* 23, no. 6 (2015): 531–536. https://doi.org/10.1002/erv.2410.

Guillaume, Sebastien, Isabelle Jaussent, Laurent Maimoun, A. Ryst, M. Seneque, L. Villain, D. Hamroun, Patrick Lefebvre, Eric Renard, and Ph. Courtet. "Associations between Adverse Childhood Experiences and Clinical Characteristics of Eating Disorders. *Scientific Reports* 6, no. 35761 (2016). https://doi.org/10.1038/srep35761.

Killeen, Therese, Timothy D. Brewerton, Aimee Campbell, Lisa R. Cohen, and Denise A. Hien. "Exploring the Relationship between Eating Disorder Symptoms and Substance Use Severity in Women with Comorbid PTSD and Substance Use Disorders." *The American Journal of Drug and Alcohol Abuse* 41, no. 6 (2015): 547–552. https://doi.org/10.3109/00952990.2015.1080263.https://doi.org/10

Lorvick, Jennifer, Alexandra Lutnick, Lynn D. Wenger, Philippe Bourgois, Helen Cheng, and Alex H. Kral. "Non-Partner Violence against Women Who Use Drugs in San

Francisco." *Violence against Women* 20, no. 11 (2014): 1285–1298. https://doi.org/10.1177/1077801214552910.

Mitchell, Karen S., Suzanne E. Mazzeo, Michelle R. Schlesinger, Timothy D. Brewerton, and Brian N. Smith. "Comorbidity of Partial and Subthreshold PTSD among Men and Women with Eating Disorders in the National Comorbidity Survey-Replication Study." *International Journal of Eating Disorders* 45, no. 3 (2012): 307–315. https://doi.org/10.1002/eat.20965.

Mitchell, Karen S., Stephanie Y. Wells, Adell Mendes, and Patricia A. Resick. "Treatment Improves Symptoms Shared by PTSD and Disordered Eating." *Journal of Traumatic Stress* 25, no. 5 (2012): 535–542. https://doi.org/10.1002/jts.21737.

Mott, Juliette M., Deleene S. Menefee, and Wendy S. Leopoulos. "Treating PTSD and Disordered Eating in the Wake of Military Sexual Trauma: A Case Study." *Clinical Case Studies* 11, no. 2 (2012): 104–118. https://doi.org/10.1177/1534650112440499.

Tagay, Sefik, Ellen Schlottbohm, Mae Lynn Reyes-Rodriguez, Nevena Repic, and Wolfgang Senf. "Eating Disorders, Trauma, PTSD, and Psychosocial Resources." *Eating Disorders* 22, no. 1 (2014): 33–49. https://doi.org/10.1080/10640266.2014.857517.

Thornley, Elizabeth, and Paul Frewen. "Posttraumatic Eating Disorders (PTED): Perceived Causal Relations between Trauma-Related Symptoms and Eating Disorders." *Personality and Individual Differences* 101 (2016): 521. https://doi.org/10.1016/j.paid.2016.05.323.

Vierling, Victoire, Sophie Etori, Lisa Valenti, Marine Lesage, Marie Pigeyre, Vincent Dodin, Olivier Cottencin, and Dewi Guardia. "Prevalence and Impact of Post-Traumatic Stress Disorder in a Disordered Eating Population Sample." *La Presse Médicale* 44, no. 11 (2015): e341–e352. https://doi.org/10.1016/j.lpm.2015.04.039.

PREGNANCY

Women often try to stay thin while pregnant and then attempt to lose weight quickly after giving birth. This obsession of wanting to stay thin during pregnancy, a natural course in a woman's life cycle, has many professionals concerned about the health of a mother and her baby. According to a recent poll on NBC's *TODAY* Moms website, approximately 49 percent of the readers selected "Why doesn't she eat more?" when asked, "When you see someone who is skinny while pregnant, are you . . ." However, 27 percent of the people chose "How does she do it?" and 24 percent selected "Wow, she looks great." In other words, 51 percent or over 4,600 people envy or are impressed by a woman who is skinny while she is pregnant. This type of mentality is driven by celebrities' fixation for the ideal body even during pregnancy (e.g., Rachel Zoe, Nicole Richie, Victoria Beckham, Bethenny Frankel), but striving for perfection can have psychological and physical consequences.

Physiological Changes during Pregnancy

A multitude of physiological changes occur during pregnancy that alter a woman's body and its functions. During the first trimester, a woman's body undergoes many changes. Hormonal changes affect every organ, with the stopping of the menstrual cycle serving as a clear sign of pregnancy. Other changes during the first trimester include extreme tiredness, tender or swollen breasts, upset stomach (morning sickness), craving or distaste for certain foods, mood swings, constipation, higher frequency of urination, headaches, heartburn, and weight gain. During the second trimester, the abdomen stretches and expands as the baby continues to grow. Some women may experience body aches (e.g., back, abdomen, groin, thigh); stretch marks on the stomach, breasts, thighs, and buttocks; patches of darker skin on the cheeks, forehead, nose, or upper lid; tingling hands; and swelling of the ankles, fingers, and face. Some of the same discomforts experienced during the second trimester may persist in the third trimester. In addition, many women will notice shortness of breath, heartburn, belly button sticking out, baby dropping or moving lower in the abdomen, and contractions.

Maternal blood supply increases by 20–50 percent during pregnancy, and cardiac output increases by 30–40 percent, which makes it one of the most important changes of pregnancy. During pregnancy heart rate increases by 10–15 beats per minute (bpm) around 28–32 weeks. The increase in blood volume provides a fetus with oxygenated blood and nutrients. Changes in ventilation also occur as early as the fourth week of gestation. Minute ventilation increases by approximately 50 percent. This is caused by an increase in tidal volume (40 percent) and respiratory rate (15 percent). In addition, many hormones are secreted during pregnancy. The hormone relaxin is responsible for relaxing ligaments as well as softening collagenous tissues; thus, relaxin is responsible for lordosis (inward curvature of the spine) during pregnancy. All these bodily changes can overwhelm an expectant mother, especially when she experiencing these changes for the first time.

Pregnancy and Body Image

As a woman experiences her pregnancy, she becomes increasingly aware of her bodily changes with each trimester. Pregnant women are likely to reevaluate their body image over time as they gain weight and as experience changes in body size and shape. The resulting body dissatisfaction that accompanies these changes during pregnancy can lead to unhealthy eating and weight loss behaviors (e.g., restricting food intake). Restrictive eating leads to complications (e.g., hypertension, premature delivery, low birth weight) for a mother and unborn child.

Researchers have examined women's changing body image during pregnancy for over 40 years. Early studies indicated body dissatisfaction increases over the course of pregnancy. However, more recent studies have reported there were no significant changes in body dissatisfaction from early to middle pregnancy, but body dissatisfaction was greater at early pregnancy compared to prepregnancy. Other researchers have found women reported higher body dissatisfaction during early and mid–second trimester. Similar to body image research with women who are not pregnant, 77 percent of pregnant women indicated they would like their bodies to be smaller. Despite being dissatisfied with their bodies, women reported being more fit and strong during pregnancy than before pregnancy, and thought they were more attractive prior to pregnancy than they did during the early, middle, and late trimesters.

Body image prior to pregnancy was also a strong predictor of negative body image in late pregnancy. Other factors that influenced women to feel less attractive and strong were depression (in late pregnancy) and comparing one's body to other people's bodies (in early pregnancy). Body comparison tendencies in early pregnancy predicted women viewing weight and shape and feeling fat as important during late pregnancy. This body comparison could lead to more body dissatisfaction and weight concerns.

Body Image and Weight Gain during Pregnancy

The relationship between body image and weight-related concerns prior to pregnancy suggests body image may be related to women gaining weight during pregnancy. For example, a 2007 study found that women who were obese before pregnancy had greater weight and body shape concerns before and during pregnancy than women who were not obese. In a 2011 study, researchers at the University of North Carolina, Chapel Hill, interviewed 1,192 women during pregnancy (at 15–20 weeks, 17–22 weeks, 24–29 weeks, 27–30 weeks) and in-hospital following delivery about health behaviors, diet, physical activity, and body image. They found that 50 percent of the women preferred a small body size, and most women who preferred the small body size were between ages 25 and 34, Caucasian, had normal BMI before pregnancy, were married, highly educated, and had a high income. In addition, the researchers identified at-risk women (i.e., women with body dissatisfaction, women who had a thin ideal body size, lower education level, and lower income) who had gained excessive weight outside the recommended guidelines from the Institute of Medicine. Gaining excessive weight outside of recommended ranges can result in poor birth outcomes due to increased maternal and fetal complications, such as increased risk of cesarean section and macrosomia (baby weighing more than 8 pounds and 13 ounces), whereas inadequate weight gain can lead to premature birth.

Effects of Pregnancy on Eating Disorders

Approximately 5–7 percent of pregnant women suffer from eating disorders. Previous studies investigated the effects of pregnancy on eating disorder symptoms, but the results were unclear. Most studies evaluating the course of eating disorder symptoms during pregnancy have reported improvement, a return to symptom levels prior to pregnancy, or even worse symptoms postpartum. Rocco and colleagues investigated the effects of pregnancy on eating attitudes and disorders in 97 women who were either pregnant with a positive history of dieting, pregnant with a clinical diagnosis of an eating disorder, or had no history of an eating disorder. They found eating attitudes and body satisfaction improved in the clinical and subclinical eating disorder groups of pregnant women during the middle phase of pregnancy. This improvement could be due to an increase in the quality of life, but the benefits were short lived, with the women returning to previous levels after delivery.

On the other hand, weight gain during pregnancy may exacerbate or reignite weight and shape concerns, which may lead to a relapse of an eating disorder postpartum. For example, researchers examined the presence of eating-disordered behaviors, body and weight concerns in women with a recent episode of eating disorder, and women with a history of eating disorder. They found that about 10 percent of the women with recent eating disorders reported dieting for weight loss at 32 weeks, a third of the women purged during pregnancy, and they had high rates of concern about weight gain during the third trimester of pregnancy. Similarly, 10 percent of women with a history of eating disorder had purged in the first 18 weeks of pregnancy and 15 percent vomited at least once daily during pregnancy.

Effects of Eating Disorders on Pregnancy

Although there is a lack of information on the effects of eating disorders on pregnancy, the limited information suggests there are many potential negative consequences for mother and baby. Eating disorders, such as anorexia nervosa and bulimia nervosa, are associated with higher rates of miscarriage, low birth weight, obstetric complications, and postpartum depression. Eating disorders are associated with nutritional, metabolic, and psychological changes that have negative effects on the development of a fetus. The most cited complications in anorexic and bulimic pregnant women include not gaining enough weight, miscarriage, and hyperemesis gravidarum during pregnancy; birth complications include low birth rate, preterm delivery, stillbirth, breech delivery, and fetal abnormality.

It has been reported that women with eating disorders gain less weight and have smaller infants than healthy women. Researchers have investigated the relationship between pregnancy outcomes and eating behaviors in women who delivered low body weight infants. Women who delivered small-for-gestational-age (SGA) infants at term reported unhealthier eating behaviors before, during, and after the pregnancy than women who delivered preterm infants (before 37 weeks). In addition, women who had low prepregnancy weight, smoked, and had bulimic tendencies tended to have a SGA infant. Factors that predicted preterm births were vomiting during pregnancy and less dietary restraint. Furthermore, the miscarriage rate seemed to be higher in women with eating disorders than in women without eating disorders.

Hyperemesis gravidarum or persistent nausea or vomiting is more common in women with eating disorders than in women without eating disorders. Researchers have reported that 10 percent of 25 women who actively engaged in bulimic behaviors had persistent nausea or vomiting during their pregnancies. One reason for higher frequency of hyperemesis gravidarum in women with bulimia is that it might be a way to rationalize the negative behaviors with more typical consequences of pregnancy. This may allow the women with bulimia to hide the bulimic behaviors behind the medical-related consequences of being pregnant.

Although there is not enough evidence to conclude why cesareans are more common in women with eating disorders, researchers have shown the rate of cesarean delivery is higher in women with eating disorders (16 percent) than in women without eating disorders (3 percent). Women with eating disorders might be viewed as higher-risk cases by physicians, which might increase the probability physicians will perform cesareans. Moreover, the behaviors of women with anorexia and bulimia might lead to more complicated labors and deliveries.

Women with eating disorders also reported having higher postpartum depression than women without eating disorders. These women have concerns healthy women might not have, such as body image concerns, weight concerns, anxiety, and disordered-eating behaviors. These concerns could make them vulnerable to postpartum depression. Investigators have reported 40 percent of women with eating disorders have a history of affective disorders, which places them at a higher risk for postpartum depression.

Postpartum and Body Image

Researchers have found postpartum women express body image concerns and are compelled to rapidly return to their pre-pregnancy weight. Body dissatisfaction may be of particular concern in postpartum women because it can lead to unhealthy dieting, which may result in impaired milk production, milk contamination, and energy deficiency. One study reported 75 percent of women were concerned about their weight in the first weeks of postpartum. Other researchers revealed women were still dissatisfied with their weight four months postpartum, six months postpartum, and one year postpartum and engaged in weight loss methods (e.g., exercise) to lose the weight gained from pregnancy. However, some postpartum women were less dissatisfied with their bodies postpartum than during pregnancy.

One noteworthy factor to examine in body dissatisfied postpartum women is weight gain. According to the Institute of Medicine, excessive gestational weight gain (i.e., over 35 pounds for normal weight women, over 25 pounds for overweight women, and over 20 pounds for the obese women) can be associated with long-term weight retention or obesity, which could lead to more body dissatisfaction. However, it is unclear which weight factor (e.g., prenatal weight, postpartum weight, or pre-pregnancy-to-postpartum weight gain) is most important in predicting body dissatisfaction. Gjerdingen and colleagues in 2009 surveyed over 500 postpartum women at the beginning of postpartum (0–1 month) and nine months later about weight, body dissatisfaction, and mental health and revealed that dissatisfaction increased over time, supporting previous research indicating that body image concerns become more negative postpartum. In addition, Gjerdingen and colleagues found mothers' body dissatisfaction at nine months postpartum was associated with increased weight gain and poorer mental health. The combination of body dissatisfaction and poorer mental health may put mothers at higher risk for developing an eating disorder postpartum.

Because postpartum women are dissatisfied with their bodies, a growing number of them are undergoing cosmetic surgery. *Mommy makeover*, a term coined by plastic surgeons, is aimed at mothers and usually involves a breast lift with or without breast implants, a tummy tuck, and some liposuction to restore or improve post-pregnancy bodies. According to the American Society of Plastic Surgery, 36 percent (*n* = 107,638) of women between 30 and 39 years of age underwent breast augmentation and 35 percent of women (n = 40,706) in this age group underwent a tummy tuck in 2010. The marketing of the mommy makeover is making women believe their bodies are worse after giving birth and they can easily fix their bodies and problems with cosmetic surgery.

Sonya SooHoo

See also: Aging and Body Image; Body Image; Cosmetic Surgery and Eating Disorders; Femininity Ideals; Infertility; Medical and Health Consequences

Bibliography

Crowell, Debra Tooke. "Weight Change in the Postpartum Period: A Review of Literature." *Journal of Nurse-Midwifery* 40, no. 5 (1995): 418–423. https://doi.org/10.1016/0091 -2182(95)00049-P.

Fairburn, Christopher G., and Sarah L. Welch. "The Impact of Pregnancy on Eating Habits and Attitudes to Shape and Weight." *International Journal of Eating Disorders* 9, no. 2 (1990): 153–160. https://doi.org/10.1002/1098-108X(199003)9:2<153::AID -EAT2260090204>3.0.CO;2-8.

Franko, Debra, and Emily B. Spurrell. "Detection and Management of Eating Disorders during Pregnancy." *Obstetrics & Gynecology* 96, no. 6 (2000): 942–946.

Gjerdingen, Dwenda, Patricia Fontaine, Scott Crow, Patricia McGovern, Bruce Center, and Michael Miner. "Predictors of Mothers' Postpartum Body Dissatisfaction." *Women's Health* 49, no. 6–7 (2009): 491–504. http://dx.doi.org/10.1080/03630240903423998.

"Is 'Skinny-While-Pregnant' a Dangerous Trend?" *Today Show: Parents.* Last modified July 28, 2011. Accessed November 18, 2016. http://www.today.com/parents/skinny -while-pregnant-dangerous-trend-1C7399086.

Mehta, Ushma, Anna Maria Siega-Riz, and Amy H. Herring. "Effects of Body Image on Pregnancy Weight Gain." *Maternal and Child Health Journal* 15, no. 3 (2011): 324–332. https://doi.org/10.1007/s10995-010-0578-7.

Micali, Nadia, Janet Treasure, and Emily Simonoff. "Eating Disorders Symptoms in Pregnancy: A Longitudinal Study of Women with Recent and Past Eating Disorders and Obesity." *Journal of Psychosomatic Research* 63, no. 3 (2007): 297–303. http://dx.doi .org/10.1016/j.jpsychores.2007.05.003.

"Pregnancy." WomensHealth.gov. Accessed November 18, 2016. https://www.womens health.gov/pregnancy/.

Rocoo, Pier Luigi, Barbara Orbitello, Laura Perini, Valentina Pera, Rossana P. Ciano, and Matteo Balestrieri. "Effects of Pregnancy on Eating Attitudes and Disorders: A Prospective Study." *Journal of Psychosomatic Research* 59, no. 3 (2005): 175–179. http://dx.doi .org/10.1016/j.jpsychores.2005.03.002.

Skouteris, Helen, Roxane Carr, Eleanor H. Wertheim, Susan J. Paxton, and Dianne Duncombe. "A Prospective Study of Factors That Lead to Body Dissatisfaction during Pregnancy." *Body Image* 2, no. 4 (2005): 347–361. http://dx.doi.org/10.1016/j.bodyim .2005.09.002.

PREVENTION

Prevention broadly refers to stopping a problem before it occurs by providing health promotion programs or education. There are several types of prevention—including primary and secondary—used to decrease unwanted behaviors and reduce diseases. Although national attention has been placed on the obesity epidemic with less funding available for eating disorder prevention efforts, it is important to consider that weight-related problems exist along a continuum and that binge eating behaviors are often present in overweight and obese individuals.

Types of Prevention

Primary prevention refers to reducing the prevalence of a disease by preventing new cases from occurring. For eating disorders, primary prevention efforts can address risk factors (e.g., dieting, body dissatisfaction) while strengthening resilience by developing protective factors (e.g., high self-esteem). Universal primary prevention refers to a program given to everyone regardless of their risk for an eating disorder. For example, National Eating Disorder Awareness Week represents community-wide campaigns to raise consciousness among diverse individuals about eating disorders. Universal prevention approaches would also include policy changes or laws to fight a particular problem. Universal prevention is often the easiest type of prevention to execute because programs can be conducted in large groups (e.g., school assemblies). However, research indicates universal prevention programs are less effective than other prevention approaches.

Selective primary prevention is geared to individuals who may be more at risk for developing eating disorder symptoms. Females have been identified as having higher body dissatisfaction and a stronger likelihood of engaging in disordered eating. Therefore, all-female prevention programs (e.g., Full of Ourselves) are implemented with these higher risk groups.

Secondary prevention refers to identifying and working with individuals who show signs of the early stages of disordered eating. This type of prevention is used to screen college athletes starting their first year for any eating concerns. Athletes who are red-flagged can get necessary support and treatment (e.g., dietitian) and receive continued monitoring throughout their athletic careers. Another example of secondary prevention is the Identity Intervention Program (IIP), which includes individual and group therapies to decrease eating disorder symptoms, improve health, and facilitate a more positive sense of self.

Lack of Prevention Programs

One study determined 41 percent of male and 61 percent of female undergraduate students thought eating disorder prevention was very important. Although many schools and students are interested in eating disorder prevention programs, very few schools offer ongoing eating disorder interventions that are incorporated into required curricula. Instead, schools tend to provide a single lesson about eating disorders in health classes; this involves lecturing about definitions or types of eating disorders and/or showing a movie about an individual (e.g., Tracey Gold) who suffered from an eating disorder. Unfortunately, these lessons can backfire, as students receive information about pathogenic weight control methods and may be triggered to engage in disordered eating. In fact, using scare tactics such as showing movies or horrifying photos (e.g., protruding rib cages and collar bones) seemed to produce an opposite of the intended effect for students. The most important consideration for any prevention effort is to avoid doing harm to participants.

History of Prevention Programs

The first generation of primary prevention programs was universally available to all participants and tended to educate them about the adverse effects of eating disorders through psychoeducation materials. As with antidrug campaigns that use scare tactics (e.g., "this is your brain on drugs") to increase one's awareness, it was assumed that any efforts to provide knowledge would be useful in preventing disordered-eating behaviors.

A second generation of prevention programs used a universal and didactic format that went beyond scare tactics by adding an educational component about sociocultural pressures (e.g., influence of media) to be thin and lose weight. These early programs were provided to everyone regardless of their sex, gender, race, or whether they were at risk for developing an eating disorder. In addition, the format was didactic and promoted an increase of knowledge without any accompanying behavioral change.

More recently, primary prevention programs (e.g., Healthy Buddies) have targeted high-risk individuals using an interactive format that goes beyond lecture. Full of Ourselves, designed for female adolescents, uses a school-based curriculum that focuses on building self-esteem, girls' leadership, and peer relationships through interactive discussions and activities. Participants have an opportunity to practice skills and receive feedback from peers in the group.

Effectiveness of Eating Disorder Prevention Programs

A recent review of published prevention programs determined 51 percent of eating disorder prevention programs decreased eating disorder risk factors and 29 percent of programs decreased current or future disordered eating. Programs using selected approaches targeted at high-risk individuals were more effective than universal approaches disseminated to everyone. Only selected programs were able to prevent future increases in eating pathology observed in control samples. Alarmingly, other studies have found universal programs were associated with increased dietary restraint and increased awareness about available eating disorder techniques that can be used to lose weight. Examples of selected prevention efforts include eating disorder prevention programs for dancers, sorority sisters, and teenage females.

According to the same review, the most effective prevention programs were interactive, rather than a lecture-only format, and used multiple sessions in the same program rather than a single session. This finding about the need for repeated exposure may explain why universal prevention programs have been largely unsuccessful. Prevention programs that separate females from males seem to produce stronger positive results than programs that have both sexes in the same group. Eating disorder prevention programs that had participants over age 15 were also more effective than programs with younger participants.

Prevention programs that included body acceptance and cognitive behavioral skills training were found to be more successful than psychoeducation programs; however, other researchers indicated psychoeducation programs were equally effective. Generally, the content of the program curriculum seemed to be less important than the characteristics of group participants (e.g., female, over 15 years). Furthermore, prevention programs that used trained interventionists who were eating disorder experts were more successful than programs that used teachers who had diverse responsibilities.

Limitations of Prevention Programs

Although selected prevention efforts were found to be significantly more effective in promoting behavior change than universal prevention programs, it is important to ensure diverse individuals are not excluded from prevention efforts. Most prevention programs rely on risk factor studies rather than on context-specific approaches to eating disorder prevention. By employing a context-specific emphasis one can avoid ignoring variables like race, social class, and sex. Interestingly, sex and other variables have been considered salient in other health promotion efforts (e.g., smoking and AIDS) but have been left out of many eating disorder prevention studies.

For example, it is important for males to have specific prevention programs to address their body image disturbances and the tendency to be at increased risk for abusing steroids and other supplements associated with a stronger drive for muscularity. Interventions should be sensitive to cultural norms and beliefs of the population being served. To avoid oversimplification, it is also important to modify programs for a target population (e.g., males) with the understanding that needs may be different for preventing anorexia nervosa compared to bulimia nervosa or binge eating disorder. These trends should be taken into consideration rather than creating a one-size-fits-all program.

Limitations for providing eating disorder prevention programs could include access and transportation. Individuals in rural areas may not be able to participate in prevention programs or may attend schools that lack the resources for or diminish the importance of eating disorder prevention. Fortunately, an alternative to providing school-based prevention programs is Internet-based preventions. For example, Student Bodies was developed to provide a forum for support and psychoeducation to individuals across the country. This 8- to 10-week program uses message boards for discussion about body image concerns. A clear advantage is that computerized formats provide support to individuals and may be more cost effective than face-to-face programs if an individual has Internet access. However, it cannot be taken for granted that every individual will have access to online prevention efforts or will have the technology expertise to use a computerized intervention.

Family-Based Prevention Efforts

The importance of involving parents and family cannot be stressed enough and obesity programs have recognized the need to change the a family system rather than solely focusing on an individual identified to be most at risk. In one study, 66 percent of male and 72 percent of female participants thought parents should be included in eating disorder prevention efforts.

For obesity interventions, family members are used to model healthy (but not excessive) physical activity and nutritional eating. The BodyWorks program provides skills to parents who learn to cook healthy snacks and meals while moving with their kids to increase physical activity. In the Health at Every Size Approach obesity prevention programs, the emphasis is on healthy behaviors rather than on losing weight. Obesity prevention efforts need not be separate from eating disorder prevention programs, and, recently, integrative approaches have successfully combined eating disorder and obesity prevention programs.

In addition to being positive role models, parents influence the body image of children and adolescents through subtle and overt messages related to size, shape, and appearance. Teasing and negative comments are triggers consistently reported by individuals with body image and eating disturbances. Therefore, programs like BodyWorks teach parents to become more aware of "fat talk" and to use statements that encourage a diet mentality with more positive statements about health. Interestingly, few eating disorder prevention programs designed for families are available. A rare exception is Off the C.U.F.F., a parent skills program to help parents manage eating disorder symptoms at home. Parents are taught about perfectionism and self-esteem to create an environment of self-acceptance.

Justine J. Reel

See also: BodyWorks; Full of Ourselves; Health at Every Size Approach; Off the C.U.F.F.; Parents; Planet Health; Protective Factors; Students Promoting Eating Disorder Awareness and Knowledge (SPEAK)

Bibliography

Becker, Carolyn Black, Anna C. Ciao, and Lisa M. Smith. "Moving from Efficacy to Effectiveness in Eating Disorders Prevention: The Sorority Body Image Program." *Cognitive and Behavioral Practice* 15 (2008): 18–27. http://dx.doi.org/10.1016/j.cbpra.2006.07.006.

Berg, Francie, Jennifer Buechner, Ellen Parham, and Weight Realities Division of the Society for Nutrition Education. "Guidelines for Childhood Obesity Prevention Programs: Promoting Healthy Weight in Children." *Journal of Nutrition Education and Behavior* 35, no. 1 (2003): 1–4.

Costin, Carolyn. *A Comprehensive Guide to the Causes, Treatments and Prevention of Eating Disorders: The Eating Disorder Sourcebook*, 3rd ed. New York: McGraw-Hill, 2007.

Fingeret, Michelle Cororve, Cortney S. Warren, Antonio Cepeda-Benito, and David H. Gleaves. "Eating Disorder Prevention Research: A Meta-Analysis." *Eating Disorders: A Journal of Treatment and Prevention* 14 (2006): 191–213. https://doi.org/10.1080/10640260600638899.

Levine, Michael P., and Linda Smolak. *The Prevention of Eating Problems and Eating Disorders: Theory, Research, and Practice.* Mahwah, NJ: Lawrence Erlbaum Associates, 2005.

Lindenberg, Katajun, Markus Moessner, Joanna Harney, Orla McLaughlin, and Stephanie Bauer. "E-Health for Individualized Prevention of Eating Disorders." *Clinical Practice & Epidemiology in Mental Health* 7 (2011): 74–83. https://doi.org/10.2174/1745017901107010074.

McMillan, Whitney, Eric Stice, and Paul Ronde. "High- and Low-Level Dissonance-Based Eating Disorder Prevention Programs with Young Women with Body Image Concerns: An Experimental Trial." *Journal of Consulting and Clinical Psychology* 79, no. 1 (2011): 129–134. http://dx.doi.org/10.1037/a0022143.

Neumark-Sztainer, Dianne. "Preventing the Broad Spectrum of Weight-Related Problems: Working with Parents to Help Teens Achieve a Healthy Weight and a Positive Body Image." *Journal of Nutrition Education and Behavior* 37, suppl. 2 (2005): S133–S139. https://doi.org/10.1016/S1499-4046(06)60214-5.

Reel, Justine J., and Joseph Halowich. "Do's and Don'ts for Eating Disorder and Obesity Prevention in Community Settings." *Utah's Health: An Annual Review* 15 (2010): 58–61.

Steiner-Adair, Catherine, Lisa Sjostrom, Debra L. Franko, Seeta Pai, Rochelle Tucker, Anne E. Becker, and David B. Herzog. "Primary Prevention of Risk Factors for Eating Disorders in Adolescent Girls: Learning from Practice." *International Journal of Eating Disorders* 32, no. 4 (2002): 401–411. https://doi.org/10.1002/eat.10089.

Stice, Eric, and Heather Shaw. "Eating Disorder Prevention Programs: A Meta-Analytic Review." *Psychological Bulletin* 130, no. 2 (2004): 206–227.

Stice, Eric, Heather Shaw, and C. Nathan Marti. "A Meta-Analytic Review of Eating Disorder Prevention Programs: Encouraging Findings." *Annual Review of Clinical Psychology* 3 (2007): 207–231. https://doi.org/10.1146/annurev.clinpsy.3.022806.091447.

Wick, Katharina, Christina Brix, Bianca Bormann, Melanie Sowa, Bernhard Strauss, and Uwe Berger. "Real-World Effectiveness of a German School-Based Intervention for Primary Prevention of Anorexia Nervosa in Preadolescent Girls." *Preventive Medicine* 52 (2011): 152–158. https://doi.org/10.1016/j.ypmed.2010.11.022.

Zucker, Nancy. *Off the C.U.F.F.: A Parents Skills Book for the Management of Disordered Eating.* Durham, NC: Duke University Medical Center, 2004.

PRO-ANA

Pro-ana is the promotion of anorexia nervosa and pro-mia is the celebration of bulimia nervosa. Both groups are in direct opposition to recovery; they offer encouragement for individuals to engage in and continue disordered-eating behaviors (e.g., fasting, restricting). Pro-ana and the celebration of anorexia nervosa has been symbolized by wearing red bracelets and pro-mia has been represented by blue bracelets. Pro-ana and pro-mia organizations have grown on the Internet with the opportunity to reach many people.

Pro–Eating Disorder Websites

Pro–eating disorder websites, which claim to be "free of judgment for one's eating disorder lifestyle," have proliferated since the late 1990s and provide online forums for discussion boards, tips and tricks, as well as *thinspirations* (i.e., pictures, quotes, and lyrics to inspire individuals to stay committed to the maintenance of anorexic behaviors). Photos on these websites portray ultrathin models with protruding collar bones and rib cages. It is also common for pro–eating disorder websites to post an Ana Creed that includes statements such as "I must weigh myself first thing every morning, and keep that number in mind throughout the remainder of that day." "Thin Commandments" consist of 10 pro-ana "truths" related to the celebration of thinness and the reinforcement of all or nothing thinking (e.g., "Losing weight is good/gaining weight is bad").

Pro–eating disorder websites are not regulated and do not represent the views of trained eating disorder professionals. Unfortunately, the content on these websites can be damaging to the treatment progress of individuals suffering from eating disorders and can trigger disordered-eating behaviors.

The Impact of Pro–Eating Disorder Websites

Pro-ana websites have created controversy because of their support for resistance against eating disorder treatment and recovery with an already difficult treatment population. Pro–eating disorder websites have been found to trigger disordered-eating behaviors and contribute to relapse in individuals with an eating disorder history.

College females who were exposed to a pro-anorexia website reported decreased self-esteem and perceived unattractiveness, thought they were overweight, and had more negative moods than when they viewed a generic home décor website. In a separate investigation of 1,575 women, researchers found females who viewed pro–eating disorder sites had higher body dissatisfaction and dysfunctional eating patterns than a control group not exposed to such sites. Alarmingly, a 2010 study found college students exposed to pro–eating disorder websites for 1.5 hours reduced weekly caloric intake from 12,167 calories to 9,697 calories. These changes in energy intake persisted for three weeks following exposure.

Parent Education about Pro–Eating Disorder Websites

Although the results of exposure to pro-ana websites have been staggering, only 52.8 percent of parents reported being aware of pro–eating disorder sites. Many parents did not know whether their children visited pro-ana websites and 62.5 percent of parents were unaware of pro-recovery sites. However, in this same study, 96 percent of adolescents who viewed pro–eating disorder websites reported learning new techniques for weight loss.

Justine J. Reel

See also: Celebrities and Eating Disorders; Children and Adolescents; Cosmetic Surgery and Eating Disorders; Internet and Eating Disorders; Media; Social Contagion Theory; Social Media and Eating Disorders; Wannarexia

Bibliography

Bardone-Cone, Anna M., and Kamila M. Cass. "Investigating the Impact of Pro-Anorexia Websites: A Pilot Study." *European Eating Disorders Review* 14 (2006): 256–262. https://doi.org/10.1002/ERV.714.

Bardone-Cone, Anna M., and Kamila M. Cass. "What Does Viewing a Pro-Anorexia Website Do? An Experimental Examination of Website Exposure and Moderating Effects." *International Journal of Eating Disorders* 40, no. 6 (2007): 537–548. https://doi.org/10.1002/eat.20396.

Giles, David. "Constructing Identities in Cyberspace: The Case of Eating Disorders." *British Journal of Social Psychology* 45 (2006): 463–477. https://doi.org/10/1348/014466605X53596.

Harper, Kelley, Steffanie Sperry, and J. Kevin Thompson. "Viewership of Pro–Eating Disorder Websites: Association with Body Image and Eating Disturbances." *International Journal of Eating Disorders* 41 (2008): 92–95. https://doi.org/10.1002/eat.20408.

Jett, Scarlett, David J. LaPorte, and Jill Wanchisn. "Impact of Exposure to Pro–Eating Disorder Websites on Eating Behaviour in College Women." *European Eating Disorders Review* 18 (2010): 410–416. https://doi.org/10.1002/erv.1009.

Lyons, Elizabeth J., Matthias R. Mehl, and James W. Pennebaker. "Pro-anorexics and Recovering Anorexics Differ in Their Linguistic Internet Self-Presentation." *Journal of Psychosomatic Research* 60 (2006): 253–256. https://doi.org/10.1016/j.psychores.2005.07.017.

Ransom, Danielle C., Jennifer G. La Guardia, Erik Z. Woody, and Jennifer L. Boyd. "Interpersonal Interactions on Online Forums Addressing Eating Concerns." *International Journal of Eating Disorders* 43, no. 2 (2010): 161–170. https://doi.org/10.1002/eat.20629.

Wilson, Jenny L., Rebecka Peebles, Kristina K. Hardy, and Iris F. Litt. "Surfing for Thinness: A Pilot Study of Pro–Eating Disorder Web Site Usage in Adolescents with Eating Disorders." *Pediatrics* 118 (2006): 1635–1643. https://doi.org/10.1542/peds.2006-1133.

PROGNOSIS

Prognosis is the potential or probable outcome of a disease or condition. It has been difficult to pinpoint a favorable prognosis rate for eating disorders due to the complexity and range of the types of disorders represented. However, preliminary findings from outcome studies provide initial prognosis estimates for anorexia nervosa and bulimia nervosa.

Prognosis Rates for Anorexia Nervosa

Anorexia nervosa is marked by frequent relapses and has the highest mortality rate of all mental disorders. Approximately 20 percent of individuals with anorexia nervosa continue to present with eating disorder symptoms. The proportion of deaths ranges from 5 percent to 16 percent across longitudinal studies. However, women with anorexia nervosa are 12 times more likely to experience mortality than women of the same age in the general population. Fifty-four percent of anorexia nervosa deaths were linked to eating disorder–related medical complications, 27 percent of deaths were suicide, and 19 percent were deaths from unknown or other causes.

The prognosis for adolescents is more optimistic than for adults with anorexia nervosa. In contrast to the 30–50 percent of adults who fully recover from anorexia nervosa, approximately 76 percent of adolescents achieved full recovery. It is expected this improved anorexia nervosa prognosis in adolescents is attributed to a shorter duration of symptoms before treatment.

Prognosis Rates for Bulimia Nervosa

The prognosis for bulimia nervosa appears to be more favorable than for anorexia nervosa. In one study, almost 60 percent of bulimia nervosa clients achieved a good outcome, 29 percent of clients realized an intermediate outcome, and 10 percent reported a poor outcome. Bulimia nervosa clients in this study had a 1.1 percent mortality rate, five times lower than anorexia nervosa clients. In a separate study, 74 percent of bulimia nervosa clients achieved full recovery compared to one-third of anorexia nervosa clients. Partial recovery was actualized by 99 percent of bulimia nervosa clients. It is estimated one-third of individuals will relapse.

The prognosis for clients with eating disorders is better for younger individuals than adults. Generally, individuals with bulimia nervosa have stronger treatment outcomes and lower mortality rates than individuals with anorexia nervosa. More research is needed to understand the prognosis for individuals who are diagnosed with binge eating disorder.

Justine J. Reel

See also: Medical and Health Consequences; Recovery; Relapse; Treatment

Bibliography

Goldstein, Mandy, Lorna Peters, Andrew Baillie, Patricia McVeagh, Gerri Minshall, and Dianne Fitzjames. "The Effectiveness of a Day Program for the Treatment of Adolescent Anorexia Nervosa." *International Journal of Eating Disorders* 44, no. 1 (2011): 29–38. https://doi.org/10.1002/eat.20789.

Keel, Pamela K., and Tiffany A. Brown. "Update on Course and Outcome in Eating Disorders." *International Journal of Eating Disorders* 43, no. 3 (2010): 195–204. https://doi.org/10.1002/eat.20810.

Miller, Catherine A., and Neville H. Golden. "An Introduction to Eating Disorders: Clinical Presentation, Epidemiology and Prognosis." *Nutrition in Clinical Practice* 25 (2010): 110–115. https://doi.org/10.1177/0884533609357566.

Zeeck, Almut, Stephanie Weber, Angelika Sandholz, Andreas Joos, and Armin Hartmann. "Stability of Long-Term Outcome in Bulimia Nervosa: A 3-Year Follow-Up." *Journal of Clinical Psychology* 67, no. 3 (2011): 318–327. https://doi.org/10.1002/jclp.20766.

PROTECTIVE FACTORS

In health and medicine, *protective factor* describes a behavior or event that reduces one's vulnerability to a specific disease or condition. A protective factor is often seen as the opposite of a risk factor, as protective factors lessen the likelihood of disease and risk factors increase the likelihood of disease. Thus, eating disorder protective factors reduce the likelihood of an individual developing an eating disorder.

Eating disorders and body image and weight problems have many of the same protective factors. This is partly because having a positive body image and following healthy weight management practices serve as protective factors for eating disorders. Thus, the factors that protect against having a negative body image would also protect against an eating disorder through a chain reaction. If a person does not develop a negative body image, they will likely not develop an eating disorder. The list of protective factors for eating disorders is quite lengthy. Most individuals who avoid developing an eating disorder have a few of these factors. It would be extremely rare for an individual to possess all the factors. Increasing the number of protective factors will decrease the likelihood of developing an eating disorder. Although there are many protective factors for eating disorders, they primarily fall into the broader categories of media exposure, psychosocial functioning, physical health, positive spirituality, and the influence of family and friends.

Media Exposure

The media perpetuates the ideal image and reinforces stereotypes about body size and weight. Magazines, television shows, and movies all display images of perfect physical appearances. Individuals who have less exposure to media are less likely to develop negative body image or eating disorders, making less media exposure a protective factor.

Psychosocial Functioning

Although lessened exposure to the media is ideal, it is impossible to completely eliminate the media. For an individual to maintain a positive body image, he or she must be able to effectively cope with the pressures of society regarding beauty and weight. Coping, or resiliency, is an especially important skill when it comes to eating disorder prevention. Beyond coping with body image challenges, an individual must be able to cope with daily tasks and challenges, negative emotions, sadness, grief, and pain. Individuals with a high level of resiliency find purpose and meaning in suffering, use appropriate coping methods, and avoid using eating disorder behaviors to mask underlying unresolved concerns.

Similarly, effective stress management is a protective factor for eating disorders. Individuals who appropriately handle the stressful demands of life are less likely to develop eating disorders. Appropriate stress management is also a protective factor for obesity, as individuals who are unable to find healthy outlets for stress more often turn to food for comfort and support.

Being able to effectively solve problems and resolve conflicts is also a protective factor for eating disorders. Self-esteem may be a confounding factor as individuals with higher self-esteem may have the internal confidence to stand up for themselves and address conflicts in an assertive manner. Individuals who lack the ability to resolve interpersonal problems are more likely to turn to dieting and weight loss.

Individual psychosocial characteristics that are protective against eating disorders include low levels of depression, high self-esteem, low levels of self-criticism, and low levels of perfectionism. An individual's ability to identify and express emotions is also correlated with fewer eating disorders. Better emotional regulation is a protective factor suggesting that effectively managing negative emotions can predict resistance to eating disorders. Individuals unable to cope effectively may be more at risk for an eating disorder as they block or numb painful or unpleasant thoughts and emotions through eating disorder behaviors and rituals. Similarly, a childhood free from abuse and/or neglect serves as a protective factor for eating disorders.

Strong social abilities make an individual less likely to develop an eating disorder. Individuals who have better social skills are less likely to have a negative body image, diet, and/or develop an eating disorder. Additionally, individuals who are socially connected to others are less likely to turn to food for an emotional release. In a common fashion, individuals with strong social support are less likely to develop an eating disorder. Individuals with a lot of close friends and family who they can turn to difficulties are less likely to use negative coping methods to deal with painful emotions.

Physical Health

Being physically healthy may be a protective factor for eating disorders. People with active lifestyles, including appropriate exercise, healthy eating, and abstinence from cigarettes and drugs, are less likely to develop an eating disorder. Although physical health is a protective factor for some, increased concern with weight and shape, dieting, and excessive levels of exercise put an individual at greater risk for an eating disorder. The protective value of physical health comes only at a level where an individual thinks well about herself and her body but is not obsessively trying to alter or change it.

Positive Spirituality

For some individuals, a high level of religion and/or spirituality is a protective factor for eating disorders. Individuals who gain acceptance and reassurance about their physical bodies from religious teachings may be less affected by media influences. This protective factor, however, is not true for all religious individuals.

Influence of Family and Friends

A positive home environment that protects children from eating disorders is one where parents are highly connected to children and can discuss topics related to appearance, body image, and weight. Parents may be needed to mediate teasing or bullying about appearance and provide a safe haven where children can be free from social pressures. Connectedness with at least one parent is a protective factor.

Eating together as a family has positive effects on weight, eating habits, and body image. The interaction between family members builds social bonds and establishes a connected relationship. Children are often able to discuss problems they are having, as well as chat about their friends and school responsibilities. The conversations at the dinner table allow parents to get to know their children, which is important because parents who are connected to their children are more likely to have a positive influence when giving counsel about weight or body image. Furthermore, adolescents who ate frequently with their families reported less use of alcohol, tobacco, and marijuana and were also more likely to get higher grades and have lower risk of depression and suicide. In addition, the typical family meal can be healthier, which can contribute to lower body mass index among adolescents.

For adolescent females, eating with the family most nights of the week protects against extreme weight loss behaviors and disordered eating.

A parent with an authoritative parenting style is also a protective factor for teens. Kids who have parents who establish rules, but allow for circumstantial changes to be made to those rules are less likely to have children with eating disorders. The increased connectedness and authoritative parenting may go together. Parents able to identify initial signs of disordered eating have an increased chance of preventing the emergence of a serious eating disorder.

The social group an adolescent associates with may have a strong influence on his or her eating disorder risk. Peer protective factors include having friends who have good self-esteem, are not interested in dieting or weight loss, and refrain from appearance-related teasing. If one peer in the group exhibits dieting or eating disorder behavior, it puts the additional members of the group at risk for initiating the same behavior. Adolescents need friends who are supportive, can identify potential eating problems, and are willing to take necessary action to ensure their friends do not engage in dangerous eating behaviors. Friends who are worried about dieting, weight, body image, and beauty put a girl at risk for an eating disorder. Similarly, for males, having friends who are overly concerned with body shape and size, muscle mass, and/or weight may put them at additional risk. Ideally, adolescents need friends who have a positive body image, are not interested in dieting or losing weight, and participate in healthy eating and exercise behaviors. Research has found girls who mature early are more likely to develop eating problems. Early breast development and menarche may place a girl at risk as she might appear different than her peers.

Having positive role models is one of the most critical protective factors for eating disorder prevention. Children and adolescents frequently look up to and admire peers and adults. They may emulate the behavior of parents or older siblings. In this way, parents may have a very direct role in the prevention of eating disorders. Many research articles have stated the influence of comments made by a mother to her daughter. Negative comments about weight and body result in an increased risk for eating disorders. Similarly, comments made by a girl's father or brothers may also increase her risk.

Parents should serve as positive role models to the children and teens around them by practicing healthy nutrition and engaging in appropriate exercise. Parents should also talk openly about the media's effect on women and the unrealistic images that are portrayed. Teaching children about media literacy from a young age may decrease the likelihood of them internalizing these ideals. Parents need to promote self-worth and compliment their children on things that are unconnected to body shape or size. They must discourage dieting behavior and weight-related teasing in the home. They need to resist the urge to make derogatory statements about their own body shape, weight, beauty, or size. If a parent is overly concerned with weight and seems upset by fluctuations, a child is more likely to mimic that behavior. Thus, a protective factor is having parents who accept their bodies and do not make negative comments about themselves.

TeriSue Smith-Jackson

See also: Children and Adolescents; Coping Skills; Family Influences; Media; Parents; Resiliency

Bibliography

Aime, Annie, Wendy M. Craig, Debra Pepler, Depeng Jiang, and Jennifer Connolly. "Developmental Pathways of Eating Problems in Adolescents." *Eating Disorders* 41, no. 8 (2008): 686–696. https://doi.org/10.1002/eat.20561.

Bardone-Cone, Anna M., Kamila M. Cass, and Jennifer A. Ford. "Examining Body Dissatisfaction in Young Men within a Biopsychosocial Framework." *Body Image* 5, no. 2 (2008): 183–194. http://dx.doi.org/10.1016/j.bodyim.2007.12.004.

Cain, Angela S., Anna M. Bardone-Cone, Lyn Y. Abramson, Kathleen D. Vohs, and Thomas E. Joiner. "Refining the Relationships of Perfectionism, Self-Efficacy, and Stress to Dieting and Binge Eating: Examining the Appearance, Interpersonal, and Academic Domains." *International Journal of Eating Disorders* 41, no. 8 (2008): 713–772. https://doi.org/10.1002/eat.20563.

Cordero, Elizabeth, and Tania Israel. "Parents as Protective Factors in Eating Problems of College Women." *Eating Disorders* 17, no. 2 (2009): 146–161. http://dx.doi.org/10.1080/10640260802714639.

Crago, Marjorie, Catherine M. Shisslak, and Anne Ruble. "Protective Factors in the Development of Eating Disorders." In *Eating Disorders: Innovative Directions in Research and Practice,* edited by R. H. Striegel-Moore and L. Smolak, 75–89. Washington, DC: American Psychological Association, 2001.

Fennig, Silvana, Arie Hadas, Liat Itzhaky, David Roe, Alan Apter, and Golan Shahar. "Self-Criticism Is a Key Predictor of Eating Disorder Dimensions among Inpatient Adolescent Females." *International Journal of Eating Disorders* 41, no. 8 (2008): 762–765. https://doi.org/10.1002/eat.20573.

Gustafsson, Sanna Aila, Birgitta Edlund, Lars Kjellin, and Claes Norring. "Risk and Protective Factors for Disturbed Eating in Adolescent Girls—Aspects of Perfectionism and Attitudes of Eating and Weight." *European Eating Disorders Review* 17, no. 5 (2009): 380–389. https://doi.org/10.1002/erv.930.

Neumark-Sztainer, Dianne. *"I'm, Like, SO Fat!" Helping Your Teen Make Healthy Choices about Eating and Exercise in a Weight-Obsessed World.* New York: Guilford Press, 2005.

Parents Toolkit. "10 Things Parents Can Do to Help Prevent Eating Disorders." *National Eating Disorders Association.* Accessed November 16, 2016. https://www.nationaleatingdisorders.org/sites/default/files/Toolkits/ParentToolkit.pdf.

Patrick, Heather. "The Benefits of Authoritative Feeding Style: Caregiver Feeding Styles and Children's Food Consumption Patterns." *Appetite* 44, no. 2 (2005): 243–249. http://dx.doi.org/10.1016/j.appet.2002.07.001.

PSYCHODRAMA

Psychodrama is a form of psychotherapy that used a variety of dramatic action methods, such as role-playing and spontaneous dramatization, to examine the problems of an individual or group, and to encourage healthy change through the development of new perceptions, behaviors, and a connection with others. Psychodrama focuses on interactive role-play as a therapeutic medium is usually in a group setting. Typically, the role-playing involves using a scenario to enact scenes from a client's life. By participating in active role-plays during group therapy, an individual can process a painful situation in a safe environment.

History of Psychodrama

Psychodrama was developed by Jacob Levy Moreno in Vienna during the early part of the 20th century to address the health of individuals and of humanity. Moreno introduced psychodrama to the United States in 1925. Moreno reported his hope for humanity was the transformation of consciousness through the integration of creative play, spontaneity, and psychological theory. Psychodrama is the vehicle he developed to facilitate this transformative process.

Description of Psychodrama in Therapy

Psychodrama sessions can last up to two or three hours and are facilitated by a trained psychotherapist who acts as a director. A psychotherapist guides participants through each phase of a session providing therapeutic support. Other key players in psychodrama sessions include a protagonist, auxiliary egos, an audience, and a stage. The protagonist is played by a group member selected to represent the theme of the group in the drama. A real life, emotionally-charged issue is enacted in the session's role-play. The auxiliary egos consist of group members who play the roles of significant others in the drama. The audience is made up of group members who witness the drama and represent the world at large; they typically do not provide feedback until the sharing phase of the session, at which time they speak of their individual experience. The stage is the actual physical space where the drama is conducted.

Each session consists of three phases: the warm-up phase, the action phase, and the sharing phase. The warm-up phase is when a group theme is identified, and a protagonist is selected. It is also a time when people in the group connect so that they can work better together. The scene is set in the action stage as the protagonist determines the scene she wants to act out and selects group members in the room to play the other roles. In the action phase the problem/painful issue is dramatized, and the protagonist examines new methods of working through it. The sharing phase is when group members are invited to express how they related to or connected with the protagonist's work.

Psychodrama and Eating Disorders

Psychodrama is a useful adjunct therapy for eating disorders. Persons with eating disorders often accommodate the wishes, demands, wants, or needs of others at the cost of developing a sense of self. Psychodrama can help individuals develop a stronger identity with role-play, as psychodrama works with the idea that one's true self develops from the role one plays. Persons with eating disorders tend to dissociate from their bodies as well as from intense memories and experiences. Psychodrama can be especially helpful to enable individuals to assume roles without necessarily experiencing them as a part of the self. Examples of this experience include enabling the protagonist to step out of the scene and watch others act out a scene or to switch her role with another, such as her sibling, to gain a different viewpoint.

Psychodrama and Bulimia Nervosa

Monica Callahan has examined the ways psychodrama is helpful for persons with bulimia nervosa and techniques to use specifically adapted to the needs of persons with bulimia. She has argued psychodrama techniques are especially useful for helping this population to break though emotional barriers and to access the hidden self. She believes psychodrama provides individuals with the tools and space to build a healthier self, and that through sharing this other people can overcome the isolation found in people with bulimia.

She has suggested three ways in which psychodrama can be adapted for people with bulimia nervosa. One modification of psychodrama involves allowing group members to work on their problems indirectly by playing roles in others' dramas. Another strategy is to capitalize on the playfulness of some psychodrama techniques. A specific example of this would be the personification of a binge food. Finally, Callahan recommends altering techniques so they are less threatening in respect to the sensitivity bulimics have about their bodies. An example would be using techniques that require limited physical movement.

Psychodrama and Anorexia Nervosa

M. Katherine Hudgins has studied the use of psychodrama with persons who have anorexia nervosa. She identified three concepts to guide the clinical treatment of anorexia using psychodrama: active experiencing, surplus reality, and empathetic bonding. *Active experiencing* is a term used in drama that indicates that the person puts herself into the role of a character. In the case of psychodrama, this occurs when auxiliary egos act out roles from a protagonist's painful memory. Active experiencing helps persons with anorexia to explore and learn to trust a part of "the self." Surplus reality is described as an intervention with the goal of giving a therapist a chance to see the internal reality of a patient. Surplus reality enables a person with anorexia to move past rigid control and rejection of sensation by enacting images in a way that appear larger than life. Hudgins reports empathic bonding is the first step in effective treatment of anorexia nervosa. Empathic bonding in therapy establishes a trusting relationship and a therapeutic alliance with a client. People suffering with anorexia often have developmental arrest and struggle to establish a working relationship in therapy. For this reason, empathic bonding often needs to occur actively, such as by mirroring nonverbal communication, with clients with anorexia.

Jessica Guenther

See also: Art Therapy; Integrative Approaches; Psychodynamic Psychotherapy Approaches; Treatment

Bibliography

American Society of Group Psychotherapy and Psychodrama. "General Information about Psychodrama." Accessed November 18, 2016. http://www.asgpp.org/.

Callahan, Monica Leonie. "Pyschodrama and the Treatment of Bulimia." In *Experiential Therapies for Eating Disorders,* edited by Lynne M. Hornyak and Ellen K. Baker, 101–120. New York: Guilford Press, 1989.

Davis, Leslie. "Acting Out Your Issues through Psychodrama." Accessed November 18, 2016. http://www.sierratucson.com/about/news-media/articles/.

Dayton, Tian. *The Living Stage.* Deerfield Beach, FL: Health Communications, 2005.

Hudgins, M. Katherine. "Experiencing the Self through Psychodrama and Gestalt Therapy in Anorexia Nervosa." In *Experiential Therapies for Eating Disorders,* edited by Lynne M. Hornyak and Ellen K. Baker, 234–251. New York: Guilford Press, 1989.

PSYCHODYNAMIC PSYCHOTHERAPY APPROACHES

Psychodynamic psychotherapy is a group of treatment approaches and techniques founded on psychoanalytic psychotherapy, the theory proposed by Sigmund Freud. Current understanding and application of Freud's ideas frequently differ from what was prevalent in the late 1800s and the early 1900s. Additionally, many psychodynamic and psychoanalytic principles (e.g., establishing a working alliance, bringing into awareness that of which a client was previously unaware) are often found in other treatment approaches.

Elements of Psychodynamic Psychotherapy

There are several different theoretical approaches to psychodynamic psychotherapy including self-psychology, object relations, and attachment theory. Although these approaches may differ in the specific focus of treatment or the language used to describe the difficulties faced by clients, there is considerable overlap of the features of these approaches. Shelder captured this when he stated that what psychodynamic psychotherapists do is help clients explore parts of themselves they may not be fully aware of, and that psychodynamic psychotherapists do this in the context of a relationship between psychotherapist and client. The elements of psychodynamic psychotherapy described below represent features that differentiate psychodynamic psychotherapy from other forms of counseling and psychotherapy.

A focus on the quality of how people relate to one another is an important aspect in psychodynamic psychotherapies. Helping clients understand why they interact with others the way they do is paramount because clients' relationships with others can be beneficial or harmful. Figuring out how and why certain relationships work and contribute to a clients' overall happiness will allow clients to identify and nurture future relationships that be satisfactory. Conversely, identifying why some relationships do not work (i.e., are harmful or distressing for a client) can allow clients to avoid developing such relationships. One of the ways by which a psychodynamic psychotherapist can help clients navigate interpersonal concerns is by using the relationship between them. Focusing on how client and psychotherapist interact with one another can provide useful information or *insight* into what works and what does not work for a client interpersonally. This is often referred to as work in the here-and-now. Working with interpersonal exchanges in the moment, rather than working with information about relationships outside of psychotherapy can help clients work through recurring themes and patterns that are apparent in every aspect of their lives (e.g., thoughts, views of themselves).

Examining how a client relates to others means addressing experiences with others. A common misconception about psychodynamic psychotherapy is that the past is an area of focus purely for the sake of figuring out what occurred during a client's childhood years. Knowing about the past, however, can help clients develop an understanding of their daily lives. Clients can then identify dysfunctional behavioral patterns (e.g., repeatedly dating the same type of person).

Finally, psychodynamic psychotherapists focus on clients' emotions. For some clients, this may mean they are helped to identify emotions when they occur. For others, focusing on emotions may mean they are helped to make sense of emotions that seem to conflict (e.g., "How can I feel angry and sad at the same time?"). Work on emotions often leads to exploration of the ways in which clients try to avoid experiencing distressing emotions.

Clients in psychodynamic psychotherapy often benefit in ways beyond symptoms remission (e.g., no longer depressed, improved relationships, decrease in anxiety). After engaging in psychodynamic psychotherapy, many clients develop and expand the resources they have to cope with life-related struggles with a goal of experiencing a greater sense of satisfaction

Evidence for the Effectiveness of Psychodynamic Psychotherapy

Research on the effectiveness of psychodynamic psychotherapy suggests this form of treatment is effective; however, the quantity of research is significantly less than for other forms of therapy such as cognitive behavioral therapy (CBT). Likewise, the evidence for the effectiveness of psychodynamic psychotherapy in the treatment of eating disorders is significantly less than for other forms of therapy. The evidence that does exist, however, suggests psychodynamic psychotherapy is effective to treat clients and the benefits seen at the end of the treatment seem to grow as time passes. This means clients continue to get better after treatment ends. In studies specifically examining the use of psychodynamic psychotherapy with clients having eating disorders, results show this form of treatment is at least as good as other forms of therapy to address eating disorders. Individuals who write about the evidence for psychodynamic psychotherapy recognize more studies are needed to compete with the vast body of research conducted on other forms of therapy. The existing evidence, however, indicates psychodynamic psychotherapy is an empirically supported therapy that performs as well as or better than other forms of therapy, and the benefits clients experience are likely to grow beyond the end of treatment.

The Application of Psychodynamic Psychotherapy for Eating Disorders

Available evidence on how and why eating disorders develop indicates there is no single cause and what may have caused an eating disorder for one person may not be the cause for another. Potential causes can include genetics, personality factors, a client's family and developmental history, co-occurring disorders, and sociocultural factors. Given the complexity and seriousness of eating disorders, attention to a client's eating-related behaviors must be the focus of treatment; however, due to the array of plausible causes of eating disorders, attention to symptoms alone is not likely to result in long-term results. Clients with eating disorders require assistance with managing their eating behaviors and help to find other ways to manage distressing emotions, improve interpersonal relationships, and come to terms with experiences (traumatic or nontraumatic) that may continue to affect them. Psychodynamic psychotherapy, or at minimum, psychodynamic technique, is perhaps best suited to address these deep and often long-standing concerns. Clients with eating disorders often struggle to manage their relationships with others and the emotions that accompany those relationships, concerns for which psychodynamic psychotherapists are specifically trained. The emphasis on the relationship between therapist and client as well as the attention to identifying and managing emotions can make psychodynamic psychotherapy an ideal form of treatment for many clients with eating disorders.

Christine L. B. Selby

See also: Causes; Cognitive Behavioral Therapy; Treatment

Bibliography

Casper, Regina C. "Integration of Psychodynamic Concepts into Psychotherapy." In *Psychobiology and Treatment of Anorexia Nervosa and Bulimia Nervosa,* edited by Katherine A. Halmi, 287–305. Washington, DC: American Psychiatric Association Publishing, 1992.

Shedler, Jonathan. "The Efficacy of Psychodynamic Psychotherapy." *American Psychologist* 65, no. 2 (2010): 98–109.

Thompson-Brenner, Heather, Jolie Weingeroff, and Drew Westen. "Empirical Support for Psychodynamic Psychotherapy for Eating Disorders." In *Handbook of Evidence-Based Psychodynamic Psychotherapy,* edited by Raymond A. Levy and Stuart J. Ablon, 67–92. New York: Humana Press, 2010.

Zerbe, Kathryn J. "Psychodynamic Management of Eating Disorders." In *Clinical Manual of Eating Disorders,* edited by Joel Yager and Pauline S. Powers, 307–334. Arlington, VA: American Psychiatric Association Publishing, 2007.

Zerbe, Kathryn J. "Psychodynamic Therapy for Eating Disorders." In *The Treatment of Eating Disorders: A Clinical Handbook,* edited by Carlos M. Grilo and James E. Mitchell, 339–358. New York: Guilford Press, 2010.

PUBERTY

Puberty is the changes in the reproductive system that occurs naturally during adolescence and leads to physical, sexual, and psychosocial maturation. Physical and sexual changes that emerge during puberty include physical growth, onset of menstruation, and development and appearance of organs and sexual characteristics (e.g., breasts and pubic hair). Among American girls, most pubertal changes occur during early adolescence. The average age of menarche (i.e., first period) is 13 years, which coincides with an increase in the amount of body fat on a girl's body. Typically, boys tend to have 1.5 times the lean body mass and bone mass of girls, while girls have twice as much body fat as boys. This significant amount of weight gain coupled with other pubertal changes has been shown to positively and negatively influence the body image of adolescents.

Pubertal Changes and Body Image

During puberty, physical appearance and body shape changes for girls and boys, and this can influence how they think about their bodies. Most girls accept pubertal changes like developing breasts and getting taller; however, some girls are distressed about gaining weight and fat during normal development. Pubertal weight gain occurs during a time when girls want to be popular and attractive to the opposite sex and are extremely self-conscious about their appearance, weight, and body shape. During early and middle adolescence, girls are more likely to judge their attractiveness based on attention from boys. This emphasis on attractiveness and popularity with the opposite sex along with normative development of fat during puberty heightens girls' awareness of their bodies and leads to increased body dissatisfaction. For example, according to a recent study, 56 percent of 9-year-olds and 43 percent of girls in the age group of 13–16 years were dissatisfied with their bodies.

Early Maturation and Stress

Adolescents may be self-critical and embarrassed about their bodies because they are maturing too early or too late, or because they are not developing according to societal expectations or the prescribed standard of beauty. Early onset or precocious puberty is defined as the beginning of the physical maturation process before age eight for girls and before age nine for boys. This condition occurs more often in girls and boys in industrialized societies. Although early physical development could occur in both girls and boys, girls are 10 times more likely to experience early onset puberty. Young girls who experience precocious puberty report identity confusion and psychological distress at higher levels than girls who experience puberty on schedule. This overall distress can result in negative body image and self-worth because of an inability emotionally and cognitively process the implications of early physical development.

For girls, researchers have reported early maturation is a risk factor for body dissatisfaction because the physical changes (e.g., weight gain, menarche) associated with puberty deviate from a Western cultural belief that the thin ideal body type is attractive and beautiful. Early maturing girls indicated a stronger desire to be thin than average or late maturing girls. In addition, early maturers reported a preference for a slenderer ideal figure than the average or late maturers when asked to choose the ideal figure they desired. Diamond recently stated girls who have larger breasts and hips are sexualized in our society. Because young girls are not mature enough to cope with this attention, they develop negative thought about their bodies well into adulthood.

Obesity and Puberty

Researchers have also found obesity tends to increase in early maturers during puberty. Females who perceived they were overweight prior to puberty reported more body dissatisfaction, desire to be thin, and eating disorder tendencies compared to females who perceived their prepubertal weight as average or underweight.

Males and Puberty

For boys, the ideal image is a muscular body with a large chest and shoulders and a slim waist. In contrast to early maturing girls, early maturing boys typically experience a developmental advantage related to societal standards for an ideal body compared to late maturing boys. Late maturing boys may appear to have a greater risk of developing body dissatisfaction and unhealthy eating and exercise behaviors. Unlike the girls, early maturing boys are viewed as more attractive and self-confident, have more positive body image, and are more popular with their peers compared to late maturing boys. A reason for this is that boys gain muscle mass and definition and their shoulder width increases, which places most boys closer to the societal standard of the ideal body shape for a man. Researchers have examined pubertal timing and body image among adolescent boys and found that late maturing boys reported more body dissatisfaction than early maturers. However, the research on the developmental trajectory of boys' body image into adulthood remains unclear.

Sonya SooHoo

See also: Adolescent Development; Body Esteem; Body Image; Body Image in Males

Bibliography

Ackard, Diann, and Carol B. Peterson. "Association between Puberty and Disordered Eating, Body Image, and Other Psychological Variables." *International Journal of Eating Disorders* 29, no. 2 (2001): 187–194. https://doi.org/10.1002/1098-108X(200103)29:2<187::AID-EAT1008>3.0.CO;2-R.

Bradley University. "Precocious Puberty and Body Image." Accessed November 18, 2016. https://bradley.edu/sites/bodyproject/sexuality/puberty/.

McCabe, Marita P., and Lina A. Ricciardelli. "A Longitudinal Study of Pubertal Timing and Extreme Body Change Behaviors among Adolescent Boys and Girls." *Adolescence* 39 (2004): 145–166.

Mendle, Jane, Eric Turkheimer, and Robert E. Emery. "Detrimental Psychological Outcomes Associated with Early Puberty Timing in Adolescent Girls." *Developmental Review* 27, no. 2 (2007): 151–171. http://doi.org/10.1016/j.dr.2006.11.001.

Pineyerd, Belinda, and William B. Zipf. "Puberty—Timing Is Everything!" *Journal of Pediatric Nursing* 20, no. 2 (2005): 75–82. http://doi.org/10.1016/j.pedn.2004.12.011.

Tremblay, Line, and Jean-Yves Frigon. "Precocious Puberty in Adolescent Girls: A Biomarker of Later Psychosocial Adjustment Problems." *Child Psychiatry and Human Development* 36 (2005): 73–91. https://doi.org/10.1007/s10578-004-3489-2.

Williams, Joanne M., and Candace Currie. "Self-Esteem and Physical Development in Early Adolescence: Pubertal Timing and Body Image." *Journal of Early Adolescence* 20, no. 2 (2000): 129–149. https://doi.org/10.1177/0272431600020002002.

PURGING

Purging refers to the purposive elimination of food and liquids using a variety of methods including self-induced vomiting, use of laxatives, diuretics, or enemas, and exercising excessively. Purging may occur to compensate for consuming trigger foods (e.g., chocolate cake), compensate for a binge eating episode, or as a continuous weight control behavior. Purging behaviors occur in the general population as well as in individuals with disordered eating or clinical eating disorders. Generally, purging behaviors are secretive and individuals attempt to hide evidence (e.g., laxative boxes).

Prevalence of Purging Behaviors

Both males and females report using purging methods to control weight. In a U.S. sample, 1.9 percent of women and 1.4 percent of men reported diuretic use, whereas 0.4 percent of women and 0.3 percent of men took laxatives. Approximately 0.1 percent of males and females admitted to self-induced vomiting to control weight. In an Australian study, adult women reported self-induced vomiting (1.4 percent) and use of laxatives (1.0 percent) or diuretics (0.3 percent) on a weekly basis. Prevalence rates of purging behaviors were even higher for adolescent boys and girls with 27.1 percent of girls and 6.5 percent of boys reporting purging to lose weight or prevent weight gain.

Alarmingly, prevalence rates for diuretic use have climbed from 0.5 percent in 1990 to 2.1 percent in 2004 as evidenced by a longitudinal investigation of female college students. Three percent of college women reported self-induced vomiting while 2.7 percent of college women misused laxatives. Meanwhile, an increase in disordered-eating behaviors was documented in both males and females in Australia over a 10-year period.

Disordered Eating and Purging Behaviors

Purging behaviors may begin as a strategy to avoid weight gain or as a supplement to dieting with the goal of weight loss. Unfortunately, these behaviors can lead to full-fledged eating disorders. Across studies, the prevalence of laxative abuse has been estimated to range from 10 percent to 60 percent for eating-disordered individuals. However, a more recent study found 67 percent of eating-disordered clients had used laxatives at some point to control weight or compensate for food intake. Purging behaviors are exhibited in individuals diagnosed with anorexia nervosa, binge eating/purging subtype, and bulimia nervosa. The current diagnostic criteria for anorexia nervosa binge eating/purging subtype is purging through self-induced vomiting or the misuse of laxatives, diuretics, or enemas at least weekly.

The bulimia nervosa diagnosis describes purging as compensatory behavior to prevent weight gain, including self-induced vomiting, laxatives, diuretics, enemas, as well as medications, fasting, or excessive exercise. Purging behaviors are important to address in treatment due to the health consequences that can result after continued use (e.g., gum erosion, dehydration, electrolyte imbalances). Additionally, outcome studies have shown individuals who continue to purge during treatment have a poorer prognosis for full recovery.

Prevention of Purging Behaviors

Of concern is the fact that many purging products (e.g., laxatives, diuretics, diet pills) are readily available over the counter. Although it is difficult to regulate whether an individual is abusing laxatives that may have initially been prescribed for a legitimate medical concern (e.g., constipation), it is recommended physicians provide natural solutions that do not require diuretic or laxative use. Another challenge associated with purging behaviors is a tendency for eating disorder education to center around a discussion of types of eating disorders. Inadvertently, lectures that discuss specific behaviors may provide purging ideas to vulnerable students who then begin to initiate pathogenic weight control behaviors.

Justine J. Reel

See also: Bulimia Nervosa: Diuretics; Laxative Abuse; Rumination Disorder

Bibliography

Ackard, Diann M., Catherine L. Cronemeyer, Lisa M. Franzen, Sara A. Richter, and Jane Norstrom. "Number of Different Purging Behaviors Used among Women with Eating Disorders: Psychological, Behavioral, Self-Efficacy and Quality of Life Outcomes." *Eating Disorders: Journal of Treatment and Prevention* 19 (2011): 156–174. https://doi.org/10.1080/10640266.2010.511909.

American Psychiatric Association. *Diagnostic and Statistical Manual of Mental Disorders*, 4th ed., rev. Washington, DC: American Psychiatric Association Publishing, 2000.

Liechty, Janet M. "Body Image Distortion and Three Types of Weight Loss Behaviors among Nonoverweight Girls in the United States." *Journal of Adolescent Health* 47 (2010): 176–182. https://doi.org/10.1016/j.jadohealth.2010.01.004.

Lock, James. "Treatment of Adolescent Eating Disorders: Progress and Challenges." *Minerva Psichiatrica* 51, no. 3 (2010): 207–216.

Roerig, James L., Kristine J. Steffen, James E. Mitchell, and Christie Zunker. "Laxative Abuse: Epidemiology, Diagnosis and Management." *Drugs* 70, no. 12 (2010): 1487–1503. https://doi.org/10.2165/11898640-000000000-00000.

R

RECOVERY

Recovery from an eating disorder has been broadly defined as the complete absence of symptoms so that an individual with an eating disorder history is indistinguishable from a person without a history. Specifically, to be fully recovered individuals should (1) no longer meet diagnostic criteria for an eating disorder; (2) not engaged in disordered-eating behaviors (e.g., vomiting, binge eating) for three months, (3) have a body mass index (BMI) of 18.5 or more; and (4) score within age-matched norms on eating disorder screening instruments.

An individual considered fully recovered from an eating disorder represents minimal risk for relapse. In contrast, *partial recovery* refers to refraining from disordered-eating behaviors and having acceptable BMI scores while not meeting the psychological criteria necessary for full recovery. Individuals in partial recovery often admit they continue to experience negative body image and eating disorder triggers.

Is Recovery from an Eating Disorder Possible?

A common belief related to addiction is that an individual who has a history of addiction will always be an addict and will remain in recovery, meaning that recovery is a lifelong process. Eating disorders differ from other addictions in that it is impossible to abstain from eating. Therefore, individuals with eating disorders must develop a healthier and more positive relationship with food to recover.

Eating disorder clinicians and researchers promote a philosophy that individuals can be *recovered from* an eating disorder rather than *in recovery*. Being recovered represents the past tense, which is more empowering for individuals and encourages disengagement from one's eating disorder identity. Furthermore, working toward full recovery or being recovered denotes optimism and the ability to improve one's condition.

It is estimated around half of all individuals with eating disorders recover. Among individuals with anorexia nervosa, 46 percent recover, 33 percent improve symptoms, and 20 percent remain disordered. Meanwhile half of individuals with bulimia nervosa recover, 30 percent improve symptoms, and 20 percent continue to meet bulimia nervosa criteria.

The controversy around whether a person can fully recovery from an eating disorder will be debated later in this book.

Justine J. Reel

See also: Relapse; Self-Care; Treatment

Bibliography

Bardone-Cone, Anna M., Megan B. Harney, Christine R. Maidonado, Melissa A. Lawson, D. Paul Robinson, Roma Smith, and Aneesh Tosh. "Defining Recovery from an Eating Disorder: Conceptualization, Validation, and Examination of Psychosocial Functioning and Psychiatric Comorbidity." *Behavioral Research Therapy* 48, no. 3 (2010): 194–202. https://doi.org/10.1016/j.brat.2009.11.001.

Darcy, Alison M., Shaina Katz, Kathleen Kara Fitzpatrick, Sarah Forsberg, Linsey Utzinger, and James Lock. "All Better? How Former Anorexia Nervosa Patients Define Recovery and Engaged in Treatment." *European Eating Disorders Review* 18, no. 4 (201): 260–270. https://doi.org/10.1002/erv.1020.

Gisladottir, M., and E. K. Svavarsdottir. "Educational and Support Intervention to Help Families Assist in the Recovery of Relatives with Eating Disorders." *Journal of Psychiatric and Mental Health Nursing* 18 (2011): 122–130. https://doi.org/10.1111/j.1365-2850.2010.01637.x.

Keifer, Ekaterina, Kevin Duff, Leigh J. Beglinger, Erin Barstow, Arnold Andersen, and David J. Moser. "Predictors of Neuropsychological Recovery in Treatment for Anorexia Nervosa." *Eating Disorders: Journal of Treatment and Prevention* 18 (2010): 302–317. https://doi.org/10.1080/10640266.2010/490120.

Turton, Penelope, Alexia Demetriou, William Boland, Stephen Gillard, Michael Kavuma, Gillian Mezey, Victoria Mountford, Kati Turner, Sarah White, Ewa Zadeh, and Christine Wright. "One Size Fits All: Or Horses for Courses? Recovery-Based Care in Specialist Mental Health Services." *Social Psychiatry and Psychiatric Epidemiology* 46 (2011): 127–136. https://doi.org/10.1007/s00127-009-0174-6.

Vanderlinden, J., H. Buis, G. Pieters, and M. Probst. "Which Elements in the Treatment of Eating Disorders Are Necessary 'Ingredients' in the Recovery Process? A Comparison between the Patient's and Therapist's View." *European Eating Disorders Review* 15, no. 5 (2007): 357–365. https://doi.org/10.1002/erv.768.

REFEEDING SYNDROME

Refeeding syndrome refers to severe electrolyte and fluid shifts that may occur when nutrition is reinstituted in a malnourished individual too rapidly, irrespective of whether it is provided orally, enterally (i.e., tube feeding), or parenterally (i.e., intravenously). During starvation the body becomes catabolic, a state in which the intracellular stores of phosphorus, potassium, and magnesium are depleted, insulin secretion decreases, and the body relies on breaking down fat for energy. During refeeding, the body shifts to an anabolic state in which insulin levels are increased to promote the synthesis of glycogen, protein, and fat. The cells require phosphorus, potassium, and magnesium for this process and these extracellular electrolytes shift into the cell, lowering serum levels. Refeeding syndrome can have profound consequences, including pulmonary, muscular, cardiovascular, hematological, gastrointestinal, and neurological complications, which can lead to death. The prevalence of refeeding syndrome in individuals with eating disorders is currently unknown and may be difficult to assess as it is multifactorial and may be underdiagnosed.

History of Refeeding Syndrome

Historically, cardiac dysfunction, edema, and other neurological conditions were observed in groups of malnourished refugees before refeeding syndrome was officially recognized. A 1940s study examined the effects of starvation and refeeding on a group of previously healthy volunteers. After a period of severe food restriction, several subjects in this study experienced cardiac problems once a normal intake of food resumed, and two study participants died due to complications associated with refeeding syndrome. Refeeding syndrome was first identified when the condition was observed in numerous prisoners of war after World War II, which further linked refeeding syndrome to starvation and prolonged fasting. Interestingly, numerous studies were conducted on people who were released from concentration camps after World War II in which documented cases of refeeding resulted in gastrointestinal problems (e.g., diarrhea), neurological complications (e.g., coma, convulsions), and heart failure symptoms.

The Minnesota Starvation Experiment

Ancel Keys, the lead investigator of the Minnesota Starvation Experiment, conducted his well-known research at the University of Minnesota beginning in 1944 to better understand the physiological and psychological effects of prolonged starvation and subsequent refeeding. The initial study participants included 36 male volunteers in the age group of 20–33 years who were subjected to a semistarvation diet and lost 25 percent of their body weight after 24 weeks on the diet. Next, the participants underwent a 24-week period of nutritional rehabilitation. After nearly three months of controlled rehabilitation from September through October of 1945, the experiment ended. Interestingly, study participants experienced physical changes including a 24 percent reduction in body weight on average as well as hair loss and edema in the knees, ankles, and face. Participants suffered complications from refeeding, including muscle cramps and soreness, increased heat tolerance, reduced tolerance to cold, episodes of vertigo, giddiness, and momentary blackouts when they stood up from a sitting position. Participants also reported decreased libido, and feeling unfocused, fatigued, weak, depressed, and apathetic.

Signs, Symptoms, and Risk Factors

Factors that place clients at a high risk for refeeding syndrome include little or no nutritional intake for greater than 7–10 days, greater than 10–15 percent weight loss in a short period, body mass index of less than 16, and a history of chronic malnutrition. Common signs and symptoms indicating a client may be developing refeeding syndrome are of electrolyte abnormalities, particularly decreases in potassium, magnesium, and phosphorus, sharp increases in blood glucose, peripheral edema, rapid weight gain of greater than 0.5 lb. per day, abnormal lung sounds, changes in pulse rate, and neurological symptoms, such as confusion, muscle weakness, tremors, and seizures. Thus, clinical and biochemical indices must be monitored for early recognition and intervention to prevent complications.

Complications of refeeding-induced hypophosphatemia involve respiratory function, the cardiovascular system, skeletal weakness, neurological problems, the endocrine system, and hematological concerns. According to McCray and colleague's work clients suffering from hypokalemia-induced refeeding syndrome usually experience cardiac dysfunction, neurological problems, metabolic complications, and gastrointestinal disorders.

Prevalence of Refeeding Syndrome

According to research, hypokalemia (associated with refeeding syndrome) has been reported in 14 percent of clients suffering from bulimia nervosa. However, based on a separate report, McCray suggested the incidence rates regarding cases of refeeding syndrome are unknown. According to a report from North Bristol NHS Trust in the United Kingdom, the general incidence rate for hospital patients with hypophosphatemia ranges from 0.2 percent to 5 percent. Refeeding syndrome has been reported in as high as 25 percent of cancer patients, due to numerous surgical procedures. Incidence rates of hypophosphatemia range from 30 percent to 38 percent in studies of patients receiving treatment through intravenous total parenteral nutrition (TPN) when phosphate was introduced. The refeeding syndrome incidence rate went up to 100 percent when parenteral nutrition was introduced to the patients in the absence of phosphate.

Management of the Client at Risk for Refeeding Syndrome

Identification of at-risk clients, close monitoring, and implementing an appropriate feeding regimen are critical to the prevention of refeeding syndrome. Nutritional rehabilitation should be advanced gradually so signs and symptoms of refeeding syndrome are recognized early and treated to prevent complications. Many hospitals and eating disorder units follow strict guidelines when refeeding a malnourished patient; the guidelines include (1) obtaining electrolyte and blood glucose levels at regular intervals, (2) assessing fluid status and body weight daily, and (3) monitoring cardiac function and blood pressure frequently. Thiamine, required for carbohydrate metabolism, is often supplemented during initial stages of refeeding due to increased demand for this nutrient. Deficiency of thiamine may result in Wernicke's encephalopathy, a neurological disorder. Initial caloric intake may be started at as little as 10 kcal/kg/day, depending on the extent of malnourishment, and increased gradually. If phosphorus, magnesium, and/or potassium levels fall, they should be corrected immediately, and caloric intake should not be advanced until electrolytes are stable. Labs may be monitored at longer intervals if they have been stable for several days.

Intravenous fluids help clients restore nutrients and hydration but should be used with caution to decrease the risk of fluid overload. It may take a few days for clients to advance to 100 percent of energy requirements, depending on biochemical stability and feeding tolerance.

Justine J. Reel, Holly E. Doetsch, and Shelly Guillory

See also: Electrolyte Imbalance; Medical and Health Consequences

Bibliography

Brynes, Matthew C., and Jessica Stangenes. "Refeeding in the ICU: An Adult and Pediatric Problem." *Current Opinion in Clinical Nutrition and Metabolic Care* 14 (2011): 186–192. https://doi.org/10.1097/MCO.ob013e328341ed93.

Cantani, Marco, and Roger Howells. "Risks and Pitfalls for the Management of Refeeding Syndrome in Psychiatric Patients." *The Psychiatrist* 31 (2007): 209–211. https://doi.org/10.1192/pb.bp.106.009878.

"Eating Disorders: Nutritional Considerations." NutritionMD.org. Accessed November 18, 2016. http://www.nutritionmd.org/health_care_providers/psychiatric/eating_disorders_nutrition.html

Fotheringham, J., K. Jackson, R. Kersh, and S. E. Gariballa. "Refeeding Syndrome: Life-Threatening, Underdiagnosed, but Treatable." *Oxford Journals, QJM: An International Journal of Medicine* 98, no. 4 (2005): 318–319. http://dx.doi.org/10.1093/qjmed/hci050.

Hearing, Stephen D. "Refeeding Syndrome Is Underdiagnosed, Undertreated, but Treatable." *British Medical Journal* 328 (2004): 908–909. https://doi.org/10.1136/bmj.328.7445.908.

Keys, Ancel. Josef Brozek, Austin Henschel, Olaf Mickelsen, and Henry Longstreet Taylor. *The Biology of Human Starvation*, Volume 1& 2. Minneapolis, Minnesota; University of Minnesota, 1950.

McCray, Stacey, Sherrie Walker, and Carol Rees Parrish. "Much Ado about Refeeding: Nutrition Issues in Gastroenterology, Series #23." *Practical Gastroenterology* (2005): 26–44.

Parrish, Carol Rees. "The Refeeding Syndrome in 2009: Prevention Is the Key to Treatment." *The Journal of Supportive Oncology* 7, no. 1 (2009): 20–21.

Prickett, Joanna. "Refeeding Syndrome." Presentation at North Bristol NHS Trust. Accessed November 18, 2016. http://slideplayer.com/slide/781738/.

"Refeeding Syndrome: The Complexity of Reintroducing Food." Bella Vita. Accessed November 18, 2016. http://www.thebellavita.com/refeeding-syndrome/.

Skibsted, Ashley. "Starvation and Refeeding Syndrome." Presentation at Concordia College, MN. Accessed November 18, 2016. http://www.slideserve.com/ananda/starvation-and-refeeding-syndrome.

Whitelaw, Melissa, Heather Gilbertson, Pei-Yoong Lam, and Susan M. Sawyer. "Does Aggressive Refeeding in Hospitalized Adolescents with Anorexia Nervosa Result in Increased Hypophosphatemia?" *Journal of Adolescent Health* 46 (2010): 577–582. https://doi.org/10.1016/j.jadohealth.2009.11.207.

REFERRING SOMEONE FOR EATING DISORDER TREATMENT

Anyone who suspects that a friend or family member has a problem faces the dilemma of how to approach that individual. Because professional help is often required, it is important to be able to refer the family member or friend for help.

Understanding and implementing strategies to increase the potential likelihood of a successful interaction are important for secretive disorders like eating disorders. Additionally, finding resources in the local community and having them available during a meeting is critical to ensure follow-through for treatment.

Denial and Eating Disorders

As with other addictions, individuals who suffer from disordered eating and eating disorders usually deny there is a problem. Common responses to being confronted about symptoms (e.g., restricting, weight loss) include making excuses (e.g., "I've had the stomach flu"), expressing anger, and adamantly denying that a problem exists. Therefore, it is important to carefully consider who will approach the person suspected of having a problem; it is also important to have that individual engage in several strategies throughout the meeting. Furthermore, this initial meeting should be viewed as an opportunity to express concern and a way to plant the seed for support. In the event an individual suspected of having a problem is open to seeking help, it is critical to locate any available local support networks and professional help. By identifying treatment resources in advance of the meeting, one can direct a friend or family member to specific treatment professionals or groups and assist to make an appointment.

Strategies for Referring Someone for Eating Disorder Treatment

Ideally, an individual who has the strongest rapport and relationship history should approach a person with a suspected eating disorder. In some cases, a sibling or friend has fewer power dynamics, is closer in age, and can be more effective than a parent or coach; however, in other instances, a concerned and respected teacher may have considerable influence. It should not be assumed someone else has already expressed concern. An individual who approaches someone suspected of having an eating disorder should show genuine concern for the well-being of an individual while identifying tangible observations (e.g., "You seem tired and sad lately.")

To avoid putting an individual on the defensive, it is recommended that the person use "I" rather than "you" statements to keep lines of communication open. As mentioned, it should be assumed a person will respond with denial. The purpose of this meeting should be to identify there is a problem and to extend support when an individual is ready to seek assistance. If the person agrees to get help for an eating disorder, the friend or family member can locate resources, make appointments, and help with transportation to treatment.

Voluntary versus Involuntary Treatment

It is important to note that regardless of the severity of an eating disorder, treatment has been found to be more beneficial when a client is admitted on a voluntary basis. Although parents may admit an individual under 18 years of age, and this is sometimes required out of medical necessity, it is important a client develop intrinsic motivation for recovery to ensure long-term success. The parallel to involuntary eating disorder treatment is court-ordered treatment associated with breaking the law. Although an individual receives treatment, he or she may only do the bare minimum required instead of making meaningful changes in cognitions or behaviors.

However, one of the advantages of getting a professional involved is a psychologist/therapist will address both the benefits and drawbacks of an eating disorder, illuminating some of the consequences of an eating disorder. A client will be forced to examine his or her readiness to address the problem and will be able to identify barriers to fully engaging in treatment.

Justine J. Reel

See also: Family Therapy; Recovery; Treatment

Bibliography

Costin, Carolyn. *A Comprehensive Guide to the Causes, Treatments and Prevention of Eating Disorders: The Eating Disorder Sourcebook*, 3rd ed. New York: McGraw-Hill, 2007.

Costin, Carolyn. *100 Questions & Answers about Eating Disorders*. Boston, MA: Jones and Bartlett, 2007.

"Eating Disorder Referral and Information Center." edreferral.com. Accessed November 18, 2016. http://www.edreferral.com.

"Something Fishy Website on Eating Disorders." Eating Disorders Anorexia, Bulimia & Compulsive Eating. Accessed November 18, 2016. http://www.something-fishy.org.

REFLECTIONS

Reflections or the Sorority Body Image Program (SBIP) refers to a body image program developed for with sorority women at universities. The Reflections initiative began in 2001 at Trinity University when a research team collaborated with an on-campus sorority group to create a program based on Dr. Eric Stice's 4-session cognitive dissonance intervention (i.e., targeting the internalization of the thin ideal standard of beauty for females).

Description of Reflections Program

Reflections or SBIP is implemented over two sessions facilitated by trained peer leaders who are active sorority members. Peer leaders receive nine hours of training before leading two 2-hour sessions. Participants engage in activities to promote positive body image and acceptance related to finding ways for sororities to change. In the initial session, participants are asked to describe the thin ideal, factors that reinforce this standard, and the costs of striving for the thin ideal. As a homework assignment, participants are asked to stand in front of a mirror and to record positive qualities about themselves including physical, emotional, and intellectual characteristics. In the second session participants share positive attributes and engage in role-plays to challenge the thin ideal. Participants are encouraged to think about changes that can occur in a sorority (e.g., policy changes) to challenge the thin ideal.

Although researchers reported challenges associated with funding and time, preliminary findings showed decreases in dietary restraint, bulimic tendencies, body dissatisfaction, and thin ideal internalization in the peer leaders for Reflections. More evaluation is needed to determine the effectiveness of the Reflections program.

Justine J. Reel

See also: Body Image; Media; Planet Health; Prevention; Sorority Women

Bibliography

Becker, Carolyn Black, Stephanie Bull, Lisa M. Smith, and Anna C. Ciao. "Effects of Being a Peer-Leader in an Eating Disorder Prevention Program: Can We Further Reduce Eating Disorder Risk Factors?" *Eating Disorders: Journal of Treatment and Prevention* 16 (2008): 444–459. https://doi.org/10.1080/10640260802371596.

Becker, Carolyn Black, Anna C. Ciao, and Lisa M. Smith. "Moving from Efficacy to Effectiveness in Eating Disorders Prevention: The Sorority Body Image Program." *Cognitive and Behavioral Practices* 15 (2008): 18–27. http://dx.doi.org/10.1016/j.cbpra.2006.07.006.

Becker, Carolyn Black, Eric Stice, Heather Shaw, and Susan Woda. "Use of Empirically-Supported Interventions for Psychopathology: Can the Participatory Approach Move Us beyond the Research to Practice Gap?" *Behavioral Research Therapy* 47, no. 4 (2009): 265–274. https://doi.org/10.1016/j.brat.2009.02.007.

RELAPSE

Relapse is the resumption of disordered-eating behaviors (e.g., purging) after completing treatment and being symptom-free for a significant period of time. Relapse rates vary from 22 percent to 63 percent for individuals with eating disorders depending on the definition of relapse and the timing of follow-up. Relapse or sliding back into disordered behaviors is often associated with shame, similar to being discovered with an eating disorder in the first place, and clients may think they have failed their treatment team, family members, and other clients in their support group.

Predictors of Relapse for Eating Disorders

Several factors are consistently associated with a greater risk for relapse, including greater body image disturbances, poor psychosocial functioning, history of suicidal ideations, higher severity of eating disorder before treatment, and comorbidity with other mental disorders (e.g., personality disorders). Furthermore, individuals who tend to excessively exercise toward the end of treatment are likely to relapse. By contrast, individuals who have the ability to abstain from disordered behaviors throughout treatment seem to be more likely to report a full recovery regardless of the initial diagnosis, suggesting clinicians should help clients avoid slip-ups during treatment.

The Impact of Body Image on Eating Disorders and Risk for Relapse: An Interview with "Tammy"

"Tammy" (pseudonym used to preserve anonymity) is a 50-year-old former competitive athlete and mother of two daughters. She articulates how negative body image and poor self-esteem contribute to her disordered eating patterns including overeating, purging, and dieting behavior. She struggled with an eating disorder from the age of 15. She also discusses how relapse and slips can occur over time throughout the recovery process.

What factors do you believe contributed to the development of your eating disorder? Was negative body image a part of this, and, if so, how did that relate to your eating behaviors?

Yes, negative body image played the biggest factor of my eating disorder. As I teenager I tended to compare my bodies to my peers. I was very envious and jealous when girls had flat stomachs and that look was very appealing to me. I was introduced by a friend to vomiting after a meal as a dieting strategy and I thought, "Great. I can eat and lose weight at the same time." Interestingly, this purging method did not really work as my weight fluctuated for years. So, with low self-esteem and a feeling of no real attachment with my parents and a negative body image these were the factors in my eating disorder. The biggest driver of my eating disorder was negative body image but other factors like my personality and family relationships did play a role.

How/when did you realize that you had a problem? Were you diagnosed as having an eating disorder?

I knew I had a problem when I could not stop and I wanted to die because I could not stop. Also, I was hiding my disease, very secretive. Since this is a shameful and secretive disease I was too embarrassed to seek help. I ended up diagnosing myself when I found an article in a magazine about bulimia. I was relieved this secret of "whatever I had" had a name and other people were bingeing and purging and I wasn't alone with this embarrassing act of bingeing and purging. I'm sure there were resources for help but if there were I was too embarrassed in sharing my secret especially living in a small town where everyone knew everybody. I was just hoping it would eventually go away. Another important point to mention is that when I was struggling with this problem, there were not all of these eating disorder–specific treatment programs like they have now all over North America.

What type of treatment did you seek for your eating disorder? What was helpful and what was less than helpful.

I had talk therapy with the therapist asking me to write a journal of my daily intake of food. Although the formal treatment did not help at the time it may have opened me up to discovering relationships with others. In fact, after seven years of struggling with bulimia nervosa, shortly after I sought therapy, I met someone and fell in love. This helped to disrupt my disordered eating behavior. My eating disorder stopped immediately. I did not continue therapy as I was no longer bingeing and purging. I suppose at the time "Love" was my antidote; it took the place of my binge and purge episodes. Little did I know I was getting into a codependent relationship. The way I understand it codependency means that I relied on my partner to meet my emotional needs and to determine my self-worth. This means that when I received positive attention from him, I felt great. But if I did not get what I needed, I was angry and felt bad about myself. As I reflect back to those years I realize that this tendency toward developing codependent relationships was a disease in itself.

I always realized the connection between my eating disorder and having an addictive personality. In the case of my eating disorder, the object of addiction was food. But it (i.e., the addiction) could easily have become sex, shopping, gambling, alcohol, prescription drugs, or something else. I've heard it referred to as "cross addiction" before. I feel cross addiction should be a key part of therapy in recovery. My eating disorder started young so that would have been helpful in recovery for me. Although I only went for a short time of therapy and would never know "the road to recovery" and if cross addiction was a part of therapy. Perhaps it is covered in therapy with certain treatment centers? I don't know. With girls and boys starting eating disorders at an early age I believe teaching and educating on and warning against cross addiction can help people for their ongoing recovery.

What did recovery look like for you? How do you feel about your relationship with food, exercise and your body now? What about relapses?

Recovery to me was great! No more spending way too much money on food to support my disease and very grateful that I no longer felt I wanted to die because I had stopped. Also the time this disease cost me, strategically planning out the entire binge process from getting or having enough money to buy the food, where I was going to buy the food, what I wanted to binge on, where to binge and purge. When all that was finally gone I finally felt free and happy, relieved, and not so tired all the time. It was exhausting when I look back and it is hard to believe how bulimia nervosa robbed me of my energy.

Life changes, body changes with age, and I'm trying to accept myself. I'm definitely not purging and bingeing and have no desire too. My relationship with food is fine, I'm not afraid of food and I eat pretty healthy.

I have not been actively engaged on a regular basis in bulimic behavior for 25 years. There have been times throughout the 25 years I have felt very uncomfortable after a meal and have thrown up, this has maybe occurred 12 or more times in a 25-year period. These purging episodes were generally triggered when I felt too full and uncomfortable. A switch tripped as I was familiar with how to "relieve" myself of the discomfort. Unfortunately each relapse was associated with intense guilt. I now work to monitor my hunger and fullness to avoid feeling triggered by feeling stuffed. I also am focusing on regulating my emotions so that I do not use my old disordered eating behaviors to cope with life's stressors.

Now that you are a parent, how do you try to be more aware about what you say and do with your daughters?

I am very conscious about what I say to my girls about their bodies, the media, and appearance in general. I explain about Photoshopped images of female and male models in magazines. How on television it is a "set" and people are constantly making you up with makeup and hair and there are scenes where they can stop filming to do touch ups. That's how they look now on television or in magazines, but it's not how they look when they wake up and even during the day when out doing errands or whatever. I wish that was explained to me growing up. I explain that they should love what they have as a body, tummy, legs that they were as Lady Gaga says "Born that way." That it is ok to have a tummy or short legs, it's what's inside. Your kindness and thoughtfulness counts. To encourage my daughters that it's ok to talk about their bodies, what you like what you don't like, and to give some empowerment. I model high self-esteem and have them learn about high self-esteem, this is all with help from a children's therapist. I do not make any remarks about other people's shape or size in front of them, but I have witnessed parents saying ignorant comments about someone's size in front of their children. I always serve as a role model to love your body no matter what.

In a unique study, eating-disordered clients were interviewed about relapse and recovery. Participants who relapsed admitted to being ambivalent about their recovery, less confident about their ability to maintain change, and more likely to seek treatment to satisfy a family member. Another finding was that participants who relapsed reported dissatisfaction with their treatment experience. For example, individuals expressed being overconfident about recovery and thought the difficult work was behind them when they discharged. Other individuals believed behavioral goals (e.g., weight restoration) were emphasized at the expense of dealing with emotional and psychological concerns during treatment.

Relapse Prevention

Knowledge of relapse predictors for eating disorders is needed to develop effective treatments and relapse-prevention strategies. A study of 51 first-admission clients with anorexia nervosa who were weight-restored when discharged from inpatient treatment revealed the overall rate of relapse was 35 percent and the highest risk period was 6 to 17 months post-discharge. This suggests some clients relapsed after remaining weight-restored for the first year, which suggests clients receive long-term follow-up care to prevent relapse after hospitalization. This study also found excessive exercise and residential concern about body shape and weight to be predictive of relapse, suggesting treatment should incorporate skills for gradually increasing physical activity and coping skills for body image disturbances.

A separate study with 140 clients treated for bulimia nervosa using cognitive behavioral therapy found 30 clients relapsed during follow-up. Specifically, 37 percent of clients reported binge or purge episodes within 17 weeks of the follow-up period and an additional 16 percent engaged in behaviors in the year following treatment. None of the relapsed clients sought additional treatments, which suggests telling clients who appear to have been successfully treated to come back if they have problems is an ineffectual relapse prevention strategy. More innovative outreach such as phone and text message follow-ups and regularly scheduled visits are warranted for relapse prevention.

Justine J. Reel

See also: Comorbidity; Protective Factors; Recovery; Self-Help Interventions; Treatment

Bibliography

Bardone-Cone, Anna M., Megan B. Harney, Christine R. Maidonado, Melissa A. Lawson, D. Paul Robinson, Roma Smith, and Aneesh Tosh. "Defining Recovery from an Eating Disorder: Conceptualization, Validation, and Examination of Psychosocial Functioning and Psychiatric Comorbidity." *Behavioral Research Therapy* 48, no. 3 (2010): 194–202. https://doi.org/10.1016/j.brat.2009.11.001.

Carter, J. C., E. Blackmore, K. Sutandar-Pinnock, and D. B. Woodside. "Relapse in Anorexia Nervosa: A Survival Analysis." *Psychological Medicine* 34 (2004): 671–679. https://doi.org/10.1017/S0033291703001168.

Federici, Anita, and Allan S. Kaplan. "The Patient's Account of Relapse and Recovery in Anorexia Nervosa: A Qualitative Study." *European Eating Disorders Review* 16 (2008): 1–10. https://doi.org/10.1002/erv.813.

Keel, Pamela K., David J. Dorer, Debra L. Franko, Safia C. Jackson, and David B. Herzog. "Postremission Predictors of Relapse in Women with Eating Disorders." *American Journal of Psychiatry* 162, no. 12 (2005): 2263–2268. http://dx.doi.org/10.1176/appi.ajp.162.12.2263.

McFarlane, Traci, Marion P. Olmsted, and Kathryn Trottier. "Timing and Prediction of Relapse in a Transdiagnostic Eating Disorder Sample." *International Journal of Eating Disorders* 41 (2008): 587–593. https://doi.org/10.1002/eat.20550.

Mitchell, James E., W. Stewart Agras, G. Terence Wilson, Katherine Halmi, Helena Kraemer, and Scott Crow. "A Trial of Relapse Prevention Strategy in Women with Bulimia Nervosa Who Respond to Cognitive-Behavior Therapy." *International Journal of Eating Disorders* 35 (2004): 549–555.

Vanderlinden, J., H. Buis, G. Pieters, and M. Probst. "Which Elements in the Treatment of Eating Disorders Are Necessary 'Ingredients' in the Recovery Process? A Comparison between the Patient's and Therapist's View." *European Eating Disorders Review* 15, no. 5 (2007): 357–365. https://doi.org/10.1002/erv.768.

RELIGION

The influence of religion on eating attitudes and body image can be highly individualized and important to understand. The influence of religion on an individual's eating disorder may be affected by personality differences, differences in religious beliefs, rigidity of religious beliefs, personal spirituality levels, and cultural religious values. Therefore, religion may play a positive or negative role in eating disorder treatment and recovery or may have no effect on an individual's eating disorder.

Positive Influence on Body Image and Eating Behaviors

As an unhealthily thin body ideal is normative for women, turning to religion to fill voids in self-esteem and body image may have a protective factor against eating disorders. Religious systems that teach adherents their bodies are acceptable regardless of size or shape may give purpose and direction to individuals. For example, many Christian sects view the body as a divine gift from God. One experimental study found women who read religious affirmations had better body esteem after exposure to a thin ideal, compared to women who read spiritual (but not religious) affirmations or information about campus topics. In clinical practice, many therapists have found religion to be a useful tool to help with eating disorder recovery, as it provides a social network and positive emotion. Additionally, residential eating disorder treatment groups may incorporate spirituality groups as part of comprehensive treatment to address the whole person. Twelve-step groups (e.g., Eating Disorder Anonymous) exemplify the use of a higher power to provide clients with strength and draw upon faith to conquer addictions and recover from an eating disorder.

Negative Influence on Body Image and Eating Behaviors

For some, religious practices or rituals may become a justification for eating disorder behaviors. Many religions speak of holy fasting or label gluttony as a sin. Throughout history, religious figures in various belief systems have often fasted or refrained from food for religious reasons and spiritual connectedness. A well-known example of this in Western culture is Jesus, who Christians believe fasted for 40 days. Furthermore, other faiths also encourage adherents to fast—such as Islam during the month of Ramadan. Fasting behavior can be viewed as holy or righteous, as an individual conquers the desires of the human body and rises to a more spiritual state. Similarly, for some, gluttony is judged to be sinful and unrighteous behavior to be avoided at all costs. Unsurprisingly, individuals with eating disorders may use religious beliefs to justify their disordered thoughts and behaviors as a spiritual quest. They may even sense a spiritual righteousness in deprivation and justify they are removing gluttony by purging.

By contrast, other individuals may view their eating disorder as wrong, selfish, and sinful, causing them to feel unrighteous and guilty for the behaviors. These negative emotions may perpetuate eating disorder behaviors as people feel unholy, sinful, and worthless. Individuals may continue to participate in eating disorder behaviors as a punishment for their unrighteousness.

When Religion Does Not Influence Body Image

Religious women may identify an element of personal strength gained by belief. Regardless, their body image may suffer when exposed to cultural stereotypes of thin ideals. Even though their religion tells them they are worthwhile and valued, they may feel inferior when bombarded by negative images from the media. This may be due to the saturation of the message and an individual's exposure to it. For example, a religious woman may spend time each day praying, reading scripture, or attending religious services, but the time she spends watching television shows that perpetuate a thin ideal is likely to be greater than the time spent on spiritual efforts. The religious convictions may not be strong enough to undo the damage from constant media exposure. Thus, religion may appear to have no effect on a woman's body image.

TeriSue Smith-Jackson

See also: Body Image; Causes; Family Influences; Protective Factors

Bibliography

Baxter, Helen. "Religion and Eating Disorders." *European Eating Disorders Review* 9, no. 2 (2001): 137–139. https://doi.org/10.1002/erv.405.

Boyatzis, Chris J., Sarah Kline, and Stephanie Backof. "Experimental Evidence That Theistic-Religious Body Affirmations Improve Women's Body Image." *Journal for the Scientific Study of Religion* 49, no. 4 (2007): 553–564. https://doi.org/10.1111/j.1468-5906.2007.00377.x.

Boyatzis, Chris J., and Katherine B. Quinlan. "Women's Body Image, Disordered Eating, and Religion: A Critical Review of the Literature." *Research in the Social Scientific Study of Religion* 19 (2008): 183–208. https://doi.org/10.1163/ej.9789004166462.i-299.61.

Grenfell, Joanne Woolway. "Religion and Eating Disorders: Towards Understanding a Neglected Perspective." *Feminist Theology* 14, no. 3 (2006): 367–387. https://doi.org/10.1177/0966735006063775.

Latzer, Yael, Faisal Azaiza, and Orna Tzischinsky. "Eating Attitudes and Dieting Behaviors among Religious Subgroups of Israeli-Arab Adolescent Females." *Journal of Religious Health* 48 (2009): 189–199. https://doi.org/10.1007/s10943-008-9189-7.

Pinhas, Leorna, Margus Heinmaa, Pier Bryden, Susan Bradley, and Brenda Toner. "Disordered Eating in Jewish Adolescent Girls." *The Canadian Journal of Psychiatry* 53, no. 9 (2008): 601–608. https://doi.org/10.1177/070674370805300907.

Smith-Jackson, TeriSue, Justine J. Reel, and Rosemary Thackeray. "Coping with 'Bad Body Image Days': Strategies from First-Year Young Adult College Women." *Body Image* 8 (2011): 335–342.

RESIDENTIAL TREATMENT

Generally, there are five levels of care for clients who have varying needs for support in treating their eating disorder. These levels of care range from outpatient, the least intensive, to inpatient treatment, the most intense form of care. Residential treatment is a step down in intensity from inpatient hospitalization. Individuals in residential treatment facilities are deemed medically stable (i.e., they do not need the continuous medical monitoring present in inpatient hospitalization) but psychologically unhealthy. Residential treatment facilities typically include continuous monitoring provided by on-site staff, including physicians, counselors, dietitians, and other mental health professionals. All meals and snacks are supervised, and residents are expected to participate in a certain amount of group and individual counseling. Counseling usually focuses on coping skills development, interpersonal development, and emotional expressivity, among other things. It is common for residential centers to offer family therapy as well. Once residents are mentally fit for discharge, the team of professionals assisting in the patient's recovery begin discharge planning, which includes a detailed plan to be followed upon a resident's return home.

Current Trends in Residential Treatment Facilities

Currently, the National Eating Disorder Association (NEDA) lists 36 residential treatment facilities in the United States. This number represents a dramatic growth;

between 2000 and 2004, the number of residential treatment centers in the United States grew 44 percent, and the number has continued to grow since then. Most of these centers are located on the West Coast (California primarily) with relatively few in the southeastern United States. The average age of individuals in a residential treatment setting is 22 years old; however, average age range is typically 14 years to 40 years old.

Although specific therapeutic processes differ between centers, residential treatment facilities typically use therapy models that are evidence based and well researched. Cognitive behavioral therapy (CBT) is the most common therapy model used. CBT targets the dysfunctional thought processes contributing to unhealthy behaviors. According to a survey of residential treatment centers, 85 percent reported using CBT as the primary form of traditional psychotherapy. Dialectical behavior therapy (DBT) is another commonly used therapy. In contrast with CBT, DBT focuses on developing specific behavioral skills (such as assertiveness training, mindfulness, and emotional expression). DBT, while the second most common therapeutic model used in residential treatment, was used by only 33 percent of the centers surveyed. Other therapy models used in residential treatment centers include twelve-step groups (based on the Twelve Steps of Alcoholics Anonymous), family therapy, trauma-focused therapies, and interpersonal therapy.

Residential treatment centers also use nontraditional therapies heavily. These nontraditional therapies provide opportunities for residents to establish interpersonal bonds outside of traditional group settings. Common nontraditional therapies are art therapy, yoga/meditation, equine therapy, recreational therapy, dance, music, journaling, and cooking. Although many of the activities central to nontraditional therapies are not psychotherapeutic in the sense of one-on-one interaction with a mental health professional, these therapies provide enrichment to a resident's day, enable them to practice self-care, develop healthy coping skills, and practice a variety of emotional skills they may have learned in traditional therapeutic settings.

Effectiveness of Residential Treatment

Given the cost associated with residential treatment centers, along with the significant disruption it can cause in an individual's life, understanding whether these treatment settings are beneficial is often a paramount concern for individuals when deciding whether to seek residential treatment. Interestingly, much of literature on residential treatment facilities focuses on patient characteristics that predict treatment outcomes or on the specific therapeutic models employed as opposed to testing whether residential treatment settings offer benefits beyond those produced by the specific therapies used or patient demographics. However, there have been a few studies that investigated whether residential treatment centers are effective without considering patient demographics or the therapeutic models used.

Studies of residential treatment center efficacy have focused on short-term outcomes (i.e., within six months of discharge). These studies have largely found positive improvements in the health of eating disorder patients, improvements in their self-reported psychological adjustment, reductions in disordered-eating behaviors, and reductions in co-occurring mental illness, such as depression and anxiety. A pair of studies that investigated the short- and long-term health outcomes of 215 patients who received residential treatment at Monte Nido Treatment Center in Malibu, California, found both short- and long-term benefits following residential treatment. Both short- and long-term outcomes were positive. In individuals with a diagnosis of anorexia nervosa, 74 percent reported short-term positive outcomes and 89 percent reported long-term positive outcomes. In residents with a diagnosis of bulimia nervosa, 95 percent reported short-term positive outcomes and 75 percent reported positive long-term outcomes. Short-term outcomes were measured in terms of the frequency individuals engaged in dysfunctional behaviors, including overexercising, self-induced vomiting, ipecac abuse, and so on. Both groups (anorexia and bulimia) were measured identically regarding short-term outcomes. Long-term outcomes were measured by the presence of regular menstruation and weight restoration (body mass index of 18 or higher) for individuals with anorexia. Long-term outcomes for individuals with bulimia nervosa were measured by a 50 percent or more reduction in the frequency of bingeing and purging behaviors.

Challenges of Residential Treatment

One of the biggest obstacles to residential treatment is the ability to afford this level of care. Many insurance policies will only cover short-term stays in residential settings; two weeks is a fairly standard length of time covered by insurance policies. Once an individual runs out of insurance funding, they are responsible for paying out of pocket for a facility. According to a study that looked at 22 of the most prominent residential facilities in the country, the average cost per day of a residential treatment facility was $956 (range: $550–$1,500). Given the average length of stay for an individual at a residential treatment facility is 83 days, the cost of an 83-day stay at $956 per day is $79,348. Even with insurance covering two to three weeks of treatment in a residential setting, the cost of a residential treatment facility is anywhere between $59,000–$65,000. For most individuals, the cost of a residential treatment facility is prohibitive and is the determining factor in how long they stay in a facility prior to discharge and dropping to a less intensive level of care. If an individual is not ready for less structured, lower levels of affordable care, the risk of relapse is higher.

Additionally, men have a more difficult time finding a residential treatment program that will accept them. Studies have shown that, while females are accepted at 100 percent of residential treatment centers, men are accepted at only 20 percent. The limited availability of programs that accept men require greater travel distances, create longer waiting lists, and can deter individuals from seeking treatment if the logistical barriers are too great. Even after being accepted and arriving, males with eating disorders differ in important ways from females, and these differences can negatively affect men's self-esteem, their ability to establish rapport with other residents, and the staff at these centers may be ill-equipped to provide necessary services to male clients. On average, men with an eating disorder diagnosis are older, have more co-occurring mental health disorders (e.g., anxiety, depression), report a higher desired BMI, struggle with dysfunctional exercise behaviors and are more likely to have been overweight prior to onset of the disorder than females. These differences, if not considered when developing treatment plans, can isolate male patients from a female-dominated treatment population and lower treatment efficacy.

Hannah J. Hopkins

See also: Health Care Costs of Eating Disorders; Levels of Care; Treatment

Bibliography

Bisbing, Zoe. "Levels of Care in Eating Disorder Treatment." Presentation at the Parent, Family, and Friends Network (PFN) Webinar Series, National Eating Disorder Association, November 20, 2014. Accessed February 24, 2017. https://www .nationaleatingdisorders.org/sites/default/files/NEDA%20Webinar%20Levels%20 of%20Treatment.pdf.

Brewerton, Timothy D., and Carolyn Costin. "Long-Term Outcome of Residential Treatment for Anorexia Nervosa and Bulimia Nervosa." *Eating Disorders* 19, no. 2 (2011): 132–144. https://doi.org/10.1080/10640266.2011.551632.

Brewerton, Timothy D., and Carolyn Costin. "Treatment Results of Anorexia Nervosa and Bulimia Nervosa in a Residential Treatment Program." *Eating Disorders* 19, no. 2 (2011): 117–131. https://doi.org/10.1080/10640266.2011.551629.

Elmquist, JoAnna, Ryan C. Shorey, Scott Anderson, and Gregory L. Stuart. "Eating Disorder Symptoms and Length of Stay in Residential Treatment for Substance Use: A Brief Report." *Journal of Dual Diagnosis* 11, no. 3–4 (2015): 233–237. https://doi.org/10.10 80/15504263.2015.1104480.

Frisch, Maria J., David B. Herzog, and Debra L. Franko. "Residential Treatment for Eating Disorders." *International Journal of Eating Disorders* 39, no. 5 (2006): 434–442. https:// doi.org/10.1002/eat.20255.

Twohig, Michel P., Ellen J. Bluett, Jeremiah G. Torgesen, Tera Lensegrav-Benson, and Benita Quakenbush-Roberts. "Who Seeks Residential Treatment? A Report of Patient Characteristics, Pathology, and Functioning in Females at a Residential Treatment Facility." *Eating Disorders* 23, no. 1 (2015): 1–14. https://doi.org/10.1080/10640266.2014.95 9845.

Weltzin, Theodore E., Tracey Cornella-Carlson, Mary E. Fitzpatrick, Brad Kennington, Pamela Bean, and Carol Jefferies. "Treatment Issues and Outcomes for Males with Eating Disorders." *Eating Disorders* 20, no. 5 (2012): 444–459. https://doi.org/10.108 0/10640266.2012.715527.

RESILIENCY

Resiliency is the ability to positively adapt to difficult circumstances. Resiliency is of interest to child and developmental psychologists who want to understand how some individuals achieve life success despite adverse childhood conditions such as poverty, abuse, and broken families. Interest in resiliency has blossomed over the past 20 years, as researchers, practitioners, and self-help authors have taken an interest in the qualities that allow people to be resilient to trauma and life obstacles. Although the increased attention to resiliency has stimulated awareness of its importance, it has also caused some confusion regarding what it means to be resilient. Most definitions of resiliency imply the action of overcoming adversity but fail to account for the underlying factors that result in resilient outcomes. To clarify the meaning of resiliency, professionals have adopted one of two views: (1) the trait view, or (2) the process view.

The Trait View: Resiliency as Something You "Have"

Resiliency is considered to be a trait, or a set of traits, possessed by certain individuals. In fact, much of the early research on resiliency adopted a trait approach. Although a few experts still believe in a singular resilient personality trait, most trait resiliency research has focused on resilient qualities, which are a type of protective factor. Protective factors are qualities and/or environmental conditions conducive to positive adaptation to stress. In a 30-year study of at-risk children born on the Hawaiian island of Kauai, it was found that children who achieved life competence (i.e., had loving relationships, a career, enjoyed a healthy amount of recreation, and were optimistic about their future) possessed several common personality characteristics that aided them to overcome life obstacles. Specifically, the at-risk children who grew to be competent adults were more self-confident, autonomous, affectionate, outgoing, and intelligent than children who failed to achieve competence as adults. Many researchers and practitioners have proposed versions the trait profile that makes a resilient personality. However, some experts caution against a solely trait view of resiliency, as this may encourage professionals who work with at-risk individuals to conclude that resiliency is something individuals either have or do not have and curb efforts to teach resiliency.

The Process View: Resiliency as a Constant Evolution

Resilience has also been described as a process. Specifically, resiliency has been defined as an ability to adapt in a functional manner despite significant challenges and adversity. A process view forms a more holistic view of resiliency by encompassing traits, environmental influences (e.g., family support, socioeconomic status), and outcomes. From the process perspective, resiliency is composed of four interrelated components: (1) risk factors, (2) protective factors, (3) vulnerability factors, and (4) positive adaptation. Risk factors are circumstances or triggering events that lead to adverse outcomes. For example, participating in a sport that emphasizes being extremely lean and includes weekly weigh-ins might be a risk factor for unhealthy eating or eating disorders. Protective factors, as defined above, are factors that buffer individuals from risk and account for positive responses. By contrast, vulnerability factors are factors that intensify the effects of risk. Depending on the context, the same factor may be considered either as protective or vulnerability. For example, positive self-esteem might protect individuals from risk, whereas negative self-esteem might make individuals more likely to succumb to risk. Finally, positive adaptation is an outcome much better than would be expected given the presence of a certain risk factor. Although the idea of positive adaptation may seem simple, it varies depending on social context. For example, dropping out of school to help support one's family may be viewed as a negative outcome in some cultures, but it is a positive outcome in others. Individuals typically experience many risk, protective, and vulnerability factors simultaneously. Positive adaptation to one risk may change how people handle future risks. Thus, the process view presents resiliency as a capacity that develops over time in the context of multiple and simultaneous life events. Researchers have proposed process views of resiliency for specific groups such as bereaved spouses, military families, couples affected by HIV/AIDS, and older adults. Some research has also been conducted examining resiliency and eating disorders.

Applying the Process View of Resiliency to Eating Disorders: A Case Example

The following case example illustrates how a process view of resiliency can be applied to the development of an eating disorder. When considering a 12-year-old girl's (Jackie) risk for, and resiliency to an eating disorder, each type of factor previously discussed would be considered. Jackie might possess several risk factors, such as a history of abuse, a family history of eating disorders, and pressure from friends to lose weight. Further, several vulnerability factors may exacerbate her risk, including low self-esteem and high perfectionism. However, a number of protective factors may buffer Jackie from developing an eating disorder, including strong social support and a deep sense of spirituality. The interaction of all factors would determine whether Jackie develops an eating disorder (i.e., negative adaptation) or does not develop an eating disorder (i.e., positive adaptation).

Body Image as a Protective/Vulnerability Factor for Eating Disorders

One of the most important protective/vulnerability factors to consider in eating disorder prevention is body image. Individuals who place high importance on body appearance and evaluate their bodies negatively are more likely to engage in restricting, purging, or bingeing behaviors. On the other hand, body image satisfaction can serve as a protective factor against eating disorders. Individuals less invested in and/or have a positive evaluation of their bodies are more likely to be accepting of the size and shape, and less likely to take drastic measures to alter their weight.

Resiliency and Body Image Dissatisfaction

Because body image dissatisfaction is a critical factor for eating disorders, it can and should be approached as an important outcome. In addition to enhanced risk for eating disorders, individuals who have poor body image are also likely to suffer from other mental health concerns, such as low self-esteem, social anxiety, and sexual inhibition. From a resiliency process perspective, viewing body image dissatisfaction as an outcome means research and practice need to identify the risk, protective, and vulnerability factors associated with poor body image.

Risk Factors for Body Image Dissatisfaction

Perhaps the most pervasive risk factor for body image dissatisfaction in Western societies is sociocultural pressure to achieve an ideal body. Both women and men are strongly influenced by the images of ultrathin women and hypermuscular men depicted in the media through television, magazines, billboards, and the Internet. Indeed, numerous studies have revealed media exposure to idealized bodies triggers body dissatisfaction for both men and women. Friends and family, another source of sociocultural body image pressure, who engage in teasing about body weight, shape, and size, can have a profoundly negative effect on a child's body image. Parents and family members also model body dissatisfaction by making self-deprecating comments about their bodies or by dieting. Peers serve as an additional risk factor due to the social comparison effect with same-aged peers who model negative body image and may tease, which is equally harmful.

Protective Factors for Body Image Dissatisfaction

Compared to risk factors, protective factors for body image dissatisfaction receive far less attention. One protective factor studied in relation to body image is quality of parental relationships. Having supportive parents has been shown to increase body image satisfaction in girls. For girls, in particular, parental encouragement to be strong, assertive, and independent may buffer sociocultural pressure to be thin. In addition to parental relationships, experts suggest several factors as potentially protecting individuals from body image dissatisfaction. First, individuals who believe they have control and can effect change over their body weight, shape, and size may be less likely to be dissatisfied with their appearance. Second, having a flexible conception of the ideal body may protect individuals from body image dissatisfaction. For example, black women have historically reported less body image dissatisfaction than white women partially because they often endorse a larger ideal body type. Finally, having a more holistic view of beauty that extends beyond body size may guard women from body image dissatisfaction.

A Model of Body Image Resiliency for Women

It stands to reason researchers and practitioners can learn a great deal from girls and women with a positive body image. A proposed model of body image resilience for females included five interrelated protective factors: (1) family-of-origin support, (2) sex role satisfaction, (3) positive physical self-concept, (4) effective coping strategies, and (5) sense of holistic balance and wellness.

Factor (1), family-of-origin support, refers to parental modeling of eating behaviors and attitudes toward food that are important predictors of body image for children. According to Choate, family-of-origin support is essential to develop the other four protective factors, as it leads directly to factors (2), (3), and (4) in the model. Factor (2), sex role satisfaction, deals with the conflict faced by women trying to meet the demands placed on them by society to be physically attractive, nurturing, and passive and at the same time fulfill their personal, social, and occupational needs. Women who internalize conflicting sex role pressures are likely to succumb to body image dissatisfaction, while women who are supported are better able to acknowledge pressures and create a personal definition of what it means to be a woman. Family support is also directly related to factor (3), positive physical self-concept. Women with a positive physical self-concept are more likely to enjoy sports, exercise, and physical activity than women with a poor physical self-concept. Although women may adopt exercise to alter their physical appearance, they often continue exercising for the psychosocial benefits such as increased awareness of their physical strength, lowered anxiety, and increased body image satisfaction. Finally, women with strong family-of-origin support develop coping strategies to ward off the negative effects of sociocultural pressure; these coping strategies include critical thinking, stress management, and assertiveness. Sex role satisfaction, positive physical self-concept, and effective coping strategies work together such that changes in one influence changes in the other. For example, being satisfied with one's sex role might contribute to positive physical self-concept, which in turn may be related to more effective coping strategies, such as using physical activity to manage stress. In addition to working together, factors (2), (3), and (4) combine to result in factor (5), holistic balance and wellness. Women who achieve physical, social, emotional, intellectual, and spiritual wellness have a diverse view of their self-worth and place less emphasis on the importance of physical appearance.

Strategies for Promoting Body Image Resilience

Based on this proposed model, several recommendations can be made to parents and school counselors on how to enhance body image resiliency in boys and girls. With regard to the influence of family and friends, parents should be educated about the strong effect their eating attitudes and behaviors have on the attitudes and behaviors of their children. Further, parents and school staff should have a no-tolerance policy for weight teasing or bullying. To increase sex role satisfaction, parents and counselors should normalize the physical changes that occur with puberty, discourage comparisons to the bodies of others, and promote acceptance of multiple body types by encouraging children to identify role models of varying shapes and sizes. To enhance physical self-concept, children should be encouraged to participate in a variety of physical activities, with an emphasis on enjoyment and health benefits rather than weight loss or aesthetic changes. Parents and counselors play a key role in teaching children effective coping strategies. Perhaps the most important strategy to promote positive body image is media literacy. Boys and girls should be taught to be critical of dominant media portrayals of the ideal male and female body. One way to promote critical thinking is by asking children to review popular magazines and to identify both helpful and harmful body messages. Although all the previously discussed strategies emphasize holistic wellness, other strategies include keeping a gratitude journal, serving as a peer mentor, and embracing spiritual beliefs. By adopting some or all strategies, boy and girls can learn to have a broader and more balanced conception of health, an increased acceptance of their bodies, and resilience to risk factors related to body image dissatisfaction.

Nick Galli

See also: Body Image; Coping Skills; Parents; Protective Factors

Bibliography

Choate, Lauren H. "Counseling Adolescent Girls for Body Image Resilience: Strategies for School Counselors." *Professional School Counseling* 10, no. 3 (2007): 317–326. http://dx.doi.org/10.5330/prsc.10.3.x47524283143v335.

Choate, Lauren H. "Toward a Theoretical Model of Women's Body Image Resilience." *The Journal of Counseling & Development* 83, no. 3 (2005): 320–330. https://doi.org/10.1002/j.1556-6678.2005.tb00350.x.

Luthar, Suniya S., Dante Cicchetti, and Bronwyn Becker. "The Construct of Resilience: A Critical Evaluation and Guidelines for Future Work." *Child Development* 71, no. 3 (2000): 543–562. https://doi.org/10.1111/1467-8624.00164.

Presnell, Katherine, Sarah Kate Bearman, and Mary Clare Madeley. "Body Dissatisfaction in Adolescent Females and Males: Risk and Resilience." *Prevention Researcher* 14 (2007): 3–6.

Stice, Eric, and Heather E. Shaw. "Role of Body Dissatisfaction in the Onset and Maintenance of Eating Pathology: A Synthesis of Research Findings." *Journal of Psychosomatic Research* 53, no. 5 (2002): 985–993. http://dx.doi.org/10.1016/S0022-3999(02)00488-9.

Werner, Emmy E. "Vulnerable but Invincible: High Risk Children from Birth to Adulthood." *European Child & Adolescent Psychiatry* 5, suppl. 1 (1996): 47–51. https://doi.org/10.1007/BF00538544.

RISK FACTORS

A risk factor is a specific element likely to lead to some condition (e.g., eating disorders). Therefore, it is reasonable to conclude intervening with a risk factor in some way (e.g., reducing its intensity or duration, or changing when it appears in one's developmental trajectory) should result in a reduced rate of the condition. Although it seems straightforward, researchers warn identifying risk factors in the field of eating disorders is not clear cut.

Alternatives to Risk Factors

The term *risk factor* has been identified by researchers as potentially problematic as it is not consistently defined across studies. Variants of this term used in the eating disorders field have included *variable risk factor*, *causal risk factor*, *proxy risk factor*, *fixed marker*, and *variable marker*. Additionally, less precise terms such as *contributor* have been used interchangeably with risk factor. Regardless of the term used, what distinguishes a risk factor from any other factor is that a risk factor must *precede* the condition in question; otherwise the factor simply co-occurs with or is a correlate of the condition. Therefore, a risk factor is one that reliably relates to the onset of a particular pathology.

In addition to how the term risk factor is defined, others have noted that simply identifying a risk factor may not be sufficiently helpful. It is likely the presence of a single risk factor may not be enough to increase the incidence of a condition. Duration, intensity, and timing of the risk factor may determine the extent to which someone is at risk for a condition. The importance of properly identifying risk factors in the field of eating disorders can aid professionals and paraprofessionals to prevent development of eating disorders, and identify and treat persons who have an eating disorder or who, at the very least, appear at risk for an eating disorder.

As noted, a true risk factor for an eating disorder must precede onset; however, some researchers have noted that distinguishing between risk factors for eating disorders and symptoms of disorders is not always clear. For example, risk factor constructs such as perfectionism, the need for control, and low self-esteem are considered symptoms of eating disorders suggesting these constructs may not precede onset but may be a part of the disorders themselves.

An additional problem in the identification of risk factors for eating disorders is that such factors do not consistently differentiate between eating disorders. For example, a factor that is considered a risk factor for bulimia nervosa may not be a risk factor for anorexia nervosa. Additionally, identification of risk factors that may distinguish between the various subtypes of eating disorders has been largely unsuccessful. Despite these apparent shortcomings, various lists of factors have been generated pointing to the types of factors, controllable and uncontrollable, that can put someone at risk for an eating disorder. These factors can be broadly classified as biological factors, sociocultural factors, and psychological factors.

Examples of Risk Factors

Specific factors nominated as putting an individual at risk for developing an eating disorder have included sex, age, ethnicity, family history, sexual abuse, life stressors, genetics, neurochemical levels, perfectionism, low self-esteem, pubertal timing, negative affect, body image dissatisfaction, internalization of the thin ideal, pregnancy complications, concern with weight and shape, and dieting. Some of these factors are regularly identified as risk factors for eating disorders. For example, dieting is sometimes referred to as a gateway behavior to an eating disorder. Individuals may begin a diet innocently enough only to find themselves engaged in a full-blown eating disorder quickly. Researchers have questioned whether dieting itself can truly be considered a risk factor when such a sizable percentage of people in Western cultures engage in dieting, but so few develop an eating disorder. That is, if dieting was a true risk factor, wouldn't the incidence of eating disorders be a lot higher? Indeed, this is often the question posed in response to many proposed risk factors.

Other risk factors such as low self-esteem are consistently identified in individuals with eating disorders; however, as noted, a problem identifying risk factors accurately is that it is not always clear whether a risk factor in question preceded an eating disorder or is a result of an eating disorder. In the case of low self-esteem, it is conceivable low self-esteem could either precede or be a consequence of an eating disorder. Moreover, low self-esteem may not necessarily be a unique risk factor for eating disorders, but it may contribute to the development of psychopathology in general. Low self-esteem has been found to relate to other mental disorders, such as depression and anxiety.

Research with Risk Factors

Studies conducted to date do not use the term risk factor consistently. Jacobi and colleagues identified the strongest risk factor was a high degree of weight and shape concerns. These researchers concluded some previously identified risk factors (e.g., family interaction styles, perfectionism) should no longer be considered risk factors for eating disorders based on more recent findings. An area of exploration that has received considerable attention by researchers is biological factors (e.g., genetics, how pregnancy and the birth process unfold, and the timing of biological developmental events). However, researchers indicate results of twin studies suggest genetics seems to be an important factor for eating disorders, but other proposed biological factors simply co-occur with eating disorders and cannot yet be reliably classified as risk factors for eating disorders.

Christine L. B. Selby

See also: Body Image; Causes; Personality Characteristics; Protective Factors; Resiliency

Bibliography

Jacobi, Corinna, and Eike Fittig. "Psychosocial Risk Factors for Eating Disorders." In *The Oxford Handbook of Eating Disorders*, edited by Stewart W. Agras, 123–136. New York: Oxford University Press, 2010.

Jacobi, Corinna, Chris Hayward, Martina de Zwaan, Helena C. Kraemer, and W. Stewart Agras. "Coming to Terms with Risk Factors for Eating Disorders: Application of Risk Terminology and Suggestions for a General Taxonomy." *Psychological Bulletin* 130, no. 1 (2004): 19–65. http://dx.doi.org/10.1037/0033-2909.130.1.19.

Keel, Pamela K., Kamryn T. Eddy, Jennifer J. Thomas, and Marlene B. Schwartz. "Vulnerability to Eating Disorders across the Lifespan." In *Vulnerability to Psychopathology*, edited by Rick E. Ingram and Joseph M. Price, 489–494. New York: Guilford Press, 2010.

Polivy, Janet, and C. Peter Herman. "Distinguishing Risk Factors from Symptoms: Are Eating Disorders Simply Disordered Eating?" In *Behavioral Mechanisms and Psychopathology: Advancing the Explanation of Its Nature, Cause and Treatment*, edited by Kurt Salzinger and Mark R. Serper, 175–198. Washington, DC: American Psychological Association, 2009.

Stice, Eric. "Risk and Maintenance Factors for Eating Pathology: A Meta-Analytic Review." *Psychological Bulletin* 128, no. 5 (2002): 825–848. http://dx.doi.org/10.1037/0033-2909.128.5.825.

ROWING

Rowing has experienced popularity as an Olympic sport and as a college sport in certain geographic areas. Like judo, wrestling, and horseracing, rowing has been classified as a weight-dependent sport due to the existence of weight classes (i.e., lightweight and heavyweight) that require athletes to make weight for competition. Although male rowing has a strong tradition in elite Ivy League schools, female rowing has only recently been made available for college athletes. It is expected rowers could experience similar pressures to lose weight as wrestlers and this could promote disordered eating and clinical eating disorders.

Eating Disorders and Male Rowers

One 1993 study found an equal prevalence of body image disturbances in male rowers and wrestlers, with 8 percent of rowers exhibiting clinical eating disorders. Rowers may engage in unhealthy weight loss methods such as fasting, restricting, purging, and dehydration strategies (e.g., saunas). However, rowing differs from other weight class sports in that the performance success is based on strength and power once the rower has achieved necessary weight requirements. Male lightweight rowers have been found to have significantly higher restrained eating behaviors and stronger body dissatisfaction than heavyweight rowers. In a separate study, male lightweight rowers were shown to have greater weight fluctuations throughout the season; they also gained more weight in the off-season. Therefore, male lightweight rowers should be considered an at-risk group for developing seasonal disordered eating patterns.

Eating Disorders and Female Rowers

Lightweight rowing for women is a more recent sport and requires college female athletes to meet a single weight class of 130 pounds. In one study comparing female and male rowers of both heavyweight and lightweight classes, female rowers displayed more disturbed eating practices and weight control methods than males. In another study comparing lightweight female rowers to female distance runners, rowers demonstrated significantly more eating restraint and higher diuretic use than runners. However, female rowers in this study seemed to have fewer body image concerns than either runners or the control group. Because female lightweight rowing is a relatively new sport, more research is needed on this potentially at-risk group of athletes.

Justine J. Reel

See also: Endurance Sports; Jockeys; Sports; Weight Pressures in Sport

Bibliography

Karlson, Kristine A., Carolyn Black Becker, and Amanda Merkur. "Prevalence of Eating Disordered Behavior in Collegiate Lightweight Women Rowers and Distance Runners." *Clinical Journal of Sport Medicine* 11 (2001): 32–37.

Nichols, David L., Charlotte F. Sanborn, and Eve V. Essery. "Bone Density and Young Athletic Women." *Sports Medicine* 37, no. 11 (2007): 1001–1014. https://doi.org/10.2165/00007256-200737110-00006.

Sykora, Cahrlotte, Carlos M. Grilo, Denise E. Wilfley, and Kelly D. Brownell. "Eating, Weight, and Dieting Disturbances in Male and Female Lightweight and Heavyweight Rowers." *International Journal of Eating Disorders* 14, no. 2 (1993): 203–211. https://doi.org/10.1002/1098-108X(199309)14:2<203::AID-EAT2260140210>3.0.CO;2-V.

Thiel, Andreas, H. Gottfried, and F. W. Hesse. "Subclinical Eating Disorders in Male Athletes: A Study of the Low Weight Category in Rowers and Wrestlers." *Acta Psychiatrica Scandinavia* 88, no. 4 (1993): 259–265. https://doi.org/10.1111/j.1600-0447.1993.tb03454.x.

Thompson, Ron A., and Roberta Trattner Sherman. *Eating Disorders in Sport*. New York: Routledge, 2010.

RUMINATION DISORDER

Rumination disorder, which has a lower prevalence than other eating disorders, has received little attention in the media. Rumination disorder (RD) is characterized by regurgitation of food that is subsequently rechewed, reswallowed, or spit out. Although research on RD is scant, it does appear to be associated with anxiety, other eating disorders, as well as certain developmental and cognitive disabilities. RD can pose significant health risks, including esophageal distress from repeated exposure to stomach acid, dental complications, malnutrition, and electrolyte imbalances. A major barrier to identifying and treating RD is the secrecy that usually accompanies this disorder based on its social unacceptability. Additionally, many people who suffer from RD do not recognize they suffer from a mental illness; therefore, they often do not seek professional treatment or medical advice.

Diagnostic Criteria for Rumination Disorder

In the latest version of the *Diagnostic and Statistical Manual of Mental Disorders* (i.e., *DSM-5*), individuals must experience repeated episodes of regurgitation for at least one month to meet criteria for rumination disorder. Regurgitation typically occurs shortly after a meal. Additionally, the regurgitation behavior must not be due to an organic biomedical condition (e.g., esophageal reflux) or another eating disorder. The important distinction in RD is the term *regurgitation*, which denotes a volitional behavior, as opposed to vomiting, which is a natural reflex. Individuals with RD often use muscular contractions in their stomach or tongue, coughing, or inserting a finger into their throat to bring food back up from their stomachs. Once the food has been regurgitated, it is either rechewed, reswallowed, spit back out, or any combination thereof. People who suffer from RD often report that it is a habit they cannot break, and some report that anxiety or tension worsens the symptoms. Rumination is also common in certain eating disorders, notably pica (ingestion of nonnutritive foods) and bulimia nervosa. However, if rumination behaviors occur in the presence of another eating disorder, the *DSM-5* clarifies a separate diagnosis of rumination disorder is not necessary.

Interestingly, RD has also been seen in infants and young children. It can be difficult to differentiate RD from nonvoluntary vomiting in young children, and it is nearly impossible to discern this behavior in an infant population. Many researchers debate whether it is appropriate to consider infants for a diagnosis of rumination disorder, as it seems unlikely an infant has the muscle control or cognitive abilities to willfully bring food back up from the stomach. For this reason, RD is often lumped into other diagnostic categories, including avoidant/restrictive food intake disorder, unspecified feeding, or eating disorder in the *DSM-5*. However, certain diagnostic categorization systems do recognize RD in infants, notably the ROME Committee, is a diagnostic system specifically for gastrointestinal disorders. Health care providers generally agree more research on rumination disorder in younger populations is needed to further clarify the boundaries between voluntary regurgitation and vomiting caused by other behaviors, such as colic or nausea/food disgust.

Frequency of Rumination Disorder

The frequency at which RD occurs in the population is unknown. Many individuals who have RD are either unaware it is considered a mental illness warranting diagnosis or are incredibly secretive about their symptoms. The secrecy of RD stems from the social rejection that many people report when they go public with their behavior. Because of this secrecy, RD can cause impairment in individual's social lives and affect the ability to hold down certain jobs. Young children may exhibit social withdrawal when at school, such as sitting alone at lunchtime or staying away from classmates so they may regurgitate without being detected.

Rumination disorder is common in individuals with developmental disabilities, including autism. Studies have shown as many as 80 percent of all individuals who have a developmental disability meet criteria for some form of eating/feeding disorder, with pica and rumination disorder among the most common. Although assessment and diagnosis may be possible in individuals with higher cognitive functioning (e.g., Asperger's syndrome), identifying RD is difficult in individuals with limited cognitive and/or verbal skills. However, caregivers should be on the lookout for tell-tale signs of RD, including halitosis and retching sounds following eating, as early diagnosis is important to prevent potentially serious health consequences.

Health Effects of Rumination Disorder

The negative health consequences associated with rumination disorder are a direct result of regurgitation. Health concerns include dental complications, such as halitosis, enamel decay, and gum disease, because of repetitive exposure to stomach acids brought back up with regurgitated food. Other concerns include malnutrition (if regurgitated food is not reswallowed), electrolyte imbalances, dehydration, and esophageal distress. If individuals facilitate regurgitation using fingers, utensils, or any other object inserted into the throat, they may also suffer from burst capillaries in the lower esophagus. All these health concerns are common to both RD and bulimia nervosa, given both disorders involve repetitive vomiting or regurgitation. When health care providers meet with individuals who present with some of these warning signs, screening for RD as well as other eating disorders should be administered.

Treating Rumination Disorder

Research on the treatment of RD is scant; however, one study found support for the efficacy of cognitive behavioral therapy (CBT). Diaphragmatic breathing has also been used to treat RD with success. Diaphragmatic breathing is a style of breathing that relaxes the abdominal muscles instrumental in regurgitation. By relaxing these muscles during and after mealtimes, individuals can control whether they regurgitate. Other studies have suggested treating a co-occurring disorder, such as generalized anxiety or bulimia nervosa, can mitigate the severity of RD. Health care providers and mental health professionals should take care to identify potential precipitators of regurgitation, as this will determine appropriate interventions. For example, if someone reports regurgitating their food is simply a habit that they cannot break, implementing a reward contingency and behavioral management treatment plan would be recommended. However, if someone reports that regurgitation seems to be more frequent during times of anxiety, CBT or mindfulness therapy would be more appropriate. Additionally, fear of certain consequences related to digestion could also play a factor in prompting regurgitation; exposure therapy would be recommended for this situation.

In individuals do not experience success from talk therapy or who are unable to participate in talk therapy (e.g., individuals with developmental disabilities), laparoscopic Nissen fundoplication surgery is an option. In this procedure, the upper portion of the stomach is wrapped and stitched around the esophageal entrance to the stomach, enhancing the esophagus's sphincter muscle in closing and blocking regurgitation. Nissen fundoplication is a common surgical procedure to treat severe acid reflux and, in some cases, may be appropriate for treating RD. However, consultation with a medical professional as well as other less invasive treatment options should be pursued first.

Hannah J. Hopkins

See also: Diagnostic and Statistical Manual of Mental Disorders; Pica; Purging

Bibliography

Bryant-Waugh, Rachel, Laura Markham, Richard E. Kreipe, and B. Timothy Walsh. "Feeding and Eating Disorders in Childhood." *International Journal of Eating Disorders* 43, no. 2 (2010): 98–111. https://doi.org/10.1002/eat.20795.

Chitkara, Denesh K., Miranda Van Tilburg, William E. Whitehead, and Nicholas J. Talley. "Teaching Diaphragmatic Breathing for Rumination Syndrome." *The American Journal of Gastroenterology* 101, no. 11 (2006): 2449–2452. http://dx.doi.org/10.1111/j.1572-0241.2006.00801.x.

Delaney, Charlotte B., Kamryn T. Eddy, Andrea S. Hartmann, Anne E. Becker, Helen B. Murray, and Jennifer J. Thomas. "Pica and Rumination Behavior among Individuals Seeking Treatment for Eating Disorders or Obesity: DSM-5 PICA and Rumination Disorder." *International Journal of Eating Disorders* 48, no. 2 (2015): 238–248. https://doi.org/10.1002/eat.22279.

Ferreira-Maia, Ana Paula, Alicia Matijasevich, and Yuan-Pang Wang. "Epidemiology of Functional Gastrointestinal Disorders in Infants and Toddlers: A Systematic Review." *World Journal of Gastroenterology* 22, no. 28 (2016): 6547–6558. https://doi.org/10.3748/wjg.v22.i28.6547.

Hartmann, Andrea S., Anne E. Becker, Claire Hampton, and Rachel Bryant-Waugh. "Pica and Rumination Disorder in DSM-5." *Psychiatric Annals* 42, no. 11 (2012): 426–430. http://dx.doi.org/10.3928/00485713-20121105-09.

Thomas, Jennifer J., and Helen B. Murray. "Cognitive-Behavioral Treatment of Adult Rumination Behavior in the Setting of Disordered Eating: A Single Case Experimental Design." *International Journal of Eating Disorders* 49, no. 10 (2016): 967–972. https://doi.org/10.1002/eat.22566.

SELECTIVE EATING DISORDER

Selective eating disorder (SED) is often referred to as picky eating or fussy eating that prevents consuming certain foods. More recently, SED has been recognized by the medical community as a problem that needs to be addressed; however, SED is not categorized as a clinical eating disorder diagnosis in the current version of the *Diagnostic and Statistical Manual of Mental Disorders.*

Symptoms of Selective Eating Disorder

Children are often identified as picky eaters, but selective eating patterns may persist into adulthood. Individuals with SED avoid certain foods based on their color, texture, or smell. In some cases, individuals with SED may be unable to eat an entire food group (e.g., fruits, vegetables). Individuals with SED may also limit consumption of foods to certain brands. Individuals with SED may prefer products that are more bland or lighter in color (e.g., plain pasta, cheese pizza). SED should be distinguished from other eating disorders such as anorexia nervosa because in SED, picky eating occurs without the accompanying body image disturbance and food preferences are not based on calorie content. Although like orthorexia, SED is a distinct condition because the food preferences are not necessarily healthy. For example, adult picky eaters have identified French fries and bacon as common food preferences.

Prevalence of Selective Eating Disorder

SED has been understudied and the exact prevalence is unknown. However, SED in toddlers may be identified as an unwillingness to try new foods, which can continue into adolescence and adulthood. SED occurs more often in boys than girls, and is thought to be more common in children who have autistic spectrum disorders. One online support group for adult picky eaters has 1,400 active members.

Consequences of Selective Eating Disorder

Individuals who suffer from SED may face consequences, such as developmental delays, problems in growth and weight gain, and malnutrition. Individuals with SED may fail to meet the body's nutrient needs due to refusing certain types of foods or entire food groups. Psychological and emotional consequences include anxiety, social avoidance, and conflict. Adults with SED may report challenges associated with food preferences that can interfere with social and professional relationships. Because individuals with SED have narrow food preferences, having inadequate nutrition to support body functions is a concern. Therefore, individuals with SED should seek help just like individuals with any other eating disorder.

Justine J. Reel

See also: Avoidant/Restrictive Food Intake Disorder; *Diagnostic and Statistical Manual of Mental Disorders*; Food Phobia; Orthorexia Nervosa; Picky Eating

Bibliography

American Psychiatric Association. *Diagnostic and Statistical Manual of Mental Disorders*, 5th ed. (*DSM-5*). Washington, DC: American Psychiatric Association Publishing, 2013.

Butchireddygari, Likhitha. "Duke Professor Links Selective Eating with Psychological Disorders." DukeChronicle.com. Last modified September 4, 2015. Accessed November 22, 2017. http://www.dukechronicle.com/article/2015/09/duke-professor-links-selective-eating-with-psychological-disorders.

"Does Extremely Picky Eating in Adulthood Signal a Mental Disorder?" *Time*. Last modified December 3, 2010. Accessed November 18, 2016. http://healthland.time.com/2010/12/03/does-extremely-picky-eating-in-adulthood-signal-a-mental-disorder/?iid=sr-link1.

Wang, Shirley S. "No Age Limit on Picky Eating." *The Wall Street Journal*. Last modified July 5, 2010. Accessed November 22, 2017. http://www.wsj.com/articles/SB10001424052748704699604575343130457388718.

SELF-CARE

Self-care refers to promoting one's health using a holistic approach. Although caring for oneself may seem self-explanatory, individuals with eating disorders often struggle with self-care. The need to develop coping strategies to address triggers and keep a positive recovery mind-set is a critical part of treatment.

Self-care has been described as using behaviors that promote health and well-being to counter the effects of stress in one's environment. Engaging in self-care practices is important to both clients who are strengthening their coping resources and mental health practitioners who support them. Unfortunately, it is widely known that clients and helping professionals struggle with a lack of adequate self-care that makes them vulnerable to mental health issues.

Identification of Self-Care Strategies

Self-care behaviors may range from specific activities that support basic needs to a more holistic look at caring for oneself. For example, it is common to refer to self-care as being synonymous with eating a nutritious and well-balanced diet or getting adequate sleep each night. However, self-care can also be represented by engaging in personal activities to reduce stress like yoga, meditation, and receiving a massage. Further, the description of self-care may be broad enough to capture one's spiritual health and well-being.

Self-care is often divided into two distinct dimensions: personal self-care and professional self-care. Personal self-care involves intentionally participating in practices that positively impact one's well-being and holistic health. By contrast, professional self-care may be related to effectively understanding the role of self in one's professional position to manage stress in a work setting. Although they are interconnected, they are both important. Having an awareness of self-care is important for clients and helping professionals to improve their practice.

Eating Disorders and Self-Care

Self-care has been promoted as an important aspect in the treatment of eating disorders. There is a tendency to put others' needs ahead of one's own needs for individuals with eating disorders. Therefore, addressing the importance of self-care and one's needs is emphasized as part of the recovery process. For example, individuals are taught how to cope with triggers (i.e., feeling vulnerable to slip into disordered-eating behaviors due to certain internal or external circumstances) using a variety of self-care strategies. The concept of self-care is related to the belief that self-love or self-compassion is indicated for individuals with eating disorders.

Justine J. Reel

See also: Coping Skills; Recovery; Treatment

Bibliography

Baker, Ellen K. "The Concept and Value of Therapist Self-Care." In *Caring for Ourselves: A Therapist's Guide to Personal and Professional Well-Being*, edited by Ellen K. Baker, 13–23. Washington, DC: American Psychological Association, 2003.

Barnett, Jeffrey E., and Natalie Cooper. "Creating a Culture of Self-Care." *Clinical Psychology: Science and Practice*, 16, no. 1 (2009): 16–20. https://doi.org/10.1111/j.1468-2850.2009.01138.x.

Lee, Jacquelyn J., and Shari E. Miller. "A Self-Care Framework for Social Workers: Building a Strong Foundation for Practice." *Families in Society: The Journal of Contemporary Social Services*, 94, no. 2 (2013): 96–103. https://doi.org/10.1606/1044-3894.4289.

National Eating Disorder Association. "Self-Care." National Eating Disorders Association. Accessed October 17, 2016. https://www.nationaleatingdisorders.org/tags/self-care.

SELF-HELP INTERVENTIONS

Self-help interventions are programs designed to be self-taught. These interventions often use a book, DVD/CD, or web-based platform to take individuals through an orderly sequence of modules on psychoeducation and skills training. Self-help interventions (SHIs) have several distinct advantages over traditional psychotherapy, including cost-effectiveness and ease of access. In the case of eating disorders, SHIs have been effective treating a variety of disordered eating problems and have provided important insight into necessary improvements that should be integrated into traditional treatment programs.

Overview of Self-Help Interventions

Self-help interventions originally gained popularity in the latter half of the 20th century, coinciding with an overall popular movement toward the values of personal responsibility and self-improvement in Western cultures. SHIs have been developed for a variety of problems, ranging from diagnosable mental illnesses (e.g., depression and anxiety) to relationship/marital dysfunction to personality deficits (e.g., lack of motivation, narcissism). Self-help treatments have also been developed to improve treatment adherence and understand of medical diagnoses, including diabetes and irritable bowel syndrome (IBS). The popularity of SHIs was also fueled by the rise of the Internet, smartphones, and mobile apps that expanded the accessibility and affordability of these programs.

SHIs take one of two primary formats: completely independent self-guided programs (referred to as *pure self-help*); or programs that are facilitated by a mental health practitioner or other clinician (*guided self-help*; GSH). In the case of more severe problems, including mental disorders and addictions, GSH is seen as a more ethical and effective option. Additionally, SHIs can be based on any number of treatment theories, ranging from cognitive behavioral therapy (CBT) to motivational interviewing to contingency management. This flexibility lends itself to a build your own approach, allowing individuals to choose the structure they prefer (pure vs. guided), the program that best matches their needs, and the ability to progress through the program at their pace.

Although the wide variety in SHIs is considered to be a strength, it also presents challenges in studying the efficacy of SHIs. Therefore, even though SHIs have been prevalent in popular culture as well as in mental health for decades, research on these programs remains sparse compared to the vast number of different self-help treatment programs available. However, SHIs have received a great deal of attention in many problem areas and have generally shown success. For example, one meta-analysis concluded SHIs for smoking cessation were as successful as traditional face-to-face treatment programs and offered an unmatched opportunity for widespread dissemination with potential positive effects on public health. Similar results have been demonstrated and replicated in depression, anxiety, problem gambling, and alcoholism. SHIs have also been incorporated into traditional treatment programs with great success in many of the same problem areas.

Results from Self-Help Interventions for Eating Disorders

Self-help intervention programs have been investigated specifically in the treatment of eating disorders and shown positive results. One of the most extensive studies to date compared a guided CBT self-help intervention to a traditional, face-to-face CBT treatment (both treatment groups were offered medication if they did not respond in a certain length of time) in bulimia nervosa. Several important findings were identified. First, the CBT guided self-help (CBTgsh) treatment was significantly more effective than traditional CBT to reduce bingeing and purging behaviors long term. Second, the CBTgsh treatment was more effective to reduce disordered-eating behaviors in participants identified as potential nonresponders compared to a traditional CBT program. Nonresponders, or participants identified as less likely to benefit from treatment, were identified as individuals who had not reported a reduction in bingeing/purging behaviors by the end of their sixth week of treatment in either group. The third and final key finding was that participants identified as severely disordered and at high risk for relapse responded significantly better to the CBTgsh treatment than to a traditional program. The authors concluded the individualization offered by the CBTgsh program was the underlying factor that contributed to the program's overall success. Taken together, these findings offer tremendous support for the efficacy of guided self-help interventions in treating bulimia, as well as for successfully treating at-risk populations (e.g., nonresponders, severely disordered).

This study is one of many that has established the efficacy of various SHIs for treating bulimia nervosa. Similarly, binge eating disorder (BED) has been widely studied in the context of self-help treatments and the results have also been positive. For example, one study comparing the efficacy of cognitive behavioral therapy guided self-help (CBTgsh) to a control condition in treating BED found CBTgsh was significantly better to reduce binge eating episodes than the control condition. Almost half of CBTgsh participants (46 percent) compared to only 13 percent of the control participants reported complete remission of bingeing following treatment. These results have been demonstrated in other studies looking at SHIs for the treatment of BED.

Although SHIs have been widely accepted as effective treatments for bulimia and binge eating disorder, the results have not been as conclusive for individuals with anorexia nervosa. Several studies have found SHIs are not effective at treating anorexia, and a minority of these studies have found individuals with anorexia report *worsening* symptoms after self-help treatments. The most commonly accepted theory for why SHIs have not been effective for treating anorexia posits that anorexia requires a more intensive and specialized treatment regimen than what is offered by self-help interventions. Given these results, researchers have been hesitant to explore SHIs in groups with anorexia nervosa for fear of resulting in negative health outcomes.

However, some studies have found individuals with anorexia nervosa respond positively to SHIs. One study investigated the efficacy of administering a pretreatment self-help program to enhance treatment adherence and engagement once individuals began a traditional outpatient intervention for eating disorders. Results showed individuals who received the self-help program were significantly more likely to engage with the traditional treatment program compared to individuals who did not receive special pretreatment program. Additionally, individuals diagnosed with anorexia and/or who reported higher levels of anorexic symptoms responded better to pretreatment SHI than individuals with other eating disorders. These results suggest SHIs may be particularly effective to enhance treatment motivation and engagement in individuals with anorexia nervosa. Another study tested a mobile self-help intervention for reducing relapse rates in individuals who previously received inpatient treatment for anorexia. The authors found the self-help intervention resulted in higher body mass index, lower rates of disordered eating and negative moods, and a decreased attention to detail in individuals with anorexia. Although these results were from a preliminary, pilot investigation, they offer support for the utility of self-help treatment programs in sustaining progress achieved during inpatient treatment.

Overall, the results strongly support the applicability of SHIs in the treatment of bulimia and binge eating disorder. SHIs have reliably reduced disordered-eating behaviors in these populations and in individuals who have not responded as positively to traditional treatment options. Although the results are not as conclusive for anorexia nervosa, studies have shown SHIs may have niches they are particularly well suited to fill for this disorder, including enhancing motivation prior to the administration of a traditional treatment program and in reinforcing positive gains made during inpatient treatment.

Positives and Negatives of Self-Help Interventions

SHIs have received attention for the positive aspects they offer. First, SHIs are much more cost-effective than traditional treatment programs. Additionally, self-help treatments can be administered by clinicians with less specialized training, which maintains the low cost of SHIs and makes these accessible to more people. Self-help interventions also allow people to progress through the program at their pace, which many researchers argue could inherently strengthen autonomy and contribute to positive outcomes. Last, SHIs are incredibly flexible and offer an unparalleled level of customization, both on behalf of a clinician who may develop or lead these interventions as well as for the patient.

Although self-help interventions have numerous benefits, there are important drawbacks to consider. First, the increasing focus on Internet- and mobile phone–based SHIs presents an opportunity for false treatments to proliferate. These programs may not be developed by trustworthy or knowledgeable sources or rigorously evaluated for their efficacy. Individuals who select a self-help intervention should carefully evaluate the source of a program and conduct background research on a program's efficacy. Self-help interventions may also not be as appropriate for certain types of disorders where breaks from reality are more common, including schizophrenia and personality disorders. Last, researchers have cautioned that SHIs are not (yet) replacements for traditional treatment programs under the direction of skilled clinicians and should be viewed as adjuncts or enrichments to professional treatment options.

Hannah J. Hopkins

See also: Cognitive Behavioral Therapy Guided Self-Help Treatment; Relapse; Treatment

Bibliography

Ambwani, Suman, Valentina Cardi, and Janet Treasure. "Mobile Self-Help Interventions for Anorexia Nervosa: Conceptual, Ethical, and Methodological Considerations for Clinicians and Researchers." *Professional Psychology: Research and Practice* 45, no. 5 (2014): 316–323. https://doi.org/10.1037/a0036203.

Brewin, Nicola, Jackie Wales, Rebecca Cashmore, Carolyn R. Plateau, Brett Dean, Tara Cousins, and Jon Arcelus. "Evaluation of a Motivation and Psycho-Educational Guided Self-Help Intervention for People with Eating Disorders (MOPED): Engagement and Completion Rates Following Use of MOPED Self-Help." *European Eating Disorders Review* 24, no. 3 (2016): 241–246. https://doi.org/10.1002/erv.2431.

Carrard, I., C. Crépin, P. Rouget, T. Lam, A. Golay, and M. Van der Linden. 2011. "Randomised Controlled Trial of a Guided Self-Help Treatment on the Internet for Binge Eating Disorder." *Behaviour Research and Therapy* 49, no. 8 (2011): 482–491. https://doi.org/10.1016/j.brat.2011.05.004.

Curry, Susan J. "Self-Help Interventions for Smoking Cessation." *Journal of Consulting and Clinical Psychology* 61, no. 5 (1993): 790–803. https://doi.org/10.1037/0022-006X.61.5.790.

Grilo, Carlos M., and Robin M. Masheb. "A Randomized Controlled Comparison of Guided Self-Help Cognitive Behavioral Therapy and Behavioral Weight Loss for Binge Eating Disorder." *Behaviour Research and Therapy* 43, no. 11 (2005): 1509–1525. https://doi.org/10.1016/j.brat.2004.11.010.

Mitchell, James E., Stewart Agras, Scott Crow, Katherine Halmi, Christopher G. Fairburn, Susan Bryson, and Helena Kraemer. "Stepped Care and Cognitive–Behavioural Therapy for Bulimia Nervosa: Randomised Trial." *The British Journal of Psychiatry* 198, no. 5 (2011): 391–397. https://doi.org/10.1192/bjp.bp.110.082172.

Wilson, G. Terence, and Laurie J. Zandberg. "Cognitive–Behavioral Guided Self-Help for Eating Disorders: Effectiveness and Scalability." *Clinical Psychology Review* 32, no. 4 (2012): 343–357. https://doi.org/10.1016/j.cpr.2012.03.001.

SELF-INJURY

Self-injurious behavior (e.g., cutting) refers to the deliberate infliction of self-harm and direct physical injury to one's body. In contrast to suicide, self-injury behaviors have no lethal intent and include both compulsive and impulsive acts of self-harm. Compulsive forms of self-injury such as hair pulling and skin picking tend to be repetitive and habitual. Impulsive self-harm is also triggered by stressful events and can include skin cutting, bruising, and burning.

Prevalence of Deliberate Self-Harm

Deliberate self-harm has often been considered an adolescent phenomenon, but self-injurious behaviors can continue into adulthood. Among U.S. adolescents, cutting was estimated to range from 26 percent to 37 percent of 9th to 12th graders with over half (51.2 percent) of cutters being female. A similar study in Canada revealed 17 percent of individuals ages 14–21 reported self-harm behaviors and the most common behaviors were cutting, scratching, or self hitting. An Irish study with 3,881 teens found females (13.9 percent) engaged in more deliberate harm than males (4.3 percent) and self-cutting was more common than overdose. A separate study of Japanese adolescents in a juvenile detention center found 16.4 percent of participants engaged in cutting and 35 percent of participants had burned themselves. Deliberate self-harm has been associated with personality disorders as well as schizophrenia, major depression, substance abuse disorders, and eating disorders.

Deliberate Self-Harm and Eating Disorders

Although deliberate self-harm behaviors are considered socially unacceptable, nonsuicidal self-injury rates were highest in eating-disordered individuals with purging behaviors (e.g., self-induced vomiting). One review showed nonsuicidal self-injury occurred in 13.6–42.1 percent of individuals with anorexia nervosa restricting subtype, 27.8–68.1 percent of individuals with anorexia nervosa binge eating/purging subtype, and 26.0–55.2 percent of individuals with bulimia nervosa. Self-harm behaviors are associated with an attempt to manage negative mood states (e.g., anger, depression) and 69.2 percent of eating-disordered individuals reported feeling better immediately after self-injurious behavior. A couple of hours after self-injurious behavior, only one-third of eating-disordered individuals felt better, and the other one-third felt worse. It is common for guilt and shame to follow a self-harm incident. Clients have reported using self-injurious behaviors to punish themselves and to sense physical rather than emotional pain.

Justine J. Reel

See also: Children and Adolescents; Comorbidity; Personality Characteristics; Risk Factors; Suicide

Bibliography

Claes, Laurence, E. David Klonsky, Jennifer Muehlenkamp, Peter Kuppens, and Walter Vandereycken. "The Affect-Regulation Function of Nonsuicidal Self-Injury in Eating Disordered Patients: Which Affect States Are Regulated?" *Comprehensive Psychiatry* 51 (2010): 386–392. https://doi.org/10.1016/j.comppsych.2009.09.001.

Claes, Laurence, Walter Vandereycken, and Hans Vertommen. "Therapy-Related Assessment of Self-Harming Behaviors in Eating Disordered Patients: A Case Illustration." *Eating Disorders: Journal of Treatment and Prevention* 10 (2002): 269–279. https://doi.org/10.1080/10640260290081858.

Favaro, Angela, and Paolo Santonastaso. "Different Types of Self-Injurious Behavior in Bulimia Nervosa." *Comprehensive Psychiatry* 40, no. 1 (1999): 57–60. http://dx.doi.org/10.1016/S0010-440X(99)90078-0.

Franko, Debra L., and Pamela K. Keel. "Suicidality in Eating Disorders: Occurrence, Correlates and Clinical Implications." *Clinical Psychology Review* 26, no. 6 (2006): 769–782. https://doi.org/10.1016/j.cpr.2006.04.001.

Franko, Debra L., Pamela K. Keel, D. J. Dover, S. S. Delinsky, K. T. Eddy, V. Charat, R. Renn, and David B. Herzog. "What Predicts Suicide Attempts in Women with Eating Disorders?" *Psychological Medicine* 34 (2004): 843–853.

Greydanus, Donald E., and Daniel Shek. "Deliberate Self-Harm and Suicide in Adolescents." *Keio Journal of Medicine* 58, no. 3 (2009): 144–151. http://doi.org/10.2302/kjm.58.144.

Hintikka, Jukka, Tommi Tolmunen, Marja-Liisa Rissanen, Kirsi Honkalampi, Jari Kylma, and Eila Laukkanen. "Mental Disorders in Self-Cutting Adolescents." *Journal of Adolescent Health* 44 (2009): 464–467. https://doi.org/10.1016/j.jadohealth.2008.10.003.

Kerr, Patrick L., Jennifer J. Muehlenkamp, and James M. Turner. "Nonsuicidal Self-Injury: A Review of Current Research for Family Medicine and Primary Care Physicians." *Journal of the American Board of Family Medicine* 23, no. 2 (2010): 240–259. https://doi.org/10.3122/jabfm.2010.02.090110.

Milos, Gabriella, Anja Spindler, Urs Hepp, and Ulrich Schnyder. "Suicide Attempts and Suicidal Ideation: Links with Psychiatric Comorbidity in Eating Disorder Subjects." *General Hospital Psychiatry* 26, no. 2 (2004): 129–135. https://doi.org/10.1016/j.genhosp psych.2003.10.005.

Pompili, Maurizio, Paolo Girardi, Giulia Tatarelli, Amedeo Ruberto, and Roberto Tatarelli. "Suicide and Attempted Suicide in Eating Disorders, Obesity, and Weight Image." *Eating Behaviors* 7, no. 4 (2006): 384–394. https://doi.org/10.1016/j.eatbeh.2005.12.004.

SELF-PRESENTATION THEORY

Self-presentation theory has been used to depict the relationship between one's emotion and perceptions about body image. According to self-presentation theory, social anxiety arises when people want to convey a particular social image to others, but have little confidence in their ability to do so. Self presentation theory (sometimes called *impression management*) has particular implications for understanding eating disorders. First, higher levels of social anxiety are associated with disordered-eating behaviors. Additionally, perfectionism (that often accompanies higher social anxiety) has been reliably linked with disordered eating as well as a greater self-reported need to present one's self in a particular way. Given the links between self-presentation theory, social anxiety, perfectionism, and disordered eating, it is important to understand self-presentation theory as well as an appreciation for its role in the etiology of eating disorders.

The Link between Social Anxiety and Eating Disorders

Anxiety disorders and eating disorders frequently co-occur. Researchers estimate as many as 85 percent of persons diagnosed with an eating disorder qualify for an anxiety disorder diagnosis. Social anxiety disorder (SAD) in particular has been shown to have an extremely high rate of co-occurrence with eating disorders. SAD is defined as an intense fear of situations where one might be evaluated, resulting in crippling embarrassment. Although it is common and even adaptive in many situations to have a certain degree of shyness or nervousness when being evaluated (e.g., giving a presentation in front of class), SAD is a maladaptive fear that results in interference with daily functioning. In extreme cases, SAD can prohibit people from being employed, engaging with friends and family, running errands, and leaving their house.

Research has found as many as 75 percent of individuals with anorexia nervosa and 68 percent of individuals with bulimia nervosa qualify for a SAD diagnosis. In comparison, only an estimated 12 percent of the general population (i.e., without an eating disorder) meet criteria for SAD. Many genetic and environmental factors are associated with both eating disorders and SAD, such as excessive perfectionism and fear of negative evaluation by others. Numerous models and studies have identified several traits found in individuals with eating disorders and high social anxiety, including low self-esteem, social skill deficits, and appearance-specific social anxiety. This last characteristic—appearance-specific social anxiety, also referred to as *social physique anxiety*—is the fear that one's physical appearance does not convey a particular desired impression to others. This fear is one of the essential ingredients of body dissatisfaction and could be a potential catalyst for engaging in weight control/loss behaviors. Social physique anxiety has been of interest for researchers who study athletes. Because certain sports (namely figure skating, gymnastics, and to a lesser extent swimming, diving, and wrestling) are usually associated with ideal body types, many athletes engage in dangerous behaviors to control or alter their body type to fit the ideal for their sport. Athletes report they are immediately assumed to be more competent or skillful in their respective sports if their body aligns with the ideal.

Understanding Self-Presentation Theory

Self-presentation theory was first proposed in the mid-1980s to explain the root of social anxiety. According to self-presentation theory, there are three critical ingredients that coalesce for a situation to provoke social anxiety in an individual. First, an individual must be concerned with how others perceive her in a social situation. Research has shown the less people care about how others view them, the less likely they are to experience social anxiety. The second critical ingredient for social anxiety is a lack of confidence in one's ability to convey the desired impression to an audience. Studies on this have found individuals with higher social anxiety also have significant social skills deficits; this relationship appears to be causal in nature, meaning the recognition of one's inadequate social skills precedes the development of social anxiety. The third and final ingredient critical to social anxiety is the determination that the appraisal received from social groups or settings are important for social status. This phenomenon can be likened to the desire to make a good impression in interviews or on first dates: certain desirable outcomes are dependent on the ability to make a positive impression.

According to self-presentation theory, eating disorders arise directly from a powerful desire to make an impression. This desire can be conscious or unconscious, and oftentimes the desired impressions speak to larger social stereotypes and prejudices. For example, many studies have identified an underlying desire for women to restrict the food they eat in social settings because eating lightly is classically associated with femininity. Conversely for men, the association between masculinity and types of food (e.g., red meat, beer) can encourage men to eat more food in social settings than they would otherwise. In some cultural traditions, it is considered rude to refuse food or not to finish your helping, which can often cause binge eating or purging to develop. A particularly jarring example can be found in online, pro-anorexia, or pro-ana, communities. The term *wannarexic* is often used as an insult when someone is deemed by a group as not a good enough or pure enough anorectic. Many individuals who have been on the receiving end of such insults reported that it often spurred them to pursue weight loss at an even greater magnitude than they had prior to being ostracized. In each of these cases, the disordered-eating behavior begins as a desire to portray a specific impression to others.

Controversy around Self-Presentation Theory as Applied to Eating Disorders

Applying self-presentation theory to eating disorders has been met with caution from the scientific community. Many researchers argue applying this theory can ignore other potentially more powerful motives for engaging in disordered-eating behaviors, including a need for control and an internalized sense of shame. Others believe self-presentation theory is best understood in the context of the early stages of eating disorders, before full-blown cognitive and emotional deficits emerge. For example, self-presentation theory could appropriately be applied to explain why a teenage girl might engage in disordered-eating behaviors in the hopes of gaining the approval of her peers, but it may be less appropriate to explain why an adult woman with an extremely limited social network and a long history of anorexia would starve herself to the point of death. However, many researchers agree that self-presentation theory is a useful and accurate interpretation of the roots of social anxiety, which often goes together with disordered eating.

Hannah J. Hopkins

See also: Body Image; Social Physique Anxiety; Wannarexia

Bibliography

Arcelus, Jon, Michelle Haslam, Claire Farrow, and Caroline Meyer. "The Role of Interpersonal Functioning in the Maintenance of Eating Psychopathology: A Systematic Review and Testable Model." *Clinical Psychology Review* 33, no. 1 (2013): 156–167. https://doi.org/10.1016/j.cpr.2012.10.009.

Britton, Lauren E., Denise M. Martz, Doris G. Bazzini, Lisa A. Curtin, and Anni LeaShomb. "Fat Talk and Self-Presentation of Body Image: Is There a Social Norm for Women to Self-Degrade?" *Body Image* 3, no. 3 (2006): 247–254. https://doi.org/10.1016/j.bodyim.2006.05.006.

Hofmann, Stefan G., and Patricia M. DiBartolo. *Social Anxiety: Clinical, Developmental, and Social Perspectives.* Amsterdam; Boston: Academic Press/Elsevier, 2010.

Levinson, Cheri A., Thomas L. Rodebaugh, Emily K. White, Andrew R. Menatti, Justin W. Weeks, Juliette M. Iacovino, and Cortney S. Warren. "Social Appearance Anxiety, Perfectionism, and Fear of Negative Evaluation. Distinct or Shared Risk Factors for Social Anxiety and Eating Disorders?" *Appetite* 67 (2013): 125–133. https://doi.org/10.1016/j.appet.2013.04.002.

McGee, Brandy J., Paul L. Hewitt, Simon B. Sherry, Melanie Parkin, and Gordon L. Flett. "Perfectionistic Self-Presentation, Body Image, and Eating Disorder Symptoms." *Body Image* 2, no. 1 (2005): 29–40. https://doi.org/10.1016/j.bodyim.2005.01.002.

Monsma, Eva V., Karin A. Pfeiffer, and Robert M. Malina. "Relationship of Social Physique Anxiety to Indicators of Physique." *Research Quarterly for Exercise and Sport* 79, no. 3 (2008): 417–422. https://doi.org/10.1080/02701367.2008.10599507.

Mori, DeAnna, Shelly Chaiken, and Patricia Pliner. "'Eating Lightly' and the Self-Presentation of Femininity." *Journal of Personality and Social Psychology* 53, no. 4 (1987): 693–702. https://doi.org/10.1037/0022-3514.53.4.693.

Striegel-Moore, Ruth H., Lisa R. Silberstein, and Judith Rodin. "The Social Self in Bulimia Nervosa: Public Self-Consciousness, Social Anxiety, and Perceived Fraudulence." *Journal of Abnormal Psychology* 102, no. 2 (1993): 297–303. https://doi.org/10.1037/0021-843X.102.2.297.

SKI JUMPING

Ski jumping is an antigravitation Olympic sport that involves flying on skis to achieve the greatest distance. Ski jumping is considered a leanness-demand sport because of the focus on weight and the perception that performance improves with reduced weight (i.e., lighter will fly further). Historically, ski jumping was limited to male athletes, but female ski jumpers trained and competed outside the Olympics. Women's ski jumping finally became an Olympic sport in Sochi, Russia, in 2014.

Weight Pressures in Ski Jumping

Because of the noted advantage of the lightest ski jumpers, ski jumping has resembled other weight class sports where athletes must make weight to improve performance. Ski jumpers may restrict certain foods, engage in fasting, purging, or excessive exercise prior to competitions. Ski jumpers tend to have petite physiques, like a jockey, and athletes are expected to remain light for competitions. Although ski jumpers wear revealing and form-fitting training and competition attire, to date no studies have explored body image concerns in these athletes.

World Cup and Olympic competitions discovered the body mass index of ski jumpers had dropped drastically during the period 1970-1995. Therefore, the Federation Internationale de Ski (FIS), the governing body for ski jumping, created regulations regarding the weight of competitors; this was dubbed the "anorexic rule" for male ski jumpers.

Anorexic Rule for Male Ski Jumpers

Prior to the 2006 Olympics, the FIS established a weight penalty for underweight ski jumpers that would result in the shortening of their skis. Because ski length affects flight, having the ski shortened creates a competitive disadvantage for underweight ski jumpers. Generally, skis can be as long as 146 percent of a ski jumper's height. Ski jumpers who are weighed in the nude and in gear must meet minimum body mass index requirements of 18.5 and 20, respectively. When a skier drops below the minimum, his skis are shortened by 2 percent for each kilogram of weight below the standard. In the 2006 Olympics, only 4 of the top 50 competitors in an individual event did not make weight, suggesting the anorexic rule has been an effective to prevent excessive weight loss. However, sports professionals have suggested athletes use the weight limit as a guide for where their weight should be, and lose weight down to the minimum requirement.

Justine J. Reel

See also: Jockeys; Sports; Weight Pressures in Sport

Bibliography

Muller, W. "Determinants of Ski Jump Performance and Implications for Health, Safety and Fairness." *Sports Medicine* 39, no. 2 (2009): 85–106. https://doi.org/10.2165/00007256-200939020-00001.

Reel, Justine J., and Katherine A. Beals, eds. *The Hidden Faces of Eating Disorders and Body Image.* Reston, VA: AAHPERD/NAGWS, 2009.

Reel, Justine J., and Holly M. Estes. "Treatment Considerations for Athletes with Disordered Eating." In *Disordered Eating among Athletes: A Comprehensive Guide for Health Professionals,* edited by Katherine A. Beals, 131–158. Champaign, IL: Human Kinetics, 2004.

Sherman, Roberta T. "Protecting the Health of Athletes: Possible Changes." Paper presented at the meeting of the International Olympic Committee Medical Commission. Monte Carlo, Monaco, 2007.

Thompson, Ron A., and Roberta Trattner Sherman. *Eating Disorders in Sport.* New York: Routledge, 2010.

SKIN TONE

Skin tone can represent a significant component of a person's body image. In the United States having a tan may be associated with a youthful glow, in contrast to other cultures that value lighter tones. One example of ways that skin tone has played a role with body image is the tendency to try to darken or lighten one's skin for perceived desirability with products or varying one's exposure to the sun. The desire to change appearance is closely correlated with body dissatisfaction, the strongest predictor of eating disorders.

Cultural Influences on Skin Tone

Many cultures desire lighter skin color, as pale skin is associated with beauty and wealth. For example, Japanese culture values white (or light) skin color, because this skin tone is believed to reflect spiritual refinement, femininity, purity, and goodness. Historically, this light skin color preference was grounded in class distinctions. Dark skin tones have been linked to the assumption that individuals were from a low social class involved in performing intense outdoor labor. By contrast, upper-class Japanese women who applied white powder to their faces to lighten their appearance were viewed as wealthy enough to protect their skin from the sun. Currently, the desire for white skin among Japanese women still exists, as white skin is considered beautiful. There are many cosmetic companies selling nonbleach skin lightening creams; the advertisements for these products claim that whiten the skin. Although it is unclear if these products actually lighten the skin, they generally do not contain chemicals associated with skin cancer.

Skin Bleaching

Throughout Asia, Latin America, and Africa, skin bleaching has become increasingly popular—particularly in areas colonized by Europe, such as Ghana, Kenya, Tanzania, Senegal, Mali, South Africa, and Nigeria—as being white equals a high social and economic status. Although both men and women report desiring a lighter skin shade, women have higher rates of skin bleaching than their male counterparts. Furthermore, women sometimes apply skin bleaching products to their children in attempts to meet the socially desirable skin tone standard.

Individuals from Africa may choose to apply skin bleaching creams to cover naturally black skin tones. Researchers suggest this practice could reflect an internalization of the discrimination experienced. Furthermore, researchers suggest descendants of enslaved Africans have not only developed negative attitudes about themselves but have also turned to skin bleaching to erase the past.

The largest effect of Western cultural values of lighter skin has been observed in Senegal and extends to other parts of Africa. In fact, the desire for lighter skin and the corresponding chemical skin bleaching behavior has resulted in skin cancer. In addition to these severe health implications, the cost of a bottle of skin bleach is $5.00, which is unattainable by a majority of the population that lives on less than $2.00 per day. Although expensive, some women in Senegal choose to spend scarce resources on potentially dangerous skin bleaching products rather than on necessary living expenses (e.g., food and clothing).

Skin Lightening Products

Skin lightening products are widely available for purchase by the public, for both clinical treatment of skin disorders and cosmetic reasons. Hydroquinone has been the standard for 40 years in treating hyperpigmentation and unaffected skin in vitiligo patients. This chemical can be found in tea, wheat, berries, beer, and coffee. Flavonoids like licorice and naturally occurring Kojic acid have also been used to lighten skin.

Advertisers tend to sell their skin lightening products to consumers by getting popular light-skinned women of color to appear in advertisements within their country of origin. For example, Halle Berry of the United States, Aishwarya Rai of India (L'Oréal), Genevieve Nnaji of Nigeria (Lux soap), and Terry Pheto of South Africa (L'Oréal) have been featured in ads. The first skin lightening cream to be targeted at men, Fair and Handsome, was created by the British company Unilever; its advertisement featured India's Bollywood celebrity Shah Rukh Khan. The advertisement led men to believe they would be more masculine if they lightened their skin. Organizers of the Miss Authentica Pageant—a beauty pageant—in Africa's Ivory Coast are aware of the dangers of skin bleaching and require pageant participants do not bleach their skin to qualify. This requirement is intended to raise awareness of the dangers of skin bleaching throughout the country. Similarly, the Jamaican government launched a campaign called Don't Kill the Skin to raise awareness about the irreversible dangers of skin bleaching.

Hailey E. Nielson

See also: Body Image; Body Image Globally; Celebrities and Eating Disorders; Cosmetic Surgery and Eating Disorders; Media; Physical Self-Perceptions

Bibliography

Charles, Christopher A. D. "Skin Bleaching, Self-Hate, and Black Identity in Jamaica." *Journal of Black Studies* 33, no. 6 (2003): 711–728. https://doi.org/10.1177/0021934703033006001.

Gillbro, J. M., and M. J. Olsson. "The Melanogenesis and Mechanisms of Skin-Lightening Agents—Existing and New Approaches." *International Journal of Cosmetic Science* 33, no. 3 (2010). 210–221. https://doi.org/10.1111/j.1168 2494.2010.00616.x.

Hall-Iijima, Christine. "Asian Eyes: Body Image and Eating Disorders of Asian and Asian American Women." *Eating Disorders* 3 (1995): 5–19. http://dx.doi.org/10.1080/10640269508249141.

Hunter, Margaret L. "Buying Racial Capital: Skin Bleaching and Cosmetic Surgery in a Globalized World." *The Journal of Pan African Studies* 4, no. 4 (2011): 142–164.

Mahe, Antoine, Fatimata Ly, Guy Aymard, and Jean Marie Dangou. "Skin Diseases Associated with the Cosmetic Use of Bleaching Products in Women from Dakar, Senegal." *British Journal of Dermatology* 148, no. 3 (2003): 493–500. https://doi.org/10.1046/j.1365-2133.2003.05161.x.

SOCIAL COMPARISON THEORY

Social comparison theory was developed in 1954 to explain how individuals are driven by a desire for self-evaluation of their abilities. According to this theory, when individuals do not have objective means to evaluate themselves, they compare their attributes and abilities to those of other people. Comparing themselves to others who are better or worse in terms of certain characteristics can strongly influence how they think about themselves, and thus lead them to engage in positive or negative behaviors.

Upward and Downward Comparisons

Unfavorable comparisons (the other person is evaluated more positively for an attribute than oneself) are *upward comparisons*. Individuals often make upward comparisons to improve themselves. For example, a woman may compare herself to someone more accomplished in school as a source of inspiration. However, the risk of upward comparison is that it may highlight her flaws (e.g., body fat) and threaten her self-esteem. Research on upward comparisons indicates people with a strong tendency to make physical appearance–related comparisons typical of societal ideals (i.e., thin ideal) experience more body dissatisfaction and disordered eating.

In contrast to upward comparisons, *downward comparisons*, or favorable comparisons (the other person is evaluated more negatively for a particular attribute than oneself) may serve to build confidence by comparing oneself with someone who is perceived to be inferior on a certain attribute. Researchers suggest people experiencing negative emotions or cognitions about themselves (e.g., low self-esteem) often try to enhance their self-regard by engaging in downward comparisons.

Social Comparison among Girls and Women

There are numerous studies showing girls and women frequently engage in social comparisons when evaluating their bodies. Social comparison theory suggests individuals may also use media images and toys as inspirational standards or models of societal attractiveness. One study found adolescent girls made more social comparisons to media models (e.g., actors) than boys, and girls who scored higher on the social comparison tendency also exhibited greater eating pathology. In another study, investigators examined the effects of playing with thin dolls (e.g., Barbie) compared to playing with realistic-sized dolls on the consumption of sweet snacks among girls ages 6–10. Approximately half the girls wanted to be thin, and the girls who played with thin dolls consumed fewer snacks than girls who played with realistic-sized dolls, suggesting real-life environmental cues that relate to body size have a powerful influence on girls' eating behaviors.

Prior research has found girls gather information on peer values, ideals, and behaviors they then use to judge their bodies and engage in weight control behaviors. Recently, researchers examined the social contexts in schools to understand what influences girls' decisions to practice weight control. They found girls are less likely to try to lose weight in schools where there are many overweight girls or where the average female BMI is high, and more likely to lose weight in schools where there are many underweight girls. However, schoolmates with a similar body size had the most powerful effect on individual girls' weight loss behaviors. This research suggests weight loss is motivated by normative standards of beauty as well as the ideals of persons like an individual.

Women who were exposed to images of ultrathin females as beautiful compared their bodies to media images, and because of this comparison, reported more negative mood and body dissatisfaction. Researchers have shown women who view images of thin women in print ads, television commercials, and music videos experience lower self-esteem and higher body dissatisfaction than women who view neutral images. Even a brief exposure to media images of the thin ideal can have a negative effect on women's body image. For women, appearance comparison was one of the strongest predictors of body dysmorphic disorder.

Social Comparison between Boys and Men

Over the past 30 years, content analyses of male media images indicate media images of men have become increasingly muscular and less realistic. Because there are more media images of what men should look like, boys and men are prone to comparing themselves to ideal images. Studies have shown adolescent boys engage in social comparison regarding their bodies, and this is related to negative body image and disordered eating. One study found social body comparison in adolescent boys predicted media use and muscle building behaviors; other researchers found social body comparison is associated with eating pathology in adolescent boys. These studies support previous findings that boys made upward comparisons of their bodies with their friends as early age eight.

For example, a study examined social comparison in adult men and found social comparisons influence body dissatisfaction indirectly through internalization (i.e., an individual accepts socially-defined ideals of attractiveness). In a separate study, researchers exposed men to television commercials with the muscular ideal and found men thought themselves less physically attractive and less satisfied with muscle shape and size than men who did not watch the commercials. The frequency of comparisons did not predict body dissatisfaction in men. It appears men engage in less social comparison to idealized media images than women. However, the direction of comparison (upward vs. downward) was principal factor influencing body dissatisfaction. The more the upward social comparison after watching commercials with images of the muscular ideal, the greater the decrease in feeling strong, weight satisfaction, and muscle satisfaction.

Sonya SooHoo

See also: Body Image; Body Image in Males; Dolls; Drive for Muscularity; Media

Bibliography

Anschutz, Doeschka J., and Rutger C. M. E. Engels. "The Effects of Playing with Thin Dolls on Body Image and Food Intake in Young Girls." *Sex Roles* 63, no. 9 (2010): 621–630. https://doi.org/10.1007/s11199-010-9871-6.

Boroughs, Michael S., Ross Krawczyk, and J. Kevin Thompson. "Body Dysmorphic Disorder among Diverse Racial/Ethnic and Sexual Orientation Groups: Prevalence Estimates and Associated Factors." *Sex Roles* 63, no. 9 (2010): 725–737. https://doi.org/10.1007/s11199-010-9831-1.

Festinger, Leon. "A Theory of Social Comparison Processes." *Human Relations* 7 (1954): 117–140. https://doi.org/10.1177/001872675400700202.

Hargreaves, Duane, and Marika Tiggerman. "Muscular Ideal Media Images and Men's Body Image: Social Comparison Processing and Individual Vulnerability." *Psychology of Men and Muscularity* 10, no. 2 (2009): 109–119. http://dx.doi.org/10.1037/a0014691.

Karazsia, Bryan T., and Janis Crowther. "Sociocultural and Psychological Links to Men's Engagement in Risky Body Change Behaviors." *Sex Roles* 63, no. 9 (2010): 747–756. https://doi.org/10.1007/s11199-010-9802-6.

Smolak, Linda, and Jonathan A. Stein. "A Longitudinal Investigation of Gender Role and Muscle Building in Adolescent Boys." *Sex Roles* 63, no. 9 (2010): 738–746. https://doi.org/10.1007/s11199-010-9819-x.

Tantleff-Dunn, Stacey, and Jessica L. Gokee. "Interpersonal Influences on Body Image Development." In *Body Image: A Handbook of Theory, Research, and Clinical Practice*, edited by Thomas Cash. New York: Guilford Press, 2002.

Warren, Cortney S., Andrea Schoen, and Kerri J. Schafer. "Media Internalization and Social Comparison as Predictors of Eating Pathology among Latino Adolescents: The Moderating Effect of Gender and Generational Status." *Sex Roles* 63, no. 9 (2010): 712–724. https://doi.org/10.1007/s11199-010-9876-1.

SOCIAL CONTAGION THEORY

A contagion is the transmission of a virus or bacteria from one human being to another, usually from close contact with an infected individual. This potential for the spreading of disease guides commonsense practices in medical treatments as well as everyday life. Similarly, the idea that mental illness symptoms are contagious and can be transmitted from one person to another is a more abstract yet well-documented phenomenon. Referred to as *social contagion* theory, research has documented mild to moderate effects of a person's social network's mental health on their mental health and well-being. One of the seminal works on this topic was conducted in a sorority and found a significant social contagion effect for disordered behaviors.

Social contagion theory states that social networks act as sites for the transmission of mental illness. This phenomenon was first demonstrated in members of a sorority whose binge eating behaviors grew more similar over time and with exposure to one another. Social contagion theory has been shown to be separate from self-selection effects and has important implications for the successful treatment of eating disorders.

The Debate between Social Contagion versus Self-Selection

One of the earliest critiques raised against this theory was that self-selection was not accounted for. Self-selection is best thought of as birds of a feather flocking together. In this case, it refers to a phenomenon where people of similar dispositions end up together because they choose to be in similar environments. This can create the illusion that social proximity influences wellness. For example, in the case of sorority women, self-selection theory would state women who opt to join sororities are more preoccupied with their weight and/or shape than their non-Greek counterparts.

As the research on this phenomenon grew more robust, the need to disentangle self-selection from social contagiousness became more pressing. Research studies were carefully designed to separate self-selection properties (usually thought of as symptoms or traits prior to group formation) from social contagion effects. Social contagion has emerged as a valid phenomenon, separate from self-selection effects. The social contagion theory has been investigated in many areas of mental health, including eating disorders, self-harm behaviors, depression symptoms, and even happiness. One research study found having a happy neighbor resulted in a 37 percent increase in individual happiness. Social contagion theory is widely accepted as an important area of study that greatly affects identification of at-risk individuals and groups, prevention efforts, treatment outcomes, and relapse/recovery prognosis.

Social Contagion Theory and Eating Disorders

It was in the field of eating disorders that social contagion theory first emerged. A research study in the late 1980s successfully demonstrated sorority women's binge eating behaviors came to resemble those of their sister members over the course of membership. Anecdotally, social contagion theory resonated with researchers, treatment providers, affected individuals, and friends/family of ill individuals. Athletic teams, close friend groups, and inpatient treatment units were all common backdrops for this phenomenon.

Over the course of the past few decades, research studies have refined social contagion theory and its effect on disordered eating. Several factors have been identified as primers for more potent social transmission of disordered eating symptoms. In research on roommates and social contagion theory, having one roommate of higher social status (i.e., thinner, higher socioeconomic status, and/or more sexually experienced) facilitates the contagion effect. Additionally, roommates with similar baseline mental health appear to be more susceptible to the influence of social contagion. Certain behaviors seem to be more easily transmitted, with self-induced vomiting the most transmittable and, perhaps surprisingly, diet one of the least transmittable behaviors.

In addition to disordered-eating behaviors, attitudes are also subject to social contagiousness. Internalization of the thin ideal, increased drive for thinness, and perfectionism have all been identified as attitudes that contribute to eating disorders and are susceptible to peer-to-peer transmission.

Implications for Treatment

One of the most salient examples of social contagion theory comes from residential treatment facilities, where individuals who are hospitalized for eating disorders (particularly anorexia nervosa) exchange tips, tricks, and motivation for maintaining their disorder. Social contagiousness can undermine treatment and recovery in situations like these, with the formation of hierarchies among patients based on weight and the detrimental effects of patients close to discharge being exposed to actively ill, newly admitted patients all playing critical roles in these situations. Research on treatment efforts with regard to inpatient units has been mixed—social contagion does appear to have a detrimental effect on patients' illness progression, but, conversely, the sense of community created by being with individuals suffering from the same affliction seems to have positive effects. Researchers have been able to offer few concrete criteria for maximizing the positive effects of residential treatment units while successfully combating social contagion effects.

Another example of social contagion in the eating disorder community manifests as "pro-ana" or "pro-mia" websites. These online venues have received a great deal of attention with the rise of social media and represent a cyberspace manifestation of social contagion theory. Pro-ana/pro-mia sites personify eating disorders (anorexia becomes "ana," bulimia becomes "mia") and celebrate eating disorders as lifestyle choices. Members frequently exchange motivational images, update each other on their progress toward desired weights, and often engage in harassment of individuals they view as not fully committed to an eating disorder lifestyle (the term *wannarexic* is often used for someone who is not considered a true anorexic). Although many official social media platforms have taken steps to regulate these online communities, the nature of the Internet allows these communities to exist relatively unchecked. This has implications for the development of eating disorders, as well as for recovered individuals at risk for relapse.

Hannah J. Hopkins

See also: Pro-Ana; Residential Treatment; Social Media and Eating Disorders; Wannarexia

Bibliography

Allison, Stephen, Megan Warin, and Tarun Bastiampillai. "Anorexia Nervosa and Social Contagion: Clinical Implications." *Australian and New Zealand Journal of Psychiatry* 48, no. 2 (2014): 116–120. https://doi.org/10.1177/0004867413502092.

Averett, Susan, Sabrina Terrizzi, and Yang Wang. "The Effect of Sorority Membership on Eating Disorders and Body Mass Index." *IZA Discussion Paper* no. 7512 (2013): 1–36. Accessed February 3, 2017. https://www.econstor.eu/bitstream/10419/80573/1/756691877.pdf.

Crandall, Christian. "Social Contagion of Binge Eating." *Journal of Personality and Social Psychology* 55, no. 4 (1988): 588–598. http://dx.doi.org/10.1037/0022-3514.55.4.588.

Eisenberg, Daniel, Ezra Golberstein, Janis L. Whitlock, and Marilyn F. Downs. "Social Contagion of Mental Health: Evidence from College Roommates." *Health Economics* 22, no. 8 (2013): 965–986. https://doi.org/10.1002/hec.2873.

Keel, Pamela K., and K. Jean Forney. "Psychosocial Risk Factors for Eating Disorders." *International Journal of Eating Disorders* 46, no. 5 (2013): 433–439. https://doi.org/10.1002/eat.22094.

Lin, Linda, Hannah McCormack, Lauren Kruczkowski, and Michael B. Berg. "How Women's Perceptions of Peer Weight Preferences Are Related to Drive for Thinness." *Sex Roles* 72, no. 3–4 (2015): 117–126. https://doi.org/10.1007/s11199-015-0446-4.

Peebles, Rebecka, Shauna Harrison, Katherine McCown, Jenny Wilson, Dina Borzekowski, and James Lock. "101. Voices of Pro-Ana and Pro-Mia: A Qualitative Analysis of Reasons for Entering and Continuing Pro–Eating Disorder Website Usage." *Journal of Adolescent Health* 50, no. 2 (2012): S62. https://doi.org/10.1016/j.jadohealth.2011.10.167.

Vandereycken, Walter. "Can Eating Disorders Become 'Contagious' in Group Therapy and Specialized Inpatient Care?" *European Eating Disorders Review* 19, no. 4 (2011): 289–295. https://doi.org/10.1002/erv.1087.

Yakusheva, Olga, Kandice A. Kapinos, and Daniel Eisenberg. "Estimating Heterogeneous and Hierarchical Peer Effects on Body Weight Using Roommate Assignments as a Natural Experiment." *Journal of Human Resources* 49, no. 1 (2014): 234–261. https://doi.org/10.1353/jhr.2014.0002.

SOCIAL MEDIA AND EATING DISORDERS

The effect of the media on body image and disordered eating has been a subject of long-standing interest to researchers and clinicians. The media have been blamed as a cause or contributing factor in the development of negative body image and eating disorders. Further, exposure to of mass media has been consistently associated with body dissatisfaction due to the internalization of an ultrathin ideal, one of the strongest predictors of disordered-eating behaviors. The role of social networking and social media sites/platforms as specific pieces of media exposure are becoming an increasing focus for research. Recent research estimates that close to 90 percent of all 18- to 29-year-olds participate in some social networking site, with Facebook, Snapchat, and Instagram the most common. Social networking platforms, websites, and apps differ in key ways that could contribute to even higher rates of image internalization and body dissatisfaction when compared to traditional mass media (e.g., magazines, television shows, movies). Additionally, various forms of social media present different challenges related to body image and eating disorders.

How Is Social Media Different from Other Forms of Media?

Social networking sites offer a fundamentally distinct experience for a user than traditional mass media. Many of these differences have important implications for understanding the role of social media on body image. First, social media platforms are inherently interactive. Users can create content, hold conversations with others, rate different content, and share with others what they are viewing, thinking, doing. This is very different from the passive role of consumers in the case of traditional mass media. Second, social media is available anytime from (almost) anywhere, making it omnipresent in the daily lives of many Western adults. More so than many other forms of media, social media has been streamlined and created specifically for constant access, with a wide array of cell phone apps offering constant connectivity for social network users.

Last, the multimedia experience of social media creates an enhanced sense of presence for its users. Social networking apps and websites present users with an immersive, audiovisual experience using images, videos, and text. This can create a sort of transportation experience where someone becomes so emotionally and psychologically invested in the world of social media that they become lost in it, similar to how many people report becoming lost in a gripping book. This psychological sensation of getting lost in the world of social media is particularly critical for body image. Research has shown that individuals report adopting beliefs and values that are consistent with the milieu in which they get lost. This has been demonstrated in the case of readers who report a psychological transportation experience when reading a book, in individuals who report a similar experience while watching a movie, and for people who report heavy social media use. By becoming lost in the world of social networking, users are much more likely to internalize the images, attitudes, and values they are exposed to on those sites.

Research on the Impact of Social Media on Body Image and Eating Behaviors

The first social networking website was created roughly two decades ago, and social media has only seen a dramatic uptick in users, popularity, and an expansion in the roles it plays in daily lives. However, research on the effect these social media sites have on body image, eating behaviors, and affect is a relatively new avenue of exploration, with most of studies on these topics emerging past several years. Social media continues to be an area of focus for researchers in these fields, and future studies will continue to expand upon our current understanding.

The initial wave of research on this topic has shown considerable support for an association between social networking and body image. One study compared the impact that browsing Facebook had on participants' self-reported mood and body satisfaction to the impact that viewing a magazine website or a neutral website had on the same measures. The participants who were exposed to their Facebook home pages for 10 minutes reported a significantly worse mood than participants in the other two groups. Effects on body satisfaction were strongest for women who reported high self-comparison tendencies in the Facebook group. Other research has shown associations between social media use and self-reported pressure to be thin, look more attractive, lose weight, or otherwise change their appearance.

Several studies have offered more nuanced results that draw connections between certain social media–specific behaviors and body image concerns. One investigation found a significant association between social grooming behaviors (i.e., liking others' pictures, conversing with others online, and checking friends' profiles) and a drive for thinness. Other variables have also been shown to correlate with greater body dissatisfaction and disordered-eating behaviors, including time spent on social media, engagement in bigger online communities (e.g., having more Facebook friends), and photo-specific behaviors, such as posting photos and liking others' photos. Additionally, research has suggested the motivation for posting content on social networking may correlate with body image dissatisfaction. For example, users who exhibited more negative feedback–seeking behaviors in their social networking usage (i.e., posted statuses or pictures with negative self-disclosures, posted content with the intent of receiving negative comments/replies from others about themselves) predicted higher dietary restraint. Similarly, users who received negative comments in response to a personal self-disclosure via reported elevated body, shape, and weight preoccupation.

Social Comparison Theory and Social Media Usage

Social comparison is the prevailing theory used to explain *how* social media impacts body image. Social comparison theory (SCT) is a long-standing hypothesis that explains how people view themselves in relation to others. SCT believes it is natural to compare ourselves to others; doing so serves to inspire us and helps us evaluate ourselves, regulate our emotions, establish connections with others, and make decisions. In SCT, there are two types of social comparisons: upward social comparisons, when we compare ourselves to those who are superior to us or possess positive characteristics; and downward social comparisons, when we compare ourselves to those who are inferior to us or who possess negative characteristics. Both forms of comparison are common, used by everyone, and have pros and cons. Upward social comparisons can often inspire us to improve ourselves but can also contribute to lower self-esteem, lower mood, and a sense of inadequacy. Conversely, downward social comparisons can make us be thankful for our status or characteristics, but can contribute to selfishness and arrogance.

Social comparisons are extremely common on social networking sites; indeed, many social media platforms can actively encourage social comparisons through the activities available to users and the design of the website/app. Many social networking sites have algorithms that offer greater visibility to posts, users, or content that receives more likes, plays, comments, and so on. Through these different algorithms, designed to encourage participation on behalf of users, individuals are more likely to be exposed to highly popular images or profiles than to less popular content, which encourages upward social comparisons. The outcomes associated with upward social comparisons match with demonstrated outcomes from frequent social media use: lower self-esteem, higher dissatisfaction with one's appearance and/or social status, and greater internalization of beauty ideals.

Differences between Social Media Platforms

Increasing diversification between the niches filled by various social networking apps is becoming more common. Facebook, Snapchat, Instagram, Twitter, have a different user profile, design, and purpose than other platforms, such as LinkedIn or Pinterest. Although research on how these different social networking platforms affect body image and/or disordered eating is scarce, it is an emerging focus in the field. One study looked at the associations between various measures of mood, body satisfaction, and disordered eating and Facebook, Instagram, and Pinterest. Facebook—which centers on connection and communication between users via statuses, messages, photos, and videos—was associated with a greater perceived pressure to attain cultural standards of beauty. Instagram is a social media platform focused specifically on sharing and editing images with others; higher reported Instagram use was associated with specifically body image concerns and body shape preoccupation. Pinterest is closely related to Instagram in that it is an image-dominated social media app; however, Pinterest is focused on *sharing* content obtained from the Internet, magazines, and other sources as opposed to *creating* original content. Higher Pinterest usage was associated with higher participation in weight management/body control methods (e.g., dieting, exercising) and higher self-reported body shame. As social media becomes an increasingly prevalent pastime of adults around the world, new platforms and apps will undoubtedly emerge that serve niche audiences. Developing an understanding of what effects these different platforms have on users, as well as how users potentially self-select into different social networking communities, will enable researchers and clinicians to effectively monitor and identify at-risk individuals.

Hannah J. Hopkins

See also: Causes; Internet and Eating Disorders; Media; Pro-Ana; Social Contagion Theory

Bibliography

Fardouly, Jasmine, Phillippa C. Diedrichs, Lenny R. Vartanian, and Emma Halliwell. "Social Comparisons on Social Media: The Impact of Facebook on Young Women's Body Image Concerns and Mood." *Body Image* 13 (2015): 38–45. https://doi.org/10.1016/j.bodyim.2014.12.002.

Green, Melanie C., Timothy C. Brock, and Geoff F. Kaufman. "Understanding Media Enjoyment: The Role of Transportation into Narrative Worlds." *Communication Theory* 14, no. 4 (2004): 311–327. https://doi.org/10.1111/j.1468-2885.2004.tb00317.x.

Greenwood, Shannon, Andrew Perrin, and Maeve Duggan. "Social Media Update 2016." *Pew Research Center: Internet and Tech.* Last modified November 11, 2016. Accessed November 22, 2017. http://www.pewinternet.org/2016/11/11/social-media-update-2016/.

Holland, Grace, and Marika Tiggemann. "A Systematic Review of the Impact of the Use of Social Networking Sites on Body Image and Disordered Eating Outcomes." *Body Image* 17 (2016): 100–110. https://doi.org/10.1016/j.bodyim.2016.02.008.

Hummel, Alexandra C., and April R. Smith. "Ask and You Shall Receive: Desire and Receipt of Feedback via Facebook Predicts Disordered Eating Concerns." *International Journal of Eating Disorders* 48, no. 4 (2015): 436–442. https://doi.org/10.1002/eat.22336.

Kim, Ji Won, and T. Makana Chock. "Body Image 2.0: Associations between Social Grooming on Facebook and Body Image Concerns." *Computers in Human Behavior* 48 (2015): 331–339. https://doi.org/10.1016/j.chb.2015.01.009.

Pepin, Genevieve, and Natalie Endresz. "Facebook, Instagram, Pinterest and Co.: Body Image and Social Media." *Journal of Eating Disorders* 3, suppl. 1 (2015): O22. https://doi.org/10.1186/2050-2974-3-S1-O22.

Perloff, Richard M. "Social Media Effects on Young Women's Body Image Concerns: Theoretical Perspectives and an Agenda for Research." *Sex Roles* 71, no. 11–12 (2014): 363–377. https://doi.org/10.1007/s11199-014-0384-6.

Vogel, Erin A., Jason P. Rose, Lindsay R. Roberts, and Katheryn Eckles. "Social Comparison, Social Media, and Self-Esteem." *Psychology of Popular Media Culture* 3, no. 4 (2014): 206–222. https://doi.org/10.1037/ppm0000047.

SOCIAL PHYSIQUE ANXIETY

Social physique anxiety refers to worry associated with having one's body evaluated by others. Social physique anxiety (SPA) was coined in the late 1980s by researchers at Wake Forest University to conceptualize body-related anxiety as perceptual, cognitive, and behavioral components of body image. Individuals with higher SPA perceive negative evaluations by others in social situations and engage in strong impression management related to their presentation of self. For example, individuals with high SPA have a stronger tendency to hide perceived bodily flaws and to avoid social situations where their body may be evaluated (e.g., fitness centers, pool parties).

Self-Presentation and Social Physique Anxiety

Self-presentation refers to ways in which people seek to present themselves favorably to make a positive impression and avoid scrutiny. Individuals experience intense social anxiety when they perceive unfavorable reactions from others. This negative evaluation specific to one's body is social physique anxiety.

SPA and self-presentation are especially relevant for exercise settings where bodies are on display and evaluation by social others is likely. Individuals who have high SPA may avoid exercise settings that promote social interactions, may seek gyms with modest clothing policies, or may exercise in private. Individuals with high SPA tend to cover their bodies with loose-fitting clothing when they are in public. A study revealed adult women expressed more favorable opinions of an exercise class when participants wore less form-fitting clothing than when participants wore revealing attire. Furthermore, high SPA exercisers tended to position themselves at the back of a group exercise class. The presence of

SPA can serve as a barrier to activities that promote bodies on display (e.g., swimming, yoga).

Social physique anxiety has also been explored in different athletes. Gymnasts with higher SPA tended to have lower confidence about sport performance and lower physical self-perceptions. Dancers and cheerleaders in aesthetic activities had higher SPA scores than swimmers. Although all the participants (i e., dancers, cheerleaders, swimmers) wore revealing team uniforms, the participants in dance and cheerleading perceived the appearance of their bodies as having a direct effect on performance.

Assessment of Social Physique Anxiety

Researchers developed a survey to measure SPA in males and females of diverse ages and abilities. The original scale (i.e., the Social Physique Anxiety Scale [SPAS]) was published in 1989 with 12 items to assess level of anxiety surrounding evaluation of one's body. More recently, researchers have advocated using a 9-item version of SPAS, but both versions of the measure are widely used with athletes, exercisers of all ages, and persons with disabilities. An example of an item from the SPA is, "In the presence of others, I feel apprehensive about my physique or figure."

Justine J. Reel

See also: Anxiety Disorders; Body Image; Self-Presentation Theory

Bibliography

Bratrud, Sharon, Marissa M. Parmer, James R. Whitehead, and Robert C. Eklund. "Social Physique Anxiety, Physical Self-Perceptions and Eating Disorder Risk: A Two-Sample Study." *Pamukkale Journal of Sport Sciences* 1, no. 3 (2010): 1–10.

Hart, Elizabeth, Mark R. Leary, and W. Jack Rejeski. "The Measurement of Social Physique Anxiety." *Journal of Sport and Exercise Psychology* 11 (1989): 94–104.

Kowalski, Kent C., Diane E. Mack, Peter R. E. Crocker, Cory B. Niefer, and Tara-Leigh Fleming. "Coping with Social Physique Anxiety in Adolescence." *Journal of Adolescent Health* 39, no. 2 (2006): 275e9–275e16.

Leary, Mark R. *Self-Presentation: Impression Management and Interpersonal Behavior.* Boulder, CO: Westview Press, 1996.

Martin, Jeffrey J. "Predictors of Social Physique Anxiety in Adolescent Swimmers with Physical Disabilities." *Adapted Physical Activity Quarterly* 16 (1999): 75–85.

Martin, Jeffrey J. "Social Physical Anxiety, Body Image, Disability, and Physical Activity." In *Social Anxiety: Symptoms, Causes and Techniques,* edited by Theresa M. Robinson, 29–46. London: Nova Science, 2010.

Martin, Jeffrey J., Amy Kliber, Pamela Hodges Kulinna, and Marianne Fahlman. "Social Physique Anxiety and Muscularity and Appearance Cognitions in College Men." *Sex Roles* 55, no. 3–4 (2006). 151–158. https://doi.org/10.1007/s11199 006 9069 0.

Reel, Justine J., and Diane L. Gill. "Psychosocial Factors Related to Eating Disorders among High School and College Female Cheerleaders." *The Sport Psychologist* 10, no. 2 (1996): 195–206.

Reel, Justine J., Sonya SooHoo, Diane L. Gill, and Kathie M. Jamieson. "Femininity to the Extreme: Body Image Concerns among College Female Dancers." *Women in Sport and Physical Activity Journal* 14, no. 1 (2005): 39–51.

SOMATIC EXPERIENCING

Somatic Experiencing offers a new and hopeful perspective on trauma. Somatic Experiencing (SE), developed by Dr. Peter Levine, is a neuroscientific-based modality that uses *bottom up* processing rather than the cognitive processing found in most forms of talk therapy. SE comes from a belief and perspective that human beings have an instinctual capacity to heal. SE is based on the theory that when a body undergoes a highly stressful situation that prevents the natural fight-or-flight system from mobilizing, the nervous system can go into a freeze state from the dysregulation. The internal stress and emotion that arises from the event becomes locked in the body, unable to be released, leading to a multitude of trauma symptoms. Trauma symptoms can occur when a perceived life threat is experienced as overwhelming and one's natural protective and/or defensive responses (fight–flight) are unavailable or inaccessible in the moment to regulate the nervous system. In other words, people experience trauma not because of the event itself, but from an individual's response to the event, in the nervous system. Trauma is the emotional and physiological aftermath of an event, not the event itself. For example, two different people may experience the same event, but one may develop traumatic symptoms, including, but not limited to Post-Traumatic Stress Disorder, while the other may be unaffected.

Somatic Experiencing and Eating Disorders

When trauma is the cause of an eating disorder, SE often is a valuable therapeutic tool. Because SE is based on the notion that trauma is a physiological, not psychological condition, the body must be included in therapy. SE works to release and neutralize negative and activating tension stored or trapped on the body. As therapy progresses, this pent-up negative, activating energy is often released in the form of trembling, sweating, crying, and even yawning. In turn, physiological changes take place, in the form of new neuropathways created in the brain. It is these neuropathways that lead to changed behavior. Just as many factors contribute to the development of an eating disorder, many therapeutic strategies, such as SE, contribute in the opposite way, so that an eating disorder is no longer needed as a protective or defensive behavior. Somatic Experiencing practitioners facilitate an increased awareness of instinctual human sensations to guide a body to heal the effects of trauma. The focus of SE treatment is on creating self-awareness, tracking internal changes to restore self-regulation, renegotiating trauma in the nervous system, and deactivating the arousal contributing to PTSD, eating disorders, insomnia, anxiety, IBS, or depression. Somatic Experiencing is a model that integrates mind and body and can be instrumental in the treatment of eating disorders. Eating disorders can be expressions of feeling very separate from others and negative towards oneself. As a person begins to listen to their body through SE, they develop a relationship and a befriend themselves. As this sensory portion of our brain is stimulated, more awareness and connection to self is experienced. Connecting deeply with this somatic sense helps to be present in the moment, to be more objective, identify less with the critical voice, and experience a more calm and peaceful way of being. Our bodies can guide us to places of healing and wisdom, if we can have compassion enough to listen.

Somatic Experiencing is a new lens through which to see and understand the functioning of eating disorders. Our nervous systems have an instinctual response to act in protect and defensive ways. These expressions are often referred to as fight, flight, and/or freeze. It is common individuals who experience continuous and or early developmental trauma to be caught in a cycle of responding to people and situations through fight, flight, or freeze, regardless of the actual presence of threat. For these individuals, their physiology is stuck in the memory of the trauma and their body's instinct to protect and defend from the trauma, even though cognitively an individual may know there is nothing to defend or protect against. Considering the symptomology of eating disorders, the model of somatic experiencing can explain the somatic expression of these symptoms. For example, an individual who struggles with anxiety, thought rumination, obsessive compulsive urges, or excessive exercise is likely caught in the cycle of flight reaction and expression. Fight energy would show up as anger towards inward, such as self-harm, purging, and/or chewing and spitting. Freeze energy tends to manifest as dissociation, numbness, depression, and a disconnection to self and others. Individuals with eating disorders often have a disconnect between mind and body. SE provides an explanation for this disconnect. An individual's nervous system, caught in their trauma memory, is stuck in its instinctual pattern of trying to protect and defend from danger. Even when an individual is intellectually aware there is no threat or danger, the body has not processed the information and released the energy of the trauma, so it is trapped in the body and cycles through various expressions of that energy. The healing in the model of SE provides space for these individuals to discharge this energy through movements and activities in a therapeutic and safe environment. Once the body releases this energy and an individual can have a different felt experience, outside of the cycle of defensive and protective energies, and learn to connect to people and the world in a completely different and positive way.

Leslie Roach

See also: Trauma; Treatment

Bibliography

Brewerton, Timothy D. "The Links between PTSD and Eating Disorders." *Psychiatric Times* 25, no. 6 (2008): 1–7. Last modified May 1, 2008. Accessed November 22, 2017. http://www.psychiatrictimes.com/articles/links-between-ptsd-and-eating-disorders.

Levine, Peter. "Somatic Experiencing." Unpublished manuscript (1992). Accessed May 26, 2017. http://healthyfuturesaz.com/images/SEHandout.pdf.

Levine, Peter. "Somatic Experiencing: Resilience, Regulation, and Self." Unpublished paper (2005).

Merwin, Rhonda M., C. Alix Timko, Ashley A. Moskovich, Krista Konrad Ingle, Cynthia M. Bulik, and Nancy L. Zucker. "Psychological Inflexibility and Symptom Expression in Anorexia Nervosa." *Eating Disorders* 19, no. 1 (2010): 62–82. http://dx.doi.org/10.1080/10640266.2011.533606.

SORORITY WOMEN

Sororities are college organizations for female college students that provide a group identity, a social outlet, as well as leadership and philanthropic opportunities for members. Sororities have been stereotyped as breeding grounds for eating disorders with suspicion that binge and purge behaviors are rampant among sisters.

Disordered Eating and Sororities

Earlier studies provide evidence that joining a sorority contributes to eating-disordered behavior. For example, one researcher found when certain eating behaviors were modeled in peer groups (i.e., sorority friends) the behaviors became normalized and accepted. Although binge eating frequency was dissimilar between friends at the beginning of the semester, binge frequency was highly related by the end of the year.

A separate study found sorority sisters tended to be more attractive, had higher family incomes, and were more willing to attempt to fit in than nonsorority college females. Specifically, sorority sisters were found to have higher alcohol use and more body dissatisfaction and fear of fatness than a nonsorority comparison group. In another study, disordered eating, body mass index, and ideal weight did not differ between sorority and nonsorority women at baseline before women joined sororities. Interestingly, by the third year, sorority women reported significantly higher levels of dieting and concern for weight than nonsorority women who showed a gradual decrease in the preoccupation with thinness throughout their college years.

Justine J. Reel

See also: Body Mass Index; Myth of the "Freshman 15"; Prevention; Reflections

Bibliography

Allison, Kelly C., and Crystal L. Park. "A Prospective Study of Disordered Eating among Sorority and Nonsorority Women." *International Journal of Eating Disorders* 35 (2004): 354–358. https://doi.org/10.1002/eat.10255.

Becker, Carolyn Black, Anna C. Ciao, and Lisa M. Smith. "Moving from Efficacy to Effectiveness in Eating Disorders Prevention: The Sorority Body Image Program." *Cognitive and Behavioral Practice* 15 (2008): 18–27. http://dx.doi.org/10.1016/j.cbpra.2006.07.006.

Becker, Carolyn Black, Eric Stice, Heather Shaw, and Susan Woda. "Use of Empirically-Supported Interventions for Psychopathology: Can the Participatory Approach Move Us beyond the Research to Practice Gap?" *Behavioral Research Therapy* 47, no. 4 (2009): 265–274. https://doi.org/10.1016/j.brat.2009.02.007.

Hoerr, Sharon L., Ronda Bokram, Brenda Lugo, Tanya Bivins, and Debra R. Keast. "Risk for Disordered Eating Relates to Both Gender and Ethnicity for College Students." *Journal of American College of Nutrition* 21, no. 1 (2002): 307–314. http://dx.doi.org/10.1080/07315724.2002.10719228.

Piquero, Nicole Leeper, Kristan Fox, Alex R. Piquero, George Capowich, and Paul Mazerolle. "Gender, General Strain Theory, Negative Emotions and Disordered Eating." *Journal of Youth Adolescence* 39 (2010): 380–392. https://doi.org/10.1007/s10964-009-9466-0.

Scott-Sheldon, Lori A. J., Kate B. Carey, and Michael P. Carey. "Health Behavior and College Students: Does Greek Affiliation Matter?" *Journal of Behavioral Medicine* 31, no. 1 (2008): 61–70. https://doi.org/10.1007/s10865-007-9136-1.

SPORTS

For anyone who has ever played or coached sports, unhealthy eating patterns are a common subject—whether working to gain weight or to lose it, when healthy methods are not effective or fast enough, some athletes resort to unhealthy behavior. Although the reasons behind these unhealthy eating behaviors are still being studied, given the complex nature of eating disorders and disordered-eating behaviors, research and practical experience have combined to shed light on the nature of eating disorders in athletes.

Prevalence of Eating Disorders in Athletes

Prevalence rates of disordered eating in athletes vary from 0 percent to 62 percent across studies (i.e., 1–62 percent for female athletes and 0–57 percent for male athletes) depending on the measure, competitive level, and sport studied. In a prevalence study, 2.0 percent of female college athletes were classified as having a clinical eating disorder and an additional 25.5 percent of athletes exhibited disordered eating patterns. Furthermore, it was estimated 0.9 percent of female athletes and 0.3 percent of male athletes suffer from anorexia nervosa and 1.5 percent of females and 0.5 percent of males suffer from bulimia nervosa.

Athletes versus Nonathletes

The question of whether athletes are more at risk for eating disorders than nonathletes is complicated. Some studies have demonstrated athletes exhibit less preoccupation with weight and lower body dissatisfaction than nonathletes. Other researchers suggest athletes have greater perceptions of self-efficacy, or self-confidence in one's ability to succeed.

However, some studies indicate athletes are at greater risk for eating disorders than nonathletes. It has been argued athletes experience the same weight pressures nonathletes experience (e.g., pressure from family, friends, media), and may further experience weight pressures unique to sport participation (e.g., pressure from coaches, subjective evaluation by judges, uniform pressures). Regardless, when reviewing numerous studies with athletes, the differences of disordered eating rates between athletes and nonathletes are small. Results indicate that athletes in lean sports (e.g., gymnastics, wrestling, distance running), are at a greater risk for disordered-eating behaviors than athletes in nonlean sports (e.g., soccer, basketball, swimming) or nonathletes.

Lean versus Nonlean Sports

Classifying sports as either lean (e.g., diving, gymnastics, dance) or nonlean sports (e.g., ball sports, track and field, swimming) has been a common way to categorize athletes and identify the potential risk for disordered eating and eating disorders. In a study on eating disorders in elite athletes, researchers found 45 percent of lean sport athletes and fewer than 20 percent of nonlean sport athletes reported disordered-eating behaviors.

Because sports types are diverse, generalizing prevalence rates is difficult and lean versus nonlean is not always an accurate portrayal of prevalence rates in every sport. Therefore, some research has been done to expand sport categories (i.e., weight class, aesthetic, endurance, and team sports) and to investigate weight-related pressures in specific sports. For instance, weight class athletes such as wrestlers and bodybuilders exhibit a disordered eating prevalence between 15 and 17 percent. Aesthetic sports, including sports like diving, gymnastics, and figure skating, had an eating disorder prevalence rate of 18 percent. This group of sports has also been associated with additional sport-specific concerns such as subjective judging and revealing attire, which may increase their risk over other sport categories. A third category of lean sports includes endurance sports (e.g., distance running, cycling). Athletes in endurance sports have reported prevalence rates of nearly 10 percent for males and 25 percent for females at an elite level. Participants in antigravitational sports (e.g., ski jumping) have also experienced increased pressure to maintain a low body weight. Ski jumpers have traditionally maintained a low body weight because lower body weight increases the distance jumped. However, because athletes were using unhealthy means to maintain that low body weight, the International Ski Federation developed rules and procedures to guard against competing at too low of a BMI (e.g., ski length deductions based on weight in kilograms, minimum BMI of 18.5). Finally, one must not forget that nonlean sport athletes are also at risk for eating disorders. In a study on youth swimmers, 15 percent of female swimmers and 4 percent of male swimmers exhibited disordered-eating behaviors.

Competitive Levels

For girls and women, the prevalence of athletes with the female athlete triad—low energy availability, change in menstrual function, and low bone mineral density—increases as competitive levels increase. In high school female athletes, the prevalence rate for the female athlete triad has been estimated to be 18.2 percent, compared to 26.1 percent in college athletes and 46.2 percent for elite female athletes. Nonetheless, a clear relationship between level of competition and eating disorders has yet to be established and results are mixed. Although competitive level may not be an individual risk factor or a protective factor, it may work in concert with other factors in an athlete's life to either prevent or exacerbate disordered-eating behaviors.

Weight Loss Methods

Methods for attempted weight loss vary across athletes. For instance, in a study of the prevalence of eating disorders in male collegiate athletes, although none were classified as eating-disordered, of the 20 percent who exhibited symptoms of eating disorders, 32 percent excessively exercised to lose weight while 14.2 percent dieted and 10 percent used laxatives, diuretics, or self-induced vomiting. For female athletes, exercise for at least two hours a day specifically to burn calories was the most frequently reported method (25.5 percent). Another 15.7 percent of athletes admitted to dieting and less than 6 percent of female athletes reported using laxatives, diuretics, or vomiting to control weight. A less commonly reported method for weight loss involves using heat to sweat out water weight (e.g., the use of saunas or heavy layering of clothing while running). The use of thermal methods to lose weight is found more often in weight-dependent sports where weight-cycling is typical (e.g., wrestling).

Sport-Specific Considerations

Weight and Performance

To understand the nature of eating disorders in athletes, it is important to consider perceptions of how weight affects performance. At present, many athletes and coaches believe reduced weight helps performance. Improved physical ability (e.g., being lighter requires less energy while running long distances) or achieving an aesthetic based on long and thin lines are among the reported benefits of lower body weight. Consequently, athletes and coaches who believe reduced weight improves performance tend to hold rigid beliefs that weight gain will always negatively affect performance. Therefore, the goal becomes to keep weight down and to lose as much weight as possible to gain a performance advantage.

Research demonstrates body weight and performance have a curvilinear relationship. Therefore, while initial weight reductions yield short-term performance improvements when that athlete "thinks he is lighter or experiences a brief increase in VO_2 max (i.e., improved cardiovascular fitness by improved processing of oxygen in the body), in the long term and with continued weight loss, performance tends to drop sharply. By reducing the amount of energy consumed by the body, an athlete experiences physical (e.g., dehydration) and psychological (e.g., irritability) detriments. Other physical detriments include loss of lean body mass, fatigue, cardiovascular damage, and bone damage, whereas another psychological effect is decreased concentration. In combination, physical and psychological detriments may increase the risk of acute injury in athletes. More long-term consequences of continued weight loss are the risk of hypertension (i.e., high blood pressure) later in life, poor basal metabolism due to the body's response of protecting food stores, damage to the reproductive system, and increased risk of coronary heart disease, renal disease and failure, and irreversible bone damage.

Personality Characteristics of Athletes

Given the complex nature of eating disorders, it is important to consider the influence of individual differences on eating disorders in athletes. One study compared the personality characteristics of individuals with eating disorders and athletes and found shared personality characteristics. This is not to say all athletes with these characteristics are guaranteed to develop an eating disorder; rather, the same characteristics that help athletes succeed in sport are also evident in nonathletes with eating disorders.

Research on the similarities between good athletes and eating-disordered nonathletes included drive for perfection, desire for control, extreme self-discipline, detachment from feelings (such as pain), and the desire to please others. For instance, good athletes make sacrifices, ignoring stress and sensations of pain, in the pursuit of success. Similarly, individuals with anorexia nervosa ignore sensations of pain and hunger in their pursuit of continued weight loss. Additionally, good athletes exhibit a strong drive for perfectionism when they continually strive for improvement, are not satisfied with their current level of success, and are driven to be the best. Individuals with anorexia nervosa exhibit similar perfectionistic tendencies when they continually strive for thinness, do not accept their current body weight, and continue to use unhealthy weight loss methods to lose weight.

Subculture of Sport

The belief that weight loss can improve performance has resulted in specific sport subcultures and weight-related traditions. For example, some sport subcultures require rookies to carry equipment or have team sweat sessions where wrestlers exercise together in rubber suits. If sport subculture encourages unhealthy weight loss methods, disordered eating may become normalized in a particular team sport. Specifically, if a sport finds pathogenic weight loss methods acceptable (e.g., weight cycling in wrestling, overtraining in gymnastics), athletes may assume coaches and other sport professionals condone these unhealthy practices.

Additionally, some athletes may understand unhealthy weight loss methods are not acceptable to the public. However, if athletes see unhealthy practices are accepted in a sport, have benefited other athletes, will help them win, and are necessary to maintain team membership, those athletes may be motivated to engage in unhealthy weight loss methods regardless of the lack of acceptance outside of sport. Athletes learn about weight loss methods from teammates, practice them, and share them with other teammates. Eventually, teams may have most team members using similar weight loss strategies. Then, if the team is successful, athletes may be reinforced in their efforts to continue to lose weight.

Other Sport Considerations

Athletes are not immune to stressors experienced by the general population. Interestingly, the media are fraught with images of thinner-than-average women and more-muscular-than-average men in contrast to body expectations for sport. For example, female track and field throwers are expected to be muscular and athletic to succeed and long-distance male runners are encouraged to be lean and light to conserve energy while running.

Additionally, some athletes are required to meet weight-related guidelines. These may be in the form of weight limits at tryout, periodic weigh-ins throughout the season, and body fat percentage monitoring. The introduction of these rigid weight ideals may encourage athletes to lose more weight to maintain their position on the team.

The very nature of sport has also been shown to influence unhealthy eating behaviors. To excel in sport, athletes must be competitive. But for some athletes, it is not enough to be as powerful, as attractive, or as successful as other athletes; they want to be the best. Because competitiveness has been found to be related to body dissatisfaction and body dissatisfaction is related to characteristics of eating disorders, competitiveness may be a risk factor for eating disorders in athletes.

Ashley M. Coker-Cranney

See also: Aerobics; Aesthetic Sports; Anorexia Athletica; Athletic Trainers; Ballet; Bodybuilding; Cheerleading; Coaches; Dancers; Distance Running; Drill Team/ Dance Team; Endurance Sports; Exercise; Female Athlete Triad; Figure Skating; Gymnastics; Jockeys; Rowing; Ski Jumping; Swimming and Synchronized Swimming; Team Sports; Weight Class Sports; Weight Pressures in Sport; Yoga

Bibliography

Beals, Katherine A. *Disordered Eating among Athletes: A Comprehensive Guide for Health Professionals.* Champaign, IL: Human Kinetics, 2004

Brownell, Kelly D., Suzan Nelson Steen, and Jack H. Wilmore. "Weight Regulation Practices in Athletes: Analysis of Metabolic and Health Effects." *Medicine and Science in Sports and Exercise* 19, no. 6 (1987): 546–556.

Dosil, Joaquin. *Eating Disorders in Athletes.* Hoboken, NJ: John Wiley & Sons, 2008.

Galli, Nick, and Justine J. Reel. "Adonis or Hephaestus? Exploring Body Image in Male Athletes." *Psychology of Men & Masculinity* 10, no. 2 (2009): 95–108. http://dx.doi.org /10.1037/a0014005.

Greenleaf, Christy, Trent A. Petrie, Jennifer Carter, and Justine J. Reel. "Female Collegiate Athletes: Prevalence of Eating Disorders and Disordered Eating Behaviors." *Journal of American College Health* 57, no. 5 (2009): 489–495. http://dx.doi.org/10.3200 /JACH.57.5.489-496.

Johns, David P. "Fasting and Feasting: Paradoxes of the Sport Ethic." *Sociology of Sport Journal* 15 (1998): 41–63.

Peden, Jamie, Beverly L. Stiles, Michael Vandehey, and George Diekhoff. "The Effects of External Pressures and Competitiveness on Characteristics of Eating Disorders and Body Dissatisfaction." *Journal of Sport & Social Issues* 32, no. 4 (2008): 415–429. https://doi.org/10.1177/0193723508325638.

Petrie, Trent A. "Differences between Male and Female College Lean Sport Athletes, Non-lean Sport Athletes, and Nonathletes on Behavioral and Psychological Indices of Eating Disorders." *Journal of Applied Sport Psychology* 8, no. 2 (1996): 218–230. http://dx.doi .org/10.1080/10413209608406478.

Petrie, Trent A., Christy Greenleaf, Justine J. Reel, and Jennifer Carter. "Prevalence of Eating Disorders and Disordered Eating Behaviors among Male Collegiate Athletes." *Psychology of Men & Masculinity* 9, no. 4 (2008): 267–277. http://dx.doi.org/10.1037 /a0013178.

Smolak, Linda, Sarah K. Murnen, and Anne E. Ruble. "Female Athletes and Eating Problems: A Meta-Analysis." *International Journal of Eating Disorders* 27 (2000): 371–380.

Sundgot-Borgen, Jorunn, and Monica Klungland Torstveit. "Prevalence of Eating Disorders in Elite Athletes Is Higher Than in the General Population." *Clinical Journal of Sports Medicine* 14 (2004): 25–31.

Thompson, Ron A., and Roberta Trattner Sherman. "'Good Athlete' Traits and Characteristics of Anorexia Nervosa: Are They Similar?" *Eating Disorders* 7, no. 3 (1999): 181–190. http://dx.doi.org/10.1080/10640269908249284.

Thompson, Ron A., and Roberta Trattner Sherman. *Eating Disorders in Sport.* New York: Routledge, 2010.

Torstveit, M. K., J. H. Rosenvinge, and J. Sundgot-Borgen. "Prevalence of Eating Disorders and the Predictive Power of Risk Models in Female Elite Athletes: A Controlled Study." *Scandinavian Journal of Medicine and Science in Sports* 18 (2008): 108–118. https://doi.org/10.1111/j.1600-0838.2007.00657.x.

STUDENTS PROMOTING EATING DISORDER AWARENESS AND KNOWLEDGE

SPEAK, stands for Students Promoting Eating Disorder Awareness and Knowledge, a student organization at the University of Utah. The group was founded by the author in 2002 as a research team when several students approached her about learning the research process while expressing an interest in body image and eating disorders. Currently, the organization has over 85 active members including undergraduate and graduate students at the University of Utah and other universities, alumni, and professional members in the community. From its inception, SPEAK has focused on research and outreach and its mission as stated on its website (www.utah.edu/speak/) is to "promote awareness of eating disorders and body image issues through educating diverse populations, developing strategies for prevention, providing resources for treatment and conducting relevant research."

Outreach Projects

SPEAK has delivered presentations to prevent eating disorders and promote health in elementary, middle, and high schools, as well as college classes, church groups, and community groups (e.g., Boys and Girls Clubs). SPEAK receives requests to conduct workshops for women in substance abuse centers and midlife clinics about body image and building body confidence. In addition to outreach presentations and health fairs, SPEAK organizes an annual Love Your Body Week in conjunction with the National Eating Disorder Awareness Week (NEDAW). The weeklong event typically includes a recovery panel (SPEAK members share their eating disorder recovery stories), a film screening about body image issues, Love Your Body yoga, and other professional speakers. Purple ribbons are worn to raise awareness about eating disorders and in 2011, SPEAK initiated its "Post-it for better body image" campaign (see Operation Beautiful for full description). For the Maximum Impact theme of 2011 LYBW, SPEAK filmed a YouTube video *What do you LOVE about your body?* to encourage appreciation of one's body and to spread a positive message about body image.

In 2009, SPEAK partnered with *Wasatch Woman* magazine to organize a Love Your Body 5K/10K walk/run event to honor Tiffany Cupit who died from an eating disorder. Over 800 walkers and runners donned purple ribbons and participated in a health fair about healthy body image.

Research Efforts

SPEAK expanded internationally in 2010 to host several hundred professionals at the Treating Bodies across the Globe event that drew doctors, nurses, social workers, psychologists, and dietitians from as far as Japan to cover recent research about eating disorders and body image. Beginning in 2009, SPEAK began offering the SPEAK Tiffany Cupit Research Award to annually support student projects about body image and eating disorders. To date, seven SPEAK members have received this award.

Future of SPEAK

University of Utah continues to serve as the host university for SPEAK. The team has supported other schools (George Washington University, SUNY–Brockport, California State University at Channel Islands, Brigham Young University, Xavier University, and Utah Valley University) to begin SPEAK chapters. SPEAK has also partnered with professionals in the community to offer ongoing education programs to parents, youth, and professionals as well as to continue to provide a yearly Love Your Body Week. SPEAK will continue to provide outreach and offer treatment referrals and resources to the community.

Justine J. Reel

See also: Advocacy Groups; Full of Ourselves; Prevention; Recovery

Bibliography

"Students Promoting Eating Disorder Awareness and Knowledge." University of Utah College of Health. Accessed November 18, 2016. http://health.utah.edu/health-kinesiology-recreation/health/opportunities/speak/.

"What Do You LOVE about Your Body?" Accessed November 18, 2016. https://www.youtube.com/watch?v=Hrmgtn7kJJ8.

SUBSTANCE ABUSE

Substance abuse refers to an unhealthy pattern of drug or alcohol use that results in significant life problems, such as failure to take care of one's responsibilities at work or home, or legal problems. Eating disorders and substance use disorders commonly co-occur. Up to 35 percent of persons with substance abuse disorders have eating disorders and up to 50 percent of persons with eating disorders have a problem with drug or alcohol abuse. This is a substantial rate as only 9 percent of the general population abuse alcohol or illicit drugs. Persons with eating disorders are up to five times likelier than persons in the general population to abuse alcohol or illegal drugs and persons who abuse alcohol or drugs are up to 11 times likelier to have an eating disorder.

Risk Factors for Substance Abuse and Eating Disorders

Eating disorders and substance use disorders share many risk factors. These include: occurrence in times of transition or stress; common brain chemistry; common family histories; low self-esteem, depression, anxiety, and impulsivity; history of sexual or physical abuse; unhealthy parental behaviors and low monitoring of children's activities; unhealthy peer norms and social pressures; and susceptibility to messages from advertising, entertainment, and other media.

Eating disorders and substance abuse also have many characteristics in common. Both disorders include a component of obsessive preoccupation with substances, food, or behaviors, and cravings. Individuals with eating disorders and individuals with substance abuse engage in compulsive behaviors, secretiveness about their behaviors, and rituals. Individuals in both groups often present with a denial of the presence and severity of a disorder. Both disorders are difficult to treat, require intensive therapy, and have a high rate of comorbidity with other psychiatric disorders. They are both life threatening and are chronic diseases with high relapse rates.

Bulimia Nervosa and Substance Abuse

Of eating disorders, bulimia nervosa, has the highest overlap with substance abuse. Researchers estimate 30–70 percent of individuals with bulimia nervosa abuse alcohol, tobacco, or drugs. One study found individuals with substance use disorders and bulimia displayed lower impulse control, greater affective lability, more stimulus seeking behavior, a higher degree of self-harm, more anxiety and conduct disorders, and more borderline or antisocial personality disorder diagnoses than persons diagnosed with bulimia nervosa alone.

Anorexia Nervosa and Substance Abuse

Research suggests 12–18 percent of individuals with anorexia nervosa also abuse drugs or alcohol. In this group, the majority with substance abuse disorders have anorexia binge/purge type as opposed to anorexia/restricting type. This is probably due to a greater link to impulsive behaviors and a novelty-seeking temperament in persons with purging subtypes of eating disorders and in persons with substance abuse histories.

Addictive Characteristics

Some researchers have claimed the comorbidity of these disorders is part of an overall addictive dimension of personality. Many researchers have argued bulimia nervosa and substance use disorder are different manifestations of an underlying predisposition to addiction. Although eating disorders and substance use disorders are separate mental health diagnoses with different approaches to addiction, the two disorders share a similarity in motivational structure and clinicians should be aware that shifting between disorders is to be expected.

Individuals with bulimia nervosa and substance use disorders have higher rates of other co-occurring psychiatric disorders, including depression, anxiety, post-traumatic stress disorder (PTSD), and personality disorders, than persons with bulimia nervosa alone. There are higher rates of sexual abuse history in persons with bulimia nervosa and persons with substance abuse disorders than the general population. Persons with bulimia nervosa and substance abuse disorders are more likely to report a history of sexual abuse than persons with bulimia nervosa alone.

The high rate of comorbidity between eating disorders and substance abuse is an area of clinical concern. Clinicians should take a careful history of substance use when clients seek treatment for eating disorders. Piran and Gadalla suggest there is a need for development and use of short screening instruments for adult women with eating disorders and substance abuse. Some researchers have asserted the risk for drug abuse in clients with eating disorders continues over time and should be continually monitored throughout treatment.

Treatment Approaches for Comorbid Substance Abuse and Eating Disorders

Treatment approaches addressing both conditions may be more effective than approaches that focus exclusively or specifically on the disorder for which a person sought treatment. Research is needed to develop strategies to address the co-occurrence of substance use and eating disorders. Clients with a dual diagnosis of a substance use disorder and an eating disorder present with unique and difficult challenges. They often have a willingness to examine only certain behaviors while denying the existence or severity of other problematic behaviors. For example, a client may be willing to examine her binge and purge behaviors while denying her alcohol use is problematic. Clients with this dual diagnosis are often resistant to letting go of unhealthy, maladaptive coping strategies such as disordered eating, purging, excessive exercise, or substance abuse. Unfortunately, there is some evidence that substance abuse is correlated with worse outcomes from eating disorder recovery.

Jessica Guenther

See also: Anxiety Disorders; Comorbidity; Personality Disorders; Self-Injury; Trauma

Bibliography

Herzog, David B., Debra L. Franko, David J. Dorer, Pamela K. Keel, Safi Jackson, and Mary Pat Manzo. "Drug Abuse in Women with Eating Disorders." *International Journal of Eating Disorders* 39, no. 5 (2006): 364–368. https://doi.org/10.1002/eat.20257.

Killeen, Therese K., Shelly F. Greenfield, Brian E. Bride, Lisa Cohen, Susan Merle Gordon, and Paul M. Roman. "Assessment and Treatment of Co-Occurring Eating Disorders in Privately Funded Addiction Treatment Programs." *The American Journal on Addictions* 20, no. 3 (2011): 205–211. https://doi.org/10.1111/j.1521-0391.2011.00122.x.

Krug, Isabel, Andrea Poyastro Pinheiro, Cynthia Bulik, Susana Jimenez-Murcia, Roser Granero, Eva Penelo, Cristina Masuet, Zaida Aguera, and Fernando Fernandez-Aranda. "Lifetime Substance Abuse, Family History of Alcohol Abuse/Dependence and Novelty Seeking in Eating Disorders: Comparison Study of Eating Disorder Subgroups." *Psychiatry and Clinical Neurosciences* 63 (2009): 82–87. https://doi.org/10.1111/j.1440-1819.2008.01908.x.

Piran, Niva, and Tahany Gadalla. "Eating Disorders and Substance Abuse in Canadian Women: A National Study." *Addiction* 102, no. 1 (2007): 105–113. https://doi.org/10.1111/j.1360-0443.2006.01633.x.

Piran, Niva, Shannon R. Robinson, and Holly C. Cormier. "Disordered Eating Behaviors and Substance Use in Women: A Comparison of Perceived Adverse Consequences." *Eating Disorders* 15, no. 5 (2007): 391–403. http://dx.doi.org/10.1080/10640260701667896.

Ram, A., D. Stein, S. Sofer, and S. Kreitler. "Bulimia Nervosa and Substance Use Disorder: Similarities and Differences." *Eating Disorders* 16, no. 3 (2008): 224–240. http://dx.doi.org/10.1080/10640260802016803.

Sinha, Rajita, and Stephanie S. O'Malley. "Alcohol and Eating Disorders: Implications for Alcohol Treatment and Health Services Research." *Alcoholism: Clinical and Emotional Research* 24, no. 8 (2000): 1312–1319. https://doi.org/10.1111/j.1530-0277.2000.tb02097.x.

Varner, Lisa M. "Dual Diagnosis: Patients with Eating and Substance-Related Disorders." *Journal of the American Dietetic Association* 95, no. 2 (1995): 224–225.

SUICIDE

Suicide is a major cause of death in individuals with anorexia nervosa and bulimia nervosa. Suicide and eating disorders have shown varying levels of comorbidity across studies but present a concern due to risk for fatality.

Prevalence of Suicide

Adolescent suicide has received increased attention as a link to bullying and other mental disorders has identified. It has been estimated that 2 million people die because of homicide or suicide. Of 877,000 suicides around the world in 2002 alone, 200,000 suicides were adolescents. Suicide is a leading cause of death for adolescents in the world and rates are increasing faster in teens than in other age categories. Of 4 million suicide attempts annually, 90,000 adolescents complete the suicide, which is one suicide every five minutes. Causes of suicide include mental health disorders such as depression, substance abuse, and eating disorders. Other triggers like loss of friends, weight-related teasing or bullying, social isolation, and academic failure are identified as links to suicidal attempts and suicide. Self-harm behaviors are associated with suicidal attempts and suicide.

Relationship between Self-Injurious Behavior and Suicide

Deliberate self-harm or self-injurious behavior refers to hurting oneself intentionally. The most common self-harm methods have included overdosing, self-poisoning, and self-cutting. Cutting among U.S. adolescents was estimated to range from 26 to 37 percent of 9th to 12th graders. Self-harm behaviors can be repetitive and are associated with increased depression, suicidal ideation, and suicide attempts. Suicide can result from either chronic conditions surrounding self-harm behaviors or by accident, if self-harm behavior (e.g., overdose) turns fatal. Specifically, the overall risk of suicide increases if self-harm persists, with a 1.7 percent increase after 5 years, 2.4 percent increase after 10 years, and 3.0 percent increase after 15 years. Five percent of self-harm clients who are hospitalized or require emergency care commit suicide within nine years of the self-harm incident. Youths who cut their wrists have higher suicide risks than individuals who cut their arms.

Anorexia Nervosa, Bulimia Nervosa, and Suicide

Eating disorders have been associated with cutting and other self-harm behaviors. Eating-disordered individuals describe self-injurious behavior as a way to cope with intense emotions or to experience their pain. Children who suffer from sexual abuse were at increased risk for developing self-cutting behavior, which is related to eating disorders and suicidal ideation. Bulimia nervosa compared to other types of eating disorders has been most clearly associated with self-harm and suicide risk with one study demonstrating a history of suicide attempts was prevalent among 16.6 percent of bulimic subjects. In fact, suicide is one of the most frequently reported causes of death in bulimic clients. Approximately 25 percent of bulimic individuals who attempt suicide report more than one suicide attempt with repeaters at greater risk of death than nonrepeaters. Another study found 22.1 percent of anorexia nervosa clients and 10.9 percent of bulimia nervosa clients had at least one suicidal attempt. Males with bulimia have been found to be especially at risk for suicide attempts and suicide; however, both males and females and individuals diagnosed with an eating disorder present a risk for comorbidity with suicide.

Justine J. Reel

See also: Comorbidity; Military; Mortality Rates; Self-Injury

Bibliography

Favaro, Angela, and Paolo Santonastaso. "Different Types of Self-Injurious Behavior in Bulimia Nervosa." *Comprehensive Psychiatry* 40, no. 1 (1999): 57–60. http://dx.doi.org/10.1016/S0010-440X(99)90078-0.

Franko, Debra L., and Pamela K. Keel. "Suicidality in Eating Disorders: Occurrence, Correlates and Clinical Implications." *Clinical Psychology Review* 26, no. 6 (2006): 769–782. https://doi.org/10.1016/j.cpr.2006.04.001.

Franko, Debra L., Pamela K. Keel, D. J. Dover, S. S. Delinsky, K. T. Eddy, V. Charat, R. Renn, and David B. Herzog. "What Predicts Suicide Attempts in Women with Eating Disorders?" *Psychological Medicine* 34 (2004): 843–853.

Greydanus, Donald E., and Daniel Shek. "Deliberate Self-Harm and Suicide in Adolescents." *Keio Journal of Medicine* 58, no. 3 (2009): 144–151. http://doi.org/10.2302/kjm.58.144.

Milos, Gabriella, Anja Spindler, Urs Hepp, and Ulrich Schnyder. "Suicide Attempts and Suicidal Ideation: Links with Psychiatric Comorbidity in Eating Disorder Subjects."

General Hospital Psychiatry 26, no. 2 (2004): 129–135. https://doi.org/10.1016/j.genhosp-psych.2003.10.005.

Pompili, Maurizio, Paolo Girardi, Giulia Tatarelli, Amedeo Ruberto, and Roberto Tatarelli. "Suicide and Attempted Suicide in Eating Disorders, Obesity, and Weight Image." *Eating Behaviors* 7, no. 4 (2006): 384–394. https://doi.org/10.1016/j.eatbeh.2005.12.004.

SWIMMING AND SYNCHRONIZED SWIMMING

Swimming is a popular sport in the United States for both males and females who compete in summer leagues, year-round programs, high schools, and colleges. Swimming events in the Summer Olympics have brought faces to the sport along with increased media attention. For example, Amanda Beard, a breaststroke champion, posed for *Playboy* magazine, representing the growing trend of sexualizing athletes and rewarding them for appearance attributes that go beyond sport prowess. Synchronized swimming represents a unique water sport that requires flexibility, strength, power, grace, and control. Although this sport has received less attention than other water sports (e.g., competitive swimming, diving), synchronized swimming has characteristics like other aesthetic and leanness-demand sports like figure skating, gymnastics, and diving. For example, competitors in synchronized swimming wear revealing team uniforms and are judged based upon an artistic aesthetic.

History of Synchronized Swimming

Synchronized swimming became an Olympic sport at the 1984 Los Angeles Summer Games. Initially, both solo and duet events were included in the Olympics; however, in 2000 at the Sydney Olympic Games, the solo event was eliminated, and the team event was added. Historically, men have not competed in synchronized swimming and feminine qualities have been valued and emphasized in the sport. Males are beginning to participate in certain geographic areas at lower levels.

Body Image and Disordered Eating in Synchronized Swimming

As a judged sport that emphasizes a particular aesthetic, synchronized swimming athletes face pressure to be thin and change their appearance. For duet and team competitions, synchronized swimming athletes are rewarded for symmetry and for appearing identical in shape with limbs of a similar length and size. A rare study that investigated body esteem of 42 elite synchronized swimming athletes found synchronized swimmers reported greater negative perceptions about appearance and had lower body mass index scores (19.2) than nonleanness-demand sport participants (21.2) or female nonathletes (19.9).

Body Image and Disordered Eating in Swimmers

Swimming is classified as a nonlean or endurance sport in eating disorder studies. In early 1987, a study found 15 percent of female and 3.6 percent of male swimmers admitted to using pathogenic weight control methods. A separate Spanish study reported 10 percent of swimmers vomited to lose weight, a higher prevalence than any of the other 17 women's sports in the sample. A Brazilian study found 45 percent of swimmers engaged in disordered-eating behaviors.

Swimmers have reported stronger body satisfaction and less social physique anxiety than athletes from other sports (e.g., aesthetic sports). However, 45 percent of Division II and III female swimmers believed a swimsuit increases body consciousness. Furthermore, swimmers wore racing suits that were a couple of sizes smaller to gain a perceived competitive advantage and reduce drag. Motivation to lose body weight was related to the perception that one's performance would improve. Another reason provided by swimmer to decrease body weight was an attempt to meet societal beauty ideals beyond the sport.

Justine J. Reel

See also: Aesthetic Sports; Endurance Sports; Sports; Team Sports; Weight Pressures in Sport

Bibliography

Ferrand, Claude, Claire Magnan, and Roberta Antonini Philippe. "Body Esteem, Body Mass Index and Risk for Disordered Eating among Adolescents in Synchronized Swimming." *Perceptual and Motor Skills* 101, no. 3 (2005): 877–884. https://doi.org/10.2466/pms.101.3.877-884.

Mountjoy, Margo. "Injuries and Medical Issues in Synchronized Olympic Sports." *Current Sports Medicine Reports* 8, no. 5 (2009): 255–261. https://doi.org/10.1249/JSR.0b013e3181b84a09.

People for the Ethical Treatment of Animals (PETA). "Amanda Beard Poses Nude to Help Save Animals on Fur Farms." Accessed November 18, 2016. https://secure.peta.org/site/Advocacy?cmd=display&page=UserAction&id=1989.

Reel, Justine J., and Katherine A. Beals, eds. *The Hidden Faces of Eating Disorders and Body Image.* Reston, VA: AAHPERD/NAGWS, 2009.

Reel, Justine J., and Diane L. Gill. "Slim Enough to Swim? Weight Pressures for Competitive Swimmers and Coaching Implications." *The Sport Journal* 4 (2001): 1–5.

Schtscherbyna, Annie, Eliane Abreu Soares, Fatima Plaha de Oliveira, and Beatriz Goncalves Ribeiro. "Female Athlete Triad in Elite Swimmers of the City of Rio de Janeiro, Brazil." *Nutrition* 25 (2009): 634–639. https://doi.org/10.1016/j.nut.2008.11.029.

Thompson, Ron A., and Roberta Trattner Sherman. *Eating Disorders in Sport.* New York: Routledge, 2010.

TANNING BEHAVIORS AND BODY IMAGE

Tanning exposes the body to ultraviolet radiation (UV) from sun, sunlamps, tanning beds, or tanning booths for cosmetic purposes. According to the Skin Cancer Foundation, a majority (70 percent) of the 1 million people who visit tanning salons are Caucasian females 16 to 49 years of age. Significantly, use of indoor tanning (e.g., tanning beds) among Caucasian female teenagers was at 30–40 percent, and in a separate study it was estimated that 2.3 million teens tan indoors using tanning salons and sunlamps. Furthermore, students 14 years and younger were significantly more likely to wear sunscreen than older high school students. Females were more likely to use sunscreen than males; however, females thought it was worth having a sunburn to achieve a tan and reported at least three sunburns the previous summer.

Body Image and Tanning Practices

Although people seem to understand the risks associated with UV exposure and skin cancer, they still choose to engage in tanning behaviors when they think having a suntan will enhance physical appearance. In fact, tanning was cited as one of the most commonly used methods to improve physical beauty along with clothing, exercise, dieting, and personality. Although other cultures (e.g., Japan) have traditionally viewed pale skin as the symbol of beauty and wealth, U.S. culture supports a notion that tanned skin represents a healthy, youthful glow.

In a rare investigation of tanning behaviors and body image in gay males, of 215 respondents, 52 participated in sun tanning, 34 frequented tanning salons, and 26 used cosmetic tanning (i.e., liquids, gels, and powders to change the color of the skin). Tanning behaviors in this study were most associated with the desire to look attractive. In a separate study of male and female college students, females reported higher appearance motives to engage in tanning practices.

Tanorexia refers to a tanning addiction, labeling individuals who engage in excessive tanning behaviors (e.g., sunbathing, use of tanning beds to the extreme, usually for the cosmetic purpose of achieving a tanned appearance). This addiction, not been formally identified in the fifth edition of the *Diagnostic and Statistical Manual of Mental Disorders*, parallels eating disorders due to the tendency to be obsessive in behaviors (e.g., tanning beds) related to body image concerns. Much media attention has been given to the case of a mother who took her five-year-old daughter into a tanning booth with her. Because unhealthy tanning practices are often linked to appearance demands, it is recommended programming for eating disorder prevention and skin cancer prevention be combined to address both skin health and body image issues.

Justine J. Reel

See also: Body Image; Body Image Globally; Cosmetic Surgery and Eating Disorders; Media

Bibliography

Cafri, Guy, J. Kevin Thompson, Paul B. Jacobsen, and Joel Hillhouse. "Investigating the Role of Appearance-Based Factors in Predicting Sunbathing and Tanning Salon Use." *Journal of Behavioral Medicine* 32 (2009): 532–544. https://doi.org/10.1007/s10865-009-9224-5.

Cafri, Guy, J. Kevin Thompson, Megan Roehrig, Ariz Rojas, Steffanie Sperry, Paul B. Jacobsen, and Joel Hillhouse. "Appearance Motives to Tan and Not Tan: Evidence for Validity and Reliability for a New Scale." *Annuals of Behavioral Medicine* 35 (2008): 209–220. https://doi.org/10.1007/s12160-008-9022-2.

Dixon, Helen G., Charles D. Warne, Maree L. Sully, Melanie A. Wakefield, and Suzzane J. Dobbinson. "Does the Portrayal of Tanning in Australian Women's Magazines Relate to Real Women's Tanning Beliefs and Behavior?" *Health Education and Behavior* 38, no. 2 (2011): 132–142. https://doi.org/10.1177/1090198110369057.

Mahler, Heike I. M., James A. Kulik, Fredrick X. Gibbons, Megan Gerrard, and Jody Harrell. "Effects of Appearance-Based Interventions on Sun Protection Intentions and Self-Reported Behaviors." *Health Psychology* 22, no. 2 (2003): 199–209. http://dx.doi.org/10.1037/0278-6133.22.2.199.

Pettijohn II, Terry F., Terry F. Pettijohn, and Kaela S. Geschke. "Changes in Sun Tanning Attitudes and Behaviors of U.S. College Students from 1995 to 2005." *College Student Journal* 43, no. 1 (2009): 161–165.

Reilly, Andrew, and Nancy A. Rudd. "Sun, Salon, and Cosmetic Tanning: Predictors and Motives." *International Journal of Humanities and Social Sciences* 2, no. 3 (2008): 170–176.

Reynolds, Diane. "Literature Review of Theory-Based Empirical Studies Examining Adolescent Tanning Practices." *Dermatology Nursing* 19, no. 5 (2007): 440–447.

TEAM SPORTS

Teams or groups share a collective sense of identity and defined roles and responsibilities. Most sports are played using teams rather than individual participation (e.g., diving or figure skating). Team sports have sometimes been defined by researchers as sports requiring anaerobic training (i.e., short-duration and high-intensity activities) and use of a ball. However, many team sports involve a variety of both aerobic and anaerobic training regimens and a range of sports equipment. Team sports can include basketball, soccer, field hockey, ice hockey, lacrosse, baseball, softball, football, and volleyball.

Team Sports, Disordered Eating, and Body Image

Some research suggests fewer team sport athletes experience clinical eating disorders compared to athletes who compete as individuals. One study revealed only 1 percent of team sport athletes reported a current or previous diagnosis of anorexia nervosa compared to 3.5 percent of endurance sport athletes and 5.6 percent of aesthetic sport athletes. Similarly, 2.1 percent of team sport athletes reported a current or previous diagnosis of bulimia nervosa compared to 1.6 percent and 5.6 percent of endurance and aesthetic sport athletes, respectively. In addition, preliminary research suggests individual sport athletes exhibit greater self-consciousness of their physique and engage in more dieting and bulimic behavior than team sport athletes. It may be argued there is far less social evaluation and exposure of one's physique in team-based athletics because performances are carried out in groups rather than individually. However, it is also plausible that athletes in team sports may already focus less on weight and self-select into a team sport environment that does not emphasize weight, body shape, and appearance.

Despite evidence suggesting team sport athletes are less at risk for clinical eating disorders than other sport types, disordered eating can be found in these athletes. Research also shows the prevalence of eating disorders in ball game sports alone, like handball, volleyball, basketball, and soccer, is 5 percent for male participants and 16 percent for female participants. Although ball game sports have not traditionally been considered high-risk sports for eating disorders, prevalence rates in female ball game participants have increased from 11 percent in 1990 to 16 percent in 1997. Researchers postulate such increases are due to a greater emphasis on appearance and body composition assessments, particularly at elite levels.

Weight Pressures

Pressures to lose or maintain weight in some team sports come from a variety of sources. In a study of 204 collegiate female athletes, the most frequently-cited sources of weight pressures were teammates (36.8 percent), the team uniform (34.3 percent), and the coach (33.8 percent). More specifically, athletes may fear teammates will notice weight gain, become self-conscious wearing the form-fitting or revealing uniforms required by a sport (e.g., tight spandex shorts in volleyball), or engage in unhealthy weight loss techniques because of a body-related comment made by a coach.

Other sources of body-related pressure may include team weigh-ins. Although weighing athletes may be strategically used to ensure a healthy weight is maintained and to avoid dehydration, performing routine weigh-ins in public can be psychologically harmful to an athlete and may lead to the adoption of pathogenic eating behaviors, such as self-induced vomiting, fasting, or the abuse of laxatives, diet pills, and diuretics.

Media exposure of team sport athletes is also a noted source of pressure to lose or maintain weight. For example, the swimsuit edition of *Sports Illustrated* is photos of female athletes around the world in suggestive positions and barely there clothing. Hundreds of magazines and other media forums publish lists of the most attractive, beautiful, or *hottest* female athletes of the year with little, if any, acknowledgment of their athletic accomplishments. Some female athletes, such as world-renowned soccer player Brandi Chastain, have explained they posed nude as a means of empowerment rather than to project sexual appeal. Other athletes have reported that they wanted to assert their femininity. Many scholars argue such behavior only further belittles women's athleticism and promotes patriarchal power. Research has shown the type of female athlete images displayed may have a negative effect on young girls. More specifically, exposure to images of female athletes performing their sport triggers a focus on what their bodies can do, while exposure to sexualized images of female athletes triggers negative statements about their bodies.

Revealing photos of female athletes promotes the notion that fitness and athletic success are equated with thinness when fitness and athletic performance cannot be determined by appearance alone. Organizations like the Women's Sports Foundation have a number of resources to promote female athletes in positive ways and prevent the objectification of female athletes through the media and other social forums.

Team Sport Subculture

Teams may be vulnerable to contagion or spreading of disordered-eating behaviors in athletes based on the norms developed by a team and coaches. For example, some teams may develop a subculture that supports weight loss, and teammates may exchange strategies on how to alter weight, shape, or appearance (e.g., how to purge). Teammates may also engage in size and shape comparisons because they often shower and dress together. Because athletes are competitive to start with, team sport athletes may compete with their peers on thinness as well. This may be especially true in aesthetic sport teams, such as collegiate gymnastics, where athletes on the same team must compete with one another for spots on a line-up that will ultimately be judged based on both performance and appearance standards. The revealing uniforms required in some team sports like volleyball may also increase size and shape comparisons between teammates because of the desire to look good while on the court. Some scholars believe female athletes may strive to meet thin ideal standards to attract fans and encourage game attendance.

Although not often studied specifically in sports, peer influence is predictive of disordered eating in nonathlete populations. Given the quantity and quality of time spent on a team, it can be anticipated a similar relationship exists between peer influence and disordered eating in the context of sports. However, while the attitudes and behaviors of teammates may create a subculture that promotes thinness and unhealthy weight loss techniques, teammates may just as easily promote an environment that supports healthy nutrition and body image with the right education and modeling from supportive adults, including coaches, as well as team captains. In addition, when a member of a team struggles with or receives treatment for an eating disorder, teammates can provide important support for an athlete. The team atmosphere, although potentially detrimental in some cases, may therefore be quite useful to prevent disordered eating and body image concerns in athletes.

Benefits of Team Sport Participation

Team sport participation is linked to a range of benefits. For example, findings from one study suggested the time spent on the team, but not individual sports, is associated with enhanced sport self-concept (i.e., improved perceptions of one's sport abilities) and, therefore, greater self-esteem. Another study revealed mothers of kindergarten through third-grade children perceived the greatest number of benefits come from team sport participation compared to individual sports, the performing arts, or community recreational activities. These benefits can include character development, improved academic achievement, and the acquisition of important social skills. Other research suggests youth sport coaches both expect and believe that youth athletes have fun, learn important life skills, and build confidence through sport participation. This is especially true when coaches promote physically and psychologically safe sport environments and use teachable moments to purposefully build character and life skills in athletes. In sum, team sports have been identified as an important avenue for building positive developmental outcomes in youth participants.

Dana K. Voelker

See also: Cheerleading; Coaches; Female Athlete Triad; Gymnastics; Sports; Swimming and Synchronized Swimming; Weight Pressures in Sport

Bibliography

Beals, Katherine A., and Melinda M. Manore. "Disorders of the Female Athlete Triad among Collegiate Athletes." *International Journal of Sport Nutrition and Exercise Metabolism* 12 (2002): 281–293. https://doi.org/10.1123/ijsnem.12.3.281.

Daniels, Elizabeth. "Sex Objects, Athletes, and Sexy Athletes: How Media Representations of Women Athletes Can Impact Adolescent Girls and College Women." *Journal of Adolescent Research* 24 (2009): 399–422. https://doi.org/10.1177/0743558409336748.

Gould, Daniel, and Sarah Carson. "Life Skills Development through Sport: Current Status and Future Directions." *International Review of Sport and Exercise Psychology* 1 (2008): 58–78. http://dx.doi.org/10.1080/17509840701834573.

Haase, Anne M. "Physique Anxiety and Disordered Eating Correlates in Female Athletes: Differences in Team and Individual Sports." *Journal of Clinical Sports Psychology* 2 (2009): 218–231.

Reel, Justine J., Sonya SooHoo, Trent A. Petrie, Christy Greenleaf, and Jennifer E. Carter. "Slimming Down for Sport: Development of Weight Pressures in Sport Measure for Female Athletes." *Journal of Clinical Sport Psychology* 4, no. 2 (2010): 99–111.

Sundgot-Borgen, Jorunn, and Monica Klungland Torstveit. "Prevalence of Eating Disorders in Elite Athletes Is Higher Than in the General Population." *Clinical Journal of Sports Medicine* 14 (2004): 25–32.

Thompson, Ron A., and Roberta Trattner Sherman. "Athletes, Athletic Performance, and Eating Disorders: Healthier Alternatives." *Journal of Social Issues* 55, no. 2 (1999): 317–377. https://doi.org/10.1111/0022-4537.00118.

TEASING

Teasing is negative commentary, such as joking and name calling. Teasing or emotional bullying is reported by one in four children and often includes social exclusion, being singled out, and being humiliated by others. Teasing related to one's weight is particularly common and can involve parents making weight-related comments.

Weight-Related Teasing among Adolescents

Weight-related teasing is reported by 26 percent of female and 22 percent of male adolescents. Adolescents who are overweight have a greater likelihood of receiving weight-related comments and teasing from peers and family members than adolescents of an average weight. For example, one study reported 45 percent of overweight adolescent girls and 50 percent of overweight adolescent boys experienced frequent weight-related teasing compared with only 19 percent of girls and 13 percent of boys who were of an average weight. In addition to teasing, overweight adolescents have also been found to be at increased risk for developing disordered-eating behaviors, possessing lower self-esteem, and reporting higher rates of depression.

Weight-Related Teasing and Disordered Eating

In one study, 46 male and 84 female adolescents were surveyed. Findings indicate frequent teasing by family and peers is associated with increased disordered eating thoughts and behaviors, depression, anxiety, anger, and decreased self-esteem. Adolescents who experience weight-related teasing place a higher value on thinness and evaluated themselves on shape and weight. High rates of teasing were predictive of severe binge eating behaviors.

Sex Differences in Teasing

Generally, female adolescents report being teased more often than male adolescents. In an Australian study examining teasing in sport and exercise contexts, females participated in organized sports less often than boys. However, adolescent girls were still teased more frequently than boys. Both girls and boys were teased by same-sex peers; however, girls were also teased by their opposite-sex peers. Teasing was associated with negative body image, which may have contributed to decreased rates of sport and exercise participation for girls.

Prevention of Teasing Behaviors

With increased awareness of the potential harms of bullying (e.g., suicide), efforts have been made to implement antibullying campaigns. Although it is important to teach healthy peer relationships and coping skills to adolescents, it is equally important to educate adults who may participate in teasing behaviors. Interventions to reduce weight-related teasing should take place in both family and school settings to prevent disordered eating and other negative consequences of teasing.

Justine J. Reel

See also: Causes; Fat Bias/Fat Discrimination; Family Influences; Obesity; Parents; Prevention

Bibliography

Benas, Jessica S., Dorothy J. Uhrlass, and Brandon E. Gibb. "Body Dissatisfaction and Weight-Related Teasing: A Model of Cognitive Vulnerability to Depression among Women." *Journal of Behavioral Therapy and Experimental Psychiatry* 41 (2010): 352–356. https://doi.org/10.1016/j.jbtep.2010.03.006.

Buhlmann, Ulrike, Laura M. Cook, Jeanne M. Fama, and Sabine Wilhelm. "Perceived Teasing Experiences in Body Dysmorphic Disorder." *Body Image* 4 (2007): 381–385. https://doi.org/10.1016/j.bodyim.2007.06.004.

Eisenberg, Maria E., Jerica M. Berge, Jayne A. Fulkerson, and Dianne Neumark-Sztainer. "Weight Comments by Family and Significant Others in Young Adulthood." *Body Image* 8 (2011): 12–19. https://doi.org/10.1016/j.bodyim.2010.11.002.

Libbey, Heather P., Mary T. Story, Dianne R. Neumark-Sztainer, and Kerri N. Boutelle. "Teasing, Disordered Eating Behaviors and Psychological Morbidities among Overweight Adolescents." *Obesity* 16, no. 2 (2008): S24–S29. https://doi.org/10.1038/oby.2008.455.

Menzel, Jessie E., Lauren M. Schaefer, Natasha L. Burke, Laura L. Mayhew, Michael T. Brannick, and J. Kevin Thompson. "Appearance-Related Teasing, Body Dissatisfaction, and Disordered Eating: A Meta-analysis." *Body Image* 7 (2010): 261–270. https://doi.org/10.1016/j.bodyim.2010.05.004.

Slater, Amy, and Marika Tiggemann. "Gender Differences in Adolescent Sport Participation, Teasing, Self-Objectification and Body Image Concerns." *Journal of Adolescence* 34 (2011): 453–463. https://doi.org/10.1016/j.adolescence.2010.06.007.

Spresser, Carrie D., Kristen M. Keune, Diane L. Filion, and Jennifer D. Lundgren. "Startle as an Objective Measure of Distress Related to Teasing and Body Image." *International Journal of Eating Disorders* 44, no. 1 (2011): 58–64. https://doi.org/10.1002/eat.20774.

TELEVISION PROGRAMS AND EATING DISORDERS

Television is a primary source of news and entertainment in modern society. Television programs are major sources of information—both overt and subliminal—regarding social norms and standards. Watching TV is also the most frequent leisure activity in the United States, accounting for over 50 percent of total leisure time for Americans 15 and older. Americans watch an average of 2.8 hours of television per day, with certain demographics such as African Americans, adults over 70 years of age, and unemployed individuals watching more. Although TV represents the average American's pastime of choice, the characters portrayed in its fictional shows are not average; one study found that less than 10 percent of all female characters in television shows are obese, while close to 40 percent of U.S. women are considered obese.

TV shows have been shown to affect body image. A recent study found 23 percent of women and 13 percent of men reported looking to television actors for beauty ideals when they were younger. Even more concerning, there is research suggesting TV programs targeted at younger audiences have significantly thinner casts than programs for adult audiences, and younger audiences take notice. Researchers found although general television viewing did not predict negative body image, specific types of television shows (namely soap operas and music videos) *did* predict more body dissatisfaction among adolescent girls.

Ways That Television Shows Relate to Eating Disorders

Pinpointing certain TV programs that deal overtly with eating disorders is easy; several popular shows such as *Glee*, *Gossip Girl*, and *Degrassi* to name just a few, have main characters that unarguably display eating disorder behavior. These portrayals generally receive criticism for their flippant, unrealistic, or in some cases normalizing treatment of these debilitating disorders. In response to one episode in the TV show, *Glee*, where a main character is clearly shown suffering from bulimia, Project HEAL (a nonprofit that raises money for eating disorder treatment and advocates for awareness) released a statement criticizing the program for its irresponsible and humorous treatment of a disorder. A number of other programs that cater to young, primarily female, audience bases have been criticized for similar depictions of eating disorders, with many showing a character magically healed the next episode.

TV shows do not have to depict a main character struggling with anorexia or bulimia to affect eating-disordered behavior, however. The sociocultural model of eating disorders claims the thin ideal is omnipresent in society and, for the majority of women, unattainable without resorting to maladaptive and destructive behaviors, like purging, overexercising, or self-imposed starvation. This thin ideal is reinforced most potently by visual media, with television as the single most powerful reinforcer of society's idealized body image. Exposure to television has been shown to correlate to higher *internalization* of the thin ideal, meaning individuals who watch more TV endorse identifying with and aspiring to the thin ideal more than individuals who watch less TV. Therefore, programs that seem completely unrelated to eating disorders may be reinforcing unhealthy ideals for body shape and weight with thin actors.

Research has also shown that internalizing *other* types of messages about body image has an important impact on disordered eating and body image. One study reported school-aged girls who internalized sexualization messages (i.e., preference for body conscious clothing) had higher body dissatisfaction. Generally, this phenomenon is thought to arise because sexualization messages tend to favor the *other's* perspective. In other words, girls and women who internalize sexualized views tend to think about their bodies from the perspective of an observer, with a harsher evaluative and judgmental perspective. This phenomenon has even broader implications for understanding how TV program affect eating disorders; clearly programs do not have to overtly reference an eating disorder or even feature noticeably thinner actors to perpetuate unhealthy messages regarding body satisfaction.

The Other Side of the Camera

Painting a picture of television shows and eating disorders would be incomplete without also recognizing the harmful effects working in the TV industry can have on its employees. Actors are routinely instructed to drastically alter their weight for various roles and their bodies are documented obsessively by paparazzi, tabloids, as well as audience bases. For child stars, this can be particularly formative. Scarlett Pomers, who was just 16 at the time she landed a starring role in the TV sitcom *Reba*, recalled how her weight became what she focused on when her personal and professional life became hectic, unstable, and an object of national gossip. Many television industry professionals have spoken out against the use of sugary candy and soda to keep child stars energetic without the subsequent weight gain that more nutritious, balanced options would have. Repeatedly, tabloids have speculated about the health of famous TV stars like Lindsay Lohan and the Olsen twins, even providing news coverage of hospitalizations and stays at treatment facilities for anorexia. It is obvious the viewing audience is not the only party to experience social pressures to be thin and maintain certain weight.

TV programs and the Masculine Body Ideal

The evidence on males and eating disorders, while steadily growing, is scarce compared to the information on women and eating disorders. However, there is ample evidence to show men too are affected by television programs and they internalize mediated images related to body image. Body ideals for men tend to favor rugged and muscular frames over the ultrathin body idealized by women. Studies on males have echoed the research done on women and media consumption: higher rates of media exposure and higher internalization of media messages regarding weight and shape correlated with more disordered-eating behaviors, a greater drive for muscularity, and leanness. Similarly, young men and boys exposed to media with more sexualizing messages also reported higher rates of body dissatisfaction and lower self-esteem. These findings parallel trends in several consumer industries, with more men (both homo- and heterosexual) paying significant sums of money for gym memberships, personal trainers, diet/weight loss supplements, waxing treatments, salon services, and styling/grooming products than ever before. Although we typically think of women as being susceptible to social pressures and media consumption regarding body image, men are also affected and in equivocal ways.

Glee

Glee was a popular American TV show aired on Fox from 2009 to 2015 and was the story of a high school glee club and its members' journeys through growing up while competing on the national show choir circuit. In Season 4, viewers were introduced to a new character, Marley (played by Melissa Benoist). Over the course of the season, Marley is bullied by her schoolmates over her mother's obesity. While practicing for her starring role as Sandy in the glee club's production of *Grease*, Marley's enemy secretly takes the waist in on Marley's costume, causing Marley to think that she's gaining weight. Marley quickly begins to restrict her eating, causing herself to vomit after meals, and abusing laxatives for weight loss purposes. Several episodes later, Marley passes out during a performance because of her eating disorder. After struggling with the disorder for several episodes, Marley finds her confidence again in a superhero-themed duet competition where she goes as *Woman Fierce*.

This portrayal of eating disorders on a television show was received poorly. Many survivors, parents, and activists thought *Glee* took a flippant and dismissive attitude toward the serious topic of eating disorders. The portrayal of Marley's eating disorder reflected an obsession with her vanity, which severely misconstrues the picture of eating disorders and downplays the severity of disorders. Additionally, many prominent figures in the field of eating disorder advocacy were troubled that *Glee* did not include a public service announcement about the content it was showing. In a statement on this topic, the cofounders of Project HEAL stated that while *Glee* had addressed many important social concerns (the show has been credited with its thoughtful treatment of bullying and virginity), the show had mocked eating disorders with the Marley storyline.

Degrassi

Degrassi: The Next Generation (referred to simply as *Degrassi*) is the fourth installment in the *Degrassi* universe, which first made its debut in 1979. *Degrassi* is a Canadian television show that follows the life of several students enrolled in junior high and high school. The show is known for its focus on primarily taboo topics, such as teen pregnancy, drug use and drinking, suicide, and sexuality. Several prominent characters on *Degrassi* dealt with eating disorders on the show, including a male character. The show generally received positive reviews for the way it handled these topics. Fans and viewers alike thought that the show conveyed the seriousness of the disorders without glorifying them or reducing eating disorders to vanity-motivated obsessions.

Starved

Starved was an American TV show that followed the stories of four friends who met in a support group for people with eating disorders. The show aired for one season on FX in 2005 and was canceled following poor critical reviews. Ann Gerhart writing from *The Washington Post* in anticipation of the show's pilot episode called the show "ultimately unpleasant," describing it as the product of the "writers [getting] together and [asking], 'Hey, what happens if you take *Seinfeld* and give them eating disorders?'" In addition to low viewer ratings and a less than positive reception among the TV critic community, advocates and survivors reacted strongly to *Starved*'s lighthearted attitude toward eating disorders. In a press release from the National Eating Disorder Association, CEO Lynn Grefe called the show an "appalling and reprehensible program." Grefe went on to claim that eating disorders are "illnesses, not choices," and that the show's comedic treatment of anorexia, bulimia, and binge eating disorder was dangerous and untrue.

Interestingly, *Starved* was created, written, coproduced and directed by Eric Schaeffer (who also played one of the show's main characters). Schaeffer reported in multiple interviews as well as promotional materials for the show that he struggles with *anorexic-thinking* and has gone through multiple self-imposed periods of starvation followed by binges in his life. Schaeffer claimed most the material in *Starved* was derived from his experience, whether personally or through witnessing the struggles of individuals he has known. In a particularly negative review in the *Los Angeles Times,* television reviewer Robert Lloyd claimed that "just because you've had an experience doesn't mean you have anything interesting to say about it," referencing Schaeffer's experience with eating disorders.

Starving Secrets

Starving Secrets premiered on Lifetime in 2011. Tracey Gold (who starred in the 1994 film about Nancy Walsh, a survivor on anorexia, *For the Love of Nancy*) hosted this documentary-style reality TV show that followed the stories of women in recovery for anorexia nervosa. The show premiered to mixed reviews, particularly in the eating disorder community. The National Eating Disorder Association had previously come out against having individual's recovery journeys or medical treatments recorded for public viewership. However, several reviews of *Starving Secrets* praised the show for breaking free of damaging stereotypes surrounding eating disorders, such as the idea that persons who struggle with eating disorders are somehow permanently damaged or that these disorders reflect a preoccupation with being skinny or staying pretty.

Hannah J. Hopkins

See also: Books about Eating Disorders; Celebrities and Eating Disorders; Media; Movies and Eating Disorders

Bibliography

"American Time Use Survey Summary." Bureau of Labor Statistics. Last modified June 24, 2016. Accessed November 22, 2017. http://www.bls.gov/news.release/atus.nr0.htm.

De Jesus, Arthur Y., Lina A. Ricciardelli, Ann Frisén, Linda Smolak, Zali Yager, Matthew Fuller-Tyszkiewicz, Phillippa C. Diedrichs, Debra Franko, and Kristina Holmqvist Gattario. "Media Internalization and Conformity to Traditional Masculine Norms in Relation to Body Image Concerns among Men." *Eating Behaviors* 18 (2015): 137–142. https://doi.org/10.1016/j.eatbeh.2015.04.004.

Derenne, Jennifer L., and Eugene V. Beresin. "Body Image, Media, and Eating Disorders." *Academic Psychiatry* 30, no. 3 (2006): 257–261. https://doi.org/10.1176/appi.ap.30.3.257.

Dumas, Daisey. "Anorexia Reality Show Starving Secrets Slammed by Eating Disorders Group for 'Putting Ill People on Television.'" *Daily Mail.* Last modified December 5, 2011. Accessed November 22, 2017. http://www.dailymail.co.uk/femail/article-2070299/Anorexia-reality-Starving-Secrets-slammed-eating-disorders-group-putting-ill-people-television.html.

Gerhart, Ann. "FX's 'Starved' Is a Bit Too Much to Stomach." *Washington Post*. Last modified August 4, 2005. Accessed November 22, 2017. http://www.washingtonpost.com /wp-dyn/content/article/2005/08/03/AR2005080302134.html.

"Glee's Take on Eating Disorders Out of Line." *HaveUHeard*. Last modified November 16, 2012. Accessed November 22, 2017. http://haveuheard.net/2012/11/glees-eating -disorders-sucks/.

Gold, Matea. "Eating Disorders, the Comedy." *Los Angeles Times*. Last modified July 31, 2005. Accessed November 22, 2017. http://articles.latimes.com/2005/jul/31 /entertainment/ca-starved31.

Krupnick, Ellie. "'Starving Secrets,' Reality Show about Eating Disorders, Comes to Lifetime." *The Huffington Post*. Last modified January 8, 2012. Accessed November 22, 2017. http://www.huffingtonpost.com/2011/11/08/starving-secrets-eating-disorders-reality -show_n_1082226.html.

Lloyd, Robert. "'Starved' for Substance." *Los Angeles Times*. Last modified August 3, 2005. Accessed November 22, 2017. http://articles.latimes.com/2005/aug/03/entertainment /et-starved3.

Lyster-Mensh, Laura Collins. "Tracey Gold's Starving Secrets Has Growing Pains." *The Huffington Post*. Last modified February 4, 2012. Accessed November 22, 2017. http:// www.huffingtonpost.com/laura-collins-lystermensh/tracey-gold-starving-secrets _b_1127899.html.

"Marley Rose." *Glee Wiki*. Accessed February 3, 2017. http://glee.wikia.com/wiki/Marley _Rose.

"National Eating Disorders Association Calls New TV Sitcom 'Starved' 'No Laughing Matter.'" Market Wired. Last modified August 1, 2005. Accessed November 22, 2017. http://www.marketwired.com/press-release/national-eating-disorders-asso-ciation -calls-new-tv-sitcom-starved-no-laughing-matter-666367.htm.

Ogden, Cynthia L., Margaret D. Carroll, Cheryl D. Fryar, and Katherine M. Flegal. "Prevalence of Obesity among Adults and Youth: United States, 2011–2014." CDC.gov. NCHS data brief, no. 219 (2015): 1–8. Accessed February 3, 2017. https://www.cdc .gov/nchs/products/databriefs/db219.htm.

Reilly, Kaitlin. "9 Women's Issues That 'Degrassi' Covered, and Got Right." *Bustle*. Last modified March 13, 2014. Accessed November 22, 2017. https://www.bustle.com /articles/18036-9-womens-issues-that-degrassi-covered-and-got-right.

Slater, Amy, and Marika Tiggemann. "Little Girls in a Grown Up World: Exposure to Sexualized Media, Internalization of Sexualization Messages, and Body Image in 6–9 Year-Old Girls." *Body Image* 18 (2016): 19–22. https://doi.org/10.1016/j.bodyim.2016.04.004.

"Starved." *Wikipedia*. 2016. Accessed February 3, 2017. https://en.wikipedia.org/wiki/Starved.

"Table 11. Time Spent in Leisure and Sports Activities for the Civilian Population by Selected Characteristics, 2015 Annual Averages." Bureau of Labor Statistics. Accessed February 3, 2017. http://www.bls.gov/news.release/atus.t11.htm.

Thomas, Ryan. "A Weighty Issue." Back Stage. Last modified May 1, 2008. Accessed November 22, 2017. http://www.backstage.com/news/a-weighty-issue/.

Thompson, J. Kevin, and Leslie J. Heinberg. "The Media's Influence on Body Image Disturbance and Eating Disorders: We've Reviled Them, Now Can We Rehabilitate Them?" *Journal of Social Issues* 55, no. 2 (1999): 339–353. https://doi.org/10.1111 /0022-4537.00119.

Vandenbosch, Laura, and Steven Eggermont. "Sexualization of Adolescent Boys Media Exposure and Boys' Internalization of Appearance Ideals, Self-Objectification, and

Body Surveillance." *Men and Masculinities* 16, no. 3 (2013): 283–306. https://doi
.org/10.1177/1097184X13477866.

Weingarten, Catherine. "Glee's Harmful Portrayal of Eating Disorders." Proud2BMe.
Accessed February 3, 2017. http://proud2bme.org/content/glees-harmful-portrayal
-eating-disorders.

THERAPEUTIC RECREATION

Therapeutic recreation views leisure as an important contributor to one's quality
of life. Recreational therapists and occupational therapists work with populations,
such as individuals with disabilities or psychiatric clients, to foster development
of a healthy leisure lifestyle. Therapeutic recreation is frequently incorporated into
comprehensive treatment programs at eating disorder facilities to provide clients
with an opportunity to engage in a variety of normal activities while in a residential
setting.

Therapeutic Recreation for Eating-Disordered Individuals

Therapeutic recreation as part of eating disorder treatment is especially important
given many eating-disordered individuals are no longer able to experience leisure
activities without strong emotions. For example, eating-disordered individuals
have often abandoned leisure physical activity (e.g., climbing) for enjoyment's sake
for activities that are more cardiovascular in nature and burn more calories (e.g.,
running). Furthermore, individuals with eating disorders have difficulty with their
emotions and handling stress. Recreational therapists can teach stress management
techniques using group activities, such as deep breathing, muscle relaxation, and
meditation. To help eating disorder clients develop social skills and enjoy the natural environment, recreational therapists may bring groups of eating-disordered
clients hiking, canoeing, fishing, and gardening. Metaphors can be used to reflect
the healing process and recovery while individuals engage in outdoor activities.
For example, the importance of being present can be stressed in an activity like
hiking that requires intense concentration with each step.

Some recreational therapy activities may use crafts, arts, and games to help clients gain personal satisfaction and achievement. An outing, such as going to a park
or a museum, can be a useful tool to promote group cohesiveness between clients
and staff as well as provide a real-world experience.

Justine J. Reel

See also: Art Therapy; Exercise; Treatment

Bibliography

Gardiner, Clare, and Naomi Brown. "Is There a Role for Occupational Therapy within a
Specialist Child and Adolescent Mental Health Eating Disorder Service?" *British Journal
of Occupational Therapy* 73, no. 1 (2010): 38–43. https://doi.org/10.4276/030802210X
1262954 8272745.

Nowell, Rhonda. "The Role of Therapeutic Recreation with Eating Disorder Patients." *Psychiatric Medicine* 7, no. 4 (1989): 285–292.

Schaffner, Angela D., and Linda P. Buchanan. "Integrating Evidence-Based Treatments with Individual Needs in an Outpatient Facility for Eating Disorders." *Eating Disorders: Journal of Treatment and Prevention* 16, no. 5 (2008): 378–392. http://dx.doi.org/10.1080/10640260802370549.

TRAUMA

Trauma refers to a single event, repeating events, enduring events, or multiple events that overwhelm an individual's ability to cope with and/or make sense of an event. Traumatic events include, but are not limited to: childhood emotional, physical, and sexual abuse; adult emotional, physical, and sexual abuse; natural disasters (i.e., hurricanes, tornados); and human-made disasters (i.e., automobile accidents, bombings). Many persons with eating disorders report histories of trauma. Researchers point to a comorbidity between eating disorders, traumatic events, and post-traumatic stress disorder (PTSD). Childhood sexual abuse is the trauma most commonly linked to later eating disorders, though certainly other forms of trauma, such as childhood or adulthood physical or verbal abuse or neglect, are also aligned with eating disorders. Studies indicate bulimia is the eating disorder most associated to trauma, but trauma histories are found in persons with other eating disorder diagnoses as well.

Eating disorders have a high comorbidity with mood disorders, anxiety disorders, somatoform disorders, personality disorders, and post-traumatic stress disorder. In one study of 101 individuals with eating disorders, 63.3 percent of the individuals with anorexia and 57.7 percent of the individuals with bulimia had experienced at least one trauma. These percentages differ from a majority of research that shows a higher correlation between bulimia nervosa and trauma than anorexia nervosa and trauma, but nonetheless exemplifies the high rate of trauma histories in eating disorder clients.

Sexual Abuse and Eating Disorders

As noted, childhood sexual abuse is trauma most correlated with eating disorders. Researchers indicate between 30 percent and 48 percent of eating disorder clients reveal a history of childhood sexual abuse. A longitudinal study conducted over 18 years found sexual abuse was a significant predictor of bulimia nervosa and other purging disorders (i.e., anorexia, binge/purge subtype). Consistent with findings on trauma, the strongest associations between sexual abuse and eating disorders have been found in individuals with bulimia nervosa. One study found that specific types of disordered eating, such as compensatory behaviors in bulimia, are associated with higher rates of sexual abuse victimization. This study reported higher rates of sexual assault and aggravated assault in individuals with bulimia nervosa than in individuals without a diagnosis, suggesting that sexual and aggravated assault may contribute to the development and/or maintenance of bulimia nervosa. Furthermore, when bulimia is present with other psychiatric comorbidities, especially substance abuse, there is a link to higher frequency and greater severity of sexual abuse.

Several researchers have found a link between sexual abuse and impulsivity and perfectionism, traits also linked to eating disorders. Wonderlich found clients with eating disorders and a history of sexual abuse report engaging in self-destructive behaviors and other impulsive behaviors. Circumstances concerning sexual abuse have been connected to heightened eating disorder symptoms, including if the sexual trauma involved parents or if was recurring. Researchers have found individuals with eating disorders and sexual trauma history often have problems of body dissatisfaction and struggle to accept their sexuality. It has been suggested eating disorders may be a way to deny sexuality and avoid painful memories and emotions associated with sexual trauma.

Childhood Abuse

Many other forms of trauma have been found in persons with eating disorders. Persons with eating disorders report a high incidence of childhood emotional abuse. Physical child abuse as well as childhood neglect are also strong predictors of eating disorders later in life. Research indicates any childhood trauma may lead to a more complex clinical presentation in an individual with an eating disorder than might otherwise be the case. Effects of childhood abuse in eating disorder clients may include low self-esteem, shame, and a negatively distorted body image. The risk of developing psychopathology including eating disorders heightens when exposure to abusive experiences is repetitive. Other traumas linked to eating disorders include adult sexual victimization, prisoner-of-war experiences, and exposure to violent environments.

PTSD and Eating Disorders

Post-traumatic stress disorder (PTSD) has a high comorbidity with eating disorders. It is important to note not every individual who has experienced trauma develops PTSD. Although researchers in one study found over half the individuals with eating disorders in the study had experienced trauma, only 12.9 percent met the criteria for diagnosis of PTSD. This is significant and of clinical concern as the lifetime prevalence of PTSD in the adult general population is 6.8 percent. PTSD has three major categories of symptoms: reliving the event, avoidance, and hyperarousal. Reliving the event disturbs day-to-day living and includes flashbacks, nightmares, and intrusive memories. Avoidance symptoms include avoiding people, places, and situations that remind the person of the trauma. Hyperarousal symptoms include a heightened startle response, hyperalertness, and sleep disturbances. Somatization in persons with comorbid eating disorders and PTSD is likely and reported more frequently than in eating-disorder clients without PTSD. Most researchers agree PTSD is more common in bulimic type eating disorders than in anorexia restricting type eating disorders.

Jessica Guenther

See also: Causes; Comorbidity; Family Influences; Post-Traumatic Stress Disorder; Somatic Experiencing

Bibliography

Brewerton, Timothy D. "Eating Disorders, Trauma, and Comorbidity: Focus on PTSD." *Eating Disorders* 15, no. 4 (2007): 285–304. http://dx.doi.org/10.1080/10640260701454311.

Briere, John, and Catherine Scott. "Assessment of Trauma Symptoms in Eating-Disordered Populations." *Eating Disorders* 15, no. 4 (2007): 347–358. http://dx.doi.org/10.1080/10640260701454360.

Johnson, Jeffrey G., Patricia Cohen, Stephanie Kasen, Judith S. Brook. "Childhood Adversities Associated with Risk for Eating Disorders or Weight Problems during Adolescence or Early Adulthood." *American Journal of Psychiatry* 159 (2002): 394–400. http://dx.doi.org/10.1176/appi.ajp.159.3.394.

Sansone, Randy A., and Lori A. Sansone. "Childhood Trauma, Borderline Personality, and Eating Disorders: A Developmental Cascade." *Eating Disorders* 15, no. 4 (2007): 333–346. http://dx.doi.org/10.1080/10640260701454345.

Smyth, Joshua M., Kristin E. Heron, Stephen A. Wonderlich, Ross D. Crosby, Kevin M. Thompson. "The Influence of Reported Trauma and Adverse Events on Eating Disturbance in Young Adults." *International Journal of Eating Disorders* 41, no. 3 (2008): 195–202. https://doi.org/10.1002/eat.20490.

Tagay, Sefik, Sandra Schlegl, and Wolfgang Senf. "Traumatic Events Post-Traumatic Stress Symptomatology and Somatoform Symptoms in Eating Disorder Patients." *European Eating Disorder Review* 18, no. 2 (2010): 124–152. https://doi.org/10.1002/erv.972.

Wonderlich, Stephen A., Ross D. Crosby, James E. Mitchell, Kevin M. Thompson, Jennifer Redlin, Gail Demuth, Joshua Smyth, and Beth Haseltine. "Eating Disturbance and Sexual Trauma in Childhood and Adulthood." *International Journal of Eating Disorders* 30, no. 4 (2001): 401–412. https://doi.org/10.1002/eat.1101.

TREATMENT

Treatment refers to a licensed professional providing care and support for a mental health concern. An exhaustive list of eating disorder treatment providers can be found at websites like www.edreferral.com, including medical, nutrition, and mental health professionals who specialize in treating eating disorders. Generally, eating disorder treatment should be comprehensive so all factors (e.g., meal plan, weight stabilization) are addressed; treatment should also be individualized to the level of care (e.g., inpatient) needed by a disordered-eating individual. Eating disorder mental health treatment may include individual therapy, group counseling, family counseling and couples counseling.

Individual Therapy

Because eating disorders are a mental health concern, it is important to address psychological and emotional concerns with a trained psychotherapist who may be a licensed clinical social worker (LCSW), a licensed professional counselor (LPC), or a licensed psychologist (LP). In individual therapy, disordered-eating clients can reveal their deepest concerns without fear or self-consciousness. Individuals may receive individual counseling in a school setting, in a more generalized counseling center, or from a private practice clinician who specializes in eating disorder treatment.

Mental Health Treatment of Eating Disorders: An Interview with Dr. Dena Cabrera

Dena Cabrera, PsyD, is a licensed clinical psychologist and a certified eating disorder specialist at Rosewood Centers for Eating Disorders, where she serves as the executive clinical director. She has personally treated hundreds of women and teens struggling with eating and body image issues. Cabrera is a well-known expert, speaker and author in the field; she has spoken at more than 20 national conferences and presented at more than 100 workshops on eating disorders and other mental health problems. At Rosewood, she manages the day-to-day programs for all levels of care and is involved in program development, staff training, and supervision throughout the Rosewood system. Dr. Cabrera is the author of *The Mom in the Mirror: Body Image, Beauty and Life after Pregnancy*.

How did you get into the mental health field and treating eating disorders?
My first year at UCLA, I discovered my roommate had an eating disorder. Growing up in a small farming community, I was not familiar with eating disorders, particularly anorexia so it was quite alarming but also intriguing. I was perplexed by why someone would want to starve themselves and destroy their bodies. I understood dieting for control and weight loss, the struggle with body image, and certainly the quest for thinness. Being a woman in this society and especially a dancer, I often wrestled with my confidence and pursued the perfect dancer's body. However, I had never gone to the extent of what I experienced from my roommate. Another close friend, I discovered, had anorexia with binge/purge type, she unfortunately lost her life to the illness. This loss created a passion in me to help those who are suffering from the illness. I immediately recognize in both of my friends, that they were not doing this on purpose. It was an illness that kept them hostage. Just as a note, my roommate went on to fully recover and has a beautiful healthy life today.

In what types of settings have you worked with clients who had eating disorders?
I have worked in all levels of care including inpatient, residential, partial hospitalization, intensive outpatient, and outpatient. My career in eating disorders spans over 19 years. Most of my career has been at the inpatient and residential level of care. I had a small private practice in between the birth of my two children. It was a good experience but I quickly realized that I really love working in a multidisciplinary team environment.

When should someone seek treatment for an eating disorder?
The earlier a person can address the disordered eating issues the better. We live in a confusing culture that sends conflicting messages when it comes to food, shape, and weight. "Healthy" is narrowly defined in this country. Therefore, when someone is distressed about their body, shape, weight, and food is being used to control feelings and stress, then it is important that the person seek help. We are almost brainwashed into believing that these negative feelings about our body or self are normal. They are not. Any stress or distress that is experienced about weight, body and food needs to be addressed. Dieting is not the answer. Level of care for someone with an eating disorder will depend on the severity of the

eating disorder. The crucial thing to remember is that when the eating disorder thoughts, feelings, and behaviors interfere with mood, daily functioning, relationships, and purpose, then it's time to seek treatment.

How can someone (or one's family) find the right treatment option?

It's important to choose a treatment provider with eating disorder experience. It would be ideal to choose a treatment provider who is certified as an eating disorder specialist. This is not always possible. Given the complexity of eating disorders, there is a need for a multidisciplinary team approach. The team should consist of a medical provider, therapist/psychologist, dietitian, and often a psychiatrist. It critical that the team utilize evidenced-based treatment modalities.

The type of treatment will be determined by the level of care that is needed, type of illness, and comorbid issues. Treatment centers vary in treatment models, approach, and care.

What are the characteristics of a solid treatment program for eating disorders?

The first and essential component of a solid eating disorder treatment program is assuring that they are Joint Commission accredited. Eating disorders have the highest mortality rate of any behavioral health disorder, making it critical that programs create the highest quality and safest care as possible. There are Joint Commission requirement that need to be followed, therefore if a facility is Joint Commission accredited you can assure that they are held to these specific eating disorder treatment standards. It's also important that the treatment program is state licensed by the behavioral health department. Other critical components include treatment providers who are credible, experienced, and recognized in the field of eating disorders and that they are delivering best practice, evidenced-based, age appropriate treatment and utilizing a comprehensive multimodal approach. A multidisciplinary approach is imperative and reflects the complex issues encompassing an eating disorder and the comorbid issues. Family involvement should be a priority in treatment whenever possible. A strong utilization review team that are experienced and qualified to work with insurances is essential. Overall, the components of successful treatment outcomes are dependent upon having a compassionate, caring treatment team who are experienced and can connect with the patients. For it is through the rapport, connection, and relationship with their team that healing begins to happen.

How do you know as a clinician that a client is on a positive path to recovery?

I believe you know when a client is on a positive path to recovery when they begin to reintegrate back into their lives and build connection with others, when they find meaning in their pain, and when they have an identity separate from their weight, size, shape, and appearance. Part of recovery constitutes the client being able to live a healthy life and have a peaceful relationship with food.

Is it possible for people to struggle with eating disorders in their 30s, 40s, 50s, and beyond?

Yes, over the past 10 years, we have seen a significant increase in women and men seeking treatment for eating disorders in their 30s, 40s, 50s, and older. If so, what are the potential triggers? There are particular issues relevant for women in their 30s and 40s and over. Hormonal changes, aging in general for women with increased body image struggles, teens leaving the home, aging parents, and relationship challenges that may appear in older years. What are some of the unique issues for mothers who struggle with eating disorders? There are medical, developmental, and psychological challenges eating disorders may pose from the beginnings of pregnancy through childbirth, the postpartum period, and parenting years. There are interferences eating disorders may have on child-rearing practices, such as breast feeding difficulties, attachment issues, feeding issues, mealtime disorganization, weight, and body image concerns in their children.

Does health insurance typically cover eating disorder treatment?
It varies from insurance to insurance. Many do cover anorexia and bulimia. However, I have experienced that some insurances exclude binge eating disorder.

Being a mother yourself, what recommendations do you give to parents who want to create a healthy home environment for food, exercise, and body image?
How we live and conduct ourselves as parents sets the tone and is the grassroots. It's important to live in a way that inspires beauty, confidence, well-being, and healthy body image. It begins with us modeling for our children and teaching them the tools so that they are equipped to handle the world.

a. Promote a Healthy Environment—Talk openly, be active, challenge negativity, and be positive
b. Teach Media Literacy
c. Balanced Eating—Don't diet! All foods fit. No "good" foods, and no "bad" foods. Balance, variety, and moderation.
d. Improve Body Image and Positive Self-Image—Monitor and curb talk about your own body and the bodies of others; challenge beliefs about thinness, exercise, "healthy," dieting, beauty, and so on.
e. Promote Overall Self-Esteem—Engage in healthy and valuable relationships; Develop talents, hobbies, and interests that make you feel good about yourself; Have fun.

How can parents tell if there is a problem and what should they do?
Parents may see a change or decompensation in their mood, behavior, and academic or sports performance before they may notice an eating disorder. Many times mood changes such as an increase in anxiety or depression may precede an eating disorder. Parents may see an increase in emotions, attitude, or behaviors (i.e., such as restricting) related to food. It is important for parents to seek help immediately for their child. The earlier the better, in terms of helping the child break the maladaptive behaviors and patterns and return to health.

Anything else you would like to add about body image or eating disorders?
It's important to model positive self-esteem, healthy confidence, and complimentary praise of self and others. Often times, we get swept into a world of judgment and comparison that only leads to measuring ourselves in a negative way. Theodore Roosevelt said that "comparison is the thief of joy." Instead of criticizing yourself or others in front of your kids, marvel humbly over the use of your legs, the fact that you have the ability to move, and the use of your five senses. Notice when loved ones make an effort to look nice; however, compliment on a child's spirit, laughter, or humor. It's not easy modeling joy and confidence while caring for self and others, but the more you demonstrate positive body image and confidence, the more you'll begin to feel it, too. The payoff is that you will help shape the future of your children and how they live in their bodies.

Individual counseling usually involves exploring triggers and contributing factors related to an eating disorder. A client is encouraged to adopt coping strategies to address stressors and replace disordered-eating behaviors. Generally, an eating-disorder client needs to work on personal boundaries in relationships and become more assertive across situations (e.g., family, work).

Group Counseling

Group counseling provides advantages over individual therapy in that individuals can provide support to one another. An eating-disordered individual may be validated when hearing similar concerns from group members rather than feeling socially isolated. Group therapy for eating-disordered individuals may focus on dialectical behavior therapy (DBT) skills and body image or body politics groups. Eating disorder treatment facilities may provide additional groups such as spirituality, assertiveness, or twelve-step groups. Group therapy is facilitated by at least one licensed professional. By contrast, support groups (e.g., Eating Disorders Anonymous, Overeaters Anonymous) provide a peer-led group environment to discuss concerns.

Family and Couples Counseling

Family and couples counseling may be offered in both outpatient and inpatient settings. Family therapy helps identify family system difficulties that contribute to eating disorder patterns and is particularly indicated for child and adolescent clients. Family therapy is also intended to act as a vehicle for educating parents and significant others about how to support an eating-disordered individual in a healthy way. For example, the role of a family member in an individual's treatment and recovery is negotiated in therapy. Some family therapy approaches (e.g., Maudsley) encourage parents to act as cotherapists and to closely monitor meal planning efforts. In other cases, family members are advised to serve solely as emotional support.

In couples counseling it may be important to address coparenting issues—such as differing parenting styles—or to work on communication skills. Couples may also need to identify how an eating disorder has affected the relationship and repair hurt feelings. Anger management and assertiveness training are commonly provided for couples as an adjunct for eating disorder treatment. The level of family involvement may depend on several factors such as family history, potential for family support, timing related to a client's treatment progress, and level of care (e.g., outpatient, residential).

Levels of Care for Eating Disorder Treatment

The type of treatment a client should pursue is determined by the severity and duration of an eating disorder. The American Psychiatric Association has identified five levels of care for clients with eating disorders. These include Level 1 (outpatient treatment), Level 2 (intensive outpatient treatment), Level 3 (partial hospitalization), Level 4 (residential treatment), and Level 5 (inpatient hospitalization). The level of care that a client should receive is based on the following criteria: medical complications, suicidal tendencies, body weight (i.e., body mass index), motivation to recover, environmental stress, purging behavior, comorbidities, treatment availability, and structure needed for eating and weight management. For example, Level 1 (outpatient treatment) involves clients who are medically stable, have no suicidal ideations, have good motivation to recover, and are self-sufficient. The most intensive level of care (i.e., Level 5, inpatient hospitalization) is recommended for individuals suffering from medical complications (e.g., low heart rate), severe electrolyte imbalances (e.g., low potassium levels), and suicidal ideations, as well as for individuals who need refeeding for weight restoration. It has been suggested anorexic individuals who are 25 percent or more below expected weight for height should be treated on an inpatient basis. Inpatient treatment should also be provided if a disordered-eating patient is at risk of engaging in self-destructive behaviors (e.g., self-mutilation) or suicidal intent and plan have been identified. Motivation to recover for individuals requiring inpatient treatment is generally poor to very poor and there is a strong need for a structured environment with full supervision. In a hospital setting, vital signs can be monitored, physical activity can be limited, and gradual weight gain can be encouraged.

Residential eating disorder treatment facilities provide a less intensive and less expensive alternative to an inpatient level of care. Many eating disorder treatment centers provide residential level of care in a campus-like atmosphere. Residential clients need to be medically stable and present with stronger motivation for recovery or have stronger social support. Residential programs often include a variety of approaches including individual therapy, group therapy, family and couples counseling, and nutritional support. A nursing staff is available to help with medication management and to police disordered-eating behaviors (e.g., purging).

Partial hospitalization (Level 3) or day treatment is a step down from the highly structured residential and inpatient treatment facilities; however, support is provided during meals. Clients generally receive group, family, and individual therapy and focus on coping skills with support and monitoring from a multidisciplinary team. Intensive outpatient (Level 2) provides a half-day version of the partial hospitalization and can be a gradual transition to traditional outpatient therapy. An eating-disordered individual should be medically stable to be appropriate for partial hospitalization or intensive outpatient levels of care.

Outpatient treatment, or traditional psychotherapy, is considered appropriate when a disordered eating client is not medically compromised. Historically, individuals with bulimia nervosa have been treated on an outpatient basis more frequently than individuals with anorexia nervosa. Outpatient therapists who specialize in eating disorder treatment can address underlying emotions such as inadequacy, lack of control, and perfectionistic tendencies. Typically, outpatient sessions last for 50 minutes once or twice weekly and most commonly involve individual therapy.

Counseling Approaches for Eating Disorders

Various theoretical frameworks have been presented for the treatment of anorexia nervosa and bulimia nervosa, including cognitive behavioral, motivational interviewing, acceptance and commitment therapy (ACT) and behavioral approaches. Although approaches vary, all approaches are to address and reduce disordered-eating symptoms.

For example, highly regarded, evidence-based cognitive behavioral approaches involve identifying dysfunctional thought patterns that trigger negative eating patterns to develop functional coping strategies that do not involve disordered eating. In cognitive behavioral therapy (CBT), a therapist helps individuals identify cognitive distortions related to body image and eating disturbances. Dialectical behavior therapy (DBT), developed by Marsha Linehan, is a type of CBT to help individuals regulate and tolerate strong emotions. A skills-based approach, DBT focuses on helping a client to increase mindfulness, improve distress tolerance, reestablish healthy interpersonal skills and relationships, and regulate emotions appropriately.

Counselors can use motivational interviewing or motivational enhancement to help clients explore their motivation for, and resistance to, recovery using the stages of change model. Using this approach, a counselor avoids labeling or judging and helps a client build self-efficacy and relevant goals according to his or her stage of change. The potential advantage in using this approach with diverse clients is it empowers an individual to increase self-awareness and to take responsibility for behaviors rather than using a formulaic approach to treatment.

Acceptance and commitment therapy (ACT) incorporates both the present (i.e., here and now) with the past contexts in which behaviors occur into psychotherapy. The acceptance component of ACT is associated with being mindful and encouraging clients to accept thoughts and emotions without judgment. The commitment component of ACT is closely tied to behavioral therapy with the goal of helping clients identify and alter specific behaviors. ACT is showing promise as a therapeutic approach for eating-disordered populations and has been adopted as an approach in many eating disorder treatment facilities (e.g., Avalon Hills Residential Eating Disorders Program).

In an intensive treatment setting, a variety of treatment modalities may be employed. The challenge of eating disorder treatment parallels court-ordered counseling cases in that a client's motivation to change affects treatment efficacy. Therefore, finding a therapeutic approach that closely fits the needs of an individual is a critical aspect of recovery. A therapeutic approach that shows promise treating eating disorders and body image disturbances in diverse individuals is the relational perspective. This perspective allows for an individual to be considered in the context of his or her relationships and was created to empower women to see their focus on connections with others as a personal strength rather than a deficit. This approach coupled with a person-centered or client-centered approach allows a counselor to listen attentively to a client's view of his or her universe without reacting too quickly. These counseling approaches (e.g., CBT, psychodynamic) are discussed in detail in separate entries.

Multidisciplinary Team Approach to Treatment

The advantage of residential and inpatient eating disorder–specific programs is medical professionals (i.e., physicians, nursing staff), dietitians, and mental health counselors are offered as part of a comprehensive treatment team. Because these facilities specialize in clients with eating disorders, they are acquainted with the complexities this population. These professionals can distinguish between occasional overeating and actual disordered-eating patterns. When a multidisciplinary team approach is implemented, it is important for team members to exhibit the following: effective communication, a willingness to meet regularly, self-awareness to avoid splitting by providing consistent messages to a client, and monitoring treatment progress.

Eating Disorder Treatment for Athletes

Researchers emphasize the importance of determining an athlete's motivation to change to increase treatment efficacy. Denial by an athlete is especially likely if an athlete is receiving positive reinforcement for disordered-eating behaviors in his or her sport and the behaviors are perceived as necessary and normal to compete. It is recommended that the counselor have a specialization in eating disorder treatment and understand the competitive athletic environment to build trust and create a strong athlete–counselor relationship. The focus should be on gradually helping an athlete increase weight and reduce eating disorder behaviors within the context of sport and on working toward relapse prevention. If eating disorder symptoms are severe and an athlete's weight loss becomes a medical concern, he or she may need to be benched. An athlete will benefit most from learning adaptive coping skills and relaxation techniques irrespective of whether he or she continues to participate in a sport, needs to take a break, or needs to ultimately leave a sport to pursue eating disorder recovery. Ideas for sequencing athlete-specific treatment sessions have been outlined.

Eating Disorder Treatment for Males

It is anticipated approximately one million males in the United States have an eating disorder. Unfortunately, most eating disorder facilities are geared to female adolescents and young adults. Two exceptions, Rosewood and Remuda Ranch, located in Wickenburg, Arizona, treat male clients in a residential setting. Barriers involved in admitting males into an eating disorder facility relate to (1) having a separation of males and females on the unit, (2) having male and female clients receive adequate privacy, (3) gender-identity and sexuality concerns of males, and (4) males and females have different concerns related to body image and disordered-eating behaviors.

Another exception, the Santé Center for Healing program (www.santecenter. com), treats males and females together using an addictions approach on a residential setting. Santé therapists find it useful to have both sexes together in body image and eating disorder group therapy so unique perspectives are offered to the opposite sex. A rare outcome study compared males and females one-year post discharge from a residential facility and discovered that while males averaged a longer length of stay (mean = 84 days; range = 25–226 days) than females (mean = 72 days; range = 23–156 days), males reported more improvement at follow-up. Differences in body image concerns were noted for male clients at Rogers Memorial Hospital, including a focus on increasing muscle rather than trying to lose weight or be thinner. Males tended to gain more weight (mean = 19 lbs.) from discharge to follow-up compared to females (mean = 7 lbs.). Using a person-centered approach and motivational interviewing has been recommended for treating males with eating disorders.

Treatment Considerations for Adult Women

The number of women over age 30 seeking treatment has increased by 400 percent and demonstrates eating disorders should not be considered a young or adolescent illness. Unfortunately, adults in midlife may be reluctant to seek treatment due to home and work responsibilities or may go underdiagnosed (e.g., it can be difficult to diagnose anorexia in postmenopausal women due to the absence of their menstrual cycle). In addition, insurance companies can be less supportive of adults in midlife than of adolescents because they sometimes take the disorder less seriously or consider it a chronic condition.

Renfrew Center in Philadelphia (www.renfrewcenter.com) provides a treatment track for women over age 35. This unique track allows older clients to have group therapy sessions geared to their unique needs as well as coffee outings together. Topics relevant to this population are addressed, including menopause, empty nest syndrome, facing the meaning of age in a youth-obsessed society, and guilt related to leaving children at home while in treatment. These women may benefit greatly from individual therapy and will probably need to educate their spouses and partners about how to support their treatment and recovery.

Cost of Treatment

Unfortunately treatment is costly. Inpatient hospitalization or residential treatment is similar in price to inpatient psychiatric stays ($1,000–$2,000/day and up), and usually a 30- to 90-day minimum stay is required for programs. Insurance companies vary widely in the willingness to cover treatment and residential stays. Insurance companies will sometimes cover a portion of the stay and then pressure the program to transition a client to a less expensive and less intensive level of care (i.e., outpatient). Another challenge is that for many clients a return visit is clinically indicated to continue the process of recovery as the step down from residential care is a difficult transition.

When one considers the comprehensive nature of treatment required for eating disorders (i.e., psychiatrist, dietician, and counselor), it is not surprising that even in an outpatient setting clients and families struggle to meet the financial demands for care. Although some outpatient services (e.g., physician, counselor) may be covered by insurance and only require the copayment, dietitians are unlikely to be covered by insurance and may be an out-of-pocket expense. In addition, many eating disorder specialists have decided against insurance panels to avoid paperwork or lower fees than what one may charge per session. Low-cost alternatives include twelve-step support groups and online message boards. However, these groups are not typically run by a trained counselor and fail to provide individualized and comprehensive treatment.

Justine J. Reel

See also: Acceptance and Commitment Therapy; Art Therapy; Cognitive Behavioral Therapy; Cognitive Behavioral Therapy Guided Self-Help Treatment; Cognitive Dissonance Interventions; Dialectical Behavior Therapy; Eating Disorders Anonymous; Equine Therapy; Family Therapy; Health Care Costs of Eating Disorders; Levels of Care; Maudsley Family Therapy; Medications and Eating Disorders; Nutrition Treatment Approaches; Overeaters Anonymous; Psychodynamic Psychotherapy Approaches; Recovery; Referring Someone for Eating Disorder Treatment; Relapse; Residential Treatment; Self-Care; Self-Help Interventions; Twelve-Step Programs; Virtual Reality

Bibliography

American Psychiatric Association. *Practice Guideline for the Treatment of Patients with Eating Disorders*, 3rd ed. Arlington, VA: American Psychiatric Association Publishing, 2006.

Calegoro, Rachel M., and Kelly N. Pedrotty. "The Practice and Process of Healthy Exercise: An Investigation of the Treatment of Exercise Abuse in Women with Eating Disorders." *Eating Disorders* 12, no. 4 (2004): 273–291. http://dx.doi.org/10.1080/10640260490521352.

Costin, Carolyn. *A Comprehensive Guide to the Causes, Treatments and Prevention of Eating Disorders: The Eating Disorder Sourcebook*, 3rd ed. New York: McGraw-Hill, 2007.

Costin, Carolyn. *100 Questions & Answers about Eating Disorders*. Boston, MA: Jones and Bartlett, 2007.

"Eating Disorder Referral and Information Center." edreferral.com. Accessed November 18, 2016. http://www.edreferral.com.

Johnson, Craig J. "Current Challenges in Recognizing and Treating Eating Disorders." *Minnesota Medicine* 86, no. 11 (2003): 34–39.

Joy, Elizabeth A., Claudia Wilson, and Steve Varochok. "The Multidisciplinary Team Approach to the Outpatient Treatment of Disordered Eating." *Current Sports Medicine Reports* 2 (2003): 331–336.

Lock, James, and Daniel Le Grange. *Help Your Teenager Beat an Eating Disorder*. New York: Guilford Press, 2005.

Lock, James, Daniel Le Grange, W. Stewart Agras, and Christopher Dare. *Treatment Manual for Anorexia Nervosa: A Family-Based Approach*. New York: Guilford Press, 2001.

Reel, Justine J., and Katherine A. Beals, eds. *The Hidden Faces of Eating Disorders and Body Image*. Reston, VA: AAHPERD/NAGWS, 2009.

Reel, Justine J., and Holly M. Estes. "Treatment Considerations for Athletes with Disordered Eating." In *Disordered Eating among Athletes: A Comprehensive Guide for Health Professionals*, edited by Katherine A. Beals, 131–158. Champaign, IL: Human Kinetics, 2004.

Renfrew Center. "Anorexia Bulimia Eating Disorder Treatment." Accessed November 18, 2016. http://www.renfrewcenter.com.

Richards, P. Scott, Randy K. Hardman, and Michael E. Berrett. *Spiritual Approaches in the Treatment of Women with Eating Disorders*. Washington, DC: American Psychological Association, 2007.

Santé Center. "Santé Center for Healing." Accessed November 18, 2016. http://www.santecenter.com.

Stewart, Tiffany M., and Donald A. Williamson. "Multidisciplinary Treatment of Eating Disorders—Part 1: Structure and Costs of Treatment." *Behavior Modification* 28, no. 6 (2004): 812–830. https://doi.org/10.1177/0145445503259855.

Thompson, J. K., L. J. Heinberg, M. Altabe, and S. Tantleff-Dunn. *Exacting Beauty: Theory, Assessment, and Treatment of Body Image Disturbance*. Washington, DC: American Psychological Association, 1999.

TWELVE-STEP PROGRAMS

Twelve-step programs are self-help programs to aid individuals in recovery from addictions, compulsions, and other behavioral problems such as relationship difficulties related to addictions. Twelve-step programs originated with Alcoholics Anonymous (AA), founded in 1935 by Bill Wilson and Dr. Bob Smith. two recovering alcoholics (i.e., sober and living a lifestyle that promoted and maintained their sobriety). They developed the AA program to assist individuals toward recovery, with the basic premise that alcoholics needed to connect to other alcoholics and a spiritual source to obtain and sustain recovery. The twelve steps used as guiding principles for recovery were first published in 1939 in the book *Alcoholics Anonymous: The Story of How More Than One Hundred Men Have Recovered from Alcoholism* (referred to as the *Big Book*). The steps as adapted for any addiction can be found at the website: www.12step.org.

Since its origin, the twelve step process has been adapted by other groups for other compulsive and behavioral problems, including Narcotics Anonymous, Gamblers Anonymous, and Debtors Anonymous. Currently, over 200 different self-help programs, often referred to as fellowships, exist worldwide. Twelve-step groups developed specifically for eating disorders and for persons struggling with disordered eating include Overeaters Anonymous, Eating Disorders Anonymous, and Anorexics and Bulimics Anonymous.

Overeaters Anonymous

Overeaters Anonymous (OA) was founded in 1960 and has fellowship groups in more than 20 countries. The premise of OA is members have a disease of compulsive overeating and an addiction to particular foods or to the way they eat. Although the fellowship group is for persons struggling with compulsive eating, members are also individuals with other eating-related problems, including anorexia nervosa, bulimia nervosa, and eating disorder not otherwise specified (EDNOS). The framework for recovery is the same for all members of OA regardless of symptomology.

Eating Disorders Anonymous

Eating Disorders Anonymous (EDA) was founded in 2000 by members of AA in Phoenix, Arizona. The EDA website states the purpose of the group is to recover from eating disorders and carry a message of recovery to others. The fellowship goal is balance as opposed to abstinence.

Anorexics and Bulimics Anonymous

Anorexics and Bulimics Anonymous (ABA) is a twelve-step group established in 1992, adapting the Twelve Steps of Alcoholics Anonymous (AA) specifically for persons with anorexia nervosa and bulimia nervosa. According to the ABA website, the only requirement for membership is "a desire to stop unhealthy eating practices." ABA is modeled after AA and originally used AA's text *Alcoholics Anonymous*, (the *Big Book*) for its text. In 2002 ABA published a text, *Anorexics and Bulimics Anonymous*, with the intention of it as a text the group could use to supplement the material in the *Big Book*. The ABA program is intended for people to gain support from a community of others struggling with the same disorders. ABA is clear the program is not intended as a substitute for professional treatment but rather as a resource to complement treatment by professional health care providers.

Research on the efficacy of twelve-step eating disorder programs is inconclusive, but some common themes regarding the benefits of programs are reported by members. Members have found comfort in the unified language of twelve-step programs and the shared conceptualization of their problem in a way that reflects their life experiences. A key focal point of the groups is emotional and spiritual healing as vital to recovery, and many members report this makes the program effective for them.

Jessica Guenther

See also: Eating Disorders Anonymous; Overeaters Anonymous; Recovery

Bibliography

Alcoholics Anonymous. *Alcoholics Anonymous*, 4th ed. New York: A. A. World Services, 2001.

Anorexics and Bulimics Anonymous (ABA). "Anorexics and Bulimics Anonymous (ABA) Welcome." Aba12steps.org. Last modified February 2, 2016. Accessed November 22, 2017. http://aba12steps.org.

Carter, Bobbi L., P. Scott Richards, Randy K. Hardman, and Michael E. Berrett. "Twelve-Step Groups for Patients with Eating Disorders." In *Spiritual Approaches in the Treatment of Women with Eating Disorders*, edited by P. Scott Richards, Randy K. Hardman, and Michael E. Berrett, 187–203. Washington, DC: American Psychological Association, 2007.

Eating Disorders Anonymous. "Eating Disorders Anonymous About." Eating Disorders Anonymous.org. Accessed November 18, 2016. http://www.eatingdisordersanonymous .org/about.html.

Johnson, Craig L., and Randy A. Sansone. "Integrating the Twelve-Step Approach with Traditional Psychotherapy for the Treatment of Eating Disorders." *International Journal of Eating Disorders* 14, no. 2 (1993): 121–134. https://doi.org/10.1002/1098-108X (199309)14:2<121::AID-EAT2260140202>3.0.CO;2-N.

McAleavey, Kristen. "Short-Term Outcomes of a 12-Step Program among Women with Anorexia, Bulimia, and Eating Disorders." *Journal of Children and Family Studies* 19, no. 6 (2010): 728–737. https://doi.org/10.1007/s10826-010-9362-y.

Russell-Mayhew, Shelly, Kristin M. von Ranson, and Philip C. Masson. "How Does Overeaters Anonymous Help Its Members? A Qualitative Analysis." *European Eating Disorders Review* 18 (2010): 33–42. https://doi.org/10.1002/erv.966.

VEGETARIANISM

Vegetarianism is a diet that avoids meat and other animal products. Vegan-type vegetarianism involves restricting all animal products (i.e., meat, fish, dairy, and eggs), whereas other forms of vegetarian diets may include dairy and eggs or fish. Strict vegetarian diets usually consist of foods low in fat but can result in deficiencies in protein, calcium, and vitamins D and B12. Therefore, vegetarians must be careful to reach the nutritional value of a well-balanced meal plan without meat products. Vegetarian diets are often associated with moral and ethical beliefs related to animal welfare; however, health reasons and the desire to lose weight also serve as motives for vegetarianism.

Eating Disorders and Vegetarian Diets

Vegetarianism has been linked with disordered eating attitudes and behaviors and having a stronger desire for thinness. In a study conducted in Minnesota, adolescents who were self-reported vegetarians were significantly more likely to report bulimic behaviors than nonvegetarian adolescents. In a separate Australian study, vegetarian teenagers expressed more concerns with being slim and higher restriction of food intake than nonvegetarian teenagers. This higher tendency for dietary restraint was also observed in college students who were vegetarians. In the same study, 37 percent of college-aged vegetarians were found to report disordered eating patterns compared to only 8 percent of nonvegetarian college peers.

In a larger study of 2,516 males and females ages 15–23, researchers found adolescent and young adult vegetarians were more likely to report binge eating with loss of control than nonvegetarian participants. Former vegetarians were more likely to engage in extreme unhealthful weight control behaviors than current vegetarians and nonvegetarian participants. Because of the confirmed link between vegetarian practices and disordered eating, self-identified vegetarianism has been used as a marker for the early detection of eating disorders.

Treatment Implications of Self-Identified Vegetarians with Eating Disorders

Because vegetarian behaviors can be related to the onset of disordered eating and eating disorders, it is important for treatment professionals to assess the timing and role of vegetarianism as it relates to eating disorder symptomatology. For example, vegetarian diets may represent one way an individual's food consumption has become more restrictive to lose weight. Many eating disorder treatment facilities do not accommodate vegetarian-diets as such food preferences are considered part of one's eating disorder. However, it is possible in an outpatient setting for dietitians to develop meal plans that limit animal product intake or replace protein with more vegetarian-friendly choices (e.g., legumes, tofu) if it is determined that vegetarianism reflects a moral or spiritual belief rather than a weight control strategy.

Justine J. Reel

See also: Disordered Eating; Fad Diets; Orthorexia Nervosa

Bibliography

Amit, M. "Vegetarian Diets in Children and Adolescents." *Pediatric Child Health* 15, no. 5 (2010): 303–308.

Barnard, Neal D., and Susan Levin. "Vegetarian Diets and Disordered Eating." *Journal of the American Dietetic Association* 109, no. 9 (2009): 1523. https://doi.org/10.1016/j.jada.2009.07.037.

Bas, Murat, Efsun Karabudak, and Gul Kiziltan. "Vegetarianism and Eating Disorders: Association between Eating Attitudes and Other Psychological Factors among Turkish Adolescents." *Appetite* 44 (2005): 309–315. https://doi.org/10.1016/j.appet.2005.02.002.

Klopp, Sherre A., Cynthia J. Heiss, and Heather S. Smith. "Self-Reported Vegetarianism May Be a Marker for College Women at Risk for Disordered Eating." *Journal of the American Dietetic Association* 103 (2003): 745–747. https://doi.org/10.1053/jada.2003.50139.

Robinson-O'Brien, Ramona, Cheryl L. Perry, Melanie M. Wall, Mary Story, and Dianne Neumark-Sztainer. "Adolescent and Young Adult Vegetarianism: Better Dietary Intake and Weight Outcomes but Increased Risk of Disordered Eating Behaviors." *Journal of the American Dietetic Association* 109 (2009): 648–655. https://doi.org/10.1016/jada.2008.12.014.

Yackobovitch-Gavan, Michal, Moria Golan, Avi Valevski, Shulamit Kreitler, Eytan Bachar, Amia Lieblich, Edith Mitrani, Abraham Weizman, and Daniel Stein. "An Integrative Quantitative Model of Factors Influencing the Course of Anorexia Nervosa over Time." *International Journal of Eating Disorders* 42 (2009): 306–317. https://doi.org/10.1002/eat.20624.

VIRTUAL REALITY

Virtual reality (VR) is a technology that creates human and computer interaction to allow individuals to experience sensations because of being immersed in life-like virtual worlds. Although VR was initially used for play and computer games intended to stimulate real-life situations (e.g., racing cars on a track), the potential for use of VR as an educational and treatment tool has recently been identified by researchers and clinicians. VR has been proposed as an innovative form of exposure therapy for individuals suffering from a variety of psychological disorders (e.g., anxiety) to practice coping skills relative to a specific triggering setting (e.g., social party). VR has effectively been used to understand and treat addictions. VR has demonstrated people with addiction respond with strong cravings to specific cues (e.g., cigarette packs, liquor bottles) and social settings (e.g., party) associated with use. Using VR, these people can learn and practice relapse prevention skills while getting experience in a lifelike but safe environment.

VR and Eating Disorder Treatment

VR is ideal for simulating food cues and environmental settings to determine an individual's emotional response and self-reported cravings/hunger. For interviewing the eating-disordered individual to better understand triggering environments, a VR high-risk eating context (e.g., restaurant) can be configured with the click of a mouse. By building upon common triggers for individuals with eating disorders, VR can be used as an assessment tool that goes beyond a standard clinical interview.

In a treatment setting, clinicians can address both negative eating behaviors and negative body image with VR technology. Currently, many eating disorder residential treatment facilities offer challenges to provide exposure to triggering situations out in the community. One's primary therapist will accompany a client to a clothing store, restaurant, or fitness center to experience exposure and practice skills. Because this is highly impractical to do on a frequent basis, most clients will only have one or two challenges during treatment. However, VR offers an opportunity to customize the setting to a client's actual home, gym, favorite restaurant, grocery, or clothing store and ensures he or she is exposed to triggering situations and is able to practice skills on a regular basis during treatment and upon discharge from a residential facility.

Body image concerns may be addressed with VR by presenting situations known to produce body dissatisfaction and body distortion. Eating-disordered individuals have an opportunity to experience these negative emotions during a counseling session and can process emotions in the moment. VR is a relatively new tool that shows great promise in the assessment and treatment of eating disorders.

Justine J. Reel

See also: Assessment; Exposure Therapy; Integrative Approaches; Treatment

Bibliography

Bordnick, Patrick S., Brian L. Carter, and Amy C. Traylor. "What Virtual Reality Research in Addictions Can Tell Us about the Future of Obesity Assessment and Treatment." *Journal of Diabetes Science and Technology* 5, no. 2 (2011): 265–271. https://doi.org/10.1177/193229681100500210.

Gorini, Alessandra, Eric Griez, Anna Petrova, and Giuseppe Riva. "Assessment of the Emotional Responses Produced by Exposure to Real Food, Virtual Food and Photographs of Food in Patients Affected by Eating Disorders." *Annals of General Psychiatry* 9 (2010): 30–41. https://doi.org/10.1186/1744-859X-9-30.

Gutiérrez-Maidonado, José, Marta Ferrer-Garcia, Alejandra Caqueo-Urizar, and Elena Moreno. "Body Image in Eating Disorders: The Influence of Exposure to Virtual-Reality Environments." *Cyberpsychology, Behavior, and Social Networking* 13, no. 5 (2010): 521–531. https://doi.org/10.1089/cyber.2009.0301.

Plante, Thomas G., Cara Cage, Sara Clements, and Allison Stover. "Psychological Benefits of Exercise Paired with Virtual Reality: Outdoor Exercise Energizes Whereas Indoor Virtual Exercise Relaxes." *International Journal of Stress Management* 13, no. 1 (2006): 108–117. https://doi.org/10.10137/1072-5245.13.1.108

Riva, Giuseppe. "The Key to Unlocking the Virtual Body: Virtual Reality in the Treatment of Obesity and Eating Disorders." *Journal of Diabetes Science and Technology* 5, no. 2 (2011): 283–292. https://doi.org/10.1177/193229681100500213.

VISCERAL SENSITIVITY

Visceral sensitivity (sometimes referred to as interoceptive awareness or interoceptive sensitivity) is an individual's ability to perceive and interpret bodily signals including sensations of fullness, hunger, heart rate, and pain. The ability to recognize and correctly interpret these signals affects the development of disordered-eating behaviors. In the case of extremely restrictive dieting, this restrictive behavior seems to represent an attempt to decrease overactive signals in the stomach an individual finds intrusive. By contrast, binge eating results from an individual unable to recognize satiety cues.

Many studies have demonstrated visceral sensitivity is a stable trait that varies between individuals and develops in early childhood. Young children who complain of frequent stomachaches, for example, may be expressing their awareness of other internal signals (e.g., hunger pains, gas pains, or constipation) but are unable to differentiate between these signals. This condition has also been implicated in the development of irritable bowel syndrome and functional gastrointestinal disorders.

Visceral Sensitivity and Intuitive Eating

One particular area of interest is the connection between visceral sensitivity and *intuitive eating*, which refers to an adaptive connection between physiological cues of satiety/hunger and eating behaviors. For example, intuitive eaters only eat when hungry and stop when they are satiated instead of relying on cues from their body to dictate when, what, and how much to eat.

Measuring visceral sensitivity usually involves heartbeat detection where individuals must sense their heartbeat (without using standard techniques like reading a pulse from the wrist) and their self-reported estimate of heart rate is compared to their actual heart rate. Many studies have demonstrated the closer an individual can estimate one's actual heart rate, the more likely he or she is to engage in intuitive eating.

Problems with Studying Visceral Sensitivity

Researchers agree visceral sensitivity occurs in three phases. The first phase is *sensation*, wherein an individual is aware of the presence of internal body signals. The second phase is *interpretation* of signals and what they mean physiologically. And last, *appraisal*, involves an individual's evaluation of signals and whether they are positive or negative, and if they are meaningful. Look at an example of an individual who is hungry. First, his or her gut would send cues to the brain through viscera, neurons and specialized cells that connect the digestive system to the central nervous system. Once an individual becomes consciously aware of a distinct signal coming from the stomach (even if unable to state precisely what a signal means), the sensation stage is reached. Next, through comparing these signals to memories of previous body signals, an individual would decide what a signal means. Is it gas pains, constipation, fullness, hunger, or something else? This is the interpretation stage. And last, how an individual reacts to these signals (both behaviorally and cognitively) is appraisal.

Two criticisms regarding the use of heartbeat detection have been raised. First, researchers have pointed out that sensing one's heartbeat is generally easier than sensing gut sensations. Most individuals in the correct environment perform moderately well on heartbeat detection tasks. Critics have pointed out that, compared to other more complicated bodily sensations, sensing one's heartbeat is simple and therefore it is problematic to use this task as a broad measure of visceral sensitivity. Second, eating-disorders researchers have noted that gut sensitivity, unlike heartbeat detection, places significant emphasis on the *appraisal* stage of interoceptive awareness. Many eating behaviors are the direct result of someone's appraisal of gut cues. Because heartbeat detection does not require any emotional reaction or behavioral response, it has been criticized as a poor substitute for gut sensitivity, particularly in eating disorder research.

The Role of Visceral Sensitivity in Specific Eating Disorders

Weak visceral sensitivity is associated with a number of behaviors and disorders, including suicidality, self-harm behaviors, chronic tinnitus (ringing in the ears), and substance abuse. In the case of body image and eating disorders, research has found poorer visceral sensitivity is correlated with body dissatisfaction and higher BMI scores. Several theories have been put forth to explain how interoception plays a role in anorexia nervosa and bulimia nervosa.

In the case of extreme dieting and anorexia nervosa, the prevailing theory suggests individuals use restrictive eating to quiet body signals. These individuals are thought to experience internal body signals as confusing, intrusive, and preoccupying to a point where they interfere with daily function. When the body is exposed to a state of chronic starvation (as is the case in anorexia nervosa), these signals tend to shut down as the body enters an extreme state of deprivation and energy conservation. Research in young children has supported this theory; chronic stomachache complaints in school-aged children (which may represent overactive internal signals) have been shown to predict the onset of anorexia nervosa in adolescence. Additionally, neuroimaging studies have shown irregular patterns of activation in areas of the brain responsible for interpreting and integrating signals from the stomach in people with anorexia, further supporting this theory.

Interoception in bulimia nervosa is more complicated. Originally, the yo-yo pattern of bingeing and purging in bulimia nervosa was thought to be the result of incorrectly interpreted body signals. For example, normative gut sensations (such as constipation and digestion) were misinterpreted as intense hunger or fullness cues. Therefore, an individual would binge or purge to address those signals.

However, more recent research has refined this model. Now, instead of bulimia seen as a result of incorrectly interpreted signals, it is thought the binge–purge pattern occurs because individuals are obsessed with gut sensations. Being unable to think about anything other than hunger and fullness sensations (even at very mild levels), they engage in extreme bingeing or purging behaviors. Research has supported this model by demonstrating individuals with bulimia are just as accurate as healthy controls at sensing their internal body cues.

Strategies to Strengthen Visceral Sensitivity

Training to be aware of one's internal body cues may seem difficult and vague, but several techniques have shown to improve visceral sensitivity. Mindfulness is a particularly well-studied and effective technique. Mindfulness is a conscious and deliberate attempt to connect with one's interior state that may include emotions, thoughts, and sensations. Yoga and meditation make use of mindfulness to enhance awareness of the body (focusing on breathing is a common tactic in many yoga classes).

Biofeedback is another strategy shown to improve visceral sensitivity. In biofeedback tasks, individuals are given real-time updates on their body processes, usually focusing on heart rate and respiration. Watching one's pulse on a heart-rate monitor is a typical task used in biofeedback. Individuals are then instructed to either elevate (raise) or depress (lower) these processes. By integrating their thoughts (i.e., mental attempts to complete the instructions given to them) with the reaction of their bodies, the brain establishes stronger connections between the prefrontal cortex (where conscious thoughts and decision making occur) and the brainstem, responsible for controlling automatic body processes.

Hannah J. Hopkins

See also: Gastrointestinal Complications Associated with Eating Disorders; Intuitive Eating; Leptin; Mindfulness

Bibliography

Ainley, Vivien, Lara Maister, Jana Brokfeld, Harry Farmer, and Manos Tsakiris. "More of Myself: Manipulating Interoceptive Awareness by Heightened Attention to Bodily and Narrative Aspects of the Self." *Consciousness and Cognition* 22, no. 4 (2013): 1231–1238. https://doi.org/10.1016/j.concog.2013.08.004.

Emanuelsen, Lene, Raechel Drew, and Ferenc Köteles. "Interoceptive Sensitivity, Body Image Dissatisfaction, and Body Awareness in Healthy Individuals." *Scandinavian Journal of Psychology* 56, no. 2 (2015): 167–174. https://doi.org/10.1111/sjop.12183.

Forrest, Lauren N., April R. Smith, Robert D. White, and Thomas E. Joiner. "(Dis)connected: An Examination of Interoception in Individuals with Suicidality." *Journal of Abnormal Psychology* 124, no. 3 (2015): 754–763. https://doi.org/10.1037/abn0000074.

Haase, Lori, April C. May, Maryam Falahpour, Sara Isakovic, Alan N. Simmons, Steven D. Hickman, Thomas T. Liu, and Martin P. Paulus. "A Pilot Study Investigating Changes in Neural Processing after Mindfulness Training in Elite Athletes." *Frontiers in Behavioral Neuroscience* 9, no. 229 (2015): 1–12. https://doi.org/10.3389/fnbeh.2015.00229.

Herbert, Beate M., Jens Blechert, Martin Hautzinger, Ellen Matthias, and Cornelia Herbert. "Intuitive Eating Is Associated with Interoceptive Sensitivity. Effects on Body Mass Index." *Appetite* 70 (2013): 22–30. https://doi.org/10.1016/j.appet.2013.06.082.

Herbert, Beate M., Cornelia Herbert, Olga Pollatos, Katja Weimer, Paul Enck, Helene Sauer, and Stephan Zipfel. "Effects of Short-Term Food Deprivation on Interoceptive Awareness, Feelings and Autonomic Cardiac Activity." *Biological Psychology* 89, no. 1 (2012): 71–79. https://doi.org/10.1016/j.biopsycho.2011.09.004.

Khalsa, Sahib S., Michelle G. Craske, Wei Li, Sitaram Vangala, Michael Strober, and Jamie D. Feusner. "Altered Interoceptive Awareness in Anorexia Nervosa: Effects of Meal Anticipation, Consumption and Bodily Arousal." *International Journal of Eating Disorders* 48, no. 7 (2015): 889–897. https://doi.org/10.1002/eat.22387.

Klabunde, Megan, Dean T. Acheson, Kerri N. Boutelle, Scott C. Matthews, and Walter H. Kaye. "Interoceptive Sensitivity Deficits in Women Recovered from Bulimia Nervosa." *Eating Behaviors* 14, no. 4 (2013): 488–492. https://doi.org/10.1016/j.eatbeh.2013.08.002.

Larauche, Muriel, Agata Mulak, and Yvette Taché. "Stress and Visceral Pain: From Animal Models to Clinical Therapies." *Experimental Neurology* 233, no. 1 (2012): 49–67. https://doi.org/10.1016/j.expneurol.2011.04.020.

Lau, Pia, Miriam Miesen, Robert Wunderlich, Alwina Stein, Alva Engell, Andreas Wollbrink, Alexander L. Gerlach, Markus Junghöfer, Thomas Ehring, and Christo Pantev. "The Relevance of Interoception in Chronic Tinnitus: Analyzing Interoceptive Sensibility and Accuracy." *BioMed Research International*. 2015, no. 487372 (2015): 1–8. https://doi.org/10.1155/2015/487372.

Merwin, Rhonda M., Nancy L. Zucker, Jennie L. Lacy, and Camden A. Elliott. "Interoceptive Awareness in Eating Disorders: Distinguishing Lack of Clarity from Non-Acceptance of Internal Experience." *Cognition and Emotion* 24, no. 5 (2010): 892–902. https://doi.org/10.1080/02699930902985845.

Moloney, Rachel D., Olivia F. O'Leary, Daniela Felice, Bernhard Bettler, Timothy G. Dinan, and John F. Cryan. "Early-Life Stress Induces Visceral Hypersensitivity in Mice." *Neuroscience Letters* 512, no. 2 (2012): 99–102. https://doi.org/10.1016/j.neulet.2012.01.066.

Pollatos, Olga, and Eleana Georgiou. "Normal Interoceptive Accuracy in Women with Bulimia Nervosa." *Psychiatry Research* 240 (2016): 328–332. https://doi.org/10.1016/j.psychres.2016.04.072.

W

WANNAREXIA

Wannarexia is a slang term used to depict an eating disorder wannabe—someone who visits pro-ana and pro-mia websites, participates in community forum discussions, and diets occasionally, but who is not considered to be dedicated to an eating-disordered lifestyle. In a question of authenticity, wannarexic individuals are sometimes called fake anorexics or wannabes by the pro-ana community, which believes wannabes undermine the credibility of the anorexia nervosa cause. Derogatory comments about wannarexics plague pro-ana discussion boards as participants attempt to weed out posers.

Wannarexia as a Warning Sign for Eating Disorders

Posts on pro–eating disorder websites are generally made by females younger than age 20. Wannarexia is often used as a label for preteen and teenage females who claim to have anorexia nervosa and view anorexia as a quick fix to lose weight and gain popularity. Although wannarexic individuals do not meet the diagnostic criteria for anorexia nervosa or other clinical eating disorders and may be overweight, visiting pro–eating disorder websites should be viewed as a warning sign for a harmful dieting mentality that usually precipitates disordered-eating behaviors. Wannabes may receive direct advice from online communities about how to develop anorexia nervosa and techniques for losing weight in an unhealthy way. Furthermore, what begins as a naive curiosity about eating disorders and a desire to become popular can lead to a genuine problem.

Justine J. Reel

See also: Femininity Ideals; Internet and Eating Disorders; Media; Pro-Ana; Self-Presentation Theory; Social Contagion Theory

Bibliography

Bardone-Cone, Anna M., and Kamila M. Cass. "What Does Viewing a Pro-Anorexia Website Do? An Experimental Examination of Website Exposure and Moderating Effects." *International Journal of Eating Disorders* 40, no. 6 (2007): 537–548 https://doi.org/10.1002/eat.20396.

Giles, David. "Constructing Identities in Cyberspace: The Case of Eating Disorders." *British Journal of Social Psychology* 45 (2006): 463–477. https://doi.org/10/1348/014466605X53596.

Hardin, Pamela K. "Shape-Shifting Discourses of Anorexia Nervosa: Reconstituting Psychopathology." *Nursing Inquiry* 10, no. 4 (2003): 209–217. https://doi.org/10.1046/j.1440-1800.2003.00189.x.

Harper, Kelley, Steffanie Sperry, and J. Kevin Thompson. "Viewership of Pro–Eating Disorder Websites: Association with Body Image and Eating Disturbances." *International Journal of Eating Disorders* 41 (2008): 92–95. https://doi.org/10.1002/eat.20408.

Jett, Scarlett, David J. LaPorte, and Jill Wanchisn. "Impact of Exposure to Pro–Eating Disorder Websites on Eating Behaviour in College Women." *European Eating Disorders Review* 18 (2010): 410–416. https://doi.org/10.1002/erv.1009.

Ransom, Danielle C., Jennifer G. La Guardia, Erik Z. Woody, and Jennifer L. Boyd. "Interpersonal Interactions on Online Forums Addressing Eating Concerns." *International Journal of Eating Disorders* 43, no. 2 (2010): 161–170. https://doi.org/10.1002/eat.20629.

Wilson, Jenny L., Rebecka Peebles, Kristina K. Hardy, and Iris F. Litt. "Surfing for Thinness: A Pilot Study of Pro–Eating Disorder Web Site Usage in Adolescents with Eating Disorders." *Pediatrics* 118 (2006): 1635–1643. https://doi.org/10.1542/peds.2006-1133.

WEIGHT CLASS SPORTS

Weight class sports include sports with divisions or categories by weight, such as wrestling, boxing, martial arts, weight lifting, power lifting, bodybuilding, and rowing. There is a weight range required per category and athletes are expected to weigh in to demonstrate eligibility. Historically, categories based on weight were created to level the playing field. Before weight classes were introduced, the stronger and larger athletes dominated competitions.

For weight class sports, categories vary based on weight and not appearance or muscularity. Categories are often named featherweight, lightweight, or middleweight. If a competitor does not make weight prior to competition, he or she is barred from competing. The timing of when a competitor is weighed in prior to competition varies by sport, and may even occur prior to season start.

Training for Weight

Generally, in weight-focused sports, the categories specify a weight range for athletes. Typically, an athlete gains a competitive advantage by weighing as close to the maximum limit of a range as possible without exceeding the class. Two methods most commonly used to achieve and maintain an athlete's ideal weight for a weight class. The first strategy is to gain as much muscle mass and strength as possible in the off-season before radically cutting weight prior to the start of the season or weigh-in. The intent behind this approach is to retain the strength and power acquired during the off-season and effectively compete with strength above that weight limit. Although not a strength-based sport, bodybuilders follow this protocol by amassing as much muscle and weight as possible in the off-season before cutting back to reduce as much body fat as possible while retaining muscle mass. A second training method that requires less weight change, involves having an athlete attain maximum strength and fitness while maintaining a competitive body weight both off-season and regular season.

Pathogenic Weight Control Methods

Unfortunately, because athletes need to be a specific weight—the heavyweight category is usually the exception, they may take unhealthy risks to cut weight for a perceived competitive edge. Such risks include caloric and fluid restriction, self-induced vomiting, excessive exercise, exercising in a sweat suit, using saunas, and using diet pills and laxatives. Therefore, athletes in weight class sports (e.g., bodybuilding, wrestling) are more likely to exhibit disordered-eating behaviors than athletes in sports that are not weight-dependent.

It is important to recognize efforts to meet weight expectations for one's sport tend to be more heavily influenced by coaches and other teammates than by socially constructed appearance standards. Thus, there is less concern about how a weight class athlete looks than about the pressure from significant others to do what it takes to be successful. Therefore, an athlete may take unhealthy risks to achieve a perceived performance advantage. In addition, any sport where physique evaluation is made or aesthetics are judged may also experience such pressures.

Timothy M. Baghurst

See also: Bodybuilding; Coaches; Sports; Weight Manipulation; Wrestling

Bibliography

Galli, Nick, Justine J. Reel, Trent Petrie, Christy Greenleaf, and Jennifer Carter. "Preliminary Development of the Weight Pressures in Sport Scale for Male Athletes." *Journal of Sport Behavior* 34 (2011): 47–68.

Lambert, Charles P., Laura L. Frank, and William J. Evans. "Macronutrient Considerations for the Sport of Bodybuilding." *Sports Medicine* 34, no. 5 (2004): 317–327. https://doi .org/10.2165/00007256-200434050-00004.

Morton, James P., Colin Robertson, Laura Sutton, and Don P. M. MacLaren. "Making the Weight: A Case Study from Professional Boxing." *International Journal of Sport Nutrition and Exercise Metabolism* 20 (2010): 80–95. https://doi.org/10.1123/ijsnem.20.1.80.

Reel, Justine, Sonya SooHoo, Trent A. Petrie, Christy Greenleaf, and Jennifer E. Carter. "Slimming Down for Sport: Developing a Weight Pressures in Sport Measure for Female Athletes." *Journal of Clinical Sport Psychology* 4 (2010): 99–111.

Shriver, Lenka H., Nance M. Betts, and Mark E. Payton. "Changes in Body Weight, Body Composition, and Eating Attitudes in High School Wrestlers." *International Journal of Sport Nutrition and Exercise Metabolism* 19 (2009): 424–432.

Thompson, Ron A., and Roberta Trattner Sherman. *Eating Disorders in Sport.* New York: Routledge, 2010.

WEIGHT MANIPULATION

Weight manipulation, sometimes referred to as weight management, is a widespread practice in many sports. This is commonly found in sports that are weight class dependent such as combat sports. Weight manipulation is defined as strategies athletes may use to alter body weight dramatically in a short time, such as fasting, overexercising, saunas, and self-induced vomiting. These strategies pose many psychological and medical risks for athletes. Additionally, many athletes risk disqualification from participation by engaging in weight manipulation behaviors as most are ruled impermissible by sports governance groups.

Sport-Specific Pressures and Prevalence of Weight Manipulation

The combat sports, martial arts, wrestling, boxing, karate, and Tae Kwon Do, are frequently associated with weight manipulation strategies. Combat sports use a weight class system to prevent mismatching opponents of vastly differing sizes, which would constitute an unfair advantage. Athletes in these sports are placed into different weight classes according to their prematch weight, which is often collected 18–24 hours before competition. These prematch weigh-ins provide an opportunity for athletes to artificially manipulate their weight and get matched with smaller, weaker opponents by qualifying for a smaller weight class. This often results in athletes who try to reduce their weight immediately prior to weighing in; after weigh-ins are complete, the athletes try to rapidly regain that lost weight to give them an advantage in the upcoming match. This cyclic pattern of rapidly losing and gaining weight—colloquially referred to as *cutting weight*—is physically harmful to the body and can also place these individuals at risk for an eating disorder.

Previous studies have found a high prevalence of weight manipulation strategies in competitive athletes at the high school, collegiate, and international levels; estimates range from 60–90 percent of combat sport athletes engaging in rapid weight loss behaviors. In a study conducted of 47 collegiate-level wrestling teams, athletes reported their teammates and coaches were a primary source of pressure, encouragement, and strategies related to weight manipulation. Of athletes surveyed, over half reported cutting weight at some point during their collegiate wrestling careers. Of those who did engage in weight manipulation, gradual dieting (79.5 percent), food and fluid restriction (45.5 percent and 20.5 percent, respectively), and increased exercise (75.2 percent) were the most common strategies. Although less common, more dangerous behaviors were reported: 7.5 percent reported fasting prior to weigh-ins, 26 percent reported practicing in a heated room to encourage sweating/water loss, 5.6 percent reported using plastic or rubber suits (to encourage sweating), 6.1 percent reported using saunas, and 9.3 percent reported excessive spitting.

Although the regularity and severity of weight manipulation in collegiate-level wrestling has decreased over the past few decades, it remains a concern for parents, coaches, and athletes. In summer 1996, several months before the Summer Olympic Games in Atlanta, Chung Se-Hoon was found collapsed in a sauna. Se-Hoon was the expected gold medalist in judo, and he was ruled dead after a heart attack following rapid weight cycling during training. Roughly a year later, in 1997, the collegiate wrestling community lost three athletes in six weeks; all deaths were the result of strenuous workouts and/or weight manipulation techniques designed to cut weight prior to precompetition weigh-ins. These deaths, among many others, have sparked outcries in the sports community and have resulted in tougher rules and regulations imposed by the National Collegiate Athletic Association (NCAA), many of which ban dramatic weight control strategies.

Physical and Psychological Consequences of Weight Manipulation

The physical repercussions of rapid weight loss strategies used in combat sports are dangerous and have short- and long-term consequences. In short-term performance, weight manipulation can lead to dehydration, an inability to regulate body temperature, electrolyte imbalances, increased heart rate, and muscle glycogen depletion. All these disturbances in physical functioning affect aerobic performance, which alters an athlete's ability to effectively maintain performance over a long period. Additionally, anaerobic performance, or short-term, intense bursts of activity, is also affected. Weight manipulation interrupts a body's ability to break down acids that accumulate in muscles during intense exercises and dramatically decrease anaerobic performance. In addition to a decrease in aerobic and anaerobic performance, athletes who use weight manipulation strategies are at higher risk for injury.

In addition to physical effects, weight manipulation poses psychological risks. Studies have found rapid weight loss has negative effects on cognitive ability, such as memory, attention, and mood. This is particularly concerning given many athletes affected by these behaviors are students. Studies have reliably documented a decreased performance on tests requiring cognitive effort during the competitive season. In addition to the cognitive effects, distraction appears to play a critical role in driving decreased academic performance. The majority of weight loss strategies used by combat sport athletes require a significant time, effort, and calculation on behalf of athletes. Intensive training sessions often occur multiple times per day for two to three hours at a time. Athletes carefully plan weight loss to coincide with precompetition weigh-ins while balancing the demands of other commitments. Precompetition diets are also carefully created to provide athletes with the maximum amount of energy and lowest amount of fat, sugar, and water to prevent unnecessary weight gain. All these factors are typically managed by athletes themselves and serve as a major distraction, which takes away from their ability to perform academically.

Athletes also report experiencing lower self-esteem, increased isolation, greater fatigue, and more depression. Many of these psychological symptoms, if not properly recognized as reflective of an underlying problem, can result in harsher treatment by coaches and peers, which often exacerbates isolation and a reduced sense of self-worth in an athlete. Additionally, weight manipulation can expose athletes to symptoms and behaviors indicative of eating disorders. A survey conducted among high school wrestlers found 10–20 percent were unable to control eating, and that rose to 30–40 percent following a competitive match. Inability to control one's eating is a classic symptom of an eating disorder. Athletes who compete in combat sports also report a higher level of preoccupation with body weight than noncombat athletes. This elevated level of body mass preoccupation coupled with other psychological symptoms, like depression and isolation, is a major risk factor for development of an eating disorder. Last, weight manipulation also poses risks for athletes after they finish their competitive careers. The use of rapid weight loss strategies often prevents these individuals from developing a stable metabolism and healthy weight management strategies, resulting in a higher rate of obesity in former combat sport athletes following retirement.

Hannah J. Hopkins

See also: Dehydration; Electrolyte Imbalance; Exercise; Weight Class Sports

Bibliography

Defeciani, Lisa. "Eating Disorders and Body Image Concerns among Male Athletes." *Clinical Social Work Journal* 44, no. 1 (2016): 114–123. https://doi.org/10.1007/s10615-015-0567-9.

Franchini, Emerson, Ciro José Brito, and Guilherme Giannini Artioli. "Weight Loss in Combat Sports: Physiological, Psychological and Performance Effects." *Journal of the International Society of Sports Nutrition* 9, no. 52 (2012): 1–6. https://doi.org/10.1186/1550-2783-9-52.

Landers, Daniel M., Shawn M. Arent, and Rafer S. Lutz. "Affect and Cognitive Performance in High School Wrestlers Undergoing Rapid Weight Loss." *Journal of Sport & Exercise Psychology* 23 (2001): 307–316. http://www.ayfcoaching.com/AcuCustom/Sitename/Documents/DocumentItem/1061.pdf.

Litsky, Frank. "WRESTLING; Collegiate Wrestling Deaths Raise Fears about Training." *New York Times.* Last modified December 19, 1997. Accessed November 22, 2017. http://www.nytimes.com/1997/12/19/sports/wrestling-collegiate-wrestling-deaths-raise-fears-about-training.html.

Oppliger, Robert A., Suzanne A. Nelson Steen, and James R. Scott. "Weight Loss Practices of College Wrestlers." *International Journal of Sport Nutrition and Exercise Metabolism* 13, no. 1 (2003): 29–46. http://dx.doi.org/10.1123/ijsnem.13.1.29.

Sansone, R. A., and R. Sawyer. "Weight Loss Pressure on a 5 Year Old Wrestler." *British Journal of Sports Medicine; London* 39, no. 1 (2005): e2. http://dx.doi.org/10.1136/bjsm.2004.013136.

WEIGHT PRESSURES IN SPORT

Sport involves multiple pressure to change body shape, size, or appearance. The pressure to lose or gain weight comes from the media, family, friends outside of sport, and personal factors, as well as teammates, coaches, judges, uniforms, and the sport-related norms associated with a sport culture. As a result, athletes are not immune to eating disorders. The media has sensationalized cases like Christy Henrich, the gymnast who weighed 47 pounds when she died from an eating disorder she developed after hearing from a judge she was too fat to excel, and Heidi Guenther, a ballerina who died at age 22 after she developed anorexia because she was told to lose five pounds in order to land the best role.

Prevalence

Lifetime prevalence estimates of clinical eating disorders are 5–10 percent in females and approximately 1 percent in males. Research indicates that many as 64 percent of female athletes and 53 percent of males report disordered-eating behaviors, placing them at risk of a clinical eating disorder. The discrepancy in lifetime prevalence rates based on sex has been observed in the athletic population as well. Collegiate female athletes, specifically, report clinical eating disorder and subclinical eating disorder occurrence rates of 2 percent and 25.5 percent, respectively. Fewer collegiate males report clinical eating disorders (0–1.8 percent), but nearly 20 percent are categorized as having subclinical eating disorders in one study. As a result, research has sought to identify the pressures athletes experience regarding weight management.

Weight Pressures Outside of Sport

In addition to sports-induced weight pressures, athletes are vulnerable to pressures typical of the general public. Although the focus of this section is on sport-specific weight pressures, it is important to remember athletes experience general social pressure from the media, family, friends, and other sources.

Media

Athletes who are successful in their sport and represent the ideal body size and shape in everyday society are often the ones who are written and reported about the most. As a result, athletes who strive for distinction may be pressures to conform to the societal idea of beauty while trying to maintain athletic excellence. These conflicting appearance ideals in greater society and in the sports world, may contribute to an athletes' willingness to resort to unhealthy eating behaviors to gain recognition.

Family

Researchers have suggested that because many individuals with disordered-eating behaviors seek approval from others, critical comments in the absence of praise from family members increase perceptions of weight-related pressure. Critical comments include remarks on physical appearance, stress on weight loss, and reinforce the thin ideal. Consequently, some athletes indicated that negative weight-related comments from family were pivotal events in the development of eating disorders.

The criteria by which comments are identified as critical are dependent upon a comment's purpose (i.e., weight loss for health vs. weight loss for appearance vs. weight loss for performance), the setting in which a comment is made (e.g., public vs. private), and the direction of a comment (i.e., weight loss vs. weight gain). Athletes most frequently tend to recall negative comments on appearance and weight loss/gain when they are communicated in a public setting. For instance, athletes have reported being affected by a family member who focused on the amount of food consumed by an athlete, being told by a family member to eat less, or being given something different to eat than others in the family.

Moreover, athletes who receive inconsistent praise for accomplishments are more likely to develop perfectionistic tendencies like those evident in individuals who exhibit disordered-eating behaviors. Subsequently, athletes may be willing to do whatever it takes, however harmful it may be, to either avoid criticism or receive praise in pursuit of success.

Self-Pressure

Although many athletes report external pressure to lose weight or maintain a low body weight, some pressure is internal. When asked if they would like to lose weight, 92 percent of figure skaters said that body weight and appearance are important to them and 94 percent responded they noticed if they gained weight. It may be that body weight and appearance are important to athletes because of influences outside of sport that emphasize the thin ideal or it might be that sport-related weight pressures contribute to the internalization of the ideal sport body type.

Sport-Specific Weight Pressures

Because athletes live in a world where they succeed or fail based on physical ability, their bodies take center stage. As such, they experience weight-related pressures in addition to the general pressures experienced by the public. Specifically, external pressure has been elevated in athletes who recalled more external weight-related pressure than athletes who recalled less external weight-related pressure. Sport-specific external pressure includes perceptions of weight-related pressure from coaches, teammates, judges, uniforms, and the sport subculture. It is perhaps not surprising then that many athletes report a desire to lose weight (e.g., 72 percent of figure skaters expressed a desire to lose weight).

Significant Others

Although athletes are influenced by others in their nonsport lives, they are also influenced daily by a number of significant others in their sport lives. Researchers have suggested the weight-related pressure athletes sense from coaches, judges, and teammates is related to the disordered-eating behaviors those athletes adopt. Thus, a growing body of research is dedicated to investigating this relationship in athletes.

Researchers have suggested coaches' weight expectations and/or weight-related comments influence athletes' disordered-eating behaviors. Coaches play a crucial role in the professional development of athletes. In some cases, they are inclined to advise their athletes on weight and appearance. Gymnastics coaches (54 percent) in one study reported determining an athlete's need for weight loss based solely on her appearance. Whereas 61 percent of competitive cheerleaders reported active dieting, 56 percent reported being told by a coach to lose weight. Likewise, 57 percent of synchronized skaters (synchronized skating is a type of figure skating) reported weight and appearance were important to a coach.

These results, and others, indicate coaches probably contribute to the adoption of disordered-eating behaviors. In a 1991 study of female athletes with clinical eating disorders, five contributing factors directly related to their coaches were identified: direct remarks, public weigh-ins, regular posting of weigh-in results, thoughts of being required to lose weight to fit a coach's ideal, and fear of losing a team position following failure to lose weight. More recently, 8.3–33.8 percent of female collegiate athletes perceived pressure from coaches to lose weight or maintain a low body weight often, usually, or always. Male athletes are not exempt from these findings. In fact, 70 percent of male collegiate athletes reported pressure from coaches to either lose or gain weight. Although a coach is not likely to be the only reason athletes adopt unhealthy weight loss behaviors, one can assume weight-related coach pressure probably contributes to dieting behaviors.

Whether athletes participate in individual or team sports, they are influenced by teammates. That is, even though athletes in individual sports do not compete with their teammates per se, they practice and compete together. This puts them in proximity with each other, increasing the flow of weight management information between team members. In a study of female athletes from a multitude of sports, 17–26.8 percent reported pressure from teammates and 5.4 percent believed their team/sport should have a weight limit. In more specific sport contexts, researchers found nearly 55 percent of synchronized skaters and 16 percent of swimmers thought weight and appearance were important to their teammates.

For male athletes, pressure from teammates related to weight may be more closely linked to increasing size and power. Regardless, 20 percent of a collegiate male athletic sample mentioned that teammates motivated them to improve fitness. However, another sample indicated weight pressure from teammates/coaches was related to higher drive for muscularity ($r = .43$) and bulimic symptomology ($r = .25$) in male athletes. This finding highlights the importance of teammate influence, regardless of weight loss intention.

Judges are often a critical part of the sport environment. In some sports, athletes are subjectively judged by a panel of judges. Subjective judging, then, leads some coaches and athletes to believe low body weight produces more appealing lines, which in turn results in higher subjective scores from judges. Divers, figure skaters, and gymnasts are judged by their skill and their ability to demonstrate grace, strength, agility, and beauty. Therefore, it is not surprising athletes in similar sports believe their weight is important to judges (e.g., 64 percent of synchronized skaters).

Uniforms

Uniforms are the most frequently reported weight pressure in many sports. Uniforms include tight swimsuits, dance attire, gymnastic leotards, volleyball shorts, or track and field spandex. Tight-fitting, revealing attire has resulted in self-consciousness and an awareness that perceived bodily flaws are apparent. In some studies, swimmers and dancers have reported uniforms were often ordered two or more sizes smaller than an athlete's typical size. Conversely, some athletes reported uniforms were ordered first and an athlete was selected to fit into whatever size was left.

For swimmers, one study indicated the most salient weight pressure was team uniform (45.2 percent), followed by teammates (16.1 percent), the crowd (12.9 percent), and perceived performance advantage (9.7 percent). More than half of college (53.5 percent) and high school (60.7 percent) cheerleaders reported their uniforms represented a weight-related pressure. Although elite divers did not report increased disordered-eating behaviors due to uniform pressure, some researchers have suggested that individuals more susceptible to these pressures retire from the sport prior to reaching an elite level, alleviating the weight-related pressure uniforms may represent.

A related pressure worth mentioning here is the presence of full-length mirrors reported by dancers. Although full-length wall-to-wall mirrors give dancers an opportunity for immediate feedback about lines and body position, they may also act as a constant reminder of body size/shape. Used consistently, the constant feedback may be distressing to many dancers.

Weight Requirements

Although some researchers suggest weigh-ins are detrimental to athletes' health, they continue to be held. In fact, one study indicated cheerleaders had a weight limit of 120 pounds and were required to have a body fat percentage between 9 percent and 17 percent at the college level. Furthermore, nearly 50 percent of college cheerleaders reported having a weight limit at tryouts and almost 40 percent indicated they had periodic weigh-ins throughout the season.

Although more recent research indicates collegiate athletes do not experience regular weigh-ins by coaches, weigh-ins still occur in some sports, like wrestling that has specific weight classes. As successful attempts to compete at a lower weight class help a wrestler gain a performance advantage, many wrestlers experience weight cycling. On average, wrestlers lose 13 pounds during a one-week weight-cutting period with some wrestlers reporting losing 9–11 pounds directly before a match using typical weight loss methods of dehydration, chronic dieting, fasting, and overtraining.

However, given the adverse effects of weight-cutting, the National Wrestling Coaches Association and National Federation of State High School Associations introduced a rule that set minimum weight class opportunities based on body composition of wrestlers prior to the start of the season. This rule stipulated wrestlers could not compete if they lost more than 1.5 percent of their body weight per week. Although it is a step in the right direction, subsequent studies have determined that this rule did not positively influence high school wrestlers' attitudes toward eating and weight loss.

Beliefs about Weight and Performance

Although several external factors associated with sports contribute to athletes' experiences of weight-related pressure, the internalization of pressure may also contribute to eating disorders and disordered-eating behaviors. In a study, 15.7 percent of athletes believed performance would improve if they lost five pounds. Whether they developed this belief from others or their experience in sport has yet to be explored, but they are probably unknowingly placing pressure on themselves to lose weight in pursuit of athletic achievement.

Ashley M. Coker-Cranney

See also: Anorexia Athletica; Ballet; Cheerleading; Coaches; Dancing; Female Athlete Triad; Figure Skating; Gymnastics; Sports; Swimming and Synchronized Swimming; Weight Class Sports; Wrestling

Bibliography

Beals, Katherine A. *Disordered Eating among Athletes: A Comprehensive Guide for Health Professionals.* Champaign, IL: Human Kinetics, 2004.

de Bruin, A. P. (Karin), Raoul R. D. Oudejans, and Frank C. Bakker. "Dieting and Body Image in Aesthetic Sports: A Comparison of Dutch Female Gymnasts and Non-Aesthetic Sport Athletes." *Psychology of Sport and Exercise* 8, no. 4 (2007): 507–520. http://dx.doi.org/10.1016/j.psychsport.2006.10.002.

"Famous Athletes with Eating Disorders." Influence Publishing. Accessed November 18, 2016. http://www.influencepublishing.com/top-20-famous-athletes-eating-disorders/.

Galli, Nick, and Justine J. Reel. "Adonis or Hephaestus? Exploring Body Image in Male Athletes." *Psychology of Men & Masculinity* 10, no. 2 (2009): 95–108. http://dx.doi.org/10.1037/a0014005.

Greenleaf, Christy. "Weight Pressures and Social Physique Anxiety among Collegiate Synchronized Skaters." *Journal of Sport Behavior* 27 (2004): 260–276.

Greenleaf, Christy, Trent A. Petrie, Jennifer Carter, and Justine J. Reel. "Female Collegiate Athletes: Prevalence of Eating Disorders and Disordered Eating Behavior." *Journal of American College Health* 57, no. 5 (2009): 489–495. http://dx.doi.org/10.3200/JACH.57.5.489-496.

Harris, M. B., and D. Greco. "Weight Control and Weight Concern in Competitive Female Gymnasts." *Journal of Sport & Exercise Psychology* 12, no. 4 (1990): 427–433.

Hausenblas, Heather A., and Diane E. Mack. "Social Physique Anxiety and Eating Disorder Correlates among Female Athletic and Nonathletic Populations." *Journal of Sport Behavior* 22 (1999): 502–512.

Kerr, Gretchen, Erica Berman, and Mary Jane De Souza. "Disordered Eating in Women's Gymnastics: Perspectives of Athletes, Coaches, Parents, and Judges." *Journal of Applied Sport Psychology* 18 (2006): 28–43. http://dx.doi.org/10.1080/10413200500471301.

Muscat, Anne C., and Bonita C. Long. "Critical Comments about Body Shape and Weight: Disordered Eating of Female Athletes and Sport Participants." *Journal of Applied Sport Psychology* 20 (2008): 1–24. http://dx.doi.org/10.1080/10413200701784833.

Peden, Jamie, Beverly L. Stiles, Michael Vandehey, and George Diekhoff. "The Effects of External Pressures and Competitiveness on Characteristics of Eating Disorders and Body Dissatisfaction." *Journal of Sport & Social Issues* 32, no. 4 (2008): 415–429. https://doi.org/10.1177/0193723508325638.

Petrie, Trent A. "Differences between Male and Female College Lean Sport Athletes, Non-lean Sport Athletes, and Nonathletes on Behavioral and Psychological Indices of Eating Disorders." *Journal of Applied Sport Psychology* 8, no. 2 (1996): 218–230. http://dx.doi.org/10.1080/10413209608406478.

Petrie, Trent A., Christy Greenleaf, Justine Reel, and Jennifer Carter. "Prevalence of Eating Disorders and Disordered Eating Behaviors among Male Collegiate Athletes." *Psychology of Men & Masculinity* 9, no. 4 (2008): 267–277. http://dx.doi.org/10.1037/a0013178.

Reel, Justine J., and Nick A. Galli. "Should Coaches Serve as the 'Weight Police' for Athletes?" *Journal of Physical Education Recreation and Dance* 77, no. 3 (2006): 6–7. http://dx.doi.org/10.1080/07303084.2006.10597836.

Reel, Justine J., and Diane L. Gill. "Psychosocial Factors Related to Eating Disorders among High School and College Female Cheerleaders." *The Sport Psychologist* 10 (1996): 195–206.

Reel, Justine J., and Diane L. Gill. "Slim Enough to Swim? Weight Pressures for Competitive Swimmers and Coaching Implications." *The Sport Journal* 4 (2001): 1–5.

Reel, Justine J., Sonya SooHoo, Katherine M. Jamieson, and Diane L. Gill. "Femininity to the Extreme: Body Image Concerns among College Female Dancers." *Women in Sport and Physical Activity Journal* 14 (2005): 39–51.

Reel, Justine J., Sonya SooHoo, Trent A. Petrie, Christy Greenleaf, and Jennifer E. Carter. "Slimming Down for Sport: Developing a Weight Pressures in Sport Measure for Female Athletes." *Journal of Clinical Sport Psychology* 4, no. 2 (2010): 99–111.

Shriver, Lenka Humenikova, Nancy Mulhollen Betts, and Mark Edward Payton. "Changes in Body Weight, Body Composition, and Eating Attitudes in High School Wrestlers." *International Journal of Sport Nutrition and Exercise Metabolism* 19 (2009): 424–432.

WEIGHT STIGMA

Concerns about an obesity epidemic or pandemic are not unfounded given that the overweight and obesity rate is estimated to be as high as two-thirds of American adults. Because of widely successful public health campaigns combating obesity the concept that *thin is good and fat is bad* is pervasive and powerful in our culture. In one study, about a fifth of adult men and a quarter of adult women reported being willing to trade three years of their life to choose their perfect weight or body size. Other individuals report adopting dangerous habits like smoking cigarettes to remain thin. These are just a few examples of the internalized belief that being overweight or obese is negative and associated with shame.

As a result of this negative association with being overweight, people who are larger may experience discrimination and prejudice. This discrimination is commonly referred to as *weight stigma* or *fat shaming* Weight stigma has been shown to have a significant psychological effect on individuals who report experiencing this negative response from others. For example, victims of weight stigma may experience increased stress and anxiety levels as well as a higher tendency to develop depression. Unfortunately, this long-term psychological stress could lead to more negative health outcomes and lower self-efficacy over weight loss. Studies have also found that weight stigma has a significant effect on a person's subsequent eating behavior, and several models for explaining the role of weight stigma in reinforcing obesity have been posited. Weight stigma is prevalent in virtually every aspect of daily life, from schooling to the workplace to health care.

Weight Stigma in Occupational, Social, and Medical Settings

Research has shown that weight stigma is the fourth most common type of prejudice experienced by individuals in the United States, after race, sex, and age. Compared with many other, less socially accepted, forms of prejudice, weight-based bias is typically seen in a much less critical light. Individuals who are overweight or obese are routinely stereotyped in the media and characterized as unmotivated,

Weight Stigma and Sizeism: An Interview with Dr. Christy Greenleaf

Dr. Christy Greenleaf is a professor in the Department of Kinesiology at University of Wisconsin at Milwaukee. She received her bachelor of arts degree in Psychology from Bowling Green State University, her master of science degree in Sport Studies from Miami University (Ohio), and her doctor of philosophy degree in Exercise and Sport Science from the University of North Carolina at Greensboro. Dr. Greenleaf's research focuses on psychosocial aspects of weight, physical activity, body image, and disordered eating. She is particularly interested in weight bias, or negative attitudes and stereotypes toward individuals who appear to be overweight, and how weight bias manifests itself within physical activity settings. Dr. Greenleaf has published 50 peer-reviewed articles, 13 book chapters, and made over 115 national/international presentations. Dr. Greenleaf is an American College of Sports Medicine Physical Activity in Public Health Specialist, a Fellow in the Obesity Society, and a Fellow in the Society of Physical and Health Educators.

What is weight stigma? Is this the same thing as sizeism and fat bias?

In my experience with research in the area of weight stigma and as an advocate who speaks against sizeism, it is important to define these terms. Individuals who look fat or larger than some socially acceptable size are judged as "less than" individuals who appear thin, lean, or fit because of the assumed negative characteristics associated with being fat. Individuals who appear fat are often thought to be lazy, have low intelligence, and lack willpower. These negative attributes are believed to be connected to an individual's weight or body shape. So weight stigma refers to the general negative perception of individuals who appear fat.

Sizeism is a form of discrimination based upon body shape or size. Size discrimination usually refers to treating individuals whose body shapes/sizes fall outside of socially accepted norms (either too thin or too fat) differently than those whose bodies "fit" within social norms. For example, someone who appears to be fat may be overlooked for a job promotion because of assumptions related to work ethic or motivation.

Fat bias refers to prejudiced attitudes held toward individuals who appear fat. Similar to the concept of weight stigma, fat bias is the generalized belief that all individuals who appear fat possess (or lack) similar personal attributes and qualities. For example, individuals who appear fat are believed to eat a lot of junk food, rarely exercise, and not care about their health. These types of beliefs can lead to size discrimination.

How are people from a young age taught that size matters and that being overweight is a bad thing?

People learn early on that their size makes a difference. Mass media certainly shapes our perceptions of what body shapes are "normal" and what body shapes are "abnormal" or "unusual." Few individuals who appear fat are included in television shows or in magazines and, when they are, they are typically portrayed as funny, silly, or the butt of a joke. Although mass media is not an accurate depiction of the real world, it certainly influences people's beliefs about what bodies are attractive, healthy, and desired.

Health promotion efforts have also (unintentionally) communicated the message that a fat body is an unhealthy body and therefore bad. Health educators, physicians, physical education teachers, etc., promote healthful eating and physical activity often in the quest of weight loss or weight maintenance. Health promotion efforts tied to weight can communicate the message that a fat body is something that must be "combated" and that a "war" is necessary ("war on obesity").

What are the most important things that parents can do to combat weight stigma within the home?

Avoid commenting on weight. Recent research indicates that weight-related comments (regardless of nature or intent) are often perceived negatively. A better approach is to discuss behaviors associated with good health (independent of weight). Parents can encourage eating nutritious foods and being physically active (but without any connection to or comments about weight).

How can we as a society fight against sizeism and weight stigma?

Embrace a philosophy of social justice. There is no evidence that making people feel bad about their bodies is an effective way of promoting health or health behaviors. Additionally, more and more evidence is coming out demonstrating that people of a variety of shapes and sizes can be healthy (some thin people have metabolic disease and some fat people do not). So we need to let go of the moral judgments we make related to bodies that appear fat and adopt a social justice philosophy whereby we (society) promote and support people of all shapes and sizes living lives that are happy and healthy.

If someone is experiencing weight stigma, what are the best strategies for coping?

It is important to seek social support when a person experiences weight stigma rather than remaining silent. Fortunately, there are a number of advocacy groups that can provide support to individuals who have received stigma about their weight or size. One group is the Association for Size Diversity and Health (ASDAH). ASDAH is committed to the Health at Every Size approach that refers to a philosophy that includes weight inclusivity, health enhancement, respectful care, eating for well-being, and life enhancing movement.

Second, it is important to become a critical consumer of media. Learn about the ways in which models' and actors' bodies and images are carefully constructed and manipulated for media. What we see in magazines and on television is not reality.

Finally, being a role model of health represents an excellent strategy for coping with weight stigma and a society that emphasizes size and thinness. A person can role model a happy and healthy life by engaging in activities that he or she loves.

---

undisciplined, unhealthy, slovenly, and lacking in willpower. This bias is present in virtually every setting and affects individuals' careers, interpersonal relationships, and even the quality of their medical care.

In the work environment, research has shown that overweight employees are routinely denigrated in comparison to their average-weight counterparts. Studies have found evidence of weight-based bias against the obese and overweight at virtually every stage of employment, including hiring, placement, compensation, promotion, discipline, and termination. Generally, overweight and obese employees are seen negatively by subordinates, coworkers, and supervisors. These individuals are often thought of as lazy, sloppy, lacking in competency, harder to get along with, and even more likely to be absent from work. Weight-based bias has been shown to exist at virtually all job levels, from entry level up through managerial, administrative, and into senior executive positions.

Overweight and obese individuals are subjected to social stigma because of their weight. Discrimination against people who are considered fat occurs across the life span, starting as young as age 3. One study conducted among high school students found 84 percent of students surveyed reported witnessing an overweight classmate being teased/bullied, socially excluded, avoided, or ignored multiple times in school. Some students also reported witnessing overweight classmates being verbally or physically threatened or hurt. Another study reported overweight adolescents have fewer friendships and are less socially integrated than their average-weight counterparts. Overweight adolescents also face more negative attitudes from teachers, a lower rate of college acceptance, and more wrongful dismissals from college. In adults, being overweight is associated with having fewer sexual partners and less satisfying sexual relationships. Overweight adults have reported being overweight is often a barrier to physical intimacy, whether by deterring potential partners or contributing to a lack of confidence that makes dating more difficult. Another study found overweight individuals are more likely to be discriminated against in decisions related to child adoption (i.e., overweight/obese adults hoping to adopt a child faced more barriers than average-weight adults).

In addition to bias in the workplace and in social settings, one of the most concerning areas where weight-based bias is prevalent is in medical settings. Health care providers commonly exhibit fat-phobic, antiobese/overweight biases; one survey of 1,100 training health care professionals found fewer than 2 percent of had positive or neutral attitudes toward overweight individuals. The other 98 percent surveyed reported either explicit (i.e., conscious) or implicit (unconscious) biases against overweight and obese individuals. The high prevalence of antiobese stigma in the medical world has been well documented. This bias is even present in health care workers who specialize in the care and treatment of overweight and obese individuals. These studies demonstrate an association between the biased attitudes of health care providers and the quality of care that obese patients report receiving. Overweight and obese individuals express being disregarded by their health care providers regularly, and this negative experience can contribute to avoidance of doctors and medical settings, lack of continuity in care, and higher levels of stress.

Causes and Consequences of Weight Stigma

Several theories have been posited to explain the origins of weight stigma. The theory that has received the most attention and is the most accurate explanation of weight stigma is psychological attribution theory. According to attribution theory, biases emerge as a result of the explanations people use. In the case of weight bias, attribution theory states people view overweight as the result of a personal failure on behalf of an individual. This line of logic reflects traditional American values that include self-discipline, individualism, and personal accountability. Because these values are ingrained into Western (specifically U.S.) culture, overweight people are often blamed for their size. Being overweight is a reflection of an inability to exercise self-control or a lack of motivation to exercise or diet, and an association between these negative personality traits and being overweight contribute to the bias against overweight individuals. This bias is often implicit (i.e., unconscious), meaning most people who adhere to this type of thinking are often unaware of it. Research has shown when people are asked to rate the personality of overweight people, they often describe them in undesirable terms such as lazy, slovenly, or gluttonous. However, if those same people are told a person is overweight due to a medical reason, such as a medication or a disease, subsequent ratings of the overweight person improve significantly.

Experiencing weight stigma has a profound psychological and physical effect on individuals. Exposure to weight stigma—particularly over a lengthy period—has identical effects as prolonged stress. Heart rate increases and the pituitary gland releases cortisol, the stress hormone. Repeated episodes of psychological stress, along with corresponding increases in cortisol levels, contribute to chronic diseases, such as heart disease, hyperglycemia (high blood sugar), high blood pressure, osteoporosis/bone density loss, and weight gain. In addition to physical effects, weight stigma has emotional and psychological effects. Individuals who are worried about being judged unfavorably on their body weight report had worsened mood, limited ability to concentrate, higher anxiety levels, more behavioral displays of self-consciousness (e.g., trying to hide one's figure through posture), lower self-esteem, and greater expectations of social rejection.

Underweight Bias

A comparatively small but growing body of research has shown bias exists against individuals who are noticeably underweight. One study surveyed over 1,000 random participants and asked them to report how likely it is they would hire, promote, terminate, recommend for adoption, or help someone following a traffic accident. Participants were shown five images of women with body mass index scores across the weight spectrum, from underweight up through obese. Results indicated bias against both the underweight and overweight/obese individuals, and in some cases the bias was stronger for underweight women than for overweight women. Although more research is needed to examine the bias against underweight individuals, it is expected underweight bias operates similarly to overweight bias.

Hannah J. Hopkins

See also: Fat Bias/Fat Discrimination; Health at Every Size Approach; Obesity; Plus-Size Models and Clothing; Teasing

Bibliography

Ali, Mir M., Aliaksandr Amialchuk, and John A. Rizzo. "The Influence of Body Weight on Social Network Ties among Adolescents." *Economics & Human Biology* 10, no. 1 (2012): 20–34. https://doi.org/10.1016/j.ehb.2011.10.001.

Blodorn, Alison, Brenda Major, Jeffrey Hunger, and Carol Miller. "Unpacking the Psychological Weight of Weight Stigma: A Rejection-Expectation Pathway." *Journal of Experimental Social Psychology* 63 (2016): 69–76. https://doi.org/10.1016/j.jesp.2015.12.003.

Carr, Deborah, Lauren F. Murphy, Heather D. Batson, and Kristen W. Springer. "Bigger Is Not Always Better: The Effect of Obesity on Sexual Satisfaction and Behavior of Adult Men in the United States." *Men and Masculinities* 16, no. 4 (2013): 452–477. https://doi.org/10.1177/1097184X13502651.

Phelan, S. M., D. J. Burgess, M. W. Yeazel, W. L. Hellerstedt, J. M. Griffin, and M. van Ryn. "Impact of Weight Bias and Stigma on Quality of Care and Outcomes for Patients with Obesity." *Obesity Reviews* 16, no. 4 (2015): 319–326. https://doi.org/10.1111/obr.12266.

Puhl, Rebecca M., and Kelly D. Brownell. "Psychosocial Origins of Obesity Stigma: Toward Changing a Powerful and Pervasive Bias." *Obesity Reviews* 4 (2003): 213–227. https://doi.org/10.1046/j.1467-789X.2003.00122.x.

Puhl, Rebecca M., Joerg Luedicke, and Cheslea Heuer. "Weight-Based Victimization toward Overweight Adolescents: Observations and Reactions of Peers." *Journal of School Health* 81, no. 11 (2011): 696–703. https://doi.org/10.1111/j.1746-1561.2011.00646.x.

Rudolph, Cort W., Charles L. Wells, Marcus D. Weller, and Boris B. Baltes. "A Meta-Analysis of Empirical Studies of Weight-Based Bias in the Workplace." *Journal of Vocational Behavior* 74, no. 1 (2009): 1–10. https://doi.org/10.1016/j.jvb.2008.09.008.

Swami, Viren, Jakob Pietschnig, Stefan Stieger, Martin J. Tovée, and Martin Voracek. "An Investigation of Weight Bias against Women and Its Associations with Individual Difference Factors." *Body Image* 7, no. 3 (2010): 194–199. https://doi.org/10.1016/j.bodyim.2010.03.003.

Swift, Judy A., S. Hanlon, L. El-Redy, Rebecca. M. Puhl, and C. Glazebrook. "Weight Bias among UK Trainee Dietitians, Doctors, Nurses and Nutritionists." *Journal of Human Nutrition and Dietetics* 26, no. 4 (2013): 395–402. https://doi.org/10.1111/jhn.12019.

Vartanian, Lenny R., and Alexis M. Porter. "Weight Stigma and Eating Behavior: A Review of the Literature." *Appetite* 102 (2016): 3–14. https://doi.org/10.1016/j.appet.2016.01.034.

Williams, Amanda L., and Michael J. Merten. "Romantic Relationships among Women Experiencing Obesity: Self-Perception and Weight as Barriers to Intimacy." *Family and Consumer Sciences Research Journal* 41, no. 3 (2013): 284–298. https://doi.org/10.1111/fcsr.12020.

WRESTLING

Competitive wrestling requires a fine balance between strength and weight. Wrestlers must be as strong and agile as they possibly can, while remaining within the weight limits of their category or class. Consequently, some athletes have taken extreme measures to make the weight. Studies investigating rapid weight loss among wrestlers began in the 1970s. Early studies found up to 80 percent of competitors engaged in a weight loss procedure. The methods used were varied and included saunas, exercising in rubberized suits, and severely curtailing caloric and fluid intake. In addition, the use of diuretics, laxatives, diet pills, self-induced vomiting, and spit cups were common methods for rapid weight loss.

History of Wrestling and Eating Disorders

In 1997, three collegiate wrestlers died from weight-related causes, which prompted the National Collegiate Athletic Association (NCAA) to implement a program to control rapid weight loss among athletes. Robert Oppliger and colleagues (2003) investigated whether the stricter guidelines worked and found 40 percent of the 741 wrestlers reported the new rules deterred extreme weight loss behaviors. However, over half of the wrestlers continued to fast to lose weight or maintain low weight, and 25 percent of wrestlers used saunas and rubberized suits to lose water weight at least once a month. Dieting behaviors among college wrestlers were more extreme than behaviors reported by high school wrestlers, but there was a clear reduction in overall pathological weight control methods compared to the 1980s. In addition, although many wrestlers admitted engaging in occasional pathogenic weight management behaviors, only 5 (of 741) met the clinical criteria for bulimia nervosa.

In 2006, the National Wrestling Coaches Association (NWCA) designed and implemented a weight management program for high school wrestlers requiring a minimum weight to be set at the start of each season. Under the guidelines, wrestlers are not permitted to compete under their minimum weight limits and cannot lose more than 1.5 percent of their body weight per week. Shriver and colleagues (2009) evaluated the efficacy of the NWCA guidelines and found that although body weight and body fat did not appear to fluctuate as widely as might be expected before these rules were introduced, wrestlers continued to report weight concerns and caloric expenditure. Thus, even though body weight and fat were more monitored using the regulations, wrestlers were not deterred from obsessing about body weight.

Future of Wrestling

Although measures have been taken to reduce the extreme weight loss during season, fluctuations in weight are reported between in-season and off-season. Typically, wrestlers experience significant weight gain during the off-season, which may indicate they are not competing at a typical or ideal body weight.

It appears wrestlers are less likely to fit the clinical eating disorder criteria than disordered eating, characterized by a focus on losing weight for short-term performance improvements. There is evidence to suggest wrestlers exhibit characteristics of anorexia nervosa (e.g., restricting food intake) or bulimia nervosa (e.g., excessive exercise). Reports of extreme dieting and use of diuretics, even with the changes implemented by the NCAA and NWCA, are still being identified. However, not all wrestlers exhibit the same eating disorder characteristics and as a group they may be similar to bodybuilders who undergo severe caloric restriction to reduce body fat prior to competition.

Timothy M. Baghurst

See also: Bodybuilding; Sports; Weight Class Sports; Weight Pressures in Sport

Bibliography

Buford, Thomas A., Stephen J. Rossi, Douglas B. Smith, Matthew S. O'Brien, and Chris Pickering. "The Effect of a Competitive Wrestling Season on Body Weight, Hydration, and Muscular Performance in Collegiate Wrestlers." *Journal of Strength and Conditioning Research* 20 (2006): 689–692.

Oppliger, Robert A., Suzanne A. N. Steen, and James R. Scott. "Weight Loss Practices of College Wrestlers." *International Journal of Sport Nutrition and Exercise Metabolism* 13 (2003): 29–46. https://doi.org/10.1123/ijsnem.13.1.29.

Shriver, Lenka H., Nance M. Betts, and Mark E. Payton. "Changes in Body Weight, Body Composition, and Eating Attitudes in High School Wrestlers." *International Journal of Sport Nutrition and Exercise Metabolism* 19 (2009): 424–432.

Steen, Suzanne N., and Kelly D. Brownell. "Patterns of Weight Loss and Regain in Wrestlers." *Medicine & Science in Sport & Exercise* 22, no. 6 (1990): 762–768.

Weissinger, Ellen, Terry J. Housh, and Glen O. Johnson. "Coaches' Attitudes, Knowledge, and Practices Concerning Weight Loss Behaviors in High School Wrestling." *Pediatric Exercise Science* 5, no. 2 (1993): 145–150.

Y

YOGA

Yoga is an integration of the body, mind, and spirit. The origins of yoga date back several thousand years in India. Yoga was created as the art, science, and philosophy of life. It is believed the vast body of knowledge, when practiced through the system of yoga, can lead to greater health, mental control, and, ultimately, self-realization.

When a body is out of alignment, the mind is rarely in control or balance. Yoga movement acts to stimulate stretching, purifying, and healing the body. Yoga movements bring balance, peace, and harmony to the mind, creating health, happiness, and fulfillment. Moreover, yoga practices readjusting negative thoughts. The emotional content of current thoughts affects future reality. By creating a conscious mind through yoga, negative conditioning of the past can be let go. This is especially critical for individuals with poor self-image and low self-esteem.

In the U.S. culture, yoga is viewed as an activity to improve health and well-being. Thus, yoga can deliver beneficial effects for a variety of medical conditions, such as blood pressure, cancer, depression, anxiety, and eating disorders. By practicing yoga regularly, the mind and body are balanced and deep relaxation is achieved. Once the balance and relaxation techniques are mastered, a sense of accomplishment is experienced along with an inner peace that may help the mind release daily worries. This mechanism may result in greater self-esteem, identified as a protective factor for individuals suffering from eating disorders.

Neurotransmitter Effects from Yoga

How yoga movement stimulates neurophysiological activities in the brain, and improves the following human functions, has been scientifically explained. First, the neurotransmitter melatonin is released through yoga movement and circadian rhythms are normalized, improving sleep and mood. Second, yoga promotes increased γ-aminobutyric acid (GABA) levels, thereby having a positive effect on depression and anxiety. Third, yoga increases dopamine levels, leading to improvements in cognition, motor behavior, motivation, reward, sleep, mood, attention, and learning. Next, increased levels of serotonins regulate anger, aggression, mood, body temperature, sleep, sexuality, metabolism, and appetite. Last, numerous studies have shown consistent evidence that positive relationships between mindfulness movements such as yoga and reduced cortisol (also known as stress hormone) levels decrease stress.

Benefits of Yoga for Eating Disorder Treatments

In the past decade, clinicians and clients have embraced the benefits of yoga for treating eating disorders. Although few studies related to eating disorders have shown the effectiveness of yoga therapy in inpatient and outpatient settings, a study conducted by Carei and colleagues demonstrated greater decreases in eating disorder symptoms and food preoccupation. Another study reported that yoga helped reduce impulsivity in clients with bulimia.

One significant benefit of practicing yoga during recovery from eating disorders is an increased level of body awareness. Clients with eating disorders are often preoccupied with food, body shape, calories, and weight. As such, yoga group therapy, through mindfulness, promotes positive thoughts, self-image, and self-talk and helps a participant stay in the present moment instead of getting preoccupied with negative thoughts and poor self-image. Yoga also initiates slow movements with attention, compassion, and awareness. This integrated approach increases a sense of well-being and calmness that results in less reactivity and increased self-care. Learning to sense the body, mind, and spirit is a powerful means to overcome personal battles with eating disorders.

Treatment Challenges Associated with Yoga

Yoga is an effective way to create a state of reflection and increased awareness for individuals experiencing intense self-hatred and suffering. Because of the nature of the disease, however, the quality of the yoga group may be dismissed if health care providers and yoga instructors are unaware of contributing factors for eating disorders. Examples of common behaviors observed in individuals with eating disorders are the comparison of one's body to those of peers and the yoga instructor, body checking by looking in the mirrors or by touching one's body, wearing extremely baggy or tight clothing, and excessively repeating yoga poses to burn extra calories. The intensity level or the types of yoga movements may trigger poor self-image and negative thoughts because of a lack of physical strength, feeling fat, or urge to overexercise. The other caution is the language used during the yoga group. The yoga instructor should be mindful while selecting terminologies of physical movements and functions (e.g., *getting toned*) and should use the yoga philosophy as a means of spiritual guidance instead of integrating religious views to create a safe and nonjudgmental atmosphere in a yoga group.

Moreover, feeling fat, ugly, shamed, and/or disgusted are described as typical emotional states in eating disorders, and facing the challenge of experiencing body awareness through yoga movements may require much effort by persons with extremely distorted self-images. Thus, some clients in inpatient or residential settings may avoid any activity guiding them to connect with their sensations, such as a yoga group. Health care providers and yoga instructors must set clear boundaries with clients who refuse or avoid yoga groups by educating them about the benefits of yoga and helping them understand the yoga experience as a part of recovery.

Considerations for Yoga Group/Therapy as Treatment for Eating Disorders

Yoga group or therapy can be an effective treatment for eating disorders. The most significant element is to select yoga instructors knowledgeable of eating disorders or who have a strong willingness to learn about and understand eating disorders. Based on a client's medical level, trained yoga instructors should have a clear understanding of how to modify poses and levels of yoga movements (i.e., power or hot yoga vs. fundamental yoga) for populations with eating disorders. When they notice common behaviors such body checking, comparisons, or overexercise during a group, they must be comfortable redirecting the actions assertively. Last, it is strongly desirable to include yoga instructors as part of a treatment team. The most crucial element of success in the treatment of eating disorders is to provide consistent messages to clients. To maintain the quality of treatment, yoga instructors and health care providers should exchange necessary client information related to yoga participation.

Maya Miyairi

See also: Exercise; Integrative Approaches; Mindfulness; Treatment

Bibliography

Bai, Bath. *Complete Guide to Pilates, Yoga, Medication, and Stress Relief.* New York: Sterling Publisher, 2006.

Carei, T. Rain, Amber L. Fyfe-Johnson, Cora C. Breuner, and Margaret A. Brown. "Randomized Controlled Clinical Trial of Yoga in the Treatment of Eating Disorders." *Journal of Adolescent Health* 46, no. 4 (2010): 346–351. http://dx.doi.org/10.1016/j.jadohealth.2009.08.007.

Douglass, Laura. "Thinking through the Body: The Conceptualization of Yoga as Therapy for Individuals with Eating Disorders." *Eating Disorders* 19 (2010): 83–96. http://dx.doi.org/10.1080/10640266.2011.533607.

Douglass, Laura. "Yoga as an Intervention in the Treatment of Eating Disorders: Does It Help?" *Eating Disorders* 17, no. 2 (2009): 126–139. http://dx.doi.org/10.1080/10640260802714555.

McIver, Shane, Paul O'Halloran, and Michael McGartland. "Yoga as a Treatment for Binge Eating Disorder: A Preliminary Study." *Complementary Therapies in Medicine* 17, no. 4 (2009): 196–202. http://dx.doi.org/10.1016/j.ctim.2009.05.002.

Price, Beverly. "Yoga as the Missing Link in Eating Disorder Recovery." *Yoga Therapy Today* 6, no. 1 (2010): 15–18.

Reel, Justine J., and Katherine A. Beals, eds. *The Hidden Faces of Eating Disorders and Body Image.* Reston, VA: AAHPERD, 2009.

ZINC

Eating disorders contribute to numerous vitamin and mineral deficiencies including deficiencies in zinc. In one study, 40 percent of individuals with bulimia nervosa and 54 percent of individuals with anorexia nervosa presented with zinc deficiencies. These deficiencies could be caused by lower dietary intake of zinc, impaired zinc absorption, vomiting, diarrhea, and binge episodes with low-zinc foods. Having a zinc deficiency is important for individuals who are at risk for eating disorders because low zinc contributes to decreased appetite and a loss of one's ability to taste foods. Therefore, restrictive behavior associated with a diet can lead to a physiological response that causes a lack of desire to eat and perpetuates anorexia nervosa.

Zinc Taste Test

The zinc taste test (ZTT) can be administered to assess for zinc deficiency in eating-disordered individuals in a noninvasive way. To follow the ZTT protocol, an individual is asked to refrain from eating, drinking, or smoking for at least 30 minutes. A client is then asked to place 1–2 teaspoons of aqueous zinc in his or her mouth, swirl for 10 seconds and spit out the solution. The client is then asked to describe the taste of the solution to test for physiological zinc status. Optimal zinc levels are represented by reports of an extremely unpleasant taste usually accompanied by a nonverbal grimace while tasting the solution; individuals deficient in zinc tend to describe the solution as tasteless or tasting like water.

Because most individuals with anorexia nervosa and bulimia nervosa are deficient in zinc, individuals can be given a supplement with liquid zinc to detect the presence of eating disorders. This is particularly useful since eating disorders are such secretive disorders and other assessment tools (e.g., questionnaires) are typically based on an individual's self-report of symptoms.

Nutritional Supplementation as Treatment

In addition to showing promise for the detection of eating disorders, zinc supplementation should be considered for the treatment of eating disorders. Specifically, preliminary studies have shown zinc supplementation leads to increased appetite, eating, and weight gain. In a frequently cited 1994 study, anorexia nervosa clients who received zinc supplementation achieved a 10 percent increase in body mass index and increased their body mass index at twice the rate of the control group.

Justine J. Reel

See also: Medical and Health Consequences; Nutritional Deficiencies

Bibliography

Birmingham, Carl L., Elliott M. Goldner, and Rita Bakan. "Controlled Trial of Zinc Supplementation in Anorexia Nervosa." *International Journal of Eating Disorders* 15, no. 3 (1994): 251–255. https://doi.org/10.1002/1098-108X.

Costin, Carolyn. *The Eating Disorder Sourcebook: A Comprehensive Guide to the Causes, Treatments and Prevention of Eating Disorders*, 3rd ed. New York: McGraw-Hill, 2007.

Costin, Carolyn. *100 Questions & Answers about Eating Disorders*. Boston, MA: Jones and Bartlett, 2007.

Humphries, Laurie, Beverly Vivian, Mary Stuart, and Craig J. McClain. "Zinc Deficiency and Eating Disorders." *Journal of Clinical Psychiatry* 50, no. 12 (1989): 456–459.

Controversies and Debates

This section of the encyclopedia provides several debate essays about controversial issues surrounding eating disorders in our society. The first essay piece will focus on whether exercise is helpful or harmful for the treatment of eating disorders. The second debate will examine whether athletes are more or less prone to develop disordered eating behaviors. The third debate dissects the sticky issue around sending body mass index report cards home to parents. The fourth debate will investigate the newer condition of orthorexia nervosa and whether it constitutes a true eating disorder or not. The fifth debate will delve into issues surrounding pro-ana websites. The final debate will focus on whether recovery is truly possible for an eating disorder.

The Paradox of Exercise: Helpful or Harmful for Treatment?

Shows like the *Biggest Loser* emphasize the need to use vigorous and intense physical exercises to drop tremendous amounts of body weight. The statement "exercise is medicine" has been a popular way of capturing the various psychological and physical benefits associated with physical activity. In fact, the American College of Sports Medicine (ACSM) promotes an Exercise Is Medicine (EIM) initiative with the intent to get physical activity into health care practices. The purpose of this initiative is to include exercise as part of the standard care a patient receives from his or her health care provider when going for a medical exam. In other words, physical activity is considered a vital sign to be checked at each doctor visit so that continuous support is provided for encouraging a healthy lifestyle and disease prevention.

The benefits of exercise are numerous. Physical activity is recommended at 150 minutes per week for adults at a moderate intensity level or 75 minutes at a vigorous intensity. Exercising at recommended levels has been synonymous with preventing overweight and obesity as well as diseases such as various cancers, diabetes, and cardiovascular problems. Physical activity helps promote bone health and can delay or prevent bone-related diseases such as osteoporosis. For all people, but especially aging adults, physical activity can assist with coordination, balance, and flexibility, which may prevent falls from occurring. From a psychological perspective, exercise has been shown to reduce depression, anxiety, and stress while improving overall mood and alertness. With so many benefits, it seems to follow that exercise be a natural part of medical care for individuals with eating disorders; however, exercise taken to the extreme can have associated detrimental effects.

Exercising at an excessive amount or being compulsive about physical activity routines can signal a problem. Specifically, individuals may develop a negative mind-set around exercise that leads to guilt, become overly obsessive about counting miles or other markers of physical activity, or begin to feel obligated to follow a rigid routine at the cost of family, social, and work obligations. This phenomenon of "too much exercise" or exercising to the extreme has been referred to as exercise dependence, obligatory exercise, compulsive exercise, excessive exercise, exercise addiction, or dysfunctional exercise. This overexercise behavior can lead to training that makes the body vulnerable for injury. Further, the exerciser in his or her attempts to disassociate from one's body will likely be at risk for exercising through pain or injury.

This dysfunctional relationship with exercise may be associated with disruptions in sleep patterns. Additionally, overexercise has been associated with irritability and mood swings. Exercise becomes the priority and other responsibilities such as job and family relationships likely suffer. Job loss, poor academic performance, and strained relationships have been reported to be correlated with having a dysfunctional relationship with exercise.

The term "exercise addiction" was coined to reflect the highs and lows associated with this negative relationship with physical activity. Initially the exerciser feels euphoria associated with physical activity, which is viewed positively. However, at some point the individual experiences exercise tolerance, which refers to needing more and more exercise to get the same euphoric effect. Furthermore, exercise becomes increasingly strict and narrow related to the types of exercise that "count" for one's routine. These routines usually get more vigorous, rigid, and demanding over time and may result in injury. The person with a dysfunctional relationship with exercise often experiences guilt surrounding not exercising the "right amount" or "being fit enough" or some other self-criticism. Interestingly, similar to other addictions, overexercisers report feeling withdrawal when they are unable to exercise.

Individuals with exercise addiction actively disregard preferences for types of movement or bodily cues of pain and discomfort as they "punch through" their brutal workout routines. Exercise is so central in their lives that they cannot take rest days even when sick or on vacation. Both physical and psychological symptoms result. Other psychological consequences include depressed mood, increased anxiety, decreased self-confidence and self-esteem, and loss of interest in eating or other activities. Importantly, physical activity no longer becomes enjoyable, which means the healthy aspect of exercise is gone.

The exact prevalence of exercise addiction is unknown. Having a negative relationship with exercise can happen in the absence of an eating disorder and has been referred to as primary exercise dependence. However, it is common for exercise addiction to occur in conjunction with disordered eating or an eating disorder as a way to compensate for food intake (i.e., a purging method). This type of exercise addiction has been referred to as secondary exercise dependence.

The focus of this debate is on how to address exercise issues within an eating disorder treatment setting. Historically, medical doctors believed that all exercise should cease and patients with eating disorders were placed on bed rest. There are some valid explanations around weight restoration operating with this approach, but should the exercise topic be broached while someone is in treatment for his or her eating disorder? Therefore, this controversy will focus on the benefits of including exercise as part of an overall treatment program. For example, what is the state of readiness required for a client to be prepared to go for a run or engage in a yoga class without abusing exercise or falling back into a negative mind-set? Should exercise behavior be extinguished entirely to allow the client to focus on recovery?

Justine J. Reel

Bibliography

Bratland-Sanda, Solfrid, Jorunn Sundgot-Borgen, Rø, Øyvind, Jan H. Rosenvinge, Asle Hoffart, and Egil W. Martinsen. "Physical Activity and Exercise Dependence during Inpatient Treatment of Longstanding Eating Disorders: An Exploratory Study of Excessive and Non-Excessive Exercisers." *International Journal of Eating Disorders* 43 (2010): 266–273. doi: 10.1002/eat.20769.

Cook, Brian, Heather Hausenblas, Ross D. Crosby, Li Cao, and Stephen A. Wonderlich. "Exercise Dependence as a Mediator of the Exercise and Eating Disorders Relationship: A Pilot Study." *Eating Behaviors* 16 (2015): 9–12. doi: 10.1016/j.eatbeh.2014.10.012.

Costa, Sebastiano, Heather A. Hausenblas, Patricia Olivia, Francesca Cuzocrea, and Rosalba Larcan. "The Role of Age, Gender, Mood States and Exercise Frequency on Exercise Dependence." *Journal of Behavioral Addictions* 2, no. 4 (2013): 216–223. doi: 10.1556/JBA.2.2013.014.

Downs, Danielle Symons, Jennifer S. Savage, and Jennifer M. DiNallo. "Self-Determined to Exercise? Leisure-Time Exercise Behavior, Exercise Motivation, and Exercise Dependence in Youth." *Journal of Physical Activity and Health* 10, no. 2 (2013): 176–184. doi: 10.1123/jpah.10.2.176.

Fleig, Lena, Rudolf Kerschreiter, Ralf Schwarzer, Sarah Pomp, and Sonia Lippke. "'Sticking to a Healthy Diet Is Easier for Me When I Exercise Regularly': Cognitive Transfer between Physical Exercise and Healthy Nutrition." *Psychology and Health* 29, no. 12 (2013): 1361–1372. doi: 10.1080/08870446.2014.930146.

Joy, Elizabeth. "Exercise Is Medicine: A Focus on Prevention." American College of Sports Medicine. Last modified October 7, 2016. http://www.acsm.org/public-information/articles/2016/10/07/exercise-is-medicine-a-focus-on-prevention.

Reel, Justine J. "The Relationship between Exercise and Eating Disorders: A Double-Edged Sword." In *Doing Exercise Psychology*, edited by Mark B. Andersen and Stephanie J. Hanrahan, 259–273. Champaign, IL: Human Kinetics, 2015.

Reel, Justine J., Jacquelyn J. Lee, and Abby Bellows. "Integrating Exercise and Mindfulness for an Emerging Conceptual Framework: The Intuitive Approach to Prevention and Health Promotion (IAPHP)." *Eating Disorders: The Journal of Treatment & Prevention* 24, no. 1 (2016): 90–97. doi: 10.1080/10640266.2015.1118951.

Reel, Justine J., and Maya Miyairi. "The Right 'Dose' of Activity: Health Educators Should Promote Mindful and Intuitive Exercise." *Community Medicine & Health Education* 2 (2012): 9–10. doi: 10.4172/2161-0711.1000e111.

Exercise Is Beneficial for Treatment of Eating Disorders

Due to the current obesity epidemic and healthy lifestyle movements, exercise has been recognized as a positive health behavior to reduce disease risk. When taken too far, however, the benefits of physical activity, including reduced risk of chronic diseases (e.g., cardiovascular disease, type 2 diabetes) and some cancers, strengthened bones and muscles, improved mental health and mood (e.g., stress, anxiety, depression), and increased chances of living longer, can be undermined and may even have deleterious effects (e.g., injury, depression, and anxiety). This tendency for excessive and harmful exercise behavior has been commonly observed among patients with eating disorders. In fact, 33–100 percent of individuals diagnosed with eating disorders reported the use of exercise as a part of their eating disorder behaviors. Specifically, overexercise is used as a compensatory behavior in response to binge episodes. Further, the relationship with exercise for these individuals with eating disorders is highly negative as they feed compelled to engage in rigid routines.

Because of his frequently reported overexercise behavior that involves a negative mind-set toward exercise, a supervised exercise education approach has become a part of a comprehensive treatment program for patients with eating disorders. According to one study conducted, 97 percent of clinicians (N = 32) in multiple countries such as the United States, Canada, Japan, China, and Australia believed that there was an association between a clients' eating disorder and physical activity. In addition, the majority of clinicians supported physical activity as an important treatment component for clients' recovery process. Although this data was published 12 years ago, recent systematic review and meta-analysis data also revealed consistent findings. Thus, many clinicians working with eating disorders tend to perceive the supervised exercise education approach as a beneficial therapeutic treatment for patients with eating disorders.

Exercise was previously prohibited in many eating disorder treatment settings until the 1990s wherein clients were put on bed rest. Moola and colleagues (2013) indicated five limitations to the current "exercise restriction" approach in their systematic review article:

1. Patients need an opportunity to redefine exercise for health-focused reasons and learn how to appropriately engage in activity in a healthy, safe, and moderate manner.
2. From the bioethical perspective, activity restrictions may be counterproductive by resulting in patients' undertaking covert and secretive activity.
3. Given the cultural mandate to be active, activity restrictions may deliver a confusing message to patients with eating disorders.
4. The current standard of care that employs refeeding in conjunction with inactivity may perpetuate the physical and psychological distress associated with the reintroduction of nutrition.
5. Activity restriction may have harmful musculoskeletal and cardiometabolic consequences.

Furthermore, it is important for patients to have opportunities to discuss exercise behaviors with their providers while they are in treatment. This treatment process will help patients work on intensive therapeutic assignments to overcome their toxic relationships with exercise as their treatment progress proceeds.

A recent meta-analysis conducted by Ng and colleagues (2013) illustrated evidence that the supervised exercise education approach helped patients with eating disorders improve psychological (e.g., body perceptions, depression, a perception of exercise) and physiological benefits (e.g., strength, cardiovascular endurance) without disrupting the patients' weight management process. In fact, research findings support the supervised exercise education approach as a reliable and safe treatment for patients with eating disorders.

To provide a safer and more effective treatment for patients with eating disorders, treatment facilities must have trained exercise educators or therapists follow reliable treatment guidelines proposed by Powers and Thompson (2008). Here are their new supervised exercise education guidelines:

1. Team Approach—a multidisciplinary team of experts in exercise, nutrition, mental health, medicine, and physical therapy should develop individually tailored exercise programs and monitor patients to ensure safety.
2. Medical Concerns/Contraindications—it is critical to monitor each patient's medical status and to ensure his or her safety to prevent harm.
3. Screen for Exercise-Related Psychopathology—identifying patients' pathological attitudes and behaviors toward exercise (e.g., exercise dependence) is important when the multidisciplinary team develops individually tailored exercise programs.
4. Create a Written Contract—a written contract that clearly states program rules, goals, outcomes, expectations, and contingencies for progression and regression of exercise activity should be agreed upon by patients and all members of the treatment team prior to allowing patients to engage in the therapeutic exercise programs.
5. Include a Psychoeducational Component—psychoeducation based on cognitive behavioral therapy needs to be implemented as a part of therapeutic exercise programs.
6. Focus on Positive Reinforcement—patients should be able to participate in therapeutic exercise programs contingent on treatment compliance and success.
7. Creating a Graded Exercise Program—graded exercise programs beginning with small amounts of low-intensity exercise should be emphasized.
8. Starting with Mild-Intensity and Slowly Build to Moderate Intensity—exercise amount and intensity level need to be very gradually increased as patients demonstrate progress with their overall eating disorder treatment, weight restoration, and any other predetermined therapeutic outcomes.
9. Tailoring the Mode of Exercise to the Needs of the Individual—exercise amounts and intensity levels should be followed by the current recommendations of the American College of Sports Medicine and tailored for patients' physiological and psychological needs.
10. Including a Nutritional Component to Account for the Physiological Needs during Exercise—registered dieticians specializing in eating disorders must monitor patients' refeeding and weight restoration progress carefully before and during patients' participation in therapeutic exercise groups. More importantly, patients should not participate in exercise until they make sufficient progress in weight stabilization and caloric and nutritional consumption to support any physical activities.
11. Debriefing after Exercise Sessions—patients should be "debriefed" regarding sensations, emotions, and thoughts evoked by exercising during or after the exercise session.

In addition, conducting a program evaluation is necessary for future supervised exercise education programs in order to prove the benefit of the supervised exercise education approach in eating disorder settings. Therefore, it is evident that the supervised exercise education approach is beneficial for patients' recovery process and potentially prevents relapse after treatment.

Maya Miyairi and Sonya SooHoo

Bibliography

"The Benefits of Physical Activity." Centers for Disease Control and Prevention. Last modified January 4, 2015. https://www.cdc.gov/physicalactivity/basics/pa-health/index.htm.

Bratland-Sanda, Solfrid, Jorunn Sundgot-Borgen, Øyvind Rø, Jan H. Rosenvinge, Asle Hoffart, and Egil W. Martinsen. "Physical Activity and Exercise Dependence during Inpatient Treatment of Longstanding Eating Disorders: An Exploratory Study of Excessive and Non-Excessive Exercisers." *International Journal of Eating Disorders* 43 (2010): 266–273. doi: 10.1002/eat.20769.

Calogero, Rachel M., and Kelly N. Pedrotty. "The Practice and Process of Healthy Exercise: An Investigation of the Treatment of Exercise Abuse in Women with Eating Disorders." *Eating Disorders: The Journal of Treatment & Prevention* 12, no. 4 (2004): 273–291. http://dx.doi.org/10.1080/10640260490521352.

Cook, Brian J., Stephen A. Wonderlich, James E. Mitchell, Ron Thompson, Roberta Sherman, and Kimberli McCallum. "Exercise in Eating Disorders Treatment: Systematic Review and Proposal of Guidelines." *Medicine & Science in Sports & Exercise* 48, no. 7 (2016): 1408–1414. doi: 10.1249/MSS.0000000000000912.

Moola, Fiona J., Sarah E. Gairdner, and Catherine E. Amara. "Exercise in the Care of Patients with Anorexia Nervosa: A Systematic Review of the Literature." *Mental Health and Physical Activity* 6, no. 2 (2013): 59–68. doi: 10.1037/t00741-000.

Ng, L. W. C., D. P. Ng, and W. P. Wong. "Is Supervised Exercise Training Safe in Patients with Anorexia Nervosa? A Meta-Analysis." *Physiotherapy* 99, no. 1 (2013): 1–11. doi: http://dx.doi.org/10.1016/j.physio.2012.05.006.

Powers, Pauline, and Ron Thompson. *The Exercise Balance: What's Too Much, What's Too Little, and What's Just Right for You!* Carlsbad, CA: Gurze Books, 2008.

Reel, Justine J. "The Relationship between Exercise and Eating Disorders: A Double-Edged Sword." In *Doing Exercise Psychology*, edited by Mark B. Andersen and Stephanie J. Hanrahan, 259–273. Champaign, IL: Human Kinetics, 2015.

Reel, Justine J., Jacquelyn J. Lee, and Abby Bellows. "Integrating Exercise and Mindfulness for an Emerging Conceptual Framework: The Intuitive Approach to Prevention and Health Promotion (IAPHP)." *Eating Disorders: The Journal of Treatment & Prevention* 24, no. 1 (2016): 90–97. doi: 10.1080/10640266.2015.1118951.

Reel, Justine J., and Maya Miyairi. "The Right 'Dose' of Activity: Health Educators Should Promote Mindful and Intuitive Exercise." *Community Medicine & Health Education* 2 (2012): 9–10. doi: 10.4172/2161-0711.1000e111.

Reel, Justine J., and Dana Voelker. "Exercise to the Extreme? Identifying and Addressing Unhealthy Exercise Behaviors." In *Athletic Insight's Writings of 2012*, edited by Robert Schinke, 301–315. Hauppauge, NY: Nova Science, 2012.

Exercise Should Not Be Incorporated into Treatment for Eating Disorders

As many as 60 percent of individuals diagnosed with an eating disorder exhibit some sort of dysfunctional exercising behavior, including exercise dependence. Individuals who use exercise as a correlate behavior to their disordered eating are often missed in traditional screenings because exercise is a socially accepted and valued activity in our society. Individuals who report using exercise to control their weight/shape have more severely disordered eating behaviors, more depression and anxiety, and more resistance to treatment. Given these trends, it is dangerous to incorporate an exercise component into eating disorder treatment.

One of the biggest threats that incorporating exercise into eating disorder treatments poses is the potential for exercise abuse or dependence. Studies have shown that as many as 70 percent of people with bulimia nervosa and 30 percent of people with anorexia nervosa have a condition called exercise dependence (also referred to as driven exercising, overexercising, and exercise abuse). Exercise dependence is described as excessive, intense exercising often driven by feelings of obligation. In both bulimia and anorexia, exercising is used as a weight loss/control strategy. For individuals who do engage in driven exercise, their eating disorder symptoms tend to be worse and more enduring; they are also at a higher risk for developing anxiety/depression. One study found that individuals diagnosed with anorexia who abused exercise had significantly longer inpatient treatment stays and relapsed more quickly than their nonexercising counterparts. Additionally, many individuals who abuse exercise often slip past traditional screening measures given that exercise is highly valued in Western societies. This is particularly true for individuals who have bulimia nervosa, as their BMIs are more likely to be in normal ranges compared to those with anorexia nervosa, who may be visibly underweight. Given the significant rates at which exercise is abused by this population and the associated risks of exercise dependence, introducing exercise as a component of treatment would expose individuals with eating disorders to an easily abused, readily concealable, and psychologically damaging potential activity.

In addition to the psychological risks associated with exercise dependence, overexercising also poses significant physical dangers for individuals with eating disorders. For individuals who maintain a very low body weight, negative impacts of continued stress on the skeletal system from compulsive exercising may result in stress fractures, scoliosis, bone breaks, and increase the risk of developing osteoporosis. In women, maintaining an underweight BMI is associated with delayed onset of menses, which can contribute to reduced bone density and failure to achieve a peak bone mass. Additionally, low body weight can put stress on the cardiovascular system and specifically the heart; that stress is compounded when heart rate is elevated during exercise. Failure to maintain a healthy, balanced, and calorically rich diet can also lead to endocrine abnormalities, malnutrition, dehydration, and electrolyte imbalances. These negative consequences are seen across all forms of eating disorders, including anorexia, bulimia, and binge eating disorder. Each of these deficits are worsened when the body is further stressed during intense exercise. Thus, individuals may experience headaches, nausea, vomiting, decreased brain functioning/development, increased risk for heart attack, heat exhaustion, amenorrhea, and organ failure. Exercise therefore exposes individuals whose bodies are already stressed as a result of their eating disorders to further damage and severe negative health consequences.

Exercise is also a potent catalyst for relapse in individuals recovering from an eating disorder. Studies have found that the presence of exercising at discharge from treatment—even if exercising under the supervision of a trained professional and/or exercising within healthy limits—predicted future relapse, a longer course of illness, and more severe symptoms. Individuals who reported exercising at discharge (completion of their treatment) had a significantly shorter amount of time between discharge and their first relapse. This pattern highlights the detrimental effects that exercising poses for individuals who are predisposed to disordered eating behavior.

Although it may be tempting to view exercise as a healthy alternative behavior to disordered eating behaviors (e.g., self-induced vomiting, laxative abuse, or food restriction), the risks associated with overexercising and the likelihood of abusing exercise in an eating disorder population are too great. A significant number of individuals with an eating disorder already overexercise, so promoting it during treatment would only increase the perception of exercise as an acceptable behavior and puts these individuals at risk of slipping back into driven exercising. Exercise is particularly dangerous in the context of the severe health dangers associated with eating disorders; individuals are at higher risk for electrolyte imbalances, malnutrition, dehydration, cardiovascular stress, irregular hormone cycles, skeletal weakness, and organ failure when exercise is coupled with low BMI and/or unhealthy diets. Last, exercise is a demonstrated predictor of relapse, even when it is supervised and done in healthy amounts. Incorporating exercise into eating disorder treatment is simply a recipe for disaster.

Hannah J. Hopkins

Bibliography

Carter, J. C., E. Blackmore, K. Sutandar-Pinnock, and D. B. Woodside. "Relapse in Anorexia Nervosa: A Survival Analysis." *Psychological Medicine* 34, no. 4 (2004): 671–679. doi: 10.1017/S0033291703001168.

Cook, Brian, Heather Hausenblas, Ross D. Crosby, Li Cao, and Stephen A. Wonderlich. "Exercise Dependence as a Mediator of the Exercise and Eating Disorders Relationship: A Pilot Study." *Eating Behaviors* 16 (2015): 9–12. doi: 10.1016/j.eatbeh.2014.10.012.

Dalle Grave, Riccardo, Simona Calugi, and Giulio Marchesini. "Compulsive Exercise to Control Shape or Weight in Eating Disorders: Prevalence, Associated Features, and Treatment Outcome." *Comprehensive Psychiatry* 49, no. 4 (2008): 346–352. doi: 10.1016/j.comppsych.2007.12.007.

Homan, Kristin. "Athletic-Ideal and Thin-Ideal Internalization as Prospective Predictors of Body Dissatisfaction, Dieting, and Compulsive Exercise." *Body Image* 7, no. 3 (2010): 240–245. doi: 10.1016/j.bodyim.2010.02.004.

Stiles-Shields, Colleen, Bryony Bamford, James Lock, and Daniel Le Grange. "The Effect of Driven Exercise on Treatment Outcomes for Adolescents with Anorexia and Bulimia Nervosa." *International Journal of Eating Disorders* 48, no. 4 (2015): 392–396. doi: 10.1002/eat.22281.

Stiles-Shields, E. Colleen, Andrea B. Goldschmidt, Leah Boepple, Catherine Glunz, and Daniel Le Grange. "Driven Exercise among Treatment-Seeking Youth with Eating Disorders." *Eating Behaviors* 12, no. 4 (2011): 328–331. doi: 10.1016/j.eatbeh.2011.09.002.

Sudi, Karl, Karl Öttl, Doris Payerl, Peter Baumgartl, Klemens Tauschmann, and Wolfram Müller. "Anorexia Athletica." *Nutrition* 20, no. 7–8 (2004): 657–661. doi: 10.1016/j. nut.2004.04.019.

Are Athletes More or Less at Risk for Eating Disorders?

Athletes are often viewed as societal role models who both are successful and have ideal physiques. Although eating disorders may occur regardless of whether someone is playing a sport and at any age, there is evidence that certain subpopulations are at greater risk than others. Because of the mental and physical demands of sport that may emphasize a particular body type, weight, or size to maximize performance, some researchers have argued that competitive athletes represent a subpopulation who may be vulnerable to the development of disordered eating behaviors such as restricting food intake and using compensatory methods such as vomiting to lose weight. In fact, several studies have supported the contention that athletes are more likely than nonathletes to suffer symptoms of eating disorders. The difference between athletes and nonathletes was especially apparent when comparing elite athletes in lean sports (e.g., distance running, gymnastics) with nonathletes. Athletes scored higher on predictors of bulimia and anorexia than nonathletes. A recent United States study that surveyed collegiate athletes revealed that 19.2 percent of males and 25 percent of females could be classified as symptomatic for an eating disorder.

However, the division between athletes and nonathletes with respect to eating disorders is not clear. Some researchers have argued that athletes might possess protective factors that prevent them from developing eating disorders. These proponents point to the physical and psychosocial health benefits of sport participation to demonstrate the ways that sport participation may serve as a buffer for eating disorder development. For example, research studies found that the collegiate athletes in their study reported significantly less dieting, were less likely to perceive themselves as overweight, had higher body esteem, and had more confidence in their bodies than nonathletes. A separate study discovered that the female athletes in their study reported less eating disorder symptomology, more positive affect, and greater emotional well-being than a matched sample of nonathletes. A recent study comparing elite Norwegian high school athletes with an age-matched nonathlete control group showed that the nonathletes exhibited more dieting and a higher incidence of disordered eating compared to the athletes.

Conflicting findings with regard to eating disorder risk between athletes and nonathletes illuminate the complex relationship between sport participation and eating disorders. Indeed, these equivocal research findings indicate that sport participation can either reduce or increase athletes' risk for an eating disorder depending on a variety of factors. Some explanations for the disparate results include the different questionnaires used to assess for eating disorder risk, which sports are included in the study, and whether the athletes represent a high level of competition. Ultimately this debate is well-positioned for evidence-based arguments on both sides of the issue. For example, researchers suggest that female athletes, such as gymnasts and figure skaters, who compete in sports that demand a certain aesthetic look for successful performance are at more risk for developing eating disorders. By contrast, male athletes who compete in a sport that does not emphasize one's body (e.g., baseball) may be relatively untouched by pressures to change one's weight, size, or shape for sport. It is expected that athletes in these sports would display low risk for eating disorders. Moreover, competitive level could play a role with respect to eating disorder risk. On the one hand, certain athletes who do not fit the desired body type for one's sport may get "weeded out" before they reach elite levels of participation. However, those athletes performing at elite levels may also be more willing to go to extremes to enhance their performance and gain an advantage over their opponents.

Justine J. Reel

Bibliography

Kerr, Gretchen, Erica Berman, and Mary Jane De Souza. "Disordered Eating in Women's Gymnastics: Perspectives of Athletes, Coaches, Parents, and Judges." *Journal of Applied Sport Psychology* 18, no. 1 (2006): 28–41. doi: 10.1080/10413200500471301.

Muscat, Anne C., and Bonita C. Long. "Critical Comments about Body Shape and Weight: Disordered Eating of Female Athletes and Sport Participants." *Journal of Applied Sport Psychology* 20, no. 1 (2008): 1–24. doi: 10.1080/10413200701784833.

Papathomas, Anthony, and David Lavallee. "Athlete Experiences of Disordered Eating in Sport." *Qualitative Research in Sport and Exercise* 2, no. 3 (2010): 354–370. doi: 10.1080/19398441.2010.517042.

Preacher, Kristopher J., and Geoffrey J. Leonardelli. "Calculation for the Sobel Test: An Interactive Calculation Tool for Mediation Tests." Quantpsy.org. Accessed January 30, 2017. http://quantpsy.org/sobel/sobel.htm.

Reel, Justine J., and Diane Gill. "Psychosocial Factors Related to Eating Disorders among High School and College Female Cheerleaders." *The Sport Psychologist* 10 (1996): 195–206. doi: 10.1123/tsp.10.2.195.

Reel, Justine J., Trent A. Petrie, Sonya SooHoo, and Carlie Anderson. "Weight Pressures in Sport: Examining the Factor Structure and Incremental Validity of the Weight Pressures in Sport—Females." *Eating Behaviors* 14, no. 2 (2013): 137–144. doi: 10.1016/j.eatbeh.2013.01.003.

Reel, Justine J., Sonya SooHoo, Trent Petrie, and Christy Greenleaf. "Slimming Down for Sport: Development of a Weight Pressures in Sport Measure for Female Athletes." *Journal of Clinical Psychology* 4, no. 2 (2010): 99–111. doi: http://dx.doi.org/10.1123/jcsp.4.2.99.

Athletes Are More at Risk for Eating Disorders

Eating disorders are serious mental health illnesses that have major health consequences for children and adults. Despite all the potential protective factors and positive health benefits that are associated with being an athlete, certain athletes face a higher risk of developing eating disorders. Disordered eating and eating disorders are more prevalent among sports in which body weight and body composition are salient aspects of the sports. In general, sports that focus on weight and body composition can be divided into three main categories: (1) aesthetic sports, (2) weight-class sports, and (3) gravitational sports.

Aesthetic sports refer to activities that value a certain "look" or physical image in the act of competing in a sport. One explanation for why athletes are more vulnerable to develop disordered eating behaviors relates to an emphasis on body weight and appearance within the sport context. Athletes in aesthetic sports such as gymnastics, diving, or figure skating report that having leaner and longer limbs can be associated with a performance advantage, and this belief seems to translate into higher rates of disordered eating. In a 2015 study, 17 percent of female athletes participating in aesthetic sports had eating disorders. For example, figure skaters are evaluated and judged on their technical elements (i.e., jumps, spins, footwork) along with their choreography, expression, style, skating dress, and overall presentation of the program. Most of the athletes in aesthetic sports are required to wear tight outfits, which can lead athletes to feel uncomfortable with their bodies. Furthermore, comments by coaches on an athlete's body shape and size are associated with a psychological pressure to lose weight. The rules and norms in these aesthetic sports place pressure on athletes to worry about their bodies, to diet and to use severe weight loss methods such as taking diet pills to be successful in the sports.

Another category of sports where there is a higher rate of eating disorders is weight-class sports, which consists of sports such as wrestling, boxing, horse racing, weight lifting, lightweight rowing, and judo. These athletes in weight-class sports engage in rapid weight loss, which is characterized by transitory weight loss of at least 5 percent of body weight in less than a week. Some athletes quickly drop the weight to be in a class where they would have a physical and mental advantage over lighter and weaker opponents. The core strategies for rapid weight loss include reducing food and fluid intake, increasing body secretions, and raising body metabolic rate to burn fat tissues. For example, wrestlers reported striving to achieve a high muscle mass and low body fat mass to complete in "weight" class, which is typically below their natural body mass. Specifically, they started restricting their diet and reducing drinking fluids a week prior to their weigh in and gradually restricted more food and liquids as it got closer to the weigh in date. On the last day before weigh in, wrestlers fasted and only sucked on chips of ice to prevent dry mouth to lose even more weight. In addition, they used severe dehydration methods or "drying out" such using wet and dry saunas, training in heated rooms, and training with plastic suits (sweat suits) to cut weight by losing water in the last hours before weigh ins. Rapid dehydration by more than 5 percent of the total body weight can result in serious health conditions such as muscle injuries, heat stroke, and even death. In 1997, three collegiate wrestlers died from using extreme weight loss methods.

Athletes participating in gravitational sports such as long-distance running, cross-country skiing, and ski jumping in which high body weight restricts performance because moving the body against gravity is an important part of these sports are at higher risk of developing eating disorders. Many athletes believe that having a thin and lean body will enhance their performance despite any scientific evidence claiming that there is a direct correlation between weight and performance, so they will pursue any measure to achieve their goals. For example, elite distance runners would run more miles (in addition to their typical training regimen), restrict their caloric intake, and engage in other unhealthy weight loss methods to have a better outcome. Not only do the athletes believe that having a lean body will propel them to the next level, coaches encourage weight loss. In a recent study, an adult elite distance runner asked her coach if she could wear the men's uniform because of chafing. Her coach responded: "Well, if you weren't so fat, you wouldn't have this problem. The reason why you're chafing is because your thighs are too big and maybe you should consider losing weight this summer."

After this comment, the distance runner lost the weight and the coach told her that she "looked stunning again." Unfortunately, these negative comments are common in sports even for adolescent athletes.

Most competition and athletic participation begin at an early age and often is the period of time when rapid change occurs in body composition and shape, especially for females. These physical developments along with emotional and psychological changes that are associated with puberty have been shown to lead young athletes to feel dissatisfied with their bodies, engage in unhealthy eating habits, and use pathogenic weight control methods to achieve the ideal weight and, ultimately, perform well and win. Recently, investigators conducted clinical interviews with adolescent elite athletes and age-matched controls and found that elite athletes had a higher rate of eating disorders than nonathletes (7.0 percent vs. 2.3 percent, respectively), supporting previous studies that athletes have a higher rate of eating disorders than nonathletes. Furthermore, adult elite athletes diagnosed with eating disorders have reported that they started dieting and developing the eating disorder during adolescence.

Due to the dangers of eating disorders and prevalence in sports, it is crucial to understand why young and adult athletes are more at risk compared to nonathletes. The risk factors of eating disorders in sports are multifactorial. General risk factors can be divided into predisposing factors, triggers factors, and perpetuating factors. The predisposing factors include biological (e.g., genetics, developmental stages of life), psychological (e.g., body dissatisfaction, low self-esteem, personality traits such as perfectionism), and sociocultural factors (e.g., peer pressure, media messages, bullying). The trigger factors are usually negative comments regarding weight, body size and shape, and traumatic experiences. The perpetuating factors could be attempts to gain approval by the coach or teammates. In addition to the aforementioned general risk factors, there are sport-specific risk factors that are unique to sports such as frequent weight regulation, dieting, early start of sport specific training, injuries, overtraining, coaching behaviors, and pressure to lose weight. For example, researchers conducted a multisite study and found that low self-esteem and exercising to be attractive and to improve appearance were significantly associated with higher eating disorder symptoms among female athletes. Some of these factors are shared with nonathletes, but the sport environment can make athletes more vulnerable to these risk factors compared to nonathletes.

Athletes regardless of age and sex are at higher risk of eating disorders. The prevalence of eating disorders among athletes could be higher but some athletes may think that disordered eating behaviors are natural parts of being an athlete and their sport.

Athletes rationalize that the pressure to achieve the perfect body shape and size will ensure optimal performance and reflect dedication to their sport rather than being viewed as a serious health problem. An untreated eating disorder can have persistent psychological and physiological effects that could be fatal. Therefore, it is crucial for parents, coaching staff, and all athletes to learn that young and adult athletes are more at risk of developing eating disorders than nonathletes and understand the general and sport-specific risk factors for preventing these insidious illnesses.

Sonya SooHoo and Maya Miyairi

Bibliography

Bar, Rachel J., Stephanie E. Cassin, and Michelle M. Dionne. "Eating Disorder Prevention Initiatives for Athletes: A Review." *European Journal of Sport Science* 16 (2016): 499–508. doi: 10.1080/17461391.2015.1013995.

Busanich, Rebecca, Kerry R. McGannon, and Robert J. Schinke. "Comparing Elite Male and Female Distance Runner's Experiences of Disordered Eating through Narrative Analysis." *Psychology of Sport and Exercise* 15 (2014): 705–712. doi: 10.1016/j.psychsport.2013.10.002.

Joy, Elizabeth, Andrea Kussman, and Aurelia Nattiv. "2016 Update on Eating Disorders in Athletes: A Comprehensive Narrative Review with a Focus on Clinical Assessment and Management." *British Journal of Sports Medicine* 50 (2016): 154–162. doi: 10.1136/bjsports-2015-095735.

Martensen, Marianne, and Jorunn Sundgot-Borgen. "Higher Prevalence of Eating Disorders among Adolescent Elite Athletes Than Controls." *Medicine & Science in Sports & Exercise* 45 (2013): 1188–1197. doi: 10.1249/MSS.0b013e318281a939.

Petrie, Trent A., Christy Greenleaf, and Justine J. Reel. "Personality and Psychological Factors as Predictors of Disordered Eating Among Female College Athletes." *Eating Disorders* 17 (2009): 302–321. doi: 10.1080/10640260902991160.

Pettersen, Ingvild, Erik Hernæs, and Finn Skårderud. "Pursuit of Performance Excellence: A Population Study of Norwegian Adolescent Female Cross-Country Skiers and Biathletes with Disordered Eating." *BMJ Open Sport & Exercise Medicine* 2:e000115 (2016): 1–6. doi: 10.1136/bmjsem-2016-000115.

Reel, Justine J., Sonya SooHoo, and Holly Estes. "Weigh-ins and Uniforms: Creating a Prevention Platform for Disordered Eating in Sport." In *Ensuring the Health of Active and Athletic Girls and Women*, edited by Linda Ransdell and Linda Petlichkoff, 253–275. Reston: National Association for Girls and Women in Sport, 2005.

Reel, Justine J., and Dana Voelker. "Sculpted to Perfection: Addressing and Managing Body Image Concerns and Disordered Eating among Athletes." In *Athletic Insight's Writings in Sport Psychology*, edited by Robert Schinke, 301–316. New York: Nova Science Publishers, 2014.

Solfrid, Bratland-Sanda, and Jorunn Sundgot-Borgen. "Eating Disorders in Athletes: Overview of Prevalence, Risk Factors, and Recommendations for Prevention and Treatment." *European Journal of Sport Science* 13 (2013): 499–508. doi: 10.1080/17461391.2012.740504

Thiemann, Pia, Tanja Legenbauer, Silja Vocks, Petra Platen, Bonnie Auyeung, and Stephen Herpertz. "Eating Disorders and Their Putative Risk Factors among Female German Professional Athletes." *European Eating Disorders Review* 23 (2015): 269–276. doi: 10.1002/erv.2360.

Athletes Are Less at Risk for Eating Disorders Than Nonathletes

Athletic participation has long been identified as a potential risk factor for the development of disordered eating. However, a growing body of scientific research actually indicates the opposite: athletes are *less* likely to develop an eating disorder than nonathletes. Athletic participation offers a number of social and emotional benefits that protect athletes from developing disordered eating behaviors, including social support and lower rates of body dissatisfaction. Understanding the protective effects that are inherent in sports participation is critical in making effective early interventions for people who are at risk for developing eating disorders. Additionally, understanding the relationship between body image, eating behaviors, and athletics can inform the way in which exercise and fitness is incorporated into treatment plans.

Numerous studies have shown that participating in sports can protect against numerous risk factors for eating disorders. This trend is seen in a variety of sports settings, including at the high school and collegiate levels and in the United States as well as internationally. Research has shown that athletes tend to endorse more body satisfaction, a more positive outlook on life, and higher ratings of self-efficacy than nonathlete counterparts. All of these traits predict a lower likelihood of developing an eating disorder, and this trend holds true for both males and females. Many researchers have sought to identify where these protective factors originate from. For example, one theory is that individuals who are more confident in their physical strength, athletic abilities, or general sportsmanship are more likely to participate in sports. Another common theory is that sport participation contributes to higher body satisfaction and confidence. The question of which comes first (i.e., sports participation or body satisfaction) has yet to be definitively answered, but it is irrefutable that participating in sports fosters greater satisfaction with one's body.

In addition to eating disorder–specific risk factors, participating in athletics contributes to better long-term mental health. One of these protective elements in athletic participation is enhanced social support. Social support has long been identified as one of the most critical and important positive influences on an individual's mental health. Within sports participation, athletes report a strong sense of community built among their teammates as well as the positive influence of their coach(es). The support that athletes report receiving from their parents has also been identified as crucial in reducing the risk of developing an eating disorder. One study found that simply playing on a sports team decreased the likelihood that someone would go on to develop depression by 25 percent and decreased the risk of suicide attempts by 12 percent. These results were found after accounting for other important variables that could contribute to mental illness, including physical disability, age, sex, race/ethnicity, and socioeconomic status.

One of the most commonly studied populations who are considered at risk for developing an eating disorder are "aesthetic" athletes. Aesthetic athletes are those who participate in judged sports, or sports where one's physique and appearance are considered important in performance. Common examples of aesthetic sports include gymnastics, dancing, and diving. Although research has shown that this particular population of athletes is at a higher risk for disordered eating behaviors, studies have pinpointed that it is *not* a result of the sport itself but the broader cultural context in which these sports occur that contribute to disordered eating. One study investigated risk and protective factors among young ballet dancers and gymnasts and found that negative comments and attitudes regarding body size expressed by the coaches was the primary risk factor for eating disorders. Coaches who made critical comments about an athlete's weight or shape, who openly endorsed or engaged in dieting/weight loss behaviors in front of their athletes, or who equated an athlete's performance with their weight/shape were reported as being the primary source of risk. This trend has been replicated among other studies as well, highlighting the importance of educating coaches and athletic training staff on modeling appropriate fitness and nutrition behaviors for their athletes.

Overall, despite a long history of being identified as a higher risk population, athletes enjoy many benefits as a result of playing sports that reduce the likelihood of developing eating disorders. These benefits include more satisfaction with their bodies, social support from their teammates, coaches, and parents, and higher ratings of self-esteem and self-efficacy. Even among sports where athletes are partially judged on their physique and appearance, the primary risk factor that contributes to dangerous eating behaviors is the attitude of the coaches and not the sport itself. These benefits indicate that sports participation should be encouraged for everyone who may be at risk for an eating disorder, but the attitude of the coaching/training staff should be carefully evaluated when choosing a team.

Hannah J. Hopkins

Bibliography

Babiss, Lindsay A., and James E. Gangwisch. "Sports Participation as a Protective Factor against Depression and Suicidal Ideation in Adolescents as Mediated by Self-Esteem and Social Support." *Journal of Developmental & Behavioral Pediatrics* 30, no. 5 (2009): 376–384. doi: 10.1097/DBP.0b013e3181b33659.

Francisco, Rita, Madalena Alarcão, and Isabel Narciso. "Aesthetic Sports as High-Risk Contexts for Eating Disorders—Young Elite Dancers and Gymnasts Perspectives." *The Spanish Journal of Psychology* 15, no. 1 (2012): 265–274. doi: https://doi.org/10.5209/rev_SJOP.2012.v15.n1.37333.

Fulkerson, Jayne A., Pamela K. Keel, Gloria R. Leon, and Trevor Dorr. "Eating-Disordered Behaviors and Personality Characteristics of High School Athletes and Nonathletes." *International Journal of Eating Disorders* 26, no. 1 (1999): 73–79. doi: 10.1002/(SICI)1098-108X(199907)26:1<73::AID-EAT9>3.0.CO;2-F.

Gaines, Stacey A., and Taylor Beth S. Burnett. "Perceptions of Eating Behaviors, Body Image, and Social Pressures in Female Division II College Athletes and Non-Athletes." *Journal of Sport Behavior* 37, no. 4 (2014): 351–369.

Goodwin, Huw, Emma Haycraft, and Caroline Meyer. "Disordered Eating, Compulsive Exercise, and Sport Participation in a UK Adolescent Sample." *European Eating Disorders Review* 24, no. 4 (2016): 304–309. doi: 10.1002/erv.2441.

Rosendahl, Jenny, B. Bormann, K. Aschenbrenner, F. Aschenbrenner, and B. Strauss. "Dieting and Disordered Eating in German High School Athletes and Non-Athletes." *Scandinavian Journal of Medicine & Science in Sports* 19, no. 5 (2009): 731–739. doi: 10.1111/j.1600-0838.2008.00821.x.

Wollenberg, Gena, Lenka H. Shriver, and Gail E. Gates. "Comparison of Disordered Eating Symptoms and Emotion Regulation Difficulties between Female College Athletes and Non-Athletes." *Eating Behaviors* 18 (2015): 1–6. doi: 10.1016/j.eatbeh.2015.03.008.

Zucker, Nancy L., Leslie G. Womble, Donald A. Williamson, and Lori A. Perrin. 1999. "Protective Factors for Eating Disorders in Female College Athletes." *Eating Disorders* 7, no. 3 (1999): 207–218. doi: 10.1080/10640269908249286.

Are Body Mass Index Report Cards a Bad or Good Thing?

Traditionally, size has been highly dependent on one's body weight. Regularly being weighed at the doctor's office and by the school nurse allowed for monitoring of body weight–related changes. Body mass index (BMI), which accounts for one's height, has been defined as a way to measure whether one is underweight, healthy weight, overweight, or obese. Approximately two-thirds of U.S. adults and one-fifth of U.S. children were considered overweight or obese based on their BMI scores. BMI is calculated by taking body weight in kilograms and dividing by height in meters squared (i.e., kg/m^2). A common criticism of using BMI as the frame of reference for one's ideal weight is that this number does not take into account the size of one's frame. Therefore, a person who genetically has a broad frame receives the same "prescription" or ideal body weight as someone with a much smaller framer. Further, body weight tends to fluctuate based on factors such as water weight and muscle weight. Therefore, someone who has a lot of muscle weight from working out or participating in sports may have a higher weight (or may gain weight). BMI does not take into account body composition or the percentage of body fat. Rather, it gives a general ballpark of where someone fits into a chart based on their height and weight.

Interestingly, BMI is not a new concept despite its apparent increase in popularity. Originally BMI was referred to as the Quetelet Index. This score was invented in Belgium between 1830 and 1850 by Adolphe Quetelet. The current term "body mass index" was popularized by Ancel Keys relative to obesity in his 1972 paper. According to the current U.S. BMI charts, having a BMI higher than or equal to 30 is considered obese. Overweight is represented by having a BMI score between 25 and 29.9 for adults. By contrast, children are measured for BMI using sex-specific, age-growth charts. In this case, children at or above the 95th percentile for sex and age are considered to be obese. Children who have a BMI between 85th and 95th percentile were considered overweight. Studies using competitive athletes have helped to illustrate the potential pitfalls associated with the BMI as the sole indicator of obesity, such as a well-known *Journal of the American Medical Association* study that found that 60 percent of National Football League players were overweight or obese. A separate study with high school varsity football players found that 28 percent of players were considered "at risk" for becoming overweight according to their BMI. Moreover, 45 percent of players were overweight and 9 percent met the criteria for being obese. Although obesity is a major societal concern for both children and adults, many researchers argue for a comprehensive approach that includes using body composition (percentage of body fat) and waist circumference (distance around the smallest point of the waist) in addition to BMI to determine whether a person is overweight or obese.

Some states have attempted to use BMI measurements as a way to prevent obesity and educate parents. Using BMI for identifying children who are at risk for weight-related problems has been a controversial practice due to the limitations of BMI and the ability to offer adequate education. Some states have introduced "BMI report cards" in the schools allowing for parents to receive a notification if their children are overweight or obese. Specifically, children are weighed, their height is measured, and then the BMI score is sent home to parents. There have been concerns about how the weighing takes place and the possibility that focusing on weight could contribute to dieting and disordered eating. Another concern is whether the parents will become the food police once they receive the BMI report card without having the tools to provide healthy meals in the home.

The body mass index formula has been popularized as a way to easily screen for overweight and obesity. However, with the focus on monitoring weight in the schools, this practice that is designed for health promotion and obesity prevention is controversial among researchers and clinicians who are concerned that children and their parents will become increasingly more focused on size and bodies. The following debate essays will argue both sides of the issue related to sending BMI report cards home.

Justine J. Reel

Bibliography

Cole, Tim J., Katherine M. Flegal, Dasha Nicholls, and Alan A. Jackson. "Body Mass Index Cut Offs to Define Thinness in Children and Adolescents: International Survey." *British Medical Journal* 335 (2007): 194–202. doi: 10.1136/bmj.39238.399444.55.

Dietz, William H., Mary T. Story, and Laura Leviton. "Introduction to Issues and Implications of Screening, Surveillance, and Reporting of Children's BMI." *Pediatrics* 124 (2009): S1–S2.

Harp, Joyce B., and Lindsay Hecht. "Obesity in the National Football League." *Journal of the American Medical Association* 293, no. 9 (2005): 1058–1062. doi: 10.1001/jama .293.9.1061-b.

Khan, Laura K., Kathleen Sobush, Dana Keener, Kenneth Goodman, Amy Lowry, Jakub Kakietek, and Susan Zaro. "Recommended Community Strategies and Measurements to Prevent Obesity in the United States." *Morbidity and Mortality Weekly Report: Recommendations and Reports* 58 (2009): 1–26.

Laurson, Kelly R., and Joey C. Eisenmann. "Prevalence of Overweight among High School Football Linemen." *Journal of the American Medical Association* 297, no. 4 (2007): 363–364. doi: 10.1001/jama.297.4.363.

Schocker, Laura. "More Schools Including Weight, BMI on Report Cards." Huffington Post. Last modified June 19, 2011. http://www.huffingtonpost.com/2011/04/19/bmi -schools_n_850776.html.

Why BMI Report Cards Have Potential for Helping Combat the Obesity Problem

In the past 30 years, rates of obesity have doubled in children and tripled in adolescents. Childhood obesity has been labeled one of the epidemics currently facing our country by the Centers for Disease Control and Prevention (CDC). Body mass index (BMI) report cards have been implemented in some states as public health measures designed to combat childhood obesity. Parents receive a report on their child's BMI categorization (underweight, normal, overweight, obese) as part of a fitness report. The intent of a BMI report card is to encourage early intervention specifically with children who are at higher risk for overweight and obesity by educating parents/families on exercise and healthy diet. BMI report cards—if implemented correctly—offer a valuable opportunity to provide targeted education and resources to families of children who are at higher risk for chronic weight-related disorders, including diabetes, obesity, and cardiovascular disease.

Currently in the United States, 25 states have some sort of procedure for documenting students' weights and heights. Although not all states require that this information be shared with parents, those that have opted to provide BMI scores to families have reported improvements. Arkansas was the first state to implement a BMI report card program in 2003 and has since reported that their childhood obesity rates have stabilized around 18 percent while the national childhood obesity rate has continued to rise. Additionally, although some stakeholders in the Arkansas BMI report cards program expressed concern over the potential for weight-related stigmatization and bullying in schools, research has shown virtually no adverse consequences related to bullying, increased dieting, or eating disorder symptomology as a result the BMI report card program.

BMI report cards also play a critical role in parental education. Interestingly, research has shown that parents are likely to misreport their child's weight or misclassify their child as a healthy weight when medical data would suggest that they are in fact overweight or obese. One study conducted in Britain found that, out of 2,976 families, only four sets of parents/caregivers reported that their child was overweight/obese; according to objective medical data (which included BMI scores), 369 of those children met criteria for overweight/obese weight classification. Clearly, parents have a tendency to overlook the severity of their child's overweight: this phenomenon has been termed "oblivobesity" by researchers and medical health professionals. Oblivobesity poses significant problems for early intervention efforts targeted at childhood obesity. First, if parents do not identify their child as overweight or obese, they may not make nutritional changes to their diet, incorporate exercise into their child's routine, or seek medical advice from their pediatrician/family physician. Additionally, research has shown a connection between parental obliviousness and child obliviousness to weight status. A study conducted by the CDC in the United States found that 70 percent of overweight boys and 80 percent of overweight girls reported their weight as normal. The percentage of children who misreported their weight as normal increased with declining socioeconomic status, highlighting the discrepancy between families with more resources in identifying weight-related health markers.

Ignoring or missing childhood overweight and obesity poses major health risks for children. One longitudinal study found that children who were overweight or at risk for overweight in the first grade were three times more likely to have hypertension by the time they were in fourth grade. Additionally, being overweight in childhood has been associated with type 2 diabetes, insulin resistance, and cardiovascular disease in children. Even for children who do not drop from the overweight or obese BMI range down into the normal BMI range, improvements in BMI scores even without dropping into the normal range were associated with health improvements. Some of these health improvements included lowered cholesterol levels, lowered blood pressure, improved insulin production, and increased aerobic fitness.

Proponents of BMI report cards have highlighted that schools represent the most significant activity in a child's day and should be on the front lines for health education. Although many researchers and public health professionals agree that BMI report cards should be one tool within a multidisciplinary approach to health education within the school systems, monitoring children's BMIs presents an invaluable opportunity for public health data tracking and early intervention possibilities. There is a demonstrated need for activities and information that heightens parental awareness of childhood obesity given the rates of misreporting and miscategorizing overweight children as normal. The health benefits associated with high BMIs and the improvements seen for BMI reductions lend further support for the incorporation of BMI report cards into public schools everywhere.

Hannah J. Hopkins

Bibliography

Crawford, Patricia B., Jim Hinson, Kristine A. Madsen, Dianne Neumark-Sztainer, and Allison J. Nihiser. "An Update on the Use and Value of School BMI Screening, Surveillance, and Reporting." *Childhood Obesity* 7, no. 6 (2011): 441–449. doi: 10.1089/chi .2011.0600.roun.

Joiner, Cynthia I. "Body Mass Index (BMI) Report Cards: Should Schools Be Responsible for Screening?" *MCN: The American Journal of Maternal/Child Nursing* 34, no. 4 (2009): 208. doi: 10.1097/01.NMC.0000357909.64863.b0.

Katz, David L. "Oblivobesity. Looking Over the Overweight That Parents Keep Overlooking." *Childhood Obesity* 11, no. 3 (2015): 225–226. doi: 10.1089/chi.2015.1131.

Kirk, Shelley, Meg Zeller, Randal Claytor, Megan Santangelo, Philip R. Khoury, and Stephen R. Daniels. "The Relationship of Health Outcomes to Improvement in BMI in Children and Adolescents." *Obesity Research* 13, no. 5 (2005): 876–882. doi: 10.1038 /oby.2005.101.

Petrou, Ilya. "'F' for 'Fat': Grading Weight Report Cards." *Contemporary Pediatrics* 32, no. 9 (2015): 35–37.

Pullis, Bridgette Crotwell, and Joe M. Pullis. "The Relationship between Body Mass Index (Weight Status) and Hypertension in a Cohort of Elementary School Students: A Retrospective Longitudinal Study." *Journal of Community Health Nursing* 26, no. 2 (2009): 64–76. doi: 10.1080/07370010902805122.

Raczynski, James M., Joseph W. Thompson, Martha M. Phillips, Kevin W. Ryan, and Herschel W. Cleveland. "Arkansas Act 1220 of 2003 to Reduce Childhood Obesity: Its Implementation and Impact on Child and Adolescent Body Mass Index." *Journal of Public Health Policy* 30 (2009): S124–S140. doi: 10.1057/jphp.2008.54.

Ruggieri, Dominique G., and Sarah B. Bass. "A Comprehensive Review of School-Based Body Mass Index Screening Programs and Their Implications for School Health: Do the Controversies Accurately Reflect the Research?" *Journal of School Health* 85, no. 1 (2015): 61–72. doi: 10.1111/josh.12222.

Vogel, Lauren. "The Skinny on BMI Report Cards." *Canadian Medical Association Journal* 183, no. 12 (2011): E787–E788. doi: 10.1503/cmaj.109-3927.

Why BMI Report Cards Are a Bad Thing

Childhood obesity remains one of the largest public health concerns in America. Since 1980, the childhood obesity rate has doubled among youths aged 6–11 (from 7 percent to 17.5 percent) and quadrupled among teens aged 12–19 (from 5 percent to 20.5 percent). Although the national childhood obesity rate has remained stable at 17 percent for the past several years, a higher rate of obesity is occurring at an earlier age. Among 2- to 5-year-olds, almost 9 percent are now obese and 2 percent are extremely obese. To combat the increase in childhood obesity, the Institute of Medicine developed an action plan in 2005, recommending schools implement annual body mass index (BMI) screenings and reports. Now 29 states and Washington, DC, have implemented BMI or other weight-related screening programs to ascertain rates of obesity and educate parents and students to live a healthier lifestyle.

The states that began giving students "BMI report cards" or "fat letters" to notify parents about their children's risk of obesity a decade ago hoped to solve the obesity epidemic by encouraging parents to increase their children's physical activity level and choose better foods. Since Arkansas's landmark legislation in 2003 that initiated the first state-level address of childhood obesity in the country, schools in Arkansas have been collecting student BMI data for the past 12 years. Although the overall statewide results remained around 39 percent of all school-aged children being classified as overweight or obese, 10th-grade students of the 2015–2016 school-year recorded the highest percentage (24 percent) of obese children for this grade since data collection began in 2003. Furthermore, 75 percent of students who were classified as obese in kindergarten remained obese by grade 10, suggesting that the "BMI report cards" are ineffective in reducing childhood obesity. Similarly, studies in California, Massachusetts, and New York found that BMI report cards had no significant effects on the students' BMI scores. Although states are mandating schools to obtain BMI data, students' BMIs are similar among schools with and without mandates.

The implementation of BMI report cards was intended to lower childhood obesity, but BMI report cards may have serious negative consequences such as anxiety about being weighed, lower self-esteem, increased weight-related teasing, and unhealthy dietary intakes and behaviors. Researchers have emphasized that privacy during measuring weight and height should be maximized to increase the comfort level and to prevent peer teasing. Announcing the child's BMI score publicly in front of peers can incite body shame and low self-esteem in the child hearing the number, and foster social comparison and weight-related teasing. Weight-related teasing refers to a specific form of peer victimization where the focus of the teasing is on the person's weight or body shape. Weight-related teasing has been shown to be associated with depression, low self-esteem, and eating disorders. After receiving BMI notifications, parents of "at risk of overweight" or "overweight" versus "normal weight" reported using riskier weight-control strategies such as asking their child to skip meals or to use diet pills to control their child's weight. These unhealthy weight-control methods can negatively affect the development of children.

Another reason to not use BMI report cards to reduce the number of overweight and obese children is that BMI is a poor indicator of obesity. It does not reflect a person's body composition accurately. For example, a very active child with large lean mass and a BMI at the 95th percentile may be classified as obese despite normal percent body fat mass. In addition, BMI classifications are skewed by maturation and race. It tends to exaggerate scores for shorter and taller than average children. Specifically, overweight is underestimated for short children and overestimated for tall children. Thus, using BMI as a screening tool for children is inaccurate because it does not account for body composition, maturation, race, and height at the upper and lower extremes among children.

Although more rigorous research studies are warranted, research on the effectiveness of using BMI notifications in combating childhood obesity indicates that sending "BMI report cards" to parents does not significantly reduce BMI scores in children and negatively affects their self-esteem, body satisfaction, and unhealthy dietary behaviors. Based on the scarce and negative results of using BMI as a motivator to encourage children and parents to increase physical activity and develop positive eating habits, the use of BMI as an obesity indicator is not justified. In addition, the inaccuracy of the BMI measurement and the cost of running BMI screening programs do not ethically justify the implementation of state mandated BMI screening programs in America. Therefore, schools should consider redirecting resources to policies and programs that have proven to improve child and adolescent health.

Sonya SooHoo and Maya Miyairi

Bibliography

Arkansas Center for Health Improvement. "Assessment of Childhood and Adolescent Obesity in Arkansas: Year 13 (Fall 2015–Spring 2016)." ACHI.net. Accessed January 30, 2017. http://www.achi.net/Content/Documents/ResourceRenderer.ashx?ID=441.

Bonthuis, Marjolein., Kitty J. Jager, Ameen Abu-Hanna, Enroco Verrina, Franz Schaefer, and Karlijn J.van Stralen. "Application of Body Mass Index According to Height-Age in Short and Tall Children." *Plos One* 8 (2013): e72068. doi: 10.1371/journal.pone.0072068.

Henningsen, Alexander, Piroska Boros, Kent Ingvalson, Fabio E. Fontana, and Oksana Matvienko. "Should Schools Send BMI Report Cards to Parents? A Review of Literature." *Journal of Physical Education, Recreation & Dance* 86 (2015): 26–32. doi: 10.1080/07303084.2015.1085340.

Himes, John H. "Challenges of Accurately Measuring and Using BMI and Other Indicators of Obesity in Children." *Pediatrics* 124 (2009): S3–S22. doi: 10.1542/peds.2008-3586D.

Kaczmarski, Jenna M., Rita D. DeBate, Stephanie L. Marhefka, and Ellen Daley. "State-Mandated School-Based BMI Screening and Parent Notification: A Descriptive Case Study." *Health Promotion Practice* 12 (2011): 797–801. doi: 10.1177/1524839911419289.

Madsen, Kathrine A. "School-Based Body Mass Index Screening and Parent Notification: A Statewide Natural Experiment." *Archives of Pediatric and Adolescent Medicine* 165 (2011): 987–992. doi: 10.1001/archpediatrics.2011.127.

Ogden, Cynthia L., Margaret D. Carroll, Cheryl D. Fryar, and Katherine M. Flegal. "Prevalence of Obesity among Adults and Youth: United States, 2011–2014." NCHS Data Brief, no. 219. Hyattsville, MD: National Center for Health Statistics, 2015.

Rankin, Jean, Lynsay Matthews, Stephen Cobley, Ahreum Han, Ross Sanders, Huw D. Wilt-shire, and Julien D. Baker. "Psychological Consequences of Childhood Obesity: Psychiatric Comorbidity and Prevention." *Adolescent Health, Medicine, and Therapeutics* 7 (2016): 125–146. doi: 10.2147/AHMT.S101631.

Ruggieri, Dominiquw G., and Sarah B. Bass. "A Comprehensive Review of School-Based Body Mass Index Screening Programs and Their Implications for School Health: Do the Controversies Accurately Reflect the Research?" *Journal of School Health* 85 (2014): 61–72. doi: 10.111/josh.12222.

Sandoval, Anna, Linsey Turner, Lisa Nicholson, Jamie Chriqui, Megan Tortorelli, and Frank J. Chaloupka. "The Relationship among State Laws, District Policies, and Elementary School-Based Measurement Children's Body Mass Index." *Journal of School Health* 82 (2012): 239–245. doi: 10.1111/j.1746-1561.2012.00693.x.

Is Orthorexia Nervosa Just Healthy Eating or a Disorder?

Orthorexia nervosa has recently been used to characterize "overly" healthy behavior related to eating that is considered extreme. Orthorexia nervosa refers to eating behavior that may include what is considered a pathological obsession for biologically pure foods that are free of herbicides, pesticides, and other artificial substances. Technically orthorexia nervosa is not a separate eating disorder diagnostic category in the *Diagnostic and Statistical Manual of Mental Disorders*, fifth edition, but clinicians identify overlaps between orthorexia nervosa and other disordered eating behaviors. Although consuming natural and organic foods is not harmful, orthorexia nervosa is marked by the excessive preoccupation or concern associated with consuming these so-called healthy foods. This term was developed in the late 1990s to capture the essence of observed disordered eating behaviors that did not seem to be accompanied with negative body image thoughts.

Orthorexia nervosa is distinct from other clinical eating disorders in that the focus is on the food itself. In other words, food is viewed as toxic or poisonous and something to be avoided but there is no associated fear of gaining weight found in anorexia nervosa. Subsequently, negative body image concerns have not been noted among individuals with orthorexia nervosa, which can create confusion at the diagnosis stage. Individuals who are prone to focus on food consumption, including athletes, medical students, physicians, dietitians, women, and teenagers, may be more vulnerable to the development of orthorexia nervosa. As mentioned above, however, orthorexia nervosa is not included as a separate diagnosis in the *DSM-5.*.

Although individuals with orthorexia nervosa are not concerned with weight loss, they experience negative moods associated with eating foods not considered healthy. Orthorexia nervosa can result in impaired social relationships, mood swings, and obsessive thoughts related to healthy food consumption. The following two debate essays will argue whether orthorexia should be considered a separate eating disorder diagnosis in the *Diagnostic and Statistical Manual of Mental Disorders*.

Justine J. Reel

Bibliography

American Psychiatric Association. *Diagnostic and Statistical Manual of Mental Disorders*, 5th ed., DSM-5. Washington, DC. American Psychiatric Publishing, 2013

Bosi, A. Tülay Bağci, Derya Camur, and Cağatay Güler. "Prevalence of Orthorexia Nervosa in Resident Medical Doctors in the Faculty of Medicine (Ankara, Turkey)." *Appetite* 49, no. 3 (2007): 661–666. doi: 10.1016/j.appet.2007.04.007.

Eriksson, Linn, A. Baigi, B. Marklund, and E. C. Lindgren. "Social Physique Anxiety and Sociocultural Attitudes toward Appearance Impact on Orthorexia Test in Fitness Participants." *Scandinavian Journal of Medicine & Science in Sports* 18, no. 3 (2008): 389–394. doi: 10.1111/j.1600-0838.2007.00723.x.

Fidan, Tulin, Vildan Ertekin, Sedat Isikay, and Ismet Kirpinar. "Prevalence of Orthorexia among Medical Students in Erzurum, Turkey." *Comprehensive Psychiatry* 51 (2010): 49–54. doi: 10.1016/j.comppsych.2009.03.001.

Kimmer, A., M. V. Dias, and A. L. Teixeira. "On the Concept of Orthorexia Nervosa." *Scandinavian Journal of Medicine & Science in Sports* 18, no. 3 (2008): 395–396. doi: 10.1111/j.1600-0838.2008.00809.x.

Kinzi, Johann F., Katharina Hauer, Christian Traweger, and Ingrid Kiefer. "Orthorexia Nervosa in Dieticians." *Psychotherapy and Psychosomatics* 75 (2006): 395–396. doi: 10.1159/000095447.

Korinth, Anne, Sonja Schiess, and Joachim Westenhoefer. "Eating Behavior and Eating Disorders in Students of Nutrition Sciences." *Public Health Nutrition* 13, no. 1 (2009): 32–37. doi: 10.1017/S1368980009005709.

Vandereycken, Walter. "Media Hype, Diagnostic Fad or Genuine Disorder? Professionals' Opinions about Night Eating Syndrome, Orthorexia, Muscle Dysmorphia and Emetophobia." *Eating Disorders: Journal of Treatment and Prevention* 19 (2011): 145–155. doi: 10.1080/10640266.2011.551634.

Orthorexia Nervosa Is an Actual Eating Disorder

Clinicians have asserted that individuals with orthorexia nervosa show an unhealthy obsession for purity of food. This obsessive tendency can lead to an overly restrictive diet, preoccupation with food preparation, and ritualized patterns of eating. For instance, typical obsessive attitudes and behaviors observed among orthorexic individuals include spending considerable time concerned about food quality. Individuals with orthorexia have concerns such as whether food items are organically grown instead of being exposed to pesticides, whether food ingredients include genetically modified sources, and whether preservatives or artificial flavors or colors are added to foods. Food packaging obsessions such as whether food labels indicate enough information to ensure the food safety and whether food ingredients contain plastic-derived carcinogenic compounds are also pervasive among individuals with orthorexia. Furthermore, these orthorexic attitudes and behaviors can often interfere with their daily and social functions as well as relationships with others.

Unfortunately, deleterious effects of an overly restrictive diet synonymous with orthorexia may involve nutritional deficiencies and medical complications similar to anorexia nervosa symptoms (e.g., osteopenia, anemia, hyponatremia, metabolic acidosis, pancytopenia, testosterone deficiency, bradycardia). In addition, there is unequivocal evidence that orthorexia nervosa and eating disorders such as anorexia nervosa have common characteristics including perfectionism, high trait anxiety, excessive controlling overeating and selection of food items and the ingredients, significant weight loss, achievement orientation, and emotional adherence to diet. Several studies have found that in general patients with anorexia nervosa do not focus on the quality of foods; however, they are not immune to the trends associated with the health food industry or certain diet foods that are marketed widely as "healthy" alternatives. In addition, previous case studies illustrated actual eating disorder cases that described pathological eating driven by a diet perceived to promote good health instead of a desire for thinness. Patients in these case studies were simply triggered by specific dieting instructions provided by health professionals due to their health conditions (e.g., eliminating fats to help control acne), and they started engaging in extreme restrictive eating patterns.

The other debatable fact is that orthorexic attitudes and behaviors can be easily overlooked as a "healthy" behavior because of recent healthy lifestyle trends (i.e., being encouraged to exercise and eat more vegetables and fruits every day) in our society. This phenomenon is similar to exercise dependence, which many individuals can view as a healthy habit. Because many orthorexic individuals do not show fear of becoming fat, extreme weight-control behavior, or overevaluation of body shape and weight, health professionals may consider that orthorexia nervosa is different from eating disorders. On the other hand, a newly recognized eating disorder diagnosis—avoidant/restrictive food intake disorder—was added to in *DSM-5* to bring attention to some of the hidden "healthy" behaviors observed among individuals with eating disorders. Avoidant/restrictive food intake disorder is defined as "an eating or feeding disturbance as manifested by persistent failure to meet appropriate nutritional and/or energy needs associated with one (or more) of the following: (1) significant loss of weight, (2) significant nutritional deficiency, (3) dependence on enteral feeding or oral nutritional supplements, and (4) marked interference with psychosocial functioning." More importantly, this type of eating disorder shows no evidence of a disturbance in the way one's body shape or weight is experienced. Although orthorexia nervosa is not currently recognized as avoidant/restrictive food intake disorder in *DSM-5*, these attitudes and behaviors are similar to what orthorexic individuals display. Therefore, orthorexia nervosa should be considered as an eating disorder for inclusion in the next edition of the *Diagnostic and Statistical Manual of Mental Disorders*.

These overlapping characteristics that orthorexia individuals may experience have raised ongoing debate surrounding whether orthorexia nervosa is a separate eating disorder since orthorexia nervosa was introduced in 1997. However, eating disorder experts, including the person who introduced orthorexia nervosa (i.e., Dr. Steven Bratman), argue that orthorexia nervosa should be recognized as a separate diagnosis from anorexia nervosa and other clinical eating disorders. Despite the ongoing debate, online resources sponsored by eating disorder organizations such as the National Eating Disorder Association and eating disorder treatment facilities recognize orthorexia nervosa as an eating disorder. Since many eating disorder cases have been overlooked in the past due to the complexity of the disease, health professionals need more careful observation and judgment when they see orthorexic attitudes and behaviors among their clients. In addition, a critical argument they must remember is that orthorexia nervosa can become not only a risk factor but also a part of eating disorders. Therefore, to prevent the aggravation of eating disorder symptoms, it is important to recognize orthorexia nervosa as an eating disorder.

Maya Miyairi and Sonya SooHoo

Bibliography

Aksoydan, E., and N. Camci. "Prevalence of Orthorexia Nervosa among Turkish Performance Artists." *Eating and Weight Disorders* 14, no. 1 (2009): 33–37. doi: 10.1007/BF03327792.

American Psychiatric Association. *Diagnostic and Statistical Manual of Mental Disorders*, 5th ed., *DSM-5*. Washington, DC: American Psychiatric Association, 2013.

Bosı, A. Tülay Bağci, Derya Çamur, and Çağatay Güler. "Prevalence of Orthorexia Nervosa in Resident Medical Doctors in the Faculty of Medicine (Ankara, Turkey)." *Appetite* 49, no. 3 (2007): 661–666. doi: 10.1016/j.appet.2007.04.007.

Bratman, Steven. "The Health Food Eating Disorder." *Yoga Journal*, September/October (1997): 42–50.

Bratman, Steven, and David Knight. *Health Food Junkies: Orthorexia Nervosa: Overcoming the Obsession with Healthful Eating.* New York: Broadway, 2001.

Brytek-Matera, Anna. "Orthorexia Nervosa—An Eating Disorder, Obsessive-Compulsive Disorder or Disturbed Eating Habit?" *Archives of Psychiatry and Psychotherapy* 14, no. 1 (2012): 55–60.

Brytek-Matera, Anna, Radosław Rogoza, Carla Gramaglia, and Patrizia Zeppegno. "Predictors of Orthorexic Behaviours in Patients with Eating Disorders: A Preliminary Study." *BMC Psychiatry* 15 (2015): 252–260. doi: 10.1186/s12888-015-0628-1.

Chaki, Biswajit, Sangita Pal, and Amit Bandyopadhyay. "Exploring Scientific Legitimacy of Orthorexia Nervosa: A Newly Emerging Eating Disorder." *Journal of Human Sport & Exercise* 8, no. 4 (2013): 1045–1053. doi: 10.4100/jhse.2013.84.14.

Donini, Lorenzo M., D. Marsili, Mariapaola Graziani, M. Imbriale, and C. Cannella. "Orthorexia Nervosa: A Preliminary Study with a Proposal for Diagnosis and an Attempt to Measure the Dimension of the Phenomenon." *Eating and Weight Disorders* 9, no. 2 (2004): 151–157. doi: 10.1007/BF03325060.

Dunn, Thomas M., and Steven Bratman. "On Orthorexia Nervosa: A Review of the Literature and Proposed Diagnostic Criteria." *Eating Behaviors* 21 (2016): 11–17. doi: 10.1016/j.eatbeh.2015.12.006.

Koven, Nancy S., and Alexandra W. Abry. "The Clinical Basis of Orthorexia Nervosa: Emerging Perspectives." *Neuropsychiatric Disease and Treatment* 11 (2015): 385–394. doi: 10.2147/NDT.S61665.

Kratina, Karin. "Orthorexia Nervosa." *National Eating Disorders Association*. Accessed January 30, 2017. http://www.nationaleatingdisorders.org/orthorexia-nervosa.

Mac Evilly, Claire. "The Price of Perfection." *Nutrition Bulletin* 26, no. 4 (2001): 275–276. doi: 10.1046/j.1467-3010.2001.00182.x

Moroze, Ryan M., Thomas M. Dunn, J. Craig Holland, Joel Yager, and Philippe Weintraub. "Microthinking about Micronutrients: A Case of Transition from Obsessions about Healthy Eating to Near-Fatal 'Orthorexia Nervosa' and Proposed Diagnostic Criteria." *Psychosomatics: Journal of Consultation and Liaison Psychiatry* 56, no. 4 (2015): 397–403. doi: 10.1016/j.psym.2014.03.003.

Park, Sang Won, Jeong Yup Kim, Gang Ji Go, Eun Sil Jeon, Heui Jung Pyo, and Young Joo Kwon. "Orthorexia Nervosa with Hyponatremia, Subcutaneous Emphysema, Pneumomediastimum, Pneumothorax, and Pancytopenia." *Electrolyte & Blood Pressure* 9, no. 1 (2011): 32–37. doi: 10.5049/EBP.2011.9.1.32.

Strand, Erik. "A New Eating Disorder?" *Psychology Today* 37, no. 5 (2004): 16.

Orthorexia Is Healthy Eating, Not an Eating Disorder

When the term "orthorexia nervosa" was first coined in the late 1990s by a medical doctor, he described the condition as a "fixation on righteous eating." In contrast to other eating disorders such as anorexia nervosa and bulimia nervosa, the focus of orthorexia nervosa (ON) is not weight loss but instead achieving a sense of purity. The fixation in ON is on only eating healthy foods that have not been tainted by modern methods of food processing, including food coloring, pesticides/herbicides, added sugars or preservatives. Although some in psychology and other medical professions argue that this set of behaviors constitutes an eating disorder, there is not enough evidence to demonstrate that ON is anything beyond an extreme form of healthy eating.

Thus far, only one questionnaire has been designed for the purposes of studying orthorexia. This questionnaire (called the ORTO-15) was given to a sample of over 400 people in Italy and included questions such as "when eating, do you pay attention to the calories in the food?" "do you think your mood affects your eating behavior?"; and "are you willing to spend more money to have healthy food?" Higher scores on the ORTO-15 indicate a higher level of health fanaticism related to food choices and therefore was interpreted by researchers as indicating the presence of ON. However, none of these questions represent disordered eating or eating patterns that are significantly different from the norm. According to a Gallup poll from 2013, almost half of all people (43 percent) reported paying significant attention to calorie counts. Additionally, the American Psychological Association reports that around a third of all U.S. adults are considered "emotional eaters" in that their mood and stress level plays a significant role in determining how much/what food they eat. Last, the willingness to spend more money on healthier food is a commonplace trend in the daily lives of almost all Americans: diets rich in fruits, vegetables, and fresh meat cost an average of $1.50 more per day than unhealthy diets high in sugar, processed foods, and "junk" foods. The ORTO-15 is an attempt to create a diagnosis out of healthy eating behaviors that are extremely commonplace in modern Western societies.

The criticism that ON represents an extreme but undisordered pattern of healthy eating has been levied against supporters of the diagnostic criteria for ON many times before. In response, researchers and clinicians who believe in the validity of ON argue that many people experience significant impairment or distress in their daily lives as a result of their behaviors, which qualifies these individuals for a diagnosis of a mental disorder and lends further support to the idea that ON is an eating disorder. Critics of ON have then rebuked this line of thinking by arguing that the distress/impairment arises not from the pattern of eating itself but instead from the obsessional element that is central to ON. Unlike in anorexia and bulimia, the diet and dietary behaviors associated with ON do not cause distress or impairment. In fact, many researchers and clinicians argue that, while perhaps unorthodox, the diet commonly found in ON is very healthy. Individuals who engage in this diet typically eat a lot of fresh fruits, vegetables, and unprocessed meats; they avoid foods that are high in sodium, added sugars, unnatural flavorings, and preservatives; and they are highly motivated to maintain this diet. In fact, research has shown that the diet associated with ON is commonly seen among individuals who have a background in nutritional science (e.g., dietitians, exercise science, athletes, medical doctors). It is the obsession with maintaining this diet—and not the diet itself—that appears to be the problematic element in ON. Many researchers have argued that this fact makes it inappropriate to categorize ON as an eating disorder and that it should be considered an element of obsessive-compulsive disorder (OCD). By thinking of ON as a corollary to OCD, researchers hope that it will emphasize the truly disordered piece of the behavior (the perfectionistic obsession with maintaining a pure diet) and discourage mental health professionals from overmedicalizing healthy behaviors, even if they are extreme.

As the debate over whether ON is indeed a bonified mental illness or just an extreme form of generally healthy behaviors continues to evolve, researchers and mental health professionals continue to develop and refine their understanding of how different individuals express the pursuit of health. By furthering the conversation around how we understand and define mental illness and eating disorders specifically, new challenges such as ON serve a crucial purpose in expanding the boundaries of our understanding of human behaviors. Ultimately, whether ON eventually becomes its own diagnosis or not, the additional attention it's garnering will only serve to improve the lives of those affected by it and similar dysfunctional behaviors.

Hannah J. Hopkins

Bibliography

Brytek-Matera, Anna. "Orthorexia Nervosa—An Eating Disorder, Obsessive-Compulsive Disorder or Disturbed Eating Habit?" *Archives of Psychiatry and Psychotherapy* 1 (2012): 55–60.

Chaki, Biswajit, Sangita Pal, and Amit Bandyopadhyay. "Exploring Scientific Legitimacy of Orthorexia Nervosa: A Newly Emerging Eating Disorder." *Journal of Human Sport and Exercise* 8, no. 4 (2013): 1045–1053. doi: 10.4100/jhse.2013.84.14.

Donini, Lorenzo, Daniela Marsili, Maria Graziani, M. Imbriale, and C. Cannella. "Orthorexia Nervosa: Validation of a Diagnosis Questionnaire." *Eating and Weight Disorders* 10, no. 2 (2005): e28–e35. doi: 10.1007/BF03327537.

Khazan, Olga. "Who Pays Attention to Calories?" *The Atlantic*, December 2, 2014. http://www.theatlantic.com/health/archive/2014/12/who-looks-at-menu-labels/383320/.

Mathieu, Jennifer. "What Is Orthorexia?" *Journal of the American Dietetic Association* 105, no. 10 (2005): 1510–1512. doi: 10.1016/j.jada.2005.08.021.

Rao, Mayuree, Ashkan Afshin, Gitanjali Singh, and Dariush Mozaffarian. "Do Healthier Foods and Diet Patterns Cost More Than Less Healthy Options? A Systematic Review and Meta-Analysis." *BMJ Open* 3, no. 12 (2013): e004277. doi: 10.1136/bmjopen-2013-004277.

Saddichha, Sahoo, Girish N. Babu, and Prabha Chandra. "Orthorexia Nervosa Presenting as Prodrome of Schizophrenia." *Schizophrenia Research* 134, no. 1 (2012): 110. doi: 10.1016/j.schres.2011.10.017.

Starcevic, Vladan. "Behavioural Addictions: A Challenge for Psychopathology and Psychiatric Nosology." *Australian & New Zealand Journal of Psychiatry* 50, no. 8 (2016): 721–725. doi: 10.1177/0004867416654009.

"Stress and Eating." APA.org. Accessed January 30, 2017. http://www.apa.org/news/press /releases/stress/2013/eating.aspx.

Should People Undergoing Eating Disorder Treatment Be Exposed to Pro–Eating Disorder Websites?

A potential trigger associated with eating disorders involves messages from media and online sites. A particularly controversial type of online messaging is represented by websites that promote eating disorders as a positive way of life that represents maintaining strong discipline over one's food intake. These dangerous websites have continued to proliferate online despite massive efforts to remove them. Pro–eating disorder efforts have been referred to as "pro-ana" and "pro-mia." Pro-ana is defined as the encouragement of anorexia nervosa while pro-mia is the promotion of bulimia nervosa. Both groups are considered to be in direct opposition to receiving treatment for and recovery from an eating disorder. Instead these websites intentionally provide a positive slant related to continuing disordered eating behaviors such as restricting one's intake or compensating for binge episodes through purging methods like vomiting. The controversial nature of these websites coupled with an inability to eliminate them entirely begs the question about how pro–eating disorder websites should be dealt with in the treatment setting. In other words, should clients be intentionally exposed to harmful websites (in a similar fashion as triggering foods or the mirror) as a therapeutic strategy?

Pro-ana and pro-mia websites use social media to reinforce messages related to intense body dissatisfaction, the need to stay ultra-thin, and the importance of appearance. Alarmingly, the forums, which include members who endorse a variety of disordered eating behaviors, can teach visitors to or members of the sites "how" to lose weight using unhealthy strategies such as severe food restriction, detoxes, cleanses, and purging methods. Photographs of anorexic-looking bodies are meant to serve as motivators for those who are supporting the cause by living the life of an anorexic. Members and visitors are urged to stay strong in spite of pressure from family, friends, or society to eat. One example of black-and-white thinking encouraged on these sites is that "losing weight is good" while "gaining weight is bad." Black-and-white thinking is also commonly reinforced with good or bad associations with particular foods or food groups.

Unfortunately, pro–eating disorder websites are not regulated. The online blogs, forums, and images directly oppose healthy views of treatment and recovery promoted by licensed eating disorder professionals. Naturally the content on these websites can undermine treatment progress of individuals suffering from eating disorders and can be triggering for disordered eating behaviors. As expected, these pro-eating disorder websites are extremely controversial. Studies have confirmed the negative effects of interfacing with a pro-ana website on the body dissatisfaction of female college students. Specifically, participants have reported feeling overweight as a result of viewing a pro-eating disorder website. Individuals who have an eating disorder history or who are seeking treatment also may be more vulnerable to being triggered by engaging with a pro-eating disorder website. Unfortunately, theses websites pop up quickly and re-emerge when removed. Perhaps most disturbing is that parents are largely unaware of the existence of pro-eating disorder websites or that their daughters and sons were participating in pro-ana chats, forums, and other online activities.

Pro-ana and pro-mia represent the promotion of eating disorders as a choice rather than a serious disease. In fact, the celebration of anorexia nervosa and thinness has led to pro-ana support groups and bracelets as symbols of the ana lifestyle. Pro-eating disorder websites offer forums for discussion boards about how to stay disordered, thinspirations, and techniques related to unhealthy weight loss. Although research over the past decade has clearly documented the damaging effects of exposure to pro-eating disorder websites, websites are difficult to regulate and have a large group of pro-ana followers. The following two debate essays will argue both sides of how to include pro-eating disorder websites as part of the treatment process. Exposure to these potentially damaging websites can represent a double-edged sword. Therefore, arguments are presented to show how pro-eating disorder websites should be properly addressed in treatment and recovery.

Justine J. Reel

Bibliography

Bardone-Cone, Anna M., and Kamila M. Cass. "Investigating the Impact of Pro-Anorexia Websites: A Pilot Study." *European Eating Disorders Review* 14 (2006): 256–262. doi: 10.1002/ERV.714.

Bardone-Cone, Anna M., and Kamila M. Cass. "What Does Viewing a Pro-Anorexia Website Do? An Experimental Examination of Website Exposure and Moderating Effects." *International Journal of Eating Disorders* 40, no. 6 (2007): 537–548. doi: 10.1002/eat .20396.

Giles, David. "Constructing Identities in Cyberspace: The Case of Eating Disorders." *British Journal of Social Psychology* 45 (2006): 463–477. doi: 10/1348/014466605X53596.

Harper, Kelley, Steffanie Sperry, and J. Kevin Thompson. "Viewership of Pro-Eating Disorder Websites: Association with Body Image and Eating Disturbances." *International Journal of Eating Disorders* 41 (2008): 92–95. doi: 10.1002/eat.20408.

Jett, Scarlett, David J. LaPorte, and Jill Wanchisn. "Impact of Exposure to Pro-Eating Disorder Websites on Eating Behaviour in College Women." *European Eating Disorders Review* 18 (2010): 410–416. doi: 10.1002/erv.1009.

Lyons, Elizabeth J., Matthias R. Mehl, and James W. Pennebaker. "Pro Anorexics and Recovering Anorexics Differ in Their Linguistic Internet Self-Presentation." *Journal of Psychosomatic Research* 60 (2006): 253–256. doi: 10.1016/j.psychores.2005.07.017.

Ransom, Danielle C., Jennifer G. La Guardia, Erik Z. Woody, and Jennifer L. Boyd. "Interpersonal Interactions on Online Forums Addressing Eating Concerns." *International Journal of Eating Disorders* 43 (2010): 161–170. doi: 10.1002/eat.20629.

Wilson, Jenny L., Rebecka Peebles, Kristina K. Hardy, and Iris F. Litt. "Surfing for Thinness: A Pilot Study of Pro-Eating Disorder Web Site Usage in Adolescents with Eating Disorders." *Pediatrics* 118 (2006): 1635–1643. doi: 10.1542/peds.2006-1133.

Pro–Eating Disorder Online Content Should Be Incorporated into Eating Disorder Treatment

Pro–eating disordered blogs have begun to surge on the Internet in the past few years as a space for anorexic or bulimic individuals to seek support from one another. The average age of individuals who subscribe to pro–eating disordered (pro-ED) content on social media is 17 years old, a particularly vulnerable age group, susceptible to the influence of provocative disordered eating content presented on social media. Although some research finds that exposure to these sites can increase dieting behaviors, other studies find that these blogs reduce levels of loneliness and help users feel greater levels of happiness. Incorporating exposure to and management of pro-ED site usage into treating for eating disorders may prove valuable in helping this population.

Individuals with eating disorders find it difficult to identify activities that are more appealing to them than their disorder. However, research has demonstrated that participation in pro-ED blogs proves to be uniquely motivating for this population, and has positive consequences after use. For instance, one study found that a third of online users who participated in online pro-ED blogs reported that these blogs were ultimately helpful toward their recovery by helping them find support and ameliorate loneliness, incidentally, two critical aspects of eating disorder treatment. Another appealing part of online pro-ED blogs is providing individuals with the ability to post about the illness with no judgment or criticism. Many users have reported that they are able to establish friendships with others who are in recovery or who are able to empathize with their experiences. Considering that this population is characterized by loneliness and isolation from previously established friend groups, participation in pro-ED sites and "friendship" obtained by like-minded users is particularly alluring. These benefits are critical to consider when building a treatment plan and determining whether these online communities should be included.

Research has also shown that safe introduction and exposure to triggering material—such as these online pro-ED websites—during the treatment process may help people with eating disorders. Within therapy, the safe incorporation of pro-ED sites can help individuals with eating disorders feel supported and stymie their curiosity of what these sites include. As opposed to forbidding pro–eating disorder site use, openness around the use and incorporating these sites into therapy can help with therapeutic rapport building as well as guide the patient's experience of the sites to be less triggering. Given this evidence, it would be a mistake to forbid using these online communities as an element of treatment as they offer benefits that many health professionals identify as critical to the recovery process.

Pro–eating disorder sites are currently more widely perceived as dangerous and triggering to eating disorder patients. However, examining these sites from a patient's perspective and incorporating open discussion around what the patient might find appealing about these sites and what they may find harmful would likely increase therapeutic alliance and allow the patient to feel less stigmatized and more understood by his or her clinician. In sum, there is evidence suggesting that the safe integration of pro-ED content in therapy would prove to be valuable in building trust between the clinician and the patient as well as foster adaptive behaviors for ill individuals.

Nandini Datta

Bibliography

Chancellor, Stevie, Tanushree Mitra, and Munmun De Choudhury. "Recovery Amid Pro-Anorexia: Analysis of Recovery in Social Media." *CHI '16* May 07–12 (2016): 2111–2123. doi: 10.1145/2858036.2858246.

Colaiori, Francesca, and Claudio Castellano. "Interplay between Media and Social Influence in the Collective Behavior of Opinion Dynamics." *Physical Review E* 92, no. 4 (2015): 042815. doi: 10.1103/PhysRevE.92.042815.

Flynn, Mark A., and Alexandru Stana. "Social Support in a Men's Online Eating Disorder Forum." *International Journal of Men's Health* 11, no. 2 (2012): 150–169. doi: 10.3149/jmh.1102.150.

Juarascio, Adrienne S., Amber Shoaib, and C. Alix Timko. "Pro-Eating Disorder Communities on Social Networking Sites: A Content Analysis." *Eating Disorders* 18, no. 5 (2010): 393–407. doi: 10.1080/10640266.2010.511918.

Meier, Evelyn P., and James Gray. "Facebook Photo Activity Associated with Body Image Disturbance in Adolescent Girls." *Cyberpsychology, Behavior, and Social Networking* 17, no. 4 (2013): 199–206. doi: 10.1089/cyber.2013.0305.

Quiles Marcos, Y., M. J. Quiles Sebastián, L. Pamies Aubalat, J. Botella Ausina, and J. Treasure. "Peer and Family Influence in Eating Disorders: A Meta-Analysis." *European Psychiatry* 28, no. 4 (2013): 199–206. doi: 10.1016/j.eurpsy.2012.03.005.

Rheinschmidt, Michelle L., and Rodolfo Mendoza-Denton. "Social Class and Academic Achievement in College: The Interplay of Rejection Sensitivity and Entity Beliefs." *Journal of Personality and Social Psychology* 107, no. 1 (2014): 101–121. doi: 10.1037/a0036553.

Rodgers, Rachel F., Siân A. McLean, and Susan J. Paxton. "Longitudinal Relationships among Internalization of the Media Ideal, Peer Social Comparison, and Body Dissatisfaction: Implications for the Tripartite Influence Model." *Developmental Psychology* 51, no. 5 (2015): 706–713. doi: 10.1037/dev0000013.

Saffran, Kristina, Ellen E. Fitzsimmons-Craft, Andrea E. Kass, Denise E. Wilfley, Craig Barr Taylor, and Mickey Trockel. "Facebook Usage among Those Who Have Received Treatment for an Eating Disorder in a Group Setting: Facebook Usage after Eating Disorder Treatment." *International Journal of Eating Disorders* 49, no. 8 (2016): 764–777. doi: 10.1002/eat.22567.

Schott, Nicole Danielle, and Debra Langan. "Pro-Anorexia/Bulimia Censorship and Public Service Announcements: The Price of Controlling Women." *Media, Culture & Society* 37, no. 8 (2015): 1158–1175. doi: 10.1177/0163443715591672.

Tan, Tina, Angeline Kuek, Shih Ee Goh, Ee Lian Lee, and Victor Kwok. "Internet and Smartphone Application Usage in Eating Disorders: A Descriptive Study in Singapore." *Asian Journal of Psychiatry* 19 (2016): 50–55. doi: 10.1016/j.ajp.2015.11.007.

Tiggemann, Marika, and Amy Slater. "NetGirls: The Internet, Facebook, and Body Image Concern in Adolescent Girls." *International Journal of Eating Disorders* 46, no. 6 (2013): 630–633. doi: 10.1002/eat.22141.

Pro–Eating Disorder Online Content Should Not Be Incorporated into Eating Disorder Treatment

The association between exposure to Western media and increased body dissatisfaction and dieting behaviors is well documented by numerous research studies. With the rise of the Internet in the past several decades, a new media form has flourished that has particular implications for eating disorders. Pro–eating disorder (pro-ED) online websites—sometimes referred to as "pro-ana" (pro-anorexia) or "pro-mia" (pro-bulimia)—have developed a devoted underground following of predominantly adolescent females. These sites enable users to share content with one another as well as message one another directly. Although some research has demonstrated that these sites enable users to forge new friendships and combat loneliness, many studies have also highlighted the detrimental effects that viewership of pro-ED content can have on body image, dieting, compensatory behaviors (e.g., exercising, purging), and on affect more generally. Given this body of evidence, it is erroneous to think that these websites should be integrated into treatment plans for eating disorders.

Although treatment plans are individualized to meet each patient's needs, the overarching goal of eating disorder treatments is to restore someone to a healthy weight and support them in maintain that weight. This is a broad goal to set, and it involves behavioral, attitudinal, and cognitive changes on behalf of the individual as well as major changes to their environment, friend group (potentially), and lifestyle. One of the most critical aspects of achieving success in treatment is eliminating "triggers" that may cause a relapse into disordered eating. Pro-ED online content is one such trigger. These websites have been shown to worsen one's mood, increase one's motivation to lose weight. In fact, many viewers report being willing to engage in some of the weight-loss strategies touted on these websites. These strategies tend to be particularly unhealthy, including grape-only diets, purging in the shower to mask the sound and odor, and halving every food item on their plate multiple times and subsequently eating only one piece (12 percent or 25 percent of the original amount).

Additionally, pro-ED communities normalize eating disorders through their exuberant proclamations that eating disorders are "lifestyle choices" and represent "purity." This trend is particularly concerning, given that a significant portion of pro-ED users are adolescents and young adults who are in the process of identity formation. By casting eating disorders as a "lifestyle choice," pro-ED content legitimizes these identities and can often mask, underplay, or completely deny the negative physical and psychological effects of eating disorders. These identities, once removed from their negative consequences, suddenly become much more appealing to the young and impressionable who are in the throes of identity formation. Research on the consequences of group dynamics and Internet communities has shown that people are far less likely to preserve a sense of moderation in their views when they are continuously presented with opinions that mirror their own. Not surprisingly, this is particularly true of pro-ED communities, who will often go to extremes to exclude users who they view as being unable to fully commit to the lifestyle (e.g., "wannarexics"). The combination of these three deadly trends — normalizing eating disorders, isolating one's self with like-minded individuals, and creating exclusivity in the communities—makes pro-ED online sites particularly worrisome for individuals with unstable identities or vulnerable personalities.

Research also indicates that many viewers who are regularly exposed to this type of content are unaware of the deleterious effects it has on their body image, self-esteem, and eating/exercising behaviors. One research study found that exposing college-aged women to a pro-ED website caused them to decrease their daily caloric intake by an average of over 2,400 calories. These results were seen after a mere 90-minute viewing of the pro-ED website, which is a negligent amount compared to the amount of time that devotees of pro-ED content spend on such sites. Many of the individuals (84 percent) who were exposed to these pro-ED sites reduced their daily caloric intake; interestingly, only 56 percent of the same subjects reported *noticing* that they had decreased their caloric intake. This is particularly troublesome for individuals who are in recovery from a past disorder and vulnerable to relapse. These effects are also long-lasting, with almost a quarter (24 percent) of the individuals exposed to 90-minutes of pro-ED content reporting that they continued to restrict their caloric intake and employ weight-loss strategies they learned about on these sites at three-weeks follow-up. Once again, these results are concerning for individuals who are recovering from eating disorders. Even if they were exposed to pro-ED content in the relative security of a treatment session, the long-lasting impact that that exposure could have on the individual may eventually catalyze a relapse once they're no longer in a treatment setting.

Therefore, despite how enticing it may be to advocate for inclusion of pro-ED content in treatment due to the community-building benefits of such communities, the risks posed by exposure to this highly triggering content are too great to warrant a place in recovery. Pro–eating disorder online content has been shown to prompt a wide number of negative consequences and be incredibly potent for young adolescents who are searching for identity and community. Perhaps even more concerning is the research showing that individuals are even unaware as to the extent that viewing this content has on their behaviors. Given these well-demonstrated and serious risks, it is inappropriate to include pro–eating disorder content in the treatment plan until the benefits of such communities can be isolated from the negative consequences.

Hannah J. Hopkins

Bibliography

Allison, Stephen, Megan Warin, and Tarun Bastiampillai. "Anorexia Nervosa and Social Contagion: Clinical Implications." *Australian & New Zealand Journal of Psychiatry* 48, no. 2 (2014): 116–120. doi: 10.1177/0004867413502092.

Bardone-Cone, Anna M., and Kamila M. Cass. "What Does Viewing a Pro-Anorexia Website Do? An Experimental Examination of Website Exposure and Moderating Effects."

International Journal of Eating Disorders 40, no. 6 (2007): 537–548. doi: 10.1002/eat.20396.

Harper, Kelley, Steffanie Sperry, and J. Kevin Thompson. "Viewership of Pro-Eating Disorder Websites: Association with Body Image and Eating Disturbances." *International Journal of Eating Disorders* 41, no. 1 (2008): 92–95. doi: 10.1002/eat.20408.

Jett, Scarlett, David J. LaPorte, and Jill Wanchisn. "Impact of Exposure to Pro-Eating Disorder Websites on Eating Behaviour in College Women." *European Eating Disorders Review* 18, no. 5 (2010): 410–416. doi: 10.1002/erv.1009.

Keel, Pamela K., David J. Dorer, Debra L. Franko, Safia C. Jackson, and David B. Herzog. "Postremission Predictors of Relapse in Women with Eating Disorders." *American Journal of Psychiatry* 162, no. 12 (2005): 2263–2268. doi: 10.1176/appi.ajp.162.12.2263.

Mulveen, Ruaidhri, and Julie Hepworth. "An Interpretative Phenomenological Analysis of Participation in a Pro-Anorexia Internet Site and Its Relationship with Disordered Eating." *Journal of Health Psychology* 11, no. 2 (2006): 283–296. doi: 10.1177/1359105306061187.

Peebles, Rebecka, Jenny L. Wilson, Iris F. Litt, Kristina K. Hardy, James D. Lock, Julia R. Mann, and Dina L. G. Borzekowski. "Disordered Eating in a Digital Age: Eating Behaviors, Health, and Quality of Life in Users of Websites with Pro-Eating Disorder Content." *Journal of Medical Internet Research* 14, no. 5 (2012): e148. doi: 10.2196/jmir.2023.

Is Recovery from an Eating Disorder Possible?

Addictions literature often emphasizes the process of being "in recovery" as ongoing. There is some dispute whether eating disorders should be classified as addictions, similar to substance use disorders or alcohol abuse, begging the question of whether recovery from an eating disorder is truly possible. Therefore, this debate will argue on one side that people who suffer from eating disorders can actually recover and eventually become "recovered." By contrast, the opposing viewpoint will argue that like other addictions, individuals with eating disorders are always "in recovery."

Recovery from an eating disorder refers to the complete absence of symptoms such as restricting and purging. In other words, an individual with an eating disorder history who is recovered should be indistinguishable from individuals who have never been diagnosed with an eating disorder. Further, in order to be considered "fully recovered" individuals should no longer meet diagnostic criteria for an eating disorder; have not engaged in any disordered eating behaviors (e.g., vomiting, binge eating) for three months; have a body mass index (BMI) of 18.5 or more; and be considered normal on eating disorder screening instruments.

An individual who is considered fully recovered from an eating disorder should be at a minimal risk for relapse or slips of disordered eating behaviors. In contrast, "partial recovery" refers to refraining from disordered eating behaviors and having acceptable BMI scores while not meeting the psychological criteria necessary for full recovery. Individuals who are in partial recovery often admit that they continue to experience negative body image and eating disorder triggers.

A common belief related to addiction is that an individual who has a history of addiction will always be an "addict" and will remain in "recovery," and that recovery represents a lifelong process. Eating disorders differ from other addictions in that it is impossible to abstain from eating. Therefore, individuals with eating disorders must develop a healthier and more positive relationship with food in order to recover from an eating disorder.

Eating disorder clinicians and researchers promote the philosophy that individuals can be "recovered from" an eating disorder rather than "in recovery." Being recovered represents past tense, which is more empowering for individuals and encourages the disengagement from one's eating disorder identity. Furthermore, working toward full recovery or being recovered denotes optimism and the ability to improve one's condition.

It is estimated that around half of all individuals with eating disorders are able to recover. Among individuals with anorexia nervosa, 46 percent recover, 33 percent improve symptoms, and 20 percent remain disordered. Meanwhile half of individuals with bulimia nervosa recover, 30 percent improve symptoms, and 20 percent continue to meet bulimia nervosa criteria.

Can individuals with eating disorders fully recover from the disease? Although being in recovery is the common language within addiction populations, many eating disorder clinicians actively promote "being recovered" from an eating disorder and individuals who are fully recovered are indistinguishable from the general population. This debate addresses the issue of "recovered" versus "in recovery" in a direct way for eating disorders.

Justine J. Reel

Bibliography

Bardone-Cone, Anna M., Megan B. Harney, Christine R. Maidonado, Melissa A. Lawson, D. Paul Robinson, Roma Smith, and Aneesh Tosh. "Defining Recovery from an Eating Disorder: Conceptualization, Validation, and Examination of Psychosocial Functioning and Psychiatric Comorbidity." *Behavioral Research Therapy* 48, no. 3 (2010): 194–202. doi: 10.1016/j.brat.2009.11.001.

Darcy, Alison M., Shaina Katz, Kathleen Kara Fitzpatrick, Sarah Forsberg, Linsey Utzinger, and James Lock. "All Better? How Former Anorexia Nervosa Patients Define Recovery and Engaged in Treatment." *European Eating Disorders Review* 18, no. 4 (2010): 260–270. doi: 10.1002/erv.1020.

Gísladóttir, M., and E. K. Svavarsdóttir. "Educational and Support Intervention to Help Families Assist in the Recovery of Relatives with Eating Disorders." *Journal of Psychiatric and Mental Health Nursing* 18 (2011): 122–130. doi: 10.1111/j.1365-2850.2010.01637.x.

Keifer, Ekaterina, Kevin Duff, Leigh J. Beglinger, Erin Barstow, Arnold Andersen, and David J. Moser. "Predictors of Neuropsychological Recovery in Treatment for Anorexia Nervosa." *Eating Disorders: Journal of Treatment and Prevention* 18 (2010): 302–317. doi: 10.1080/10640266.2010.490120.

Turton, Penelope, Alexia Demetriou, William Boland, Stephen Gillard, Michael Kavuma, Gillian Mezey, Victoria Mountford, Kati Turner, Sarah White, Ewa Zadeh, and Christine Wright. "One Size Fits All: Or Horses for Courses? Recovery-Based Care in Specialist Mental Health Services." *Social Psychiatry and Psychiatric Epidemiology* 46 (2011): 127–136. doi: 10.1007/s00127-009-0174-6.

Vanderlinden, J., H. Buis, G. Pieters, and M. Probst. "Which Elements in the Treatment of Eating Disorders Are Necessary 'Ingredients' in the Recovery Process? A Comparison between the Patient's and Therapist's View." *European Eating Disorders Review* 15, no. 5 (2007): 357–365. doi: 10.1002/erv.768.

No, People Are Always in Recovery from an Eating Disorder

A common tenet in addictions literature is the idea that people are always "in recovery" from their addiction, as opposed to ever being fully "recovered." The debate over these two viewpoints has been ongoing for decades; however, with the popularity of twelve-step groups like AA that are built on the idea of recover*ing* (versus recover*ed*), the former viewpoint has become the dominant one within the world of addictions. This is not to say that finding a fulfilled life is never possible for individuals with a history of addictions, nor is it to disparage the importance of seeking treatment for this class of disorders. Rather, it is to say that certain characteristics of these disorders persist beyond treatment and represent lasting and permanent patterns of behavior, thoughts, and emotions. These long-lasting patterns require constant vigilance on behalf of the affected individual and can trigger relapses or setbacks in a person's well-being. Eating disorders have often been thought of as close cousins of the addictive disorders, and therefore the debate over recover*ed* (medical model) versus recover*ing* (twelve-step model) has also received attention in eating disorders. Given the abundant evidence showing important similarities between eating disorders and addictions along with the demonstrated persistence of certain key features of eating disorders throughout recovery, eating disorders must be understood using the twelve-step model of recovery.

Addictions and eating disorders have traditionally been thought of as closely related. Co-occurrence of these disorders is common, even at subclinical levels, and the frequency at which these two disorders are seen together has prompted many researchers to hypothesize that they share underlying personality, physiological, and behavioral qualities. Studies have demonstrated that individuals with eating disorders share certain traits found in addiction disorders, including elevated sensitivity to stress, risk seeking tendencies, and self-harming behaviors. Key neurotransmitters involved in substance abuse disorders—such as dopamine, serotonin, endogenous opioids, and neuropeptide Y—have been shown to correlate with eating disorders (particularly binge eating disorder and bulimia nervosa) and play similar roles in the development of both addiction and eating disorders.

In addition to the demonstrated similarities between addictions and eating disorders, the twelve-step model of recovery in eating disorders is further supported by the persistence of core symptoms past the point of weight restoration. Weight restoration is often considered to be the benchmark of recovery in eating disorders, and it refers to the maintenance of a healthy BMI for an extended period of time in the absence of disordered eating behaviors. Even in individuals who have been maintaining a healthy BMI for extended periods of time (years, in many cases), elevated levels of perfectionism, obsessions, body dissatisfaction, anxiety, and depression are still reported. This pattern is almost identical to the progression of addictive disorders: even though the behaviors that comprised the disorder are no longer present, core psychological symptoms that are considered essential to a diagnosis during the actively ill stage persist. This pattern is one of the primary reasons why the twelve-step model has been considered so important to the understanding of addictions.

Research has also shown that, in addition to personality and mood variables, certain cognitive patterns persist in individuals with eating disorders through the recovery phase. Studies have demonstrated that women who are considered recovered from anorexia nervosa and bulimia nervosa exhibit abnormal neuronal activation patterns in the ventral striatum, a brain region responsible for assigning emotional significance to events and stimuli. Cognitive deficiencies have also been found among individuals classified as recovered from eating disorders, including heightened sensitivity to visual information about one's body and difficulty integrating multiple sources of information into a coherent context (process referred to as *coherence*). These traits have been identified in individuals during the active stages of eating disorders, as well as persisting throughout weight restoration.

In conclusion, conceptualizing eating disorders within the twelve-step framework of recovering is widely supported by the evidence. Eating disorders and addictions have been reliably linked by common personality types and cognitive patterns, supporting the appropriateness of applying the twelve-step model of addiction recovery to eating disorders. Additionally, research has demonstrated that core features of eating disorders are present before the onset of a disorder and persist through weight restoration, suggesting that eating disorders are simply one stage in a lifelong progression of certain personality and cognitive profiles. The high relapse rate in eating disorders, which cannot be sufficiently explained by the medical model, is yet another indication of the long-term nature of these disorders and the appropriateness of using the twelve-step model in understanding these disorders.

Hannah J. Hopkins

Bibliography

Blinder, Barton J., Mary C. Blinder, and Visant A. Sanathara. "Eating Disorders and Addictions." *Psychiatric Times* 15, no. 12 (1998). Accessed January 30, 2017. http://web4health.info/en/med/docs/ed-disorders-addiction.html.

Davis, Caroline, and Gordon Claridge. "The Eating Disorders as Addiction: A Psychobiological Perspective." *Addictive Behaviors* 23, no. 4 (1998): 463–475. doi: 10.1016/S0306-4603(98)00009-4.

Eshkevari, Ertimiss, Elizabeth Rieger, Matthew R. Longo, Patrick Haggard, and Janet Treasure. "Persistent Body Image Disturbance Following Recovery from Eating Disorders." *International Journal of Eating Disorders* 47, no. 4 (2014): 400–409. doi: 10.1002/eat.22219.

Keel, Pamela K., David J. Dorer, Debra L. Franko, Safia C. Jackson, and David B. Herzog. "Postremission Predictors of Relapse in Women with Eating Disorders." *The American Journal of Psychiatry* 162, no. 12 (2005): 2263–2268. doi: 10.1176/appi.ajp.162.12.2263.

Lopez, Carolina, Kate Tchanturia, Daniel Stahl, and Janet Treasure. "Weak Central Coherence in Eating Disorders: A Step towards Looking for an Endophenotype of Eating

Disorders." *Journal of Clinical and Experimental Neuropsychology* 31, no. 1 (2009): 117–125. doi: 10.1080/13803390802036092.

Wagner, Angela, Howard Aizenstein, Vijay K. Venkatraman, Amanda Bischoff-Grethe, Julie Fudge, J. Christopher May, Guido K. Frank, Ursula F. Bailer, Lorie Fischer, Karen Putnam and Walter H. Kaye. "Altered Striatal Response to Reward in Bulimia Nervosa after Recovery." *International Journal of Eating Disorders* 43, no. 4 (2010): 289–294. doi: 10.1002/eat.20699.

Wagner, Angela, Nicole C. Barbarich-Marsteller, Guido K. Frank, Ursula F. Bailer, Stephen A. Wonderlich, Ross D. Crosby, Shannan E. Henry, Victoria Vogel, Katherine Plotnicov, Claire McConaha, and Walter H. Kaye. "Personality Traits after Recovery from Eating Disorders: Do Subtypes Differ?" *International Journal of Eating Disorders* 39, no. 4 (2006): 276–284. doi: 10.1002/eat.20251.

Wolfe, Wendy L., and Stephen A. Maisto. "The Relationship between Eating Disorders and Substance Use: Moving beyond Co-Prevalence Research." *Clinical Psychology Review* 20, no. 5 (2000): 617–631. doi: 10.1016/S0272-7358(99)00009-4.

People Can Recover from an Eating Disorder

Recovery and being recovered from an eating disorder is possible. For many years, some professionals and individuals struggling with eating disorders believed that their eating disorders were a lifelong battle. According to this traditionally adopted medical model of recovery, the focus was on reducing the symptoms; that is, any presence of the symptoms denied the individuals with eating disorders a "recovered" status even if they lived a meaningful life. After the debate whether this symptom-focused medical model approach truly reflected the meaning of recovery in eating disorders, the evolution of the recovery model emerged. Today, the notion that someone can be recovered from an eating disorder is supported by lived experiences of individuals who have completely recovered from eating disorders. Further, guidelines set by national and state organizations align with this optimistic and positive approach to recovery.

Because recovery can be subjective and has been inconsistently used and defined by numerous professionals and organizations, the Substance Abuse and Mental Health Services Administration (SAMHSA) developed a unified working definition of *recovery* to advance recovery opportunities for individuals with mental health illness and substance abuse disorders. Recovery is defined as "a process of change through which individuals improve their health and wellness, live a self-directed life, and strive to reach their full potential." Recovery has become the primary goal of mental health care. Therefore, national and state organizations are transforming their traditional, medical model of pessimism that mental illness is a lifelong sentence to focus on recovery-oriented guidelines and evidence-based programs to provide opportunities for people to completely recover. For example, states such as Connecticut and Maine created practice guidelines for mental health practitioners to follow to encourage and support clients to take ownership of their efforts to manage and overcome their mental illnesses. These principles and guidelines instill hope and expectation that recovery is possible and mental illness does not have to be a lifelong process.

After the implementation of the recovery-oriented guidelines at the national and state level, researchers examined whether this approach is effective for people with eating disorders. The recovery-oriented model emphasizes the importance of hope. Hope has been reported as a salient psychological construct in helping people recover from anorexia nervosa. For example, hope was a reflection of the "possibility to change" among individuals who were recovered from anorexia nervosa (with or without the experience of another eating disorder). In addition, hope was linked to "desire for recovery" among the individuals, and the role of hope was to alleviate the mental and physical pain for them.

Another principle of the recovery-oriented model that is associated with successful outcome of eating disorders is that there is no single pathway to recovery. The model suggests that change is not limited to only professional intervention and emphasizes the importance of external factors and the interactions between the individual and the environment. First, while receiving a treatment, it is critical to have "positive experiences in treatment" (i.e., a meaningful process of therapy sessions with a therapist, compatible with medication or type of therapy). Second, finding a new hobby or activity (e.g., playing an instrument, yoga) can play a significant role in one's recovery. Last, positive and helpful experiences with new or renewed relationships (e.g., individuals with an eating disorder, family and partners, friends, a spiritual relationship) are also an important component in recovery.

In contrast to the medical model (e.g., focusing on symptom reduction), researchers examining eating disorder programs that incorporate the recovery-oriented model for eating disorder treatment have found more positive treatment outcomes. One study focused on quality of life instead of weight gain and collaboratively articulating treatment goals for patients found a very low dropout rate. Another eating disorder program integrated the new approach by focusing on better quality of life, lower levels of distress, and more hope for the future. As a result of this new recovery-oriented approach, individuals in the program experienced significantly less eating disorder symptoms, more valuable relationships, and less hopelessness and distress. From these findings, treatments based on the recovery-oriented model had more promising treatment outcomes and helped more individuals who had not responded well to traditional symptom-focused treatments recover from eating disorders.

The evolution of the recovery-oriented approach in eating disorders has demonstrated that recovery can be described as multidimensional factors rather than one single factor such as symptom reduction. Recovery has diverse pathways, and hope for recovery plays a critical role in recovery. Despite the complexity of recovery in eating disorder, the new notion of a recovery-oriented model in eating disorders has extended the understanding and validation of recovery for eating disorders. Furthermore, using this newly recognized recovery-oriented approach, many who have suffered from eating disorders can holistically broaden their views toward recovery and build more confidence to believe that they can be recovered from eating disorders.

Sonya SooHoo and Maya Miyairi

Bibliography

Bachner-Melman, Rachel, Ada H. Zohar, and Richard P. Ebstein. "An Examination of Cognitive versus Behavioral Components of Recovery from Anorexia Nervosa." *Journal of Nervous and Mental Disease* 194, no. 9 (2006): 697–703. doi: 10.1097/01. nmd.0000235795.51683.99.

Dawson, Lisa, Paul Rhodes, and Stephen Touyz. "The Recovery Model and Anorexia Nervosa." *Australian and New Zealand Journal of Psychiatry* 48, no. 11 (2014): 1009–1016. doi: 10.1177/0004867414539398.

Ellison, Marsha Langer, Lindsay K. Belanger, Barbara L. Niles, Leigh C. Evans, and Mark S. Bauer. "Explication and Definition of Mental Health Recovery: A Systematic Review." *Administration and Policy in Mental Health and Mental Health Services Research* (2016): 1–12. doi: 10.1007/s10488-016-0767-9.

Federici, Anita, and Allan S. Kaplan. "The Patient's Account of Relapse and Recovery in Anorexia Nervosa: A Qualitative Study." *European Eating Disorders Review* 16, no. 1 (2008): 1–10. doi: 10.1002/erv.813.

Hay, Phillipa J., and Kenneth Cho. "A Qualitative Exploration of Influences on the Process of Recovery from Personal Written Accounts of People with Anorexia Nervosa." *Women & Health* 53, no. 7 (2013): 730–740. doi: 10.1080/03630242.2013.821694.

Kordy, Hans, Beatrice Krämer, Robert L. Palmer, Hana Papezova, Jacques Pellet, Matthias Richard, and Janet Treasure. "Remission, Recovery, Relapse and Recurrence in Eating Disorders: Conceptualization and Illustration of a Validation Strategy." *Journal of Clinical Psychology* 58, no. 7 (2002): 833–846. doi: 10.1002/jclp.2013.

"SAMHSA's Working Definition of Recovery." Substance Abuse and Mental Health Services Administration. Accessed February 6, 2017. http://store.samhsa.gov/product /SAMHSA-s-Working-Definition-of-Recovery/PEP12-RECDEF.

Touyz, S., D. Le Grange, H. Lacey, P. Hay, R. Smith, S. Maguire, B. Bamford, K. M. Pike, and R. D. Crosby. "Treating Severe and Enduring Anorexia Nervosa: A Randomized Controlled Trial." *Psychological Medicine* 43, no. 12 (2013): 2501–2511. doi: 10.1017 /S0033291713000949.

Wonderlich, Stephen, James E. Mitchell, Ross D. Crosby, Tricia Cook Myers, Kelly Kadlec, Kim LaHaise, Lorraine Swan-Kremeier, Julie Dokken, Marnie Lange, Janna Dinkel, Michelle Jorgensen, and Linda Schander. "Minimizing and Treating Chronicity in the Eating Disorders: A Clinical Overview." *International Journal of Eating Disorders* 45, no. 4 (2012): 467–475. doi: 10.1002/eat.20978.

Case Illustrations

In this section, 10 separate scenarios will be presented that illustrate a particular case example of someone who has a problem with some aspect of eating. Each case study will depict a particular situation as well as practical responses and recommendations based on the evidence found in the literature.

Case Illustration #1: Pregnancy and Body Dissatisfaction

Patty has always eaten what she wanted for the most part. She considered her relationship with food to be healthy growing up and has never had an eating disorder. Unlike her friends in high school who constantly dieted, Patty ate foods in moderation. She attributed her ability to balance food groups appropriately to her family environment. Her parents both modeled eating a variety of foods and trying new types of dishes. This resulted in her being adventurous and not really expressing fear around experimenting but also meant Patty had a balanced diet.

The other thing going in Patty's favor has been her height. At five foot nine she was in a constant state of growth during her adolescence. Now that she is in her late 20s, she has stopped growing but still has the luxury to consume more calories than her shorter girlfriends who complain about their weight incessantly.

Two months ago, Patty, at 29 years of age, delivered a baby girl named Isabelle. Throughout her pregnancy Patty maintained a laser focus on meeting nutritional needs for her and the baby. However, she was ravenous throughout the pregnancy and remains hungry all of the time. Patty also found herself to be stressed throughout the pregnancy due to worries that she was not prepared to be a parent. She reports that when she felt hungry, she tended to reach for high sugar or salty foods rather than healthy snacks. Patty believes her inability to regulate her hunger has contributed to higher than average weight gain during her pregnancy. She believed that this was normal given her height and that she would lose the weight once she had her baby but that has not been the case.

Now Patty finds herself becoming increasing fixated on her body weight. She weighs herself several times throughout the day and engages in body checking often. She stands in front of a mirror and criticizes a variety of body parts that she feels are too heavy. For the first time in her life she feels out of control with her weight and is experiencing negative body image. This body dissatisfaction could drive her to take drastic measures but Patty is unsure how to solve the problem of her food consumption as well as her obsession with body shape and size. What is she to do?

Recommendations and Interpretations

Pregnancy serves as an important milestone for women that can have implications for one's body image. Although most pregnant females are able to understand the gradual and minimal weight gain that occurs during pregnancy, the biggest risk can come once the baby is delivered and the expected weight loss has not occurred. For women who have never dealt with eating or body image issues, this newfound body dissatisfaction linked to stubborn weight gain can be frustrating. Further, this negative body image can put some women at risk for developing disordered eating even when they do not have a history of eating disorder behavior. Therefore, it is very important that Patty seek help to cope with this difficult time.

Therapy sessions with a mental health professional will help Patty address her body image and focus on body weight. She will likely benefit from a therapeutic approach such as acceptance commitment therapy (ACT) that incorporates self-acceptance and mindfulness into the process. Patty will need to learn to stay patient with her body and develop coping skills to deal with emotions associated with eating, body weight, and her body scrutiny. It may also be helpful for her to discuss her transition to the new identity as "mom" and how she will engage in important self-care as challenges present themselves.

In addition to the psychology behind the eating, Patty may want to work with a dietitian to address her mind-set around eating. Patty will want to avoid a tendency to restrict food or diet in an attempt to lose weight. Instead she could benefit from some education around intuitive eating to get back in touch with her physiological hunger and fullness. She may need to accept that her hunger will remain for a while before it begins to even out. She will also learn how to moderate her eating so that she eats healthy and filling meals throughout the day. She will be encouraged to eat mindfully and chew food into small bites in order to taste her food. For Patty it will take time to feel like herself again, but she can be confident because she has achieved a healthy relationship with food in the past.

Case Illustration #2: Muscle Dysmorphia

Zachary is proud of the fact that he can bench 205 pounds. Being able to lift more than his peers at the gym motivates him to push harder and load more weight onto the barbell. Anyone looking at Zachary from the outside would see a muscular and extremely fit college student who works out a lot. On the inside, Zachary feels very different from the image he portrays. For starters Zachary is intensely dissatisfied with his body. He feels like his muscles are too small and that his pectoral muscles (chest) are droopy. He feels like his arms look like "chicken wings" and are too thin for the rest of his body. Although he is striving to achieve the V-shaped muscular body, when Zachary looks in the mirror he sees a shape that seems disproportionate in his regular workout. His stomach still seems to retain some of that stubborn fat even though he has cut most fat out of his extremely strict diet. He often stands in front of the room with thoughts of hatred toward his body. Additionally, he tends to engage in body checking behaviors that involve pulling at his skin and touching his muscles.

Zachary is religious with his dietary plan and protein powders. He has a different potion he uses for a smoothie that he consumes during each meal of the day. He has eliminated carbohydrates from his diet as much as possible and primarily consumes lean proteins like chicken and fish. For exercise, Zachary engages in cardiovascular exercise by working out on the elliptical five days of the week. His long workout involves a combination of CrossFit exercises like pushing a tire or weight bench across the floor and free weight exercises. He spends an hour a day focusing on an aspect of his upper body (arms, shoulders, chest, and back) with separate time devoted to his core and lower body. He tries not to deviate from his lifting routines as he fears he will lose muscle quickly. He already feels like he is underweight and lacks muscle.

Zachary attempts to camouflage his body by wearing baggy clothing. He has added tattoos to his arms in the hopes that he will appear larger. He obsesses about his size, weight, exercise, and diet. This compulsion to work out has interfered with his ability to date people or to keep a regular work schedule. He has also missed class when he was driven to stay at the gym to continue a workout. His level of dissatisfaction is high but he does not feel able to continue increasing his repetitions and lengthening the duration of his workouts. He is unsure what to do. What should Zachary do?

Recommendations and Interpretations

The literature would suggest that Zachary displays the telltale signs for muscle dysmorphia. Muscle dysmorphia is characterized by an intense body dissatisfaction and feeling that one is too small. This condition is often associated with an extremely distorted view of one's body. In Zachary's case when he looks in the mirror he sees arms and legs that are underweight. To outside observers, however, he appears fit and muscular. The concern is that Zachary's negative body image has led to a compulsive workout routine and strict dietary program. He is also experiencing shame associated with his physique that has resulted in wearing baggy clothing.

Experts would recommend that Zachary see a mental health professional to discuss his body image concerns. Because his muscle dysmorphia has negatively impacted his personal life by becoming a barrier to dating, school, and work, he will want to identify some healthy coping strategies. It is likely that Zachary could benefit from a combination of exposure therapy and cognitive behavior therapy to develop more comfort in front of a mirror and to decrease body checking behaviors. He will also need to work on his overall self-confidence and self-worth. Although the work will not happen overnight, Zachary's long-term goal should be to place less emphasis on appearance and working out. He should be encouraged to take on new hobbies and activities so that he can begin to develop healthy coping skills and a broader identity.

A nutrition expert might be helpful to provide Zachary with guidance about his food intake. He will likely be encouraged to reduce his consumption of protein powders and replace them with whole foods that can provide the necessary nutrients as part of an overall healthy diet.

Case Illustration #3: Picky Eating

Holly just turned 10 years old and is in fifth grade. She is a flamboyant and engaging little girl who is a loyal friend. She is doing well in school and likes her teachers. Her favorite subject is social studies and she loves learning about history. She has several friends who get together for sleepovers. In every way Holly appears like the "normal" 10-year-old except when it comes time for meals. Holly becomes visibility frustrated when it is time to eat. In fact, she tries to postpone the inevitable by continuing activities, even her homework.

Once Holly sits down she has a very narrow list of foods she is willing to eat. She refuses to try new foods claiming they are "gross" and "disgusting." She has eliminated most foods that contain fat or sugar. She proudly exclaims that she hates pizza and burgers. The only foods she really likes are ice cream milkshakes, chicken noodle soup, collard greens, and mashed potatoes. Although the restrictive behavior got worse when Holly had braces put on, she has not returned to a more varied diet in months. Her parents attempt to tease her into eating other types of food and creating fun concoctions but Holly is stubborn about what she consumes. To add further concern, she rarely finishes her plate or eats enough calories to sustain her needed intake for growth requirements. Her pediatrician has noted that she is at the lowest percentile for body weight among her peers while being of average height for her age. In general, the doctor does not seem concerned and states she will likely "grow out of it." Other parents talk to Holly's mother and say, "at least your child is not overweight." Holly's mother is still concerned and feels powerless to help her child expand her dietary choices. What can she do?

Recommendations and Interpretations

All signs point to Holly being what is called a picky eater. Holly's mother is rightly concerned as picky eating can result in nutritional deficits and being unable to get the body's caloric needs met. Holly's mom may consider taking her to a dietitian who specializes in pediatric nutrition and has an understanding of eating disorders. This dietitian can help determine whether mental health treatment is necessary along with nutritional counseling. If Holly's mother is aware that a trauma has occurred in Holly's childhood, she can enlist the support of a mental health professional immediately. It will be important to explore when the picky eating started. Did it follow a particular event or has Holly been picky even since she was an infant? Understanding any root or underlying causes will be helpful for moving forward to slowly add new foods.

The mental health professional and/or dietitian will likely engage in exposure therapy to slowly introduce Holly to new tastes, textures, and foods of different colors. The process will be slow but necessary to expand foods that Holly consumes throughout the day. The dietitian will explore safe foods versus scary foods. It will also be important for the mental health professional to determine whether the restrictive eating behaviors are accompanied by negative body image thoughts. Even though Holly is only 10 years old, the research suggests that children as young as 6, 7, and 8 years old are engaging in dieting behaviors. The comments about disliking their bodies begin at a similar age as they hear early that being larger in size is considered shameful in society.

Another important step moving forward will be building the self-esteem of Holly and her ability to be involved in a number of activities. Girls on the Run has been a helpful program for young girls. The Girls on the Run program, which espouses a positive health message, involves having mothers and daughters participate together in lessons that promote self-confidence and working up to running a race together.

Being able to determine whether Holly fits the clinical criteria for being a picky eater will be important moving forward. There may be some risk for future disordered eating behaviors such as anorexia nervosa and selective eating disorder if the problems persist. It is also important that she receive her necessary nutritional requirements. The dietitian will likely add supplements like the nutritional drink BOOST until she is ready to have a more varied and well-rounded diet. It is important to normalize eating as much as possible, so that Holly does not feel scrutinized at every meal. Ideally, Holly can be supported to expand the food she consumes and can even begin to enjoy the meals.

Case Illustration #4: Disordered Eating as a Coping Strategy

Veronica is 14 years old and her family just moved from Nevada to Alabama for her mother's career. She is facing culture shock and a number of challenges due to the move across country. Although she was pretty well adjusted and had a stable mood when she lived in Henderson, Nevada, she now finds that everything is new to her. Many of her peers at her new high school have never even been to Las Vegas and consider her a "freak." It has also been a challenge for her academically. The statewide curricula from Nevada to Alabama are drastically different. Courses that she took in Nevada are not offered in Alabama, which means she is behind in school. She is also finding that teachers are not willing to help her catch up in her studies due to the overpacked classrooms. The teachers' attention seems to be focused on disciplining the problem students.

The students in Alabama are also very different from those in her hometown of Henderson. Whereas Henderson served as a melting pot for all kinds of transplants or families from out of state, Alabama has people who have lived there proudly since birth. They are not particularly welcoming to an outsider from a strange place. Some kids have joked that she "hails from sin." Veronica feeling sensitive interprets that to mean that she is sinful or bad in some way. Given that students seem to talk about religion a lot, it creates strong feelings of discomfort that Veronica's family does not attend church or belong to a particular denomination. The one person who has been friendly to Veronica is Jenny, her next door neighbor. Jenny invited her to her Baptist church last week. Veronica wants to make friends, but she is unsure whether that is the proper route to building relationships. Everything seems out of Veronica's control. She feels depressed and unable to regulate her emotions.

In attempts to cope with her difficult situation and to gain control again, Veronica has started to become strict with what she allows herself to eat. This restrictive behavior surrounding food started off as a diet so that she could be in charge of what she put in her body. Veronica refuses to eat the fried Southern chicken, black-eyed peas, and collard greens they serve at the lunchroom each day as a way to rebel against her new culture. Instead she brings an apple and some sliced vegetables with hummus dip. The other students look at her lunch choice like she is from another planet. The problem is that her "alternative lunch" has burgeoned into a restrictive breakfast and dinner. Most days she skips breakfast entirely. Dinner is harder to control because she eats with her father, but she has cut back on her portions significantly. Her body weight has begun to drop fairly dramatically in the short time since her family moved to Alabama. She has never struggled with eating or body weight in the past.

Veronica feels fatigued and is struggling with sleep. She is hungry all of the time but suppresses her urge to eat. Now her parents are complaining that she has a problem. What should Veronica and her parents do to address this issue?

Recommendations and Interpretations

It is to be expected that Veronica is having some difficulty adjusting to her new state and school. Some of her response reflects the natural reaction to a transition to a new place and the accompanying culture shock. However, the concern is that her negative emotions and mood have contributed to the development of unhealthy coping strategies and disordered eating behaviors. She may benefit from seeing a mental health counselor or school counselor to discuss the stress associated with the move that seems to be linked to her eating behavior and depressed move. She may also want to work through the challenges associated with her new culture and religious pressures with a neutral person. It is also important that Veronica have the opportunity to participate in activities that will allow her to meet some people. If she has an interest in certain sports, crafts, or community groups, this might be a good start to encourage the social interaction.

Although Veronica is at an age that increases her risk for developing a full-blown eating disorder, it does not appear that she has used these behaviors in the past. Further, her mood was well-adjusted prior to her move to Alabama. Therefore, it is critical to provide support while not going overboard on identifying Veronica as a "patient." Her behaviors and weight should be monitored carefully but it is expected that with time she will adjust to her new environment and make new friends.

Case Illustration #5: Gastric Bypass Surgery and Disordered Eating

Mason just celebrated his 45th birthday. Mason was always overweight as a child for as long as he can remember. The other kids would eat the same amount but somehow he would gain the weight. He realizes his childhood obesity was most likely linked to genetics in his family—all his relatives were heavy. Also, his family tended to serve foods that were prepared with butter, mayonnaise, and lard. During his 20s and 30s, his weight slowly crept up. By his late 30s, he was told by his physician that he was morbidly obese according to the body mass index standards that consider height and weight. By that point Mason was having trouble climbing stairs and with normal everyday mobility. Entering an exercise program was going to be challenging. Moreover, he had tried and failed many different types of diets over the years.

When his weight climbed to well above 300 pounds, his physician claimed that Mason was the ideal candidate for gastric bypass surgery. He thought about it for several months, tried again to lose the weight on his own, and being unsuccessful decided to undergo the surgery. Postsurgery Mason was elated to discover that he was unable to eat as much and that the weight was magically melting away. He lost the first 40 pounds very easily. The challenge was that Mason's mind-set toward food and eating had not changed despite the surgery and his size. He still feels like the "fat guy." He has also become obsessed with keeping the weight off to the point that people are concerned he is losing too much weight. He restricts many types of foods but then finds that he emotionally eats in moments of perceived weakness or when he feels intensely stressed or overwhelmed. On a more dangerous side, Mason has started smoking to relieve stress and he believes it will prevent him from putting food in his mouth. Mason doubts he will ever experience a stable body weight and balanced diet. What should he do?

Recommendations and Interpretations

Clinicians and researchers would argue that gastric bypass surgery patients may be at risk for developing disordered eating and eating disorders postsurgery. This is logical considering that the candidates for weight loss surgery most likely have had an unhealthy relationship with food for their entire lives. Many of them were chronic dieters who vacillated between periods of severe restriction, fasting, and sticking to a particular fad diet and overeating episodes that represented consuming large amounts of food. In fact, it has been estimated that approximately one-third of overweight and obese individuals suffers from binge eating disorder, which has been included in the latest version of the *Diagnostic and Statistical Manual of Mental Disorders*. Binge eating disorder refers to having frequent binge episodes that feel uncontrollable and involve the consumption of excessive amounts of food. Mason and other patients who undergo gastric bypass surgery should receive plenty of counseling prior to taking the drastic medical measures to lose weight. Weight loss surgery should be viewed as the last resort. Further, individuals should be educated about the nutritional content of foods as well as the psychology behind their eating behavior. Individuals like Mason should be taught to eat mindfully so that they are conscious of the food they are consuming and their feelings of fullness. They should participate in a support group before and after the surgery. Groups like Overeaters Anonymous (OA) can be helpful for receiving validation for feelings about food.

Now that Mason has had the surgery, he needs to transform his self-image. He is facing a transition to a new identity and will want to explore how he can see himself in a new light. Picking up some new hobbies that encourage him to engage in enjoyable physical activity would be beneficial to Mason. He will need to deal with other people adjusting to his new weight also. Family members, friends, and the public are likely to treat him differently than when he was a larger man prior to the surgery. He seems to have a lot of fear behind gaining weight again and he will need to learn to trust himself and his body. He may need to participate in a smoking cessation program to alleviate that dysfunctional coping method. Finally, he will want to develop eating behaviors that can be part of a regular and long-term lifestyle rather than yo-yo diets.

Case Illustration #6: Internet Dating and Body Image

Hayley just turned 30 years old. She teaches at a midsized university and is working toward tenure. She is experiencing pressures related to publishing her research along with balancing a high teaching load of three classes per semester. Time management seems to be out of the question given that her students are demanding of her attention. They text, e-mail, and call at all hours of the night with questions about assignments and their grades. She is also new to teaching, which means she spends a lot of effort developing slides and applied learning activities for her classes. She reports feeling like she is "only one week ahead of the students." Meanwhile Hayley often feels intimidated that she is the youngest faculty member in her department and they do not seem to take her viewpoints seriously. "I guess it doesn't help that I'm blonde, but I did earn my PhD fair and square, so give me a break," she exclaims.

Hayley moved to this city for her job and is single. The only way she can think of to meet new people, especially potential bachelors is through online dating. She has become obsessed with building the "perfect" online profile to attract the man of her dreams. The problem is that she finds the online dating community to be extremely focused on looks. The anonymity seems to allow people to behave poorly. One potential suitor requested that she take a selfie of her front, back, and side profile before they went on a date. He explained, "I don't want to date a fat chick." After being part of dating websites for the past year, Hayley has discovered that her self-esteem has dropped and she is experiencing intense body dissatisfaction. She feels like she is "old" for the dating scene and "all the good ones are already paired up." Being a faculty member means that she interacts with a lot of young people and gets asked out but students are off-limits. She does not have a lot of time to develop friendships and she is finding herself lonely. Her family has always kept her grounded. However, her hometown is a 12-hour drive away, which does not help matters since it is difficult to go home during the holiday breaks.

Hayley's body dissatisfaction has affected her in multiple ways. First, when she has "bad body image days," which seem to be more and more frequent, Hayley wears baggy clothing to hide her figure and perceived body flaws. She constantly checks her appearance in the mirror and pulls at her skin. She has also begun to weigh herself several times throughout the day. By having an awareness of her body weight, she is feeling more conscience of her diet. Mainly she is limiting her food intake to raw vegetables and salads. Hayley has installed a mobile application to track her calorie intake and help her stay disciplined in her plight to lose weight. She believes that if she loses 25 pounds she will be more "marketable" in the online dating world. In reality, Hayley's weight represents a healthy number for her height. To lose weight, she is drinking detox potions, restricting foods except for a narrow list of "allowable" items, and she exercises twice a day. At first, her energy was up and she felt a renewed sense of purpose. But lately, she is having sleep issues and feels fatigued all of the time. She also feels irritable toward her students and the other faculty members. They have noticed that she has lost weight and refer to her as the "waif prof," which is annoying to her. Don't they realize it is not possible to be too thin?

Recommendations and Interpretations

Hayley is struggling with a difficulty in her life transition. In addition to moving to a new state, she is working in a new job and does not have a lot of social support. Her family, which has always kept her grounded, are a great distance. Her feelings of isolation and loneliness are potentially contributing to negative body image and disordered eating behavior. It is important that Hayley build her social support network in a few ways. First, it is recommended that Hayley find ways to meet people outside of work and the university. There are often newcomers' clubs or book clubs that she can join in the community. She might benefit from seeking out other young faculty members who are new to the university. They are likely experiencing some of the same challenges associated with time management and feelings of isolation. As a group they can discuss their stressors and strategies for being successful as a young faculty member.

It is advised for Hayley to see a mental health counselor to process her feelings related to the transition. The counseling setting is ideal for talking through the loneliness and feelings of inadequacy resulting from Internet dating sites. She would likely benefit from taking a break from the Internet dating sites especially since they are not positively impacting her well-being and sense of self. She needs to rely on herself to inform her self-worth rather than individuals on the Internet sites.

The disordered eating behaviors and dieting may dissipate if she addresses the stress and negative self-image. However, if the disordered eating behavior continues she may need to receive some specific treatment related to the feeling-food connection. A dietitian can help her devise an eating plan that will fit into her work day and broaden the types of foods she consumes.

Case Illustration #7: Life of the Party

Ariana is in her late 20s and living in her parents' condo in Park City, Utah. She moved to Utah after finishing college in Georgia. Her family still lives in Atlanta but will fly out to see her in their private jet. At first, Ariana was nervous about meeting new people since she was an outsider and gets anxious in social settings. She finds that drinking some wine before going out blunts her nerves and lowers her inhibitions. This allows her to be more social when she goes out. To that end, Ariana has met a lot of people her age who are single and want to have a good time. She enjoys the party atmosphere and finds herself at a new restaurant and drinking on a nightly basis. She often has too much to drink while she is out.

Many mornings she will wonder how she got home and will not remember what happened the night prior.

She is also meeting a lot of people but does not want to get into a relationship at the moment. Her parents have not pressured her to get a full-time job but have encouraged her to take classes or pick up a part-time position. Jobs are scarce in the tourist town where seasonal work is often occupied by individuals from across the globe. Ariana is enrolled for an online class at the University of Utah but she has fallen behind in her assignments because she is not really motivated.

Ariana has dieted most of her life. Now that she is going out most nights she continues to restrict her food intake. Sometimes when she has too much to drink she will force herself to vomit telling herself it will speed her feeling better. She often wakes up with a hangover and her weight has decreased. Family members on their last visit expressed concern with her eating and with her drinking behavior. They have given her a choice to see a life coach, admit to eating disorder treatment, or attend a twelve-step program. To appease them Ariana agreed to see a life coach to discuss her plans moving forward.

Recommendations and Interpretations

It is not uncommon for a life coach to be a licensed mental health professional and hopefully that is what happens in this case for Ariana. A licensed professional will recognize the need to assess for both an eating disorder and a substance use disorder. It seems that Ariana is engaging in some risky behaviors and abusing alcohol with binge drinking. An important step will be to determine which mental health disorder should be the primary diagnosis so that Ariana can seek appropriate treatment. However, a challenge in this case is that Ariana's family is driving the treatment rather than Ariana. Ariana does not seem motivated to change her behaviors or to develop healthy coping mechanisms to address her anxiety and stress. It may be useful for the clinician to use an approach called motivational interviewing to determine where Ariana is related to stages of change and readiness for treatment. If she decides to embrace treatment, Ariana will likely benefit from a multidisciplinary treatment team that includes a mental health professional, dietitian, and medical provider. The mental health professional can help Ariana process her feelings of anxiety around social situations and meeting new people. A therapist who specializes in addiction will be helpful for addressing the comorbid conditions of disordered eating and alcohol abuse.

A dietitian can assess whether her nutritional intake is adequate but she has lost weight signaling that she is restricting at an unhealthy level. As her parents have suggested, she may decide to attend a twelve-step program to participate in an ongoing support group. By going out nightly with individuals who binge drink, it is likely that alcohol abuse has become normalized. Ariana may need to meet some new friends and develop some hobbies that do not involve partying. For example, when she moved to the area, Ariana was excited to ski the powder in Utah. She has not done any skiing since her arrival several months ago.

Her status as a part-time student should also be examined. If it is not too late, Ariana should work to withdraw from the online course so that her grade is not negatively affected. She can explore other options for classes once she is ready to go back to school. It might be helpful for her to engage in some career counseling to determine her path as Ariana has felt like she is without direction since she graduated from college. Picking up a part-time job would give her some structure in her day.

Case Illustration #8: Sexual Identity and Body Image

Tommy has grown up in a traditional home in Idaho with religious parents. He is 20 years old and has recently come out to his friends and family. He has been attending the same church throughout his teenage years, but he does not feel supported now. In fact, his Mormon bishop has encouraged him to go to conversion school to "straighten him out." He feels like he has been rejected due to his sexual identity and abandoned by the church. In fact, other teenagers that go to his ward (i.e., church in his particular neighborhood) are already getting engaged and looking to start a family. He feels alienated and believes they are whispering behind his back. One of the younger brothers of his former friend from the ward blurted out "what is a flamer?" Now he has stopped attending church services and interacting with church members. He feels a little lost and directionless. To cope with his stress he has restricted his eating and has become a vegetarian to avoid eating fatty meats. He counts calories and is obsessive about checking food labels.

Tommy has also started to exercise to control his weight. He now runs around the track daily and lifts weights in efforts to become lean. In order to fit in with his new peer group he has cut his hair and is spending massive amounts of money on clothing. He feels pressure to keep up with the latest trends, which also means wearing skinny jeans. His form-fitting clothing makes him feel more self-conscious of his body and he is particularly dissatisfied with his midsection. He wants to lose his "beer belly" but has found that while everywhere else on his body is slimming down, his stomach remains. He is unhappy with the photos taken and posted on social media (i.e., Instagram) as well as the videos posted on Snapchat because they stir up his intense body dissatisfaction. One of his friends has offered him an easy fix for his body concerns: diet pills. Tommy has found that taking the diet pills makes his heart race but he likes to think that the fat is melting away. He feels like he is spiraling out of control. His family is encouraging him to go to counseling but Tommy is scared to talk to anyone. He also does not want to have anyone tell him to change what he is doing in attempts to lose weight.

Recommendations and Interpretations

Tommy is undergoing a number of transitions in his life. Tommy should see a therapist who will empower him to explore the relationship between his identity, self-worth, and body image. His thoughts and feelings about himself and his body are translating to unhealthy behaviors and dysfunctional coping strategies. It will be necessary for Tommy to receive support as he builds his confidence and addresses the conflicts he is experiencing from his church and family. He will benefit from discussing the rejection he feels so that he can move forward to create a new support network. His new peer group seems to represent a double-edged sword for Tommy. Although he feels liberated to find individuals who share his sexual identity, he also is picking up some dangerous habits such as the diet pills. He is also dealing with immense pressure to be skinny and to "look the part." Tommy will want to uncover how he can be himself on his life journey.

Tommy's therapist can help him examine the way that he is using restrictive eating and excessive exercise as dysfunctional coping strategies. He will want to develop healthy relationships with food and exercise. He may be encouraged to see a dietitian to develop a more balanced approach to eating that includes a wide variety of foods. Tommy can explore the types of movement he enjoys rather than exercising solely with a weight loss motive. Yoga and meditation may prove to be healthy outlets he can try as stress reduction methods. Tommy will need to stop taking the diet pills that likely carry some hazardous side effects. Finally, when Tommy is ready, he may want to consider family therapy to mend his relationship with his parents and siblings. It will be important for him to determine a mutual understanding so that he can move forward.

Case Illustration #9: Codependency and Disordered Eating

Janet is 55 years old and has been married and divorced twice. In both cases, her relationships began as torrid love affairs marked with excitement and passion. Janet realizes that she thrives on attention from men and finds that her mood is affected by those around her. When she receives compliments on her looks she reports feeling "heady," but when it seems like no one notices her, she feels down. Growing up, her father was distant, ignored the children, and primarily focused on working to support the family. He worked long hours and would come home to watch the nightly news and boxing matches. When she was a teenager, her father left the family suddenly for another women who was an administrative assistant at his office. They moved to Florida, which meant that she rarely saw him. Janet remembers feeling personally betrayed and abandoned by her father's indiscretion.

Throughout her life, Janet has engaged a pattern of "serial monogamy" that is represented by a string of consecutive relationships. She always feels "off kilter" unless the guy she is dating smothers her with affection and is "more into me than I am into him." She cannot remember any time that she has been "single" for longer than one month at a time. She also tends to settle for someone who is not necessarily "her type" just to be in a relationship.

Unfortunately, this tendency to always be in a romantic relationship has resulted in an inability for Janet to develop a healthy identity. She finds that she relies on others to feel happy and is constantly feeling disappointed by the men that she dates (and eventually marries). She also has stayed in relationships past their "shelf life" due to a fear of being alone. She would rather be in a doomed relationship that is unhealthy than become single again. To avoid getting hurt, Janet continues to flirt with other men while she is in a relationship. In some cases, she meets her next boyfriend and is not faithful in her current relationship. The early part of her relationships tend to be exciting and adventure-filled, but then Janet finds herself feeling unfulfilled once again. She experiences depression and anxiety tied to her relationship struggles and her fear of abandonment issues. By focusing on her appearance and engaging in dieting, Janet is able to achieve a sense of being in control despite the chaos in her life.

To address her insecurities around aging, Janet has spent thousands of dollars on antiaging creams and serums. She has gotten cosmetic surgery to address perceived skin imperfections and receives Botox injections religiously. At age 50, her birthday present to herself was new breast implants. Not being satisfied with the result, she had the new ones removed and asked for a larger size. She is worried that the skin around her knees is sagging and that she has developed a little belly. She is contemplating more cosmetic surgery but has already racked up considerable credit card debt.

She is an emotional eater and a yo-yo dieter. Janet tends to be on the slim side. When she is undergoing a breakup or beginning a new relationship, Janet finds she does not have an appetite. When first becoming attracted to a man, she describes a feeling of euphoria associated with the male attention and the excitement around meeting a new person. As the newness wears off Janet finds that she starts to eat more normally again. When the relationship starts to fall apart, she notices that she becomes an emotional eater, often overeating salty snacks or ice cream. Now that she is aware of this cycle with eating and relationship, she is ready to get help. Given that she has been divorced twice, she would like to change her life and break the pattern.

Recommendations and Interpretations

Janet has clearly developed a pattern of codependency in her relationship that stems from childhood issues. Codependency in a relationship has been defined as having an unhealthy and destructive overreliance on one's partner for emotional and other needs. People who are insecure and have not fully formed a unique identity are at increased risk for codependency. Janet may be attempting to get closure on issues surrounding her dysfunctional relationship with Dad but seems stuck in a cycle of unhappy relationships.

It is recommended that Janet use a holistic approach to addressing her problems around codependency and relationships. First, she should seek the support of a licensed mental health professional to address her feelings of depression and anxiety. She can also explore the relationship between feelings in her childhood and her insecurities as an adult. The therapist will likely encourage Janet to spend some time alone before embarking on another relationship. Because Janet can slip into the pattern quite easily, she will need to work on becoming aware of her internal triggers and mood. She should be discouraged from behaviors such as flirting that may contribute to the likelihood of her obtaining male attention.

Activities geared to encouraging independence are recommended. Janet should explore new hobbies and work to develop healthy friendships with women. Maybe she can invite girlfriends to take a cooking class together or start a book club. It is recommended that Janet continue to look at redefining her identity as a "stand-alone person" outside of a romantic relationship. A recommendation around codependency is to view yourself as the "cake" and when you are ready for a significant other, he or she represents the "icing" on the cake.

Her financial health should be addressed as part of a holistic approach along her journey of self-discovery. She should meet with a financial planner or obtain software to help her track expenses and devise a plan for tackling the debt. Finally, Janet could benefit from meeting with a dietitian to address her inconsistent patterns of eating that are often emotionally based behaviors. She would be well-served by learning and practicing the concept of intuitive eating to allow her to stay in touch with feelings of hunger and fullness.

Case Illustration #10: Food Phobia

Ryan has reported a history of problems with food. He discusses having a supportive family and parents who have a normal relationship with food. His only sibling, a younger sister, also is described as eating normally. Despite being 13 years old and having a healthy appetite, he refuses to eat any foods with lumps or that could be difficult to swallow. Ryan describes what seems to be having a psychological block to eating most foods. With his growth spurt, he has found it challenging to maintain his body weight. He likely does not consume enough calories to sustain his continued growth.

The food he has been willing to eat needs to be blended thoroughly with a smooth texture. He has been consuming blended versions of food for the past three years as his sole means of receiving nutritional intake. Upon probing about the genesis of his resistance to chewing foods and to better understand his problem, it becomes apparent that his behavior is linked to a past event. Specifically, several years ago Ryan witnessed a stranger in a restaurant choke on food. That person lost consciousness and died. As a result of observing that traumatic incident, he has been unable to eat anything with texture and has preferred soft foods ever since.

His parents are concerned that he will not be able to grow normally and maintain an adequate weight to support his growth. Further, as he matures it does not seem realistic to continue to have all food sources blended. They would like him to be able to eat normally and socialize over food with friends and family. Furthermore, they have become aware that Ryan is being teased for his "weird food behaviors" by the other kids in his class. Ryan seems extremely resistant to changing his ways and trying new foods or anything with texture. What should they do?

Recommendations and Interpretation

It is important for Ryan to see a mental health therapist to work through this difficulty that is affecting his life on a daily basis. What Ryan is suffering from resembles a food phobia. The technical term for this problem, "functional dysphagia," refers to a fear of swallowing foods. Foods that are solid and lumpy usually are associated with the largest concern. It is important to note that functional dysphagia is differentiated from other eating disorders like anorexia nervosa that involve restricting. Specifically, the avoidance of foods has nothing to do with calories or fear of weight gain. With Ryan there is no concern about his body or negative body image present. Instead, he is afraid of the food itself. People with this type of phobia are fearful of eating food due to worries of experiencing gagging, choking, vomiting, or being poisoned.

Experiencing a traumatic event has directly contributed to his fears that he may choke on food. Generally, the natural response to having anxiety about something is to avoid the triggering event as much as possible. Therefore, Ryan has gone out of his way to prevent himself from choking on foods. He will likely be frightened and resistant to enter therapy and to try new foods. Therefore, it is imperative that Ryan work with an extremely patient therapist who can earn his trust.

The first step in his treatment should involve learning some anxiety reduction strategies. If Ryan is able to work toward achieving a deep state of relaxation, he can build confidence in his ability to control his feelings of anxiety. Likely Ryan will engage in some form of exposure therapy (often called cognitive desensitization therapy) to gradually reduce his phobia around specific foods. There will be small steps to try scary foods coupled with support and anxiety reduction techniques he has learned. He will gradually be able to extinguish his fears around swallowing and choking, but it will take time. His family support and reinforcement of small successes will be important for his treatment. Addressing the anxiety and trauma will be necessary to deal with the eating-related behaviors.

Food phobias are often misunderstood. Children and adults who avoid certain foods or who eat narrow diets of soft foods are seen as picky eaters. They may be teased or given a hard time for not eating like everyone else. The root of the problem is often an incident surrounding the individual who had a scary choking experience or observed it with someone else (as in Ryan's case). Therefore, to avoid having the issue minimized, it is necessary for the food phobia to receive attention in a medical setting.

Glossary

Alexithymia: Defined as the inability to identify and describe one's feelings.

Angular Cheilosis: A complication associated with self-induced vomiting referring to lesions or sores on the angles of the lips.

Average American Woman (AAW): A project undertaken by the U.S. government in the 1930s through the 1950s in hopes of standardizing clothing sizes across garment types, manufacturers, and materials.

Biofeedback: A strategy to improve visceral sensitivity, in which individuals are shown real-time updates on their body processes, usually focusing on heart rate and respiration.

Bradycardia: A slowed heart rate defined as a resting heart rate of less than 60 beats per minute.

Congestive Heart Failure: Results when the body is unable to effectively pump blood into the body.

Dental Caries: Refers to tooth decay or cavities associated with some people with eating disorders.

Diaphragmatic Breathing: A particular style of breathing that relaxes the abdominal muscles that are instrumental in causing regurgitation.

Dissonance-Based Interventions (DBIs): Considered particularly potent because they motivate change based on an individual's self-concept, which produces longer lasting change than using an external motivator.

Eating Disorders Coalition (EDC): A special interest eating disorders group created in 2000 and dedicated to advocating for more legislative action within Congress.

Endocrine System: Composed of glands that produce and secrete hormones. These hormones are involved in metabolism, growth, and development and in sexual development and function.

Food Cravings: Typically independent of any physiological need and considered to be psychological in nature.

Gum Disease: Refers to gingivitis and is caused by irritation to the gums from the acid that results from vomiting.

Hegemonic Masculinity: Refers to the dominant conceptions of what it means to be a man.

Hypercholesterolemia: Elevated cholesterol that is commonly identified in individuals with anorexia nervosa.

Hypotension: Decreased blood pressure resulting from a decrease in cardiac output, arterial tone, and effective arterial blood volume.

Interoception: Refers to an individual's ability to perceive and interpret bodily signals including sensations of fullness, hunger pains, heart rate, and pain (sometimes referred to as interoceptive awareness or interoceptive sensitivity).

Metabolic Alkalosis: Results in an increased serum bicarbonate level, which is almost always the result of purging through self-induced emesis or diuretic abuse.

Mindful Eating: Involves focusing on the food itself and slowing down while eating, incorporating the senses of sight and smell to fully enjoy the meal.

Mitral Valve: Involved in the blood flow in the cardiac muscle between chambers in the heart.

Noxious Stimuli: Something used in exposure therapy that is feared or unwanted by the individual.

Orthostatic Hypotension: A form of hypotension in which the individual's blood pressure suddenly falls when he or she shifts from a sitting to a standing position.

Perimolysis: The erosion of enamel on the teeth's surface.

Pro-Mia: The celebration of bulimia nervosa using websites and social media that can result in the perpetuation of unhealthy behaviors.

Prognosis: One's potential to improve from a particular condition and demonstrate favorable treatment outcomes.

Project HEAL: A nonprofit that raises money for eating disorder treatment and advocates for awareness.

Sialadenosis: An enlargement or hypertrophy of the salivary glands.

Sizeism: A form of discrimination based upon body shape or size.

Sugar Addiction: The object (i.e., food with high sweetness) of one's addiction is desired as a way to soothe emotions or feel comfort. Often considered a myth rather than a scientifically supported type of addiction.

Thyroid Hormone: Primarily responsible for regulation of metabolic processes and thermoregulation of body temperature.

Directory of Resources

Books

Ogden, Jane. *Psychology of Eating: From Healthy to Disordered Behavior*. 2nd ed. Hoboken, NJ: Wiley-Blackwell, 2010.

Steiner-Adair, Catherine, and Lisa Sjostrom. *Full of Ourselves: A Wellness Program to Advance Girl Power, Health, and Leadership*. New York: Teachers College Press, 2005.

Tribble, Evelyn, and Elyse Resch. *Intuitive Eating: A Revolutionary Program That Works*. New York: St. Martin's Griffin, 2012.

Journals

Eating Disorders: The Journal of Treatment & Prevention
http://www.tandfonline.com/loi/uedi20#.VfbBx9JVhBc

International Journal of Eating Disorders (IJED)
http://onlinelibrary.wiley.com/journal/10.1002/(ISSN)1098-108X

Journal of Clinical Sport Psychology (JCSP)
http://journals.humankinetics.com/JCSP

Journal of Nutrition (JN)
http://jn.nutrition.org/

Organizations

Academy for Eating Disorders (AED)
www.aedweb.org
Global access to knowledge, research, and best treatment practice for eating disorders.

Academy of Nutrition and Dietetics (Eat Right Pro)
www.eatright.org
World's largest organization of food and nutrition professionals.

American Nutrition Association (ANA)
www.americannutritionassociation.org/
Nutrition professionals and students who promote nutrition and wellness in the community.

American Psychiatric Association
www.psych.org
Organization of psychiatrists working together to ensure humane care and effective treatment for all persons with mental illness, including substance use disorders.

American Psychology Association (APA)
www.apa.org
Scientific and professional organization representing psychology in the United States.

American Society for Nutrition (ASN)
www.nutrition.org
Nutrition scientists who conduct nutrition research and translate findings into practice.

Binge Eating Disorder Association (BEDA)
www.bedaonline.com
Provides research and resources for binge eating.

Centers for Disease Control and Prevention (CDC): Physical Activity/Healthy Living
www.cdc.gov/physicalactivity and www.cdc.gov/HealthyLiving
Information on exercise and health.

Council on Size and Weight Discrimination
www.cswd.org
Council working to change public policies and people's attitudes concerning body weight.

Eating Disorders Anonymous (EDA)
www.eatingdisordersanonymous.org
A fellowship of individuals who share their experiences, strength, and hope with each other to help others recover from their eating disorders.

Eating Disorders Coalition (EDC)
www.eatingdisorderscoalition.org
Advancing the recognition of eating disorders as public health priority in the United States.

F.E.A.S.T. (Families Empowered and Supporting Treatment of Eating Disorders)
www.feast-ed.org
International organization of and for caregivers of eating disorder patients by providing information and mutual support, promoting evidence-based treatment, and advocating for research and education to reduce the suffering associated with eating disorders.

Food Addicts Anonymous
www.foodaddictsanonymous.org
Resources for individuals with a food addiction.

Food Nutrition Service: USDA (United States Department of Agriculture)
www.fns.usda.gov
Information to increase food security and reduce hunger by providing children and low-income people access to food.

International Association of Eating Disorders (IAED)
www.iaedp.com
Members and resources for international multidisciplinary groups and professionals working in the eating disorder field.

Multi Service Eating Disorders Association (MEDA)
www.medainc.org
Serves as a support network and resource for clients, loved ones, clinicians, educators, and the general public.

National Association for Males with Eating Disorders (NAMED)
www.namedinc.org
Providing support for males affected by eating disorders.

National Association of Anorexia Nervosa and Associated Disorders (ANAD)
www.anad.org
Resources for people to overcome their fears and issues with eating and body image.

National Association of Student Personnel Administrators (NASPA)
www.naspa.org
Organization for advancement of student affairs profession.

National Eating Disorders Association (NEDA)
www.nationaleatingdisorders.org
Organization with resources for individuals and supporting families affected by an eating disorder.

National Institute of Mental Health (NIMH)
www.nimh.nih.gov
Information for aid in understanding and treating mental illness.

National Institutes of Health (NIH)
www.nih.gov
Nation's medical research agency, supporting scientific studies that turn discovery into health.

National Sexual Violence Resource Center (NSVRC)
www.nsvrc.org
Advocates and sex offender treatment professionals' network.

National Suicide Prevention Lifeline
1-800-273-8255
www.suicidepreventionlifeline.org
Provides 24/7 free and confidential support for people in distress, prevention and crisis resources for you and your loved ones, and best practices for professionals.

Overeaters Anonymous (OA)
www.oa.org
Worldwide resources for individuals who struggle with overeating problems.

School Nutrition Association
www.schoolnutrition.org
School nutrition professionals focused on improving the quality of school meals through education and advocacy.

SHAPE America (Society of Health and Physical Educators)
www.shapeamerica.org
Organization of professionals involved in physical education, physical activity, dance, school health and sport.

World Health Organization (WHO)
www.who.int
Resources about global projects, initiatives, activities on health, and development topics.

Websites

Anorexia Nervosa & Related Eating Disorders (ANRED)
www.anred.com
Comprehensive information about anorexia nervosa, bulimia, binge eating disorder, and less well-known eating disorders.

Body Positive
www.bodypositive.com
Tools and resources to feel good about our bodies.

Caring Online
www.caringonline.com
Resources for eating disorder treatment.

Diabulimia
www.diabulimiahelpline.org
Resources on education, support, and advocacy for diabetics with eating disorders and their loved ones.

EDReferral.com (Eating Disorder Referral and Information Center)
www.edreferral.com
Provides names of eating disorder professionals across the country by region that can take referrals.

Gurze Books
www.gurzebooks.com
A trade book publishing company that specializes in eating disorders since 1980.

Healthy Weight Network
www.healthyweight.net
Resources for research and information on obesity, eating disorders, weight loss, and healthy living at any size.

In Her Image: Producing Womanhood in America
www.inherimage.juliabarry.com
Information on a multimedia exploration of how popular images represent and shape female life in America.

Intuitive Eating
www.intuitiveeating.org
Resources about intuitive eating from the authors.

Love Your Body Project, NOW Foundation
www.now.org
The NOW Foundation focuses on a broad range of women's rights issues, including women's health and body image and women with Massachusetts Eating Disorder Association (MEDA).

Maudsley Parents
www.maudsleyparents.org
An organization of parents who helped their children recover from anorexia and bulimia through the use of family-based treatment.

Media Influence on Body
www.about-face.org
Tools for understanding and resisting harmful media messages that affect self-esteem and body image.

Mirror Mirror
www.mirror-mirror.org
Resources and information for people with eating disorders.

National Eating Disorder Information Centre
www.nedic.ca
Canadian nonprofit providing resources on eating disorders and weight preoccupation.

New Moves
www.newmovesonline.com
Support to help girls learn healthy eating and physical activity habits while improving self-esteem and body image.

Project Look Sharp
www.projectlooksharp.org
Media literacy initiative to provide lessons, media materials, training, and support in the classroom.

Promoting Active & Healthy Lifestyles (PE Links 4 U)
www.pelinks4u.org
Resources for healthy lifestyles.

Pro-Recovery Movement
www.eatingdisorderhope.com
Support to help those in eating disorder recovery.

Recover Your Life
www.recoveryourlife.com
Self-harm support communities on the Internet.

Screening for Mental Health, Inc.
www.mentalhealthscreening.org
Screening and mental health programs to reach individuals at all stages of their life.

Something Fishy
www.something-fishy.org
Resources for awareness and support for people with eating disorders and their loved ones.

We Are Diabetes
www.wearediabetes.org
Promoting support, education, and awareness for type 1 diabetics who suffer from eating disorders.

About the Editor and Contributors

About the Editor

Justine J. Reel, PhD, LPC, CMPC, serves in the role of associate dean for Research and Innovation at the University of North Carolina Wilmington. She also has a faculty appointment as a professor in Exercise Science. She is a licensed professional counselor and a certified sport psychology consultant. She received her bachelor's degree from North Carolina State University and completed her doctoral and two master's degrees from the University of North Carolina at Greensboro. She has treated eating disorder clients across inpatient, residential, partial, intensive outpatient, and outpatient settings. She has conducted research about body image and eating disorders for the past 23 years.

Dr. Reel is the author of *The Hidden Faces of Eating Disorders and Body Image*; *Eating Disorders: An Encyclopedia of Causes, Treatment, and Prevention*; *Working Out: The Psychology of Sport and Exercise*; and *Filling Up: The Psychology of Eating*. She has published over 100 papers and has delivered over 200 presentations about body image and eating disorders.

About the Contributors

Timothy M. Baghurst, PhD, is an assistant professor in the Department of Health and Human Performance at Oklahoma State University. He has published research articles on male body image and muscle dysmorphia.

Robert A. Bucciere, MSW, LCSW, is a mental health and health care consultant who resides in North Carolina. Formerly he served as a hospital manager for the Department of Clinical Social Work and Chaplaincy program at the University of Utah: Health Care. Prior to his position as a manager, he was the lead licensed clinical social worker at the University Health Care: Neurobehavior HOME Program. He graduated from the University of Maryland at Baltimore and the University of North Carolina at Greensboro. He has published and presented on eating disorders while providing individual, couples, and group psychotherapy to thousands of individuals in a variety of populations across the life span. He served as the editorial assistant for this book project.

Ashley M. Coker-Cranney, MS, PhD, is a Visiting Instructor of Sport and Exercise Psychology in the Department of Sport Sciences at West Virginia University. She received her master's degree in the Department of Exercise and Sport Science at the

University of Utah, her master's degree in Community Counseling at West Virginia University and her doctoral degree in Sport and Exercise Psychology from West Virginia University. She previously served as the head coach for the University of Idaho cheerleading and dance squads.

Juliann Cook Jeppsen, LCSW, PhD, is a licensed clinical social worker who works at the University of Utah Neuropsychiatric Institute. She is advanced-trained and certified in EMDR (eye movement desensitization and reprocessing) and maintains a part-time private practice in Salt Lake City.

Nandini Datta is a fourth-year graduate student at Duke University's Clinical Psychology program. Her research focuses primarily on the impact of interpersonal impairment in anorexia nervosa. She is currently working on her dissertation, a study looking at the impact of meal skipping on cognitive ability. She is also pursuing a study looking at the role of social media use in eating disordered individuals. Prior to moving to Durham, she worked at Stanford's Eating Disorder Lab as a research assistant, involved with a genetic study on adolescents with anorexia nervosa. She has also had the opportunity to be involved in a variety of projects through her lab, including a qualitative study on friendships among individuals with anorexia nervosa. Her clinical work focuses on a child population, and she hopes to continue working with eating disorders after graduation.

Holly E. Doetsch, MS, RD, is a clinical dietitian at Primary Children's Medical Center in Salt Lake City, Utah, where she assists with the inpatient management of eating disorders. She holds master's degrees in Exercise and Sport Science and Nutrition from the University of Utah. Her presentations and publications have addressed such topics as nutrition therapy for eating disorders, the female athlete triad, and disordered eating among the diabetes population.

Nick Galli, PhD, is a Lecturer in the Department of Health, Kinesiology, and Recreation at the University of Utah. Previously he served as assistant professor in Sport Studies at California State University at Northridge. He received his doctoral degree in the Department of Exercise and Sport Science from the University of Utah.

Christy Greenleaf, PhD, is an associate professor in the Department of Kinesiology at the University of Wisconsin at Milwaukee. She received her bachelor of arts degree in Psychology from Bowling Green State University, her master of science degree in Sport Studies from Miami University (Ohio), and her doctor of philosophy degree in Exercise and Sport Science from the University of North Carolina at Greensboro. Dr. Greenleaf's research focuses on psychosocial aspects of weight, physical activity, body image, and disordered eating.

Jessica Guenther, MSW, is a primary therapist who works with eating disordered clients at the Eating Recovery Center in Denver, Colorado. She holds a bachelor's degree in Science with majors in Addiction Counseling and Social Work from the

University of Mary in Bismarck, North Dakota, and a master's of Social Work with a certificate in Women's Health from the University of Utah.

Shelly Guillory, RN, BSN, earned bachelor's degrees in nursing and journalism from the University of Utah. She is the director of Nursing at a nonprofit substance abuse treatment center, Odyssey House, located in Salt Lake City.

Hannah J. Hopkins is finishing her a master's degree at the University of North Carolina Wilmington in the school of Social Work. She is specializing in substance abuse and hopes to work in the addictions field. Prior to beginning her master's studies, Hannah received her bachelor's of science degree in Psychology from Duke University. During her undergraduate career, Hannah got involved in the Duke Center for Eating Disorders through research, and this sparked her passion for research in this field. Following graduation from Duke, Hannah remained at the Center for Eating Disorders for a year where she worked on a clinical trial testing a new treatment for childhood picky eating and anxiety. She was responsible for recruiting children and their families for this study, as well as leading them through much of the research protocol over the course of several months. She also had the opportunity to be involved in several side projects, including a study investigating friendships in anorexia nervosa.

Amelia McBride, MS, RD, CD, practices as an outpatient dietitian at Primary Children's Medical Center in Salt Lake City, Utah. She received a bachelor's of science in Dietetics from the University of Arizona, and a master's of science in Nutrition from the University of Utah.

Maya Miyairi is an assistant professor in the Department of Kinesiology and Health Science at Utah State University at Brigham City campus. She currently teaches courses for health education/health science programs through broadcast and online. She received her master's degree in Exercise and Sport Science and her doctoral degree in Health Promotion and Education at the University of Utah. She previously developed and implemented exercise education programs at eating disorders residential facilities in Utah. Her current research interests include weight bias, intuitive exercise, cross-cultural comparisons of disordered eating behaviors, and weight-related teasing as a form of bullying behaviors.

Hailey E. Nielson, MS, CHES, is a certified health education specialist and received her master's degree from the University of Utah in Health Promotion and Education with an emphasis in Weight Management, Body Image, and Eating Disorders in addition to a graduate certificate in Global Health and a minor in Nutrition. She has conducted research related to nutrition globally. Currently, she works for the International Rescue Committee addressing nutrition with refugees.

Leslie Roach is currently a master's student at the University of North Carolina Wilmington in the school of Social Work. She is focusing on the impact of trauma and trauma-informed care through the specialization of somatic experiencing. She also has a special interest in eating disorders and the connection between trauma, attachment, and eating disorders. She and three other colleagues from North Carolina wrote and published a meta-review, in the *Journal of Trauma, Violence & Abuse*, on using yoga as a treatment for trauma in 2015. Upon graduation, she hopes to work in the eating disorder field in a somatically focused way. Prior to beginning her master's studies, Leslie worked for UNC-Health Care as a massage and body-work therapist, as well as a yoga teacher. She received her bachelor's of science degree in Psychology and Exercise Sport Science from the University of North Carolina at Chapel Hill. She has always had a passion and curiosity for the mind–body connection and sees the need and benefit to incorporating both in the therapeutic process.

Christine L. B. Selby, PhD, CC-AASP, is an assistant professor of Psychology at Husson University in Bangor, Maine. She also maintains a limited private practice as a licensed psychologist, sport psychologist, and eating disorder specialist. Dr. Selby is active in a number of professional organizations including the Academy for Eating Disorders where she serves on the Fitness Industry Guidelines Task Force and the Association for Applied Sport Psychology where she cofounded and cochairs the Eating Disorder Special Interest Group.

TeriSue Smith-Jackson, PhD, MPH, is an assistant professor at Utah Valley University in Orem, Utah. She received her doctoral degree in the Department of Health Promotion and Education from the University of Utah. Her primary research interests are body image, the "freshmen 15," and intuitive eating.

Sonya SooHoo, PhD, received her bachelor's degree from the University of California at Berkeley, her master's degree from the California State University at East Bay, and her doctorate from the University of Utah. She currently lives in San Francisco and works with clients on performance-related issues. Previously, she worked at the Department of Veterans Affairs at Palo Alto as a Research Health Science Specialist examining the prospective relationships between pain, depression, and mental health disorders, and evaluating the woman veteran's comprehensive health care program. Her other research interests include body image and disordered eating among athletes.

Dana K. Voelker, PhD, is an assistant professor in the Department of Sciences at West Virginia University. Prior to that, she was an assistant professor in the Department of Kinesiology, Sports Studies, and Physical Education at the College at Brockport, State University of New York. Prior to her position at Brockport, she was a doctoral student and university fellow at the Institute for the Study of Youth Sports, Michigan State University. She teaches sport sociology and sport psychology, studies eating and exercise behaviors in athletes, and works as a consultant assisting athletes at all levels to develop to their fullest both as athletes and people.

Index

Page numbers in **boldface** indicate location of main entries.

Abdul, Paula, 107, 124
Abuse. *See* Child abuse, eating disorders and; Sexual abuse, child
Academy for Eating Disorders, **1**, 10, 63, 115, 301, 671
Acceptance and Commitment Therapy, **2–3**, 572, 654
Achievement orientation, 428–429
Acrocyanosis, 346, 347
Action figures
    drive for muscularity/muscle dysmorphia and, 187–188, 371
    male body image and, 97, 180–181
    See also Dolls, body image and; G.I. Joe
Active at Any Size, 237
Acupressure and acupuncture, 293
Adler, Alfred, 226
Adolescent development, **4–9**
    cognitive, 5–6
    moral, 6
    parent-adolescent relationship and, 6–7
    peer relationships and, 7–8
    physical, 4–5
    self, 8–9
    social, 6–8
    See also Puberty
Adolescent identity theory, Erikson's, 8
Advocacy groups, eating disorder, **10–15**
    See also specific eating disorder advocacy groups
Aerobic exercise training, endurance sports and, 203
Aerobics, **16–17**
    body image and, 16
Aesthetic sports, **18–21**, 240
    athlete perfectionism, 21
    benefits, 21

body image concerns and disordered eating, 18–19
coach comments and eating disorder risk, 19–20, 623, 627
diet pill use, 623
disordered eating and eating disorders in, 18–19, 538
eating disorder risk, 622, 623, 626–627
judges and athlete body image, 20
males, 20–21
parents and body image, 20
rules and norms and eating disorder risk, 623
teammates and body image, 20
uniforms/apparel and eating disorder risk, 623
See also Bodybuilding; Cheerleading; Dancing; Diving; Figure skating; Gymnastics
Africa, body image in, 86–88, 521–522
Aging and body image, **22–25**
    antiaging products, 22
    cosmetic surgery, 22, 24
    eating disorders, 23
    life transitions, 24
    media, 22–23
    menopause, 24
    mirror checking, 660
    See also Botox; Emotional eating; Overeating; Overexercise; Thin ideal
Airbrushing, **26**
Alcoholics Anonymous, 418, 493, 576, 577
Alexithymia, **27–28**, 34, 40, 669
Alpha-theta (deep state) training, 383
Amenorrhea, **28–29**

anorexia nervosa diagnosis, 28, 32, 34, 345

avoidant/restrictive food intake disorder, 52

bone mass and, 412

calcium deficiency, 396

causes, 28–29

DSM-5 removal, 28, 33, 44, 93, 166, 274

exercise-induced, 326

health consequences, 29

hypothalamic, 326

leptin and, 326

management, 29

osteoporosis and, 415

primary, 28, 44, 240

secondary, 28, 33, 44, 240

vascular function and, 412

See also specific sports; Female athlete triad; Osteoporosis

American Anorexia Bulimia Association, 381

American Psychiatric Association, 82, 672

See also *Diagnostic and Statistical Manual of Mental Disorders* (DSM); Eating disorders assessment guidelines, APA; Levels of care

America's Next Top Model, 244

Angular cheilosis, 155–156, 347–348, 669

Aniston, Jennifer, 366

Anorexia athletica, **30–31**, 56

Anorexia hysterica, 286

Anorexia nervosa, **32–35**

alexithymia, 34

anxiety and mood disorders, 34

body image distortion, 33

as coping skill, 145

DSM-III, 164

DSM-III-R, 165

DSM-IV-TR , 44, 191

DSM-5, 32, 41

effects on unborn child, 455

ego-syntonic disorder, 409

emotional disease view, 286

endocrine problem view, 286

exercise and, 207, 212, 619

fashion model prevalence, 357

female prevalence, 128, 274

gay males, 35

health consequences, 34, 195–196, 271–272, 338, 396, 415, 416

infertility, 291

intellectually disabled people, 295

leptin and, 325–326

males, 34–35, 275

maturity fears and, 428

medication, 339–340

1970s view of, 286

nutrition treatment goals, 390–391

obsessive-compulsive disorder and, 407, 409

obsessive-compulsive personality disorder and, 432

perfectionism, 34, 112, 636

personality characteristics, 34, 540

personality disorders and, 34

poor visceral sensitivity, 582

pregnancy and childbirth, 455

prognosis rates, 464

purging methods, 477

recovery, 479, 647, 649, 651

relapse, 489

social anxiety disorder and, 517

symptoms, 33–34

treatment and therapies, 333–334, 364, 471, 513–514

vitamin and mineral deficiencies, 396, 397

See also names of specific athletes, celebrities, fashion models, and sports; Amenorrhea; Borderline personality disorder; Celebrities and eating disorders; Deaths, eating disorder-related; Laxative abuse; Maudsley Family Therapy; Pro-ana, websites/online communities; Refeeding syndrome; Self-injury; Substance abuse; Suicide

Anorexic rule, 520

Anorexics and Bulimics Anonymous, 576, 577

Antidiet movement, 301

Anxiety disorders, **36–38**

anorexia nervosa and, 34

binge eating disorder and, 60

bulimia nervosa and, 109

eating disorders and, 37, 214

fear extinction, 215

generalized, 37
panic attacks and panic disorder, 36, 37
types, 37
See also Appearance anxiety; Social
physique anxiety
Appearance anxiety, 404
Art therapy, **38–39**, 128, 230, 493
Assertiveness training, **39–40**
alexithymia and, 40
group approach, 39
role-play, 40
strategies, 39
Assessment, **40–46**
belief system, 45–46
clinical, 40–41
cognitions, 45–46
eating disorder criteria, 41–42
eating disorders, 43–44
interpersonal functioning, 46
mental health and medical professionals,
41
methods, 42–43
physical and medical symptoms, 44–45
registered dietitians, 41
research-based, 40
self-report measures, 42
semistructured instruments, 42
structured instruments, 42
*See also specific assessment methods and
instruments; Diagnostic and Statistical
Manual of Mental Disorders (DSM);
Diagnostic interview*
Association for Size Diversity and Health,
280, 600
See also Health at Every Size® approach
ATHENA, **47**
Athletes, eating disorder risk in, 621–627
adolescent elite athletes, 624
perceived performance advantage and,
625
perpetuating and predisposing factors,
624
social support, 626
trigger factors, 624
versus general population, 621–627
*See also specific sports and types of sports;
Athletes, eating disorders and*
Athletes, eating disorders and, 537–541
amenorrhea and, 29

coaches, 553
competitive levels, 538
female team sports, 553
lean versus nonlean sports, 537–538
male team sports, 553
media exposure, 553–554
perceived performance advantage, 539
personality characteristics, 539–540
prevalence, 537–539
required weight-related guidelines,
540–541
sport-specific considerations, 539–541
sport subcultures and weight loss
methods, 540
team sports versus individual sports,
552–555
versus nonathletes, 537–538
weigh-ins, 553
weight loss methods, 539
weight pressures, 537
*See also specific sports, categories of sports,
and names of athletes; Athletes, eating
disorder risk in; Female athlete triad;
Weight pressures in sport*
Athletic trainers, **48–49**
Atkins Diet, 221
Attachment theory, 7
Atypical eating disorder, 165
Autism spectrum disorder
avoidant/restrictive food intake disorder
and, 50, 51
pica and, 437
picky eating and, 443, 509
rumination disorder and, 505
selective eating disorder and, 509
Avalon Hills Residential Eating Disorders
Program, 572
Average American Woman project, 446,
669
Avoidant/restrictive food intake disorder,
50–54
adults, 52
amenorrhea and, 52
autism and, 50, 51
aversion to specific characteristics of
food, 51
children, 51–52
diagnostic criteria, 51
DSM-5, 50, 53, 166, 262, 636

eating-related fears, 51
emotional barriers to eating, 51
symptoms, 50–51
versus picky eating, 51
See also Food phobia; Picky eating

Bacon, Linda, 280, 304
Balanchine, George, 55
Ballet, **55–56**, 151
    amenorrhea and, 56
    anorexia athletica in, 56
    anorexia nervosa in, 56
    body image, 55
    bulimia nervosa in, 56
    eating disorders in, 19, 56, 151
    teacher comments and student eating
        disorders, 627
    weight loss strategies, 56
    See also Guenther, Heidi
Banting, William, 221
Barbie
    body image and, 180, 181, 245
    Dove *Playing with Beauty* activity,
        182–183
    social comparison theory, 523–524
Bariatric surgery, **57**
Basketball, 538, 553
Bateman, Justine, 107
Bateson, Gregory, 226
Beard, Amanda, 548
Beauty, modeling industry and cultural
        standards of, 357–358
Beck, Aaron, 133
Beck Scales, 133
Becker, Anne, 251
Beckham, Victoria, 33, 59
Behavioral therapy, 572
    rumination disorder and, 506
Belly dance, body satisfaction and, 152
Berger, Hans, 382
Best Little Girl in the World, The (film), 368
Best Little Girl in the World, The (Steven
        Levenkron novel), 104
Biggest Loser, 233, 613
Bigorexia, **58–59**, 95, 369
    body image disturbances, 58–59
    male bodybuilders, 58
    mirror checking, 58
    symptoms, 58

See also Body dysmorphic disorder;
    Muscle dysmorphia
Binge, 43, 44, 108
Binge eating
    coping skill, 144, 145
    negative physical self-perception, 435
    neuroticism, 429
    poor visceral sensitivity, 582
    social contagion theory and sorority,
        526, 536
    Stunkard, Albert, studies and report, 59
    See also Binge eating disorder
Binge eating disorder, **59–62**
    bariatric surgery and, 57
    coexisting conditions, 60–61
    DSM-IV appendix, 286
    DSM-IV-TR, 59, 165
    DSM-5, 32, 42, 59–60, 63, 286, 659
    Fijians, 252
    health consequences, 61, 274, 338, 391
    impulsivity and, 289, 290
    infertility, 291
    leptin and, 326
    medication, 339
    mortality rate, 362
    neurotransmitters, 648
    nutrition treatment goals, 391
    overweight individuals, 121, 659
    prevalence, 60, 274, 275
    PTSD and, 450
    symptoms, 59–60
    treatment and therapies, 300, 364, 513,
        514
    Type 1 diabetics, 315
    versus bulimia nervosa, 59
    weight stigma, 63
    *See also names of specific athletes and
        celebrities*; Celebrities and eating
        disorders; Emotional eating; Obesity
Binge Eating Disorder Association, 1,
    63–64, 672
Binge foods, 108
Biofeedback, 584, 669
    See also Neurofeedback
Biofeedback Certification Institute of
        America, 384
Birth defects, mother's eating disorder and,
        291
Body alienation, **64–66**

adolescence and, 64
at-risk populations, 65
contributing factors, 66
eating disorders and, 65
in health care settings, 66
self-harming behaviors and, 65
sexual abuse and, 64
Body avoidance, **67–68**
assessment, 67–68
body dysmorphic disorder and, 72
bulimia nervosa and, 108
treatment and therapies, 67
Body checking, 67, **68–69**
assessment, 69
associated behaviors, 68
bulimia nervosa and, 108
treatment and therapies, 69
See also Body dissatisfaction; Body
dysmorphic disorder; Mirror checking
Body Checking Questionnaire, 69
Body dissatisfaction. *See* Body image
dissatisfaction
Body distortion, 33, **70–71**
measurement, 70–71
therapies, 71
versus body dissatisfaction, 70
virtual reality technology and measuring,
71
See also Body dysmorphic disorder;
Muscle dysmorphia
Body dysmorphic disorder, 58, **72–73**, 83
cosmetic surgery and, 72
DSM criteria, 72
social comparison theory, 524
suicide and suicidal ideation, 72, 73
treatment, 72–73
See also Bigorexia; Body avoidance;
Muscle dysmorphia
Body esteem, **74–75**
adolescent programs, 74–75
measurement, 75
pregnancy, 75
puberty, 74–75
sex differences, 74
Body Esteem Scale, 75
Body image, 70, **76–80**
aging and, 22–24, 318
Americans, 82
culturally defined beauty, 77

eating disorder relapse, 487–489
etiology, 82–83
health, 80
influences, 77–79
masculinity ideals, 332
media, 77, 79, 83
peers and family, 77–78
self-awareness, 78
self-esteem, 78
sex differences, 92, 95
social media, 528–531
See also Aerobics; Ballet; Body image,
global; Body image, male; Body image
dissatisfaction; Body image globally;
Body image in males
Body image globally, **81–91**
Africa, 86–88
China, 85–86
Europe, 83–84
food availability and, 81–82
India, 86
Japan, 84–85
Mexico, 88–89
South America, 88
Westernization, 82–85
See also Body image; Body distortion
Body image in males, **92–98**
action figures and, 97
athletes, 94
causes of dissatisfaction, 96
eating disorders, 93–94
media images as influences, 97
muscularity, 95
parents and peers as influences, 96–97
programs to promote positive, 97–98
research, 92, 95
sexual identity, 663–664
weight, 95
See also Bigorexia; Drive for muscularity;
Muscle dysmorphia
Body Image Avoidance Questionnaire,
67–68
Body image dissatisfaction, 70, 76–77, 83
body checking, 68
females, 75, 83
hegemonic masculinity, 96
Internet dating, 660–661
males, 75, 83, 92
media ideal body image, 498

parent body self-deprecation, 498
protective factors, 498
resiliency and, 497
risk factors, 498
social comparison theory, 524–525
weight teasing, 498
See also Body distortion; Body
    dysmorphic disorder; Body image;
    Body image in males; Media; Muscle
    dysmorphia; Parents
Body mass index (BMI), **98–100**, 393, 628
changes in children, 394
criticism, 628
eating disorders, 99
health concerns, 448
obese and overweight U.S. adults and
    children, 628
obese BMI, 628
as obesity indicator, 633
overweight BMI, 628
See also Body mass index report cards;
    Obesity; Obesity rates; Overweight
    rates
Body mass index report cards, 99–100,
    628–633
Arkansas, 630, 632
criticisms, 632–633
early obesity intervention, 631
intent, 630
negative consequences, 632, 633
obesity prevention tool, 628–631, 632
parental education, 630
public health data tracking tool, 631
weight-related teasing, 632
See also Body Mass Index (BMI);
    Obesity; Obesity rates
Body shame
cosmetic surgery and, 404
self-objectification and, 403
Bodybuilder Image Grid, 372
Bodybuilding, 18, **100–102**
aesthetic sport, 18
anabolism, 101–102
body image, 101
competitive, 100
disordered eating and eating disorders
    in, 101–102, 275, 538, 604
mirror checking, 101
weight class sport, 538, 588, 589

yo-yo dieting, 102
See also Bigorexia; Drive for muscularity;
    Muscle dysmorphia; Schwarzenegger,
    Arnold
BodyWorks, **102–103**, 400, 426, 461
Books about eating disorders, **104–106**
See also titles of specific books
Borderline personality disorder, 431–432
anorexia nervosa and, 432
bulimia nervosa and, 432
See also Impulsivity; Personality
    disorders
Botox, 22, 665
Bowen, Murray, 230
Boxing, 588, 623
Boyle, Caitlin, 413
Bradycardia, 342, 669
Bratman, Steven, 414, 636
Breast augmentation, 146, 665
aging and, 22
Brazil, 88
mommy makeover, 456–457
Brief Wondrous Life of Oscar Wao, The (Junot
    Diaz), 106
Brown, Barbara, 383
Bruch, Hilde, 285
Bulimia nervosa, 33, **107–110**, 165, 286
anxiety and mood disorders and, 109
binge methods, 108
as coping skill, 144, 145
DSM-III, 107, 164, 286
DSM-III-R, 165
DSM-IV-TR, 191
DSM-5, 32, 41, 107
effects on unborn child, 455
emotional eating and, 200
exercise dependence, 619
femininity ideals and, 245
health consequences, 45, 109, 196, 271,
    272–273, 338, 505
infertility, 291
intellectual disabilities, 295
leptin and, 326
medication, 339, 340–341, 349
neurotransmitters and, 648
nutrition treatment goals, 391
obsessive-compulsive disorder and, 407
onset, 109
personality disorders and, 109

post-binge guilt, 108
pregnancy and childbirth, 455
prevalence, 108–109, 128, 274, 275
prognosis rates, 464–465
PTSD and, 450, 565
purging methods, 477
recovery, 479, 649
relapse, 489
rumination and, 504
self injury and, 516
sexual promiscuity and, 109
sexual trauma and, 109
social anxiety disorder and, 517
substance abuse and, 109, 544, 545
substance abuse and child sexual abuse
    and, 564
suicide, 547
symptoms, 107, 435
treatment and therapies, 47, 109, 333,
    364, 512–513, 514
Type 1 diabetics, 315
versus binge eating disorder, 59
visceral sensitivity, 582–583
zinc deficiency, 397
*See also names of specific athletes,
    celebrities, fashion models, and sports*;
    Ballet; Body avoidance; Body
    checking; Borderline personality
    disorder; Celebrities and eating
    disorders; Deaths, eating disorder-
    related; Diuretics; Laxative abuse;
    Maudsley Family Therapy; Pro-mia,
    websites/online communities; Self-
    injury; Substance abuse; Suicide
Bullying, PTSD and, 450
    See also Teasing, weight-related

Cabrera, Dena, 567–569
Calcium supplementation, osteoporosis
    and, 416–417
Calorie counting, 392–393
Canopy Cove program, 287
Cardiovascular complications, eating
    disorders and, 337, 338, 342–343
    bradycardia, 342
    congestive heart failure, 343
    electrocardiogram abnormalities, 337
    hypotension, 342–343
    mitral valve prolapse, 337, 342

Care. *See specific types of treatment*; Levels
    of care; Treatment
Caro, Isabelle, 359–360
Carpenter, Karen, 33, **111**, 116, 286, 361
Catherine of Siena, Saint, 285
Causes. *See* Eating disorders, causes/factors
    contributing
Celebrities and disorders, 33, 59, **116–121**
    public disclosure, 116
    *See also names of specific athletes and
        celebrities*; Celebrity culture, impact of
        on public health
Celebrity culture, impact of on public
    health, 120–121
Center for Change, 328
Centers for Disease Control and
    Prevention, 258, 447, 629, 672
Chastain, Brandi, 553
Cheerleading, 18, **122–125**
    aesthetic sport, 18, 123
    body image, 123–125
    coach and weight pressure, 124–125,
        593
    eating disorders in male, 21
    flyers, 123, 124
    male, 122–123, 125
    uniforms as weight pressure, 124, 125,
        595–596
    weight pressures, 123–125, 593,
        595–596
Child abuse, eating disorders and
    emotional, 126, 228, 450, 564, 565
    physical, 223, 439, 450, 564, 565
    See also Sexual abuse, child
Children and adolescents with eating
    disorders, **125–129**, 439–441
    adolescents, 440
    anorexia nervosa mortality rates, 125,
        128
    barriers to treatment, 128
    chaotic/dysfunctional home
        environment, 439
    family mental illness, 439
    hospitalizations, 125
    infants and babies, 440
    interview of mother, 264–267
    parents, 126–127
    pre-school and school aged, 440
    prevalence, 125, 128

treatment, 128–129, 440
See also Child abuse, eating disorders
and; Sexual abuse, child
China, body image in, 85–86
cosmetic surgery, 83, 85
males, 86
mother-daughter relationship, 85–86
Christian, Jo, 206
Chung Se-Hoon, 590
Church, Ellen, 253
Clarkson, Kelly, 107
Client-centered therapy, 572, 574
Climbing, anorexia athletica and, 30
Coaches, 19–20, **129–131**
coach-athlete relationship, 131
weight pressures, 130–131, 592, 593,
594–595, 623, 624, 627
See also specific sports
Codependency, 665
disordered eating case study, 664–666
treatment recommendations, 665–666
Cognitive behavioral therapy, **132–135**
anorexia nervosa and, 133–134
binge eating disorder and, 134
body avoidance, 67
body checking, 71
body dissatisfaction, 83
bulimia nervosa and, 133, 134
coping skills training, 143, 145
eating disorders and, 388, 572
family, 230
mental disorders and, 132–133
muscle dysmorphia treatment, 655
obstacles to using, 134
residential treatment centers, 493
rumination disorder and, 506
techniques, 133
See also Cognitive behavioral therapy
guided self-help treatment
Cognitive behavioral therapy guided self-
help treatment, **135–138**, 512–513
binge eating disorder and, 135, 513, 514
bulimia nervosa and, 136–137,
512–513, 514
cross-cultural effectiveness, 137
Internet-based protocol, 137
research, 136–137
treatment protocol and content, 135–136
Cognitive defusion, 2

Cognitive desensitization therapy
food phobia and, 263
functional dysphasia and, 667
See also Exposure therapy
Cognitive development theory, Piaget's,
5–6
Cognitive dissonance interventions,
138–141
anorexia nervosa, 141
bulimia nervosa, 141
dissonance-based interventions, 139,
140–141
obesity, 141
results, 140–141
Stice's, 485
Cognitive dissonance theory, 139
Comaneci, Nadia, 276
Comorbidity, **141–142**
anxiety disorders, 142
bipolar disorder, 142
case study, 661–663
mood disorders, 141, 142
obsessive-compulsive disorder, 142
personality disorders, 142
self-harming behaviors, 142
substance abuse, 142
trauma history, 142
Conditioned learning, 214–215
Congestive heart failure, 343, 669
Conscious eating, 301
Cooper, Kenneth, 16
Coping skills, **143–145**
anorexia nervosa dietary restriction,
145, 657–658
avoidance-oriented, 143
coping self-efficacy, 144
binge eating and, 144
bulimia nervosa and, 144
eating disorders and, 144–145
emotion-oriented, 143
maladaptive, 144
task-oriented, 143
types, 143
See also Cognitive behavioral therapy;
Dialectical behavior therapy;
Interpersonal therapy
Cortisol, 345–346
Cosmetic surgery and eating disorders,
146–149

aging and, 22, 24, 665
body dysmorphic disorder and, 72
body shame and, 404
China, 83, 85
eating disorders and, 148
invasive, 146
Japan, 84–85
mental health and, 147–148
mommy makeover, 456–457
most common, 146
noninvasive, 146
popularity in Western countries, 146
postpartum, 456–457
research, 146–147
South America, 88
See also Breast augmentation;
    Liposuction
Couric, Katie, 120
Crandall, Chris S., 234
Cross-country runners. See Distance
    running
Cross-country skiing, 201, 623
Cupit, Tiffany, 543
Curtis, Jamie Lee, 26
Cutting. See Self-injury
Cutting weight, 94, 203, 590, 596, 623
    See also specific weight class sports; Sports,
        combat; Weight manipulation
Cycling
    anorexia athletica in, 30
    eating disorders in, 538
    endurance sport, 201, 538
    weight pressures, 202

Dancers, 18, **151–153**
    aesthetic sport, 18, 626
    eating disorders in males, 21
    full-length mirrors and weight pressure,
        596
    lean sport, 538
    therapy, 493
    See also Ballet; Belly dance, body
        satisfaction and; Modern dance; Street
        dancers, body satisfaction and
Dare, Christopher, 333
Deaths, eating disorder-related
    athletes, 20, 287, 311, 590, 604, 623
    ballet dancers, 56, 287
    elderly anorexics, 318

fashion models, 287, 356, 358–360
    See also Caro, Isabelle; Carpenter, Karen;
        Chung Se-Hoon; Elmalich, Hila;
        Gillitzer, Jeremy; Guenther, Heidi;
        Henrich, Christy; Mortality rates;
        Ramos, Eliana; Ramos, Luisel; Reston,
        Ana; Sanchez, Emanuel Jose
Dehydration, **153–155**
    clinical manifestations, 154
    diuretic and laxative abuse and, 154
    eating disorders and, 154
    orthostatic hypotension, 154
    treatment, 154–155
Dental complications, **155–157**
    angular cheilosis, 155–156, 347–348,
        669
    dental caries, 155, 156, 669
    dental erosion, 272, 274
    gingivitis, 155, 156, 669
    hyperamylasemia, 155, 157
    perimolysis, 155, 156, 670
    salivary gland enlargement, 155, 157
Depression, **157–158**
    anorexia nervosa and, 157
    binge eating disorder and, 60–61
    bulimia nervosa and, 157
    eating disorders and, 157, 158
    emotional eating and, 200
    late-onset eating disorders and, 318
    See also Comorbidity
Detox diets and cleanses, **158–159**
Developmental disabilities
    bulimia nervosa and, 295
    pica and, 437
    rumination disorder and, 505
    See also Intellectual disabilities, body
        image and
Diabetes, **160–163**
    binge eating disorder and, 315
    bulimia nervosa and, 160, 315
    health consequences of eating disorder
        behaviors with, 161–162
    insulin omission as weight control
        behavior, 160–161
    managing eating disorders, 162
    preoccupation with food, 161
    risk factors for individuals with eating
        disorders, 160
    stressor related to management, 161

weight loss and, 160
    See also Ketoacidosis
*Diagnostic and Statistical Manual of Mental
    Disorders* (DSM), **164–166**
    DSM-5 removal of amenorrhea as
        anorexia nervosa requirement, 28, 33,
        44, 166, 274
    See also specific eating disorders
Diagnostic interview, 42, **166–167**
Dialectical behavior therapy, **168–170**
    binge eating disorder, 169–170
    bulimia nervosa, 170
    cognitive behavioral therapy, 168
    comorbidities with eating disorders, 169
    coping skills training, 143, 145
    diary cards, 168
    distress tolerance skills, 169
    eating disorders, 169–170, 388, 570, 572
    mindful eating, 169
    mindfulness, 168–169, 355
    mindfulness mediation, 169
    personality disorders, 432
    residential treatment centers, 493
    targets, 168
Diana, Princess, 116, 118, 119
Diana Effect, 118
Diaphragmatic breathing, 669
    rumination disorder and, 506
Dichotomous thinking, 429
Diet industry, 233
Diet pills, **171–172**, 663
Dietary Guidelines for America, MyPlate
    and, 392
Dietary restraint, **173–174**
    disinhibiting eating, 173
    measurement, 173–174
Dieticians
    fat bias, 234, 237
    eating disorder specialists, 617
    on eating disorders treatment team, 574
    picky eating treatment, 444
    sport nutrition specialists, 94
    See also Assessment; Nutrition treatment
        approaches
Dieting
    child, 84
    emotional eating and, 200
    post-1950s, 286
    sorority women, 536

yo-yo, 102
    See also Diet industry; Diet pills; Dietary
        restraint; Fad diets
Dietsch, G., 382–383
DioGuardi, Kara, 59
Disinhibiting eating, 173
Disordered eating, 20, **175**
    case study, 657–658
    internalization of thin ideal and, 245
    lean versus nonlean sports and,
        537–538
    purging and, 477
    weight-related teasing and, 112–113,
        556
    See also Aesthetic sports; Bodybuilding;
        Distance running; Diving; Endurance
        sports; Energy availability; Fad diets;
        Figure skating; Gymnastics; Jockeys;
        Rowing; Swimming; Weight class
        sports; Wrestling
Dissonance-based interventions, 139, 140,
    669
    results, 140–141
Distance running, **176–177**
    anorexia athletica in, 30
    coach comments and eating disorder
        risk in, 624
    disordered eating and eating disorders
        in, 94, 176, 202, 538
    eating disorder risk, 623–624
    endurance sport, 201, 538
    gravitational sport, 623
    lean sport, 537
    weight pressures, 177, 202
Diuretics, **177–179**
    abuse, 154, 177, 178
    cardiac complications, 178
    clinical manifestations, 178–179
    edema treatment, 194
    electrolyte abnormalities, 178, 197, 198
    loop, 178
    potassium-sparing, 178
    prevalence of purging use, 477
    Pseudo-Bartter syndrome, 179
    thiazide, 178
    treatment for abuse, 179
    See also Dehydration; Electrolyte
        imbalance; Hypocalcemia;
        Hypokalemia; Hypomagnesemia

Diving
  aesthetic sport, 18, 538, 623, 626
  disordered eating and eating disorders,
    94, 538
  lean sport, 538
Dolls, **180–181**
  Dove *Playing with Beauty* activity,
    182–183
  See also Action figures; Barbie; G.I. Joe
Dove Campaign for Real Beauty, 79,
    181–183, 447
  activities and workbook, 182–183
  advertisements, 182
  workshops, 182–183
Drill team/dance team, **183–184**
Drive for muscularity, **184–189**
  assessment, 185–186
  athletes, 187
  behavior component, 185
  biological factors, 187
  body image component, 185
  gay men, 186
  media and, 187, 188
  measuring, 372
  negative consequences, 186
  personality factors, 187
  physical attributes, 187
  prenatal testosterone exposure, 187
  race and ethnicity, 186
  sex differences, 186
  sex role perceptions, 187
  social comparison theory, 524
  social environment, 187
  weight pressure from coach and
    teammates, 595
  See also Action figures; Bigorexia; Muscle
    dysmorphia
Drive for Muscularity Attitudes
    Questionnaire, 185
Drive for Muscularity Scale, 185, 372
Dual diagnosis. *See* Comorbidity
Duncan, Margaret Carlisle, 335
Dutch Eating Behavior Questionnaire, 174
Dying to Be Thin, 367

Eating Disorder Diagnostic Scale, 42
Eating Disorder Examination, 42
Eating Disorder Examination-
    Questionnaire, 42

Eating disorder not otherwise specified,
    191
  diagnosis examples, 191
  DSM-III-R, 165
  DSM-IV, 128, 165
  DSM-IV-TR, 128, 165, 191, 318
  elimination from *DSM-5,* 191
  females, 318
  intellectual disabilities, 295
  males, 275
Eating Disorder Sourcebook (Carolyn
    Costin), 105–106
Eating disorders
  aging and body image, 23
  culture-bound syndromes, 114
  DSM-5 criteria, 32, 41–42, 164
  prevalence in United States, 82
  related behaviors, 43
  substance abuse and, 543–545
  See also specific types of eating disorders;
    Eating disorders, causes/factors
    contributing to; History of eating
    disorders
Eating disorders, causes/factors
    contributing to, 94, **112–115**
  abuse, 112, 113
  body dissatisfaction, 112, 113
  co-occurring disorders, 473
  cognitive factors, 112
  developmental history, 473
  familial, 114-115, 473
  genetic, 115, 473
  interpersonal experiences, 112
  media, 113–114
  obsessive thoughts, 112
  peers, 114
  perfectionistic thinking, 112
  personality factors, 473
  psychological, 112–113
  regulation of emotions, 113
  sociocultural, 113–114, 473
  teasing, 112–113
  trauma, 112, 113
  See also Body image dissatisfaction;
    Child abuse, eating disorders and;
    Media; Sexual abuse, child; Thin
    ideal; Teasing, weight-related;
    Trauma, eating disorders and;
    Ultrathin ideal

Eating Disorders: Obesity, Anorexia Nervosa, and the Person Within (Hilda Bruch), 285

Eating Disorders Anonymous, **192–193,** 491, 576, 577, 672

Eating disorders assessment guidelines, APA, 43

Eating Disorders Awareness and Prevention Program (New York State), 13, 322, 381

Eating Disorders Coalition, 10, 13, 321, 669, 672

Eating for Life Alliance, 14

Edema, **193–194**
    body areas affected, 193
    causes, 193–194
    management and treatment, 194
    peripheral, 347
    pitting, 193
    purging and, 193
    reproductive hormones and, 194
    See also Refeeding syndrome

Ego-dystonic belief system, 45–46

Ego-syntonic belief system, 45

Elderly individuals. *See* Late life and late-onset eating disorders

Electrocardiogram, **195–196**
    abnormalities, 337
    anorexia nervosa and changes in, 195–196
    bulimia nervosa and changes in, 196
    changes and refeeding, 196

Electrolyte imbalance, **197–199**
    bulimia nervosa and, 197–198
    clinical manifestations, 198–199
    diuretic and laxative misuse and, 197, 198
    eating disorders and, 197–198
    medical complications, 396
    metabolic acidosis, 198
    metabolic alkalosis, 198, 199
    serum bicarbonate increase and decrease, 197
    See also Hypochloremia; Hypokalemia; Hypomagnesemia; Hyponatremia; Refeeding syndrome

Ellis, Albert, 133, 230

Elmalich, Hila, 356, 359

Emotional eating, **200–201**
    aging and body image and, 24, 665
    binge eating disorder, 200
    body image and, 200
    bulimia nervosa, 200
    depression and, 200
    dieting and, 200
    eating disorders, 200–201
    intuitive eating versus, 200
    low self-esteem and, 200
    obesity and, 201
    overweight and, 201
    perfectionism and, 200
    post-bariatric surgery, 57
    trigger foods, 200
    U.S. adults, 638
    yoyo weight cycling and, 200

Emotional Freedom Technique, 293

Endocrine system, 669
    complications, 344–346

Endurance sports, endurance, **201–203**
    athlete energy deficits, 201–202, 203
    benefits, 203
    coaches, 203
    disordered eating and eating disorders, 202–203, 538
    female athlete triad and, 203
    female athletes, 202
    stress fractures, 203
    weight pressures, 202
    See also Cross-country skiing; Cycling; Distance running; Rowing

Energy availability, 175, **204–205,** 239–240
    female athlete triad and, 204, 239–240, 242
    low, 204–205, 240

Energy psychology, 293

Equestrian athletes, eating disorders and, 312
    See also Horseback riding; Jockeys

Equine therapy, **205–206,** 493
    adolescents with eating disorders, 128
    benefits for eating disorder treatment, 205–206

Europe, body image in, 83–84
    banning of underweight models, 83
    eating disorders, 84
    males, 84

Exercise, **206–210**

anaerobic, 207
anorexia nervosa and, 207
benefits, 305
debriefing feelings following, 209–210
dysfunctional, 207
eating disorders and, 306–308
health benefits, 207
eating disorder history treatment and, 207
individualized, 209
negative relationship with eating disorders, 206–207
nutrition therapy and, 395
osteoporosis and, 417
physical self perceptions, 435–436
positive relationship with eating disorders, 206–207
prescribed, 208
psychological benefits, 207
recommendations for eating disorder treatment, 208–210
screening for dysfunctional, 210
structured, 208
supervised, 208–209
types, 210
See also specific forms of exercise; Exercise addiction; Exercise dependence; Exercise education, eating disorder treatment and; Intuitive exercise; Obligatory exercise
Exercise, appearance-motivated, 405
Exercise, compulsive, 30, 389, 614, 619, 655
See also Anorexia athletica
Exercise, dysfunctional, 308, 614
Exercise, eating disorder treatment and, 613–620
benefits, 613, 615–618
problems, 614, 616, 618–620
relapse, 620
supervised exercise education guidelines, 617
See also specific types and forms of exercise; Exercise; Exercise addiction; Exercise dependence; Intuitive exercise; Obligatory exercise
Exercise, mindful, 307, 355
Exercise addiction, 308, 614
Exercise dependence, 211–213, 614, 619

aerobics instructors, 17
anorexia nervosa and, 212
eating disorders and secondary, 212
identifying characteristics, 211
perfectionism, 212
physical complications, 211
primary versus secondary, 212
psychological characteristics, 212–213
psychological symptoms, 211
Exercise dependence scale, 309
Exercise education, eating disorder treatment and, 207–208
Exercise is Medicine initiative, 237, 613
Experiment in Love, An (Hilary Mantel), 106
Exposure therapy, 214–216
anorexia nervosa, 215–216
anxiety disorders, 214
binge eating disorder, 216
bulimia nervosa, 216
eating disorders, 215–216
fear extinction, 215
functional dysphasia, 667
goal, 214
muscle dysmorphia, 655
Pavlovian learning theories and, 214
rumination disorder, 506
theoretical basis, 214–215
virtual reality as, 216
See also Cognitive desensitization therapy; Exposure with response-prevention therapy
Exposure with response-prevention therapy, 216
Eye movement desensitization and reprocessing, 217–219
eating disorder treatment phases, 218–219

F.E.A.S.T., 10, 14, 673
Facebook, 528, 529, 531
Fad diets, 221–222
eating behavior strategies, 221
problems, 221
types, 221-222
weight gain after, 222
See also specific diets
Family-based treatment. See Family therapy; Maudsley Family Therapy
Family influences, 222–225

body image, 77–78
British Asian families, 225
Caucasian families, 224–225
ethnicity, 224–225
family dynamics, 223
Fijian families, 225
Maori and Pacific Islander families, 225
maternal influence, 223
paternal influence, 223–224
positive body image culture, 13
relationship with adolescents, 6–7
sibling influence, 224
single-parent families, 223
thin ideal, 245
See also Parents
Family therapy, **226–232**, 388, 570
Adlerian, 226
experiential, 230
family systems, 230–231
feminist, 231
operant conditioning, 230
residential treatment centers, 493
strategic, 231
structural, 231–232
See also Art therapy; Cognitive
behavioral therapy; Maudsley Family
Therapy; Role playing
Fat bias/fat discrimination, **233–239**, 280,
599
as acceptable, 233–234
binge eating and, 235, 236
body image and, 235
depression and, 235
experiences, 234–235
fitness preprofessionals and
professionals, 234–235
health behaviors and, 235–236
health care providers and, 234, 237
ideology of blame, 234
obesity empathy suit, 237
pervasiveness, 234
physical educators and, 235
psychological well-being and quality of
life, 235
reducing, 236–237
resources, 237
school peers and, 235
self-esteem, 235
settings, 234

teachers and, 235, 237
See also Weight stigma
Fat shaming. See Fat bias/fat
discrimination; Teasing, weight-
related; Weight stigma
Feeding disorder of infancy and early
childhood (DSM-IV-TR), 52
Female athlete triad, **239–243**
amenorrhea, 239, 240, 241
athlete education and, 242
bone health, 239, 240–241, 242, 416
coach education and, 242
eating disorders, 239, 538
endothelial dysfunction, 241–242
endurance sports and, 203
energy availability, 204, 239–240, 242
menstrual status, 239, 240, 241, 242
osteopenia, 240–241
osteoporosis, 239, 241, 416
parent education and, 242
prevalence, 242
prevention and treatment, 242–243
screening, 242–243
social support, 243
stress fractures, 241
Female Athlete Triad Coalition, 242
Females. See names of specific athletes,
eating disorders, and females;
Amenorrhea; Barbie; Breast
augmentation; Celebrities and eating
disorders; Cosmetic surgery; Dolls;
Female athlete triad; Femininity
ideals; Gender and sex; Infertility;
Liposuction; Media; Modeling
industry; Models; Models and
eating disorders; Oligomenorrhea;
Osteoporosis; Plus-size models and
clothing; Pregnancy; Puberty; Sizes,
women's clothing; Sorority women;
Thin ideal; Ultrathin ideal
Femininity ideals, **244–246**
athletes, 245–246
bulimia nervosa and, 245
contemporary models, 244
flappers, 244
Gibson Girl, 244
history of ideal female body, 244
movie stars, 244
1960s models, 244

See also Barbie; Dolls, body image and; Thin ideal; Ultrathin ideal
Ferrigno, Lou, 100
Field, Sally, 120
Figural rating scales, **247**
Figure Rating Scale, 70–71, 247
Figure skating, 18, **248–250**
    aesthetic sport, 18, 538, 623
    amenorrhea and, 250
    attire and costumes, 248, 250
    coaches, 19, 250
    disordered eating and eating disorders in, 19, 248–250, 538
    eating disorder risk and, 622
    evaluative nature of and disordered eating in, 249, 250
    first world championship, 248
    International Judging System, 250
    pairs skating, 18, 249
    physical demands and disordered eating in, 249–250
    stress fractures, 250
    U.S. Figure Skating membership, 248
    weight pressures and disordered eating in, 249, 250
    See also names of specific figure skaters; Figure skating, synchronized
Figure skating, synchronized, 249
    weight pressure from coach, 593
    weight pressure from teammates, 595
Fiji study, **251–253**, 357
    anorexia and bulimia rates, 252
    binge eating disorder, 252
    eating disorders and television, 252–253
    influence of television on body image, 252, 253
    macake, 252
    obesity, 252–253
    traditional Fiji culture and body image, 251–252
Films. *See* Movies and eating disorders
"Finish your plate" mentality, 421
Flight attendants, **253–255**
    body image dissatisfaction, 254
    disordered eating, 254
    Thai Airways International BMI and waist standards, 255
    weight restrictions, 253–254
Flow experiences, 403

Fonda, Jane, 16, 107, 120
Food addiction, **255–256**
    cravings, 255–256, 669
    eating disorders, 256
    reasons to classify in DSM, 256
    support groups, 256
    See also Binge eating; Binge eating disorder; Bulimia nervosa; Obesity; Obesity rates; Overweight rates
Food Addicts Anonymous, 256, 673
Food allergies, **257–258**
    deadly, 258
    diagnosing, 258
    eating disorders, 258
    most common, 257
    prevalence in United States, 257
    versus food intolerance, 257, 258
Food cravings, 255–256, 669
Food desert, **259–261**
    academic achievement and, 259
    causes, 259–260
    ethnic minorities and, 261
    health outcomes, 259
    obesity and, 259
    problems with studying, 260–261
    USDA definition, 259
    See also Food swamp
Food diary/journal, 441, 487
Food Guide Pyramid, 392
Food insecurity, 267
Food phobia, **262–263**
    case study, 666–667
    cognitive desensitization therapy, 263
    functional dysphagia, 262, 666–667
    treatment, 263
    versus picky eating, 262
    See also Avoidant/restrictive food intake disorder
Food security, **263–267**
Food swamp, 261
For the Love of Nancy, 367–368, 561
Forgiveness meditation, 292
Fraser, Katie, 11–13
"Freshman 15" myth. *See* Myth of the "Freshman 15"
Freud, Sigmund, 472
Full of Ourselves, 74–75, **268–269**, 458, 459
    evaluation, 269

mindful eating, 268
Functional dysphagia, 262, 666–667
   recommended treatment, 666–667
   See also Food phobia

G.I. Joe, 97, 180, 181
   See also Action figures
Garland, Judy, 244
Gastric bypass surgery
  post-surgery disordered eating case study,
    658–660
Gastrointestinal complications, **271–274,**
   343–344
   abnormal liver enzymes, 272
   acute gastric dilation, 272, 273, 274
   anorexia nervosa and, 271–272
   binge eating disorder and, 274
   bulimia nervosa and, 271, 272–273
   constipation, 271
   esophageal, 273
   gastroparesis, 272–273
   heartburn, 273, 274
   hypovolemia and electrolyte
     disturbances, 273
   impaired colon function, 273
   parotid gland swelling, 272–273
   See also Dental complications
Gay males
   anorexia nervosa, 35
   drive for muscularity, 186
   sexual identity, 663–664
   tanning behaviors, 551
Gender and sex, **274–275**
   differences in eating disorders and body
     image disturbances, 275
   eating disorder prevalence rates,
     274–275
   See also specific eating disorders; Drive
     for muscularity; Female athlete triad;
     Muscle dysmorphia
Gibson, Charles Dana, 244
Gibson Girl, 244
Gillitzer, Jeremy, 287
Gold, Tracey, 368, 561
Gottman, John, 230
Graham, Ashley, 446, 447
Greenleaf, Christy, 599–600
Grefe, Lynn, 560
Guenther, Heidi, 6, 287, 592

Gull, William, 32, 34, 285–286
Gum disease, 155, 156, 669
Gymnastics, 18, **276–278**
   aesthetic sport, 18, 277, 538, 554, 623,
    626
   anorexia athletica in, 30
   coach and weight pressures, 19, 277,
    593, 627
   disordered eating and eating disorders
    in, 19, 276–277, 538
   eating disorder risk, 622
   judges, 277
   lean sport, 537
   peers, 277
   team subculture and eating disorders in,
    554
   uniforms as weight pressure, 277
   See also names of specific gymnasts;
    Gymnastics, rhythmic
Gymnastics, rhythmic, 18, 277
   disordered eating in, 277

Hale, Lucy, 120
Haley, Jay, 231
Hamwi, George, 393
Hamwi equation, 393
Hattou shin ideal, 85, **279**
Hawks Intuitive Eating Scale, 303
Health at Every Size® approach, **280–281,**
   400, 447–448, 461, 600
   body image, 280–281
   evaluation, 281
   intuitive eating, 301, 304
   philosophy, 280
Health care costs of eating disorders,
   282–284
   impaired social functioning, 283
   inpatient hospital treatment, 282–283
   insurance, 283
   loss of employment, 282, 283
   lower educational attainment, 282, 283
   outpatient, 283
   residential treatment facilities, 283
   secondary individual, 283
   societal-level economic burden, 284
   treatment and medical expenses, 282–283
Healthy Buddies, 459
Hegemonic masculinity, 670
   male body image dissatisfaction and, 96

Henie, Sonja, 248
Henrich, Christy, 276, 287, 592
History of eating disorders, **285–287**
  Africa, 285
  ancient Egypt, 285
  ancient Rome, 285
  first freestanding treatment center, 286
  recognition of male sufferers, 287
  17th century, 285
  treatment centers and male sufferers,
    287
  12th and 13th centuries, 285
  20th century, 286–287
  21st century, 287
  See also specific eating disorders; Catherine
    of Siena, Saint; Internet and eating
    disorders
Holliday, Tess, 446, 447
Hope, Help, and Healing for Eating Disorders
  (Gregory Jantz), 106
Hornbacher, Marya, 104
Horseback riding, eating disorder patients
  and, 210, 312
  See also Equine therapy
Hospitalization
  inpatient, 282–283, 328, 492, 571
  partial, 328, 571
  See also Health care costs of eating
    disorders; Treatment
Huffine, Candice, 447
Hull, Clark, 132
Hypercholesterolemia, 345, 670
Hypocalcemia
  clinical manifestations, 199
  diuretic use, 178
  laxative abuse, 320
Hypochloremia, 344
  electrolyte imbalance, 197, 198
Hypokalemia, 344
  clinical manifestations, 198–199
  diuretic use, 178
  electrolyte imbalance, 197, 198
  ketoacidosis, 315–316
  laxative abuse, 320
  Pseudo-Bartter syndrome, 179, 339
  refeeding syndrome, 199, 482
  torsade de pointe, 196
Hypomagnesemia
  clinical manifestations, 199

  diuretic use, 178
  electrolyte imbalance, 197
  laxative abuse, 320
  refeeding syndrome, 199
Hyponatremia, 344
  electrolyte imbalance, 197
  laxative abuse, 320
  treatment, 199
Hypophosphatemia, 199
  refeeding syndrome, 199, 482
Hypotension, 342–343, 670
Hypovolemia, 273

Identity Intervention Program, 458
IMPACT Act, 13
Impulsivity, **289–290**
  binge eating and, 289, 290
  child sexual abuse history and, 565
  coping ability and, 289
  eating disorder severity and, 289, 290
  eating disorders and, 289, 290, 427,
    428, 565
  multi-impulsivity versus uni-impulsivity,
    289–290
  personality disorders and, 289, 431
  psychological functioning, 289
  purging behavior and, 428
  substance abuse and, 428
  See also Reward-sensitivity
India, body image in, 86
Infertility, **290–291**
  eating disorders and, 291
  polycystic ovarian syndrome and, 291
  prevalence in United States, 290–291
  See also specific eating disorders;
    Amenorrhea
Instagram, 528, 531
Integrative approaches, **291–293**
  acupuncture, 293
  energy psychology, 293
  interdisciplinary team of professionals,
    292
  meditation, 292
  spiritual wisdom exercise, 292
  therapeutic massage/touch, 292–293
Integrative health, 291–292
  See also Integrative approaches
Intellectual disabilities and body image,
  294–296

eating disorders, 294–295
female desire to be thinner, 295–296
male desire for bigger muscles, 295
obesity rate, 295
See also names of specific eating disorders;
Developmental disabilities
International Association of Eating
Disorder Professionals, 1, 63,
297–298, 381
International Journal of Eating Disorders, 1,
59
Internet, eating disorders and, 287,
298–300, 336
body image, 336
dangers, 298–299
fitspiration websites, 299
misinformation, 299
Student Bodies program, 300
thinspiration websites, 299, 336
thintention websites, 299
triggering images, 298
web-based treatment and prevention
programs, 298, 299–300
See also Internet dating, case study of
body image dissatisfaction and; Pro-
ana, websites/online communities;
Pro-eating disorder website exposure,
eating disorder treatment and; Pro-
mia, websites/online communities;
Social media, eating disorders and
Internet dating, case study of body image
dissatisfaction and, 660–661
Interoception, 670
See also Interoceptive awareness, eating
disorders and poor; Visceral sensitivity
Interoceptive awareness, eating disorders
and poor, 428, 582
See also Interoception; Visceral
sensitivity
Interpersonal therapy
coping skills training, 143, 145
residential treatment centers, 493
Intuitive eating, **301–304**, 305, 393
antidiet movement and, 301
assessment, 303–304
benefits, 304
emotional eating versus, 200, 666
goal, 301
males, 304

obese eating and, 304
poor visceral sensitivity, 582
post-partum education about, 654
premise, 301
principles, 302–303
See also Health at Every Size® approach
Intuitive Eating (Elyse Resch and Evelyn
Tribole), 301–303, 304
Intuitive eating scale, Tylka, 303
Intuitive exercise, **305–309**
assessment, 309
diverse movement, 308
residential treatment settings, 308
Intuitive exercise scale, 309
Invisible Man, The (John Morgan), 106
Iron deficiency, medical complications of,
397

Jahn, Friedrich, 276
James, Lilly, 367
Japan, body image in, 84–85
child dieting, 84
cosmetic eyelid surgery, 84
eating disorders, 84
geisha stereotype, 84
hair coloring, 84
skin tone, 521, 551
social anxiety, 84
Jockeys, **311–312**
disordered eating and eating disorders,
275, 311–312
"flipping," 311, 312
"Hot Box" weight loss method, 311, 312
rapid weight loss strategies, 623
smoking as appetite suppressant, 311
weight restrictions, 311
John, Elton, 107, 116, 119
Johnson, Craig, 1
Johnson, Kathy, 276
Jones, Mary Cover, 132
Journaling, **313–314**, 493
Joyner, Kati, 388–390
Judo
rapid weight loss strategies, 623
training death, 590
weight class sport, 502, 623

Kamiya, Joseph, 383
Kerrigan, Nancy, 248

Ketoacidosis, **315–316**
  clinical manifestations, 315
  eating disorders and Type 1 diabetes,
    315
  hypokalemia and, 315–316
  skipping insulin, 315
  starvation, 316
  treatment, 315–316
  See also Diabetes
Keys, Ancel, 99, 481, 628
Kilmer, Val, 367
Kirk, Jenny, 248–249
Knightley, Keira, 367
Kohlberg, Lawrence, 6
Kournikova, Anna, 245

Lady Gaga, 107, 119
Lanugo, **317**, 347
Lasegue, Charles, 286
Late life and late-onset eating disorders,
    318
  See also specific types of eating disorders
Lawley, Robyn, 447
Laws. See Legislation on eating disorders
Laxative abuse, **319–320**
  medical complications, 198, 273, 320,
    338, 344
  prevalence, 477
  treatment considerations, 320
  See also Electrolyte imbalance
Legislation on eating disorders, **321–324**
  Eating Disorders Awareness, Prevention
    and Education Act of 2000, 323
  Federal Response to Eliminate Eating
    Disorders (FREED) Act, 322–323,
    324
  laws, 321–322, 324
  2014 New York State law, 322, 324
  2016 Missouri law, 322, 324
  under consideration, 322–323
  See also Mental Health Parity and
    Addiction Equity Act, Paul Wellstone
    and Pete Domenici; Patient Protection
    and Affordable Care Act; 21st Century
    Cures Act
Leigh, Jennifer Jason, 368
Leptin, **325–326**
  See also specific eating disorders;
    Amenorrhea; Obesity

Let's Move!, **327**, 400
Levels of care, **329**
  APA, 43, 570–571
  See also specific types of treatment;
    Treatment
Levine, Peter, 534
Linehan, Marsha, 168, 571
Liposuction, 22, 146, 147
  Brazil, 88
  postpartum, 456
  promotional ads, 79
  as purging behavior, 148
Liquid nutrition supplementation, 394
Little Girl Who Didn't Want to Get Fat, The
    (Isabelle Caro), 359–360
Little Girls in Pretty Boxes (Joan Ryan),
    277
Little Miss Perfect, 79
Lohan, Lindsay, 559
Lombard, Carole, 244
Love Your Body 5K/10K, 543
Love Your Body Week, 542

Male Body Attitudes Scale, 185
Male Body Checking Questionnaire, 69
Males. See specific eating disorders, sports,
    and types of sports; Action figures;
    Athletes, eating disorders and;
    Bigorexia; Body image in males;
    Body image dissatisfaction; Drive
    for muscularity; Gay males; Gender
    and sex; Hegemonic masculinity;
    Masculinity ideals; Muscle
    dysmorphia; Puberty
Martial arts, 588
Masculinity ideals, **331–332**
  body image, 332
  muscularity, 331
  television programs and, 559
  traditional masculinity archetypes,
    331–332
  See also Drive for muscularity
Maturity fears, anorexia nervosa and, 428
Maudsley Family Therapy, 232, **333–334**,
    421
  anorexia nervosa, 333–334
  bulimia nervosa, 333
McCarthy, Melissa, 367
McCreary, Donald, 184–185

Meal planning, eating disorder clients and, 391–392
  exchange list, 392
Meals on Wheels, food desert and, 259
Media, **334–336**
  aging and body image, 22–23
  body dissatisfaction, 335
  body image, 77, 83, 528
  digital manipulation, 335, 365, 366
  eating disorders, 528
  internalization of ultrathin ideal and, 528
  male body image, 97
  modern versus historical, 365
  Monroe, Marilyn, body ideal, 334
  portrayal of female athletes, 245
  self-objectification, 403
  sexualization of body, 402
  television and body image, 335
  Twiggy body ideal, 335
  vehicle for portraying body ideals, 74
  weight stigma, 599, 600
  See also Fiji study; Internet and eating disorders; Media literacy, parents teaching children; Thin ideal; Ultrathin ideal
Media exposure, female athletes and eating disorders, 553–554
Media literacy, parents teaching children, 468, 499, 569
Medical and health consequences, **337–348**
  cardiovascular, 337, 338, 342–343
  dermatological, 346–347
  endocrine, 344–346
  gastrointestinal, 338, 343–344
  hematological, 346
  interview with O'Melia, Dr. Anne, about, 338–342
  neurological, 346
  oral, 338, 347–348
  renal, 344
  See also specific eating disorders; Cardiovascular complications; Dental complications; Gastrointestinal complications
Medications and eating disorders, **349–350**
  anorexia nervosa, 339–340
  antianxiety medications, 350

antidepressants and binge eating disorder, 349
antidepressants and bulimia nervosa, 339, 349
attention-deficit drugs, 250
attention-deficit drug for binge eating disorder, 339
weight gain as side effect, 350
Meditation, 292, 493
  forgiveness meditation, 292
  guided, 292
  mindfulness meditation, 292
  self-care stress reduction strategy, 510, 563, 664
  transcendental meditation, 292
  visceral sensitivity training, 584
Meditative breathing, 292
Menopause, **350–351**
  body image, 24
  eating disorder trigger, 351
  increased BMI and weight gain, 351
  See also Aging and body image; Late life and late-onset eating disorders
MentorCONNECT, 15
Meridian tapping, 293
Metabolic acidosis, 198, 316, 344
Metabolic alkalosis, 154, 178, 179, 198, 199, 344, 670
Metadevelopment and Research Institute, 217
Mental Health Parity and Addiction Equity Act, Paul Wellstone and Pete Domenici, 13, 323, 324
Metropolitan Life Insurance weight charts, 393–394
Mexico, body image in, 88–89
Middle-aged women, eating disorders in. *See* Late life and late-onset eating disorders
Military, **352–353**
  contributing factors, 352
  risk factors, 353
Mindful eating, 301, 354–355, 670
  See also Dialectical behavior therapy; Full of Ourselves
Mindful exercise. *See* Exercise, mindful
Mindfulness, **354–355**
  Acceptance and Commitment Therapy core principle, 2

body image, 355
dialectical behavior therapy, 355
eating disorders treatment, 355
visceral sensitivity training, 584
See also Exercise, mindful; Mindful eating;
    Mindfulness meditation; Mindfulness
    therapy, rumination disorder and
Mindfulness meditation, 292
See also Dialectical behavior therapy
Mindfulness therapy, rumination disorder
    and, 506
Minnesota Starvation Experiment, 104–
    105, 481
Minuchin, Salvador, 231
Mirasol Eating Disorder Treatment Center,
    383
Mirror checking
    aging and, 660
    bigorexia, 58
    bodybuilding, 101
    muscle dysmorphia, 95, 373, 654
    pregnancy, 653
    yoga, 608
Mitral valve, 670
Mitral valve prolapse, 337, 342
Miyairi, Maya, 306–308
Modeling industry
    cultural standards of beauty and,
        357–358
    regulation attempts, 358
    See also Models; Models and eating
        disorders
Models
    weight and BMI versus average woman,
        356
    See also names of specific models;
        Modeling industry; Models and eating
        disorders; Plus-size models and
        clothing
Models and eating disorders, 356–361
    anorexia nervosa, 357
    deaths, 287, 356, 358–360
    See also names of specific models
Modern dance, 151–152
    body image, 151
    eating disorders, 152
    weight pressures, 151
Mom in the Mirror, The (Dena Cabrera), 567
Monroe, Marilyn, 244, 334

Monte Nido Treatment Center, 494
Mood disorders
    anorexia nervosa and, 34
    bulimia nervosa and, 109
Moreno, Jacob Levy, 470
Mortality rates, 361–362, 568
    anorexia nervosa, 34, 125, 215, 362,
        464, 465
    bulimia nervosa, 362, 465
    eating disorders, 323, 361–362, 568
Moss, Kate, 244
Motivational interviewing, 363–364
    eating disorder treatment, 363–364,
        388, 572
    males with eating disorders and, 574
    Stages of Change model, 363–364
Movies and eating disorders, 365–368
    documentaries, 367
    professional actors, 366–367
    See also names of specific actors, actresses,
        and films; Celebrities and eating
        disorders; Media
Muscle Appearance Satisfaction Scale, 185,
    372
Muscle dysmorphia, 73, 95, 275, 332,
    369–373
    action figures and, 371
    behavioral symptoms, 95
    body image and, 370
    bodybuilders, 73, 95
    case study, 654–655
    cognitive symptoms, 95
    lack of DSM-5 classification, 370
    measuring, 372–373
    mirror checking, 95, 373, 654
    parents and, 371
    peers and, 371
    perfectionism and, 371
    physical consequences, 371
    physique protection, 372, 373
    possible causes, 371
    psychological consequences, 371
    social/recreational consequences,
        371–372
    treatment, 655
    See also Bigorexia; Body image
        dissatisfaction; Body image in males;
        Drive for muscularity; Masculinity
        ideals

Muscle Dysmorphia Inventory, 372–373
Muscularity, 331
  See also Drive for muscularity; Muscle dysmorphia
Music therapy, 493
MyPlate, 392
MyPyramid, 392
Myth of the "Freshman 15," **374–378**
  alcohol consumption, 376
  communal dining, 375
  contradictory evidence, 376
  dietary freedom, 375
  eating disorders and obesity, 377–378
  fast food and vending machines, 375
  physical activity, 376
  prevention, 378
  stress, 377
  weight dissatisfaction, 377

National Association for Males with Eating Disorders, 15, 673
National Association of Anorexia Nervosa and Associated Disorders, 14, 673
National Athletic Trainers' Association, 48–49
National Eating Disorders Association, 322, **381–382**, 390, 673
  criticism of television shows about eating disorders, 560, 561
  formation, 286
National Eating Disorders Awareness Week, 286, 381, 458, 542
National Institutes of Health, 445, 674
Neurofeedback, **382–384**
  complementary therapy, 383
  goal, 382
  professional standards, 384
  typical session, 383–384
  See also Biofeedback
Neuroticism, eating disorders and, 429
Nia, **384–385**
  eating disorder treatment, 208, 209, 210, 385
  forms and principles, 384
Night Eating Questionnaire, 386–387
Night eating syndrome, **385–387**
  assessing, 386–387
  DSM-IV-TR exclusion, 191

DSM-5 other specified feeding or eating disorder, 385
  obesity, 385, 386
  prevalence, 386
  proposed diagnostic criteria, 386
Nissen fundoplication, 506
Normal eating, 301
Noxious stimuli, 670
  exposure therapy and, 443
Nutrition treatment approaches, **387–395**
  anorexia nervosa-specific, 390–391
  binge eating disorder-specific, 391
  bulimia nervosa-specific, 391
  calorie counting, 392–393
  determining target weight range, 393–394
  eating disorder clients, 390
  exercise and, 395
  intuitive eating, 393
  meal planning, 391–392
  MyPlate, 392
  nutrition assessment, 390
  registered dieticians, 387, 390
  ultimate goals, 390
  weight restoration techniques, 394
Nutritional deficiencies, **395–397**
  calcium, 396
  electrolytes, 395–396
  iron, 397
  thiamine (vitamin B1), 396
  vitamin C, 397
  vitamin D, 396
  zinc, 397
  See also specific eating disorders

Obama, Michelle, 327, 400
Obamacare. *See* Patient Protection and Affordable Care Act
Obesity, **399–401**
  adults, U.S., 399
  binge eating disorder and, 401, 659
  biological factors, 399
  black women, U.S. non-Hispanic, 399
  BMI as poor indicator, 633
  causes, 399–400
  children, U.S., 399
  eating disorders and, 400–401
  emotional eating and, 201
  family-based treatment, 400

Fijians, 252–253
food insecurity and, 267
genetic factors, 399
health concerns, 448
leptin and, 326
lifestyle factors, 399
night eating syndrome and, 385, 386
prevalence, 399
prevention, 400, 461
puberty and, 475
risks for children, 630
screen time and, 399–400
treatment, 400
Uganda, 267
See also Obesity rates
Obesity rates, 598
adolescent, 629, 632
child, 629, 632
See also Obesity
Objectification theory, **402–404**
sexualization of body, 402
See also Media; Self-objectification
Obligatory exercise, **405–406**, 614
drive for thinness, 405
eating-disordered behaviors, 405–406
motivational drive, 406
sense of control, 406
Oblivobesity, 630
Observing self, 2–3
Obsessive-compulsive disorder (OCD), 37,
407–409
anorexia nervosa and, 407, 409
bulimia nervosa and, 407
differences with eating disorders, 409
DSM-5 classification, 407
eating disorder severity and, 408
eating disorders and, 407–408
ego-dystonic disorder, 409
perfectionism and, 408
similarities with eating disorders,
408–409
Obsessive-compulsive personality disorder,
431
anorexia nervosa and, 432
perfectionism and, 432
Off the C.U.F.F., **410–411**, 426, 461
evaluation, 411
Oligomenorrhea, **411–412**
health consequences, 412

management, 412
primary cause, 411
Olsen, Mary Kate, 120, 559
Operation Beautiful, **413**, 542
Orthorexia nervosa, 191, 287, **414–415**,
634–639
anorexia nervosa comparisons, 635–636
at-risk groups, 415
medical complications, 635
obsessive-compulsive disorder and, 639
perceived as eating disorder, 635–637
perceived as healthy eating, 638–639
potential eating disorder risk factor, 637
prevalence, 414–415
versus other eating disorders, 414
Orthostatic hypotension, 342–343, 670
dehydration, 154
ORTO-15 questionnaire, 638
Osbourne, Sharon, 107
Osteopenia, 44–45, 345
anorexia nervosa and, 416
female athlete triad and, 240–241
Osteoporosis, 345, **415–417**
in advanced age, 415
amenorrhea and, 415
anorexia nervosa and, 415, 416
calcium supplementation, 416–417
exercise, 417
hormone therapy, 416
prevalence in eating-disordered
individuals, 416
treatment, 416–417
weight restoration therapy, 416
See also Female athlete triad
Other specified feeding or eating disorder
(*DSM-5*), 41, 166, 385
night eating syndrome, 385
Overcoming Binge Eating (Christopher
Fairburn), 135–136, 137
See also Cognitive behavioral therapy
guided self-help treatment
Overeaters Anonymous (OA), 192,
417–418, 576–577, 659, 674
Overeating
aging and, 24
fat bias and, 235, 236
food addiction and, 256
See also Binge eating; Binge eating
disorder; Bulimia nervosa;

Disinhibiting eating; Myth of the
"Freshman 15"; Obesity; Overeaters
Anonymous
Overexercise, 24, 614, 616
    See also Exercise, compulsive; Exercise,
    dysfunctional; Exercise addiction;
    Exercise dependence
Overtraining. See Obligatory exercise
Overweight rates, 233, 598

Page, Bettie, 244
Paleo Diet, 222, **419**
Panic attacks and panic disorder, 36, 37
    DSM-5, 36
Parentectomy, 14
Parenteral nutrition, 394
Parents, **421–426**
    of adult daughter with eating disorder,
        422–424
    child and teen body image and, 421
    child and teen eating disorders/restraint
        and, 421, 468
    eating disorder education, 426, 499
    father weight talk and dieting impact on
        child, 424, 468, 499
    impact of child's eating disorder on, 423,
        425–426, 468, 499
    mother weight talk and dieting impact
        on child, 421, 424, 468, 499
    parenting style and child eating
        disorders, 421, 468
    treatment-related financial concerns, 425
    weight teasing, 421, 424–425, 499
Patient Protection and Affordable Care Act
    eating disorder coverage, 322, 324
Pavlov, Ivan, 132, 214
Pavlovian learning, 214
Peak motivational states, 403
Peers
    adolescent relationships, 7–8
    body image and, 78
    thin ideal and, 245
    See also specific sports
Perfectionism
    aerobics instructors, 17
    athletes, 540
    child sexual abuse history and, 565
    conscientious, 21
    depression and anxiety and, 126

diabetes and eating disorders and, 160,
    161
eating disorders and, 23, 427, 501, 517,
    527, 565
low self-esteem and, 427, 430
resiliency risk factor, 497
self-evaluative, 21
self-oriented, 427
socially prescribed, 427
    See also Aesthetic sports; Anorexia nervosa;
    Emotional eating; Exercise dependence;
    Muscle dysmorphia; Obsessive-
    compulsive disorder; Obsessive-
    compulsive personality disorder
Perimolysis, 155, 156, 670
Personality characteristics, **427–430**
    achievement orientation, 427, 428–429
    dichotomous thinking, 427, 429
    maturity fears, 428
    need for approval, 429–430
    neuroticism, 429
    See also specific eating disorders;
    Impulsivity; Interoceptive awareness,
    eating disorders and poor;
    Perfectionism
Personality disorders, **431–432**
    bulimia nervosa and, 109
    dialectical behavior therapy, 432
    DSM-5 category, 431
    treatment implications for eating
        disorders, 432
    types, 431
    See also specific eating disorders;
    Borderline personality disorder;
    Impulsivity; Obsessive-compulsive
    personality disorder
Physical Self-Perception Profile, 435
Physical self-perceptions, **433–436**
    assessment, 435–434
    binge eating and negative, 435
    bulimic symptoms and negative, 435
    enhancement strategies, 435–436
    female, 433
    physical activity and, 435–436
    physical attractiveness, 433–434
    physical competence, 434
    physique control and eating behaviors,
        434–435
    sex differences, 434

Pica, **437**
    DSM-5 classification, 437
    intellectual disability and, 437
    pregnant women and, 437
    risk factors, 437
    rumination disorder and, 504, 505
    treatment, 437
Picky eating, 51, **438–444**, 667
    abnormal breastfeeding behaviors and,
        442
    adults, 442–443
    anorexia nervosa and, 442
    anxiety disorders and, 442
    behavioral training, 443
    case study, 656–657
    children, 442, 443
    children with autism, 443
    cognitive behavioral therapy, 444
    DSM-5 avoidant/restrictive food intake
        disorder, 438
    exposure therapy, 443
    versus food phobia, 262
    versus selective eating disorder, 287
    treatment approaches, 441, 443–444,
        656–657
    See also Food phobia; Selective eating
        disorder
Pinterest, body control/body shame and,
    531
Planet Health, 401, **444–445**
    evaluation, 445
    goal, 444
Plus-size models and clothing, **446–448**
    eating disorders, 447–448
    fashion industry clothing sizing and, 446
    redefining term "plus size," 446–447
    See also names of plus size models
Polizzi, Nicole "Snooki," 124–125
Pomers, Scarlett, 559
Pope, Harrison, 95
Post-traumatic stress disorder, **449–451**
    binge eating disorder and, 450
    bulimia nervosa and, 450, 565
    bullying and teasing and, 450
    combat veterans and military personnel,
        449, 450
    domestic violence witnesses and
        survivors, 449
    emotional abuse and, 450

eating disorders and, 449–450, 565
    first responders, 450
    losing parent while child/teen and, 450
    military sexual assault/harassment
        survivors, 450
    parental separation/discord witnesses,
        450
    physical abuse and, 450
    prevalence, 565
    sexual assault survivors, 449, 450
    somatic experiencing, 534
    substance abusers, 450–451
    symptoms, 449, 565
    treatment, 451
Postpartum depression, eating disorders
    and, 456
Power lifting, 588
Pregnancy, **452–457**
    body dissatisfaction case study, 653–654
    body dissatisfaction during and
        postpartum, 453, 456–457
    body esteem, 75
    body image and weight gain, 454
    body image during and postpartum, 24,
        453, 456–457
    celebrity fixation with ideal body, 452
    cosmetic surgery postpartum, 456–457
    eating disorders and, 291, 453
    effects of eating disorders on, 455–456
    effects of on eating disorders, 454–455
    mirror checking, 653
    physiological changes, 452–453
    pica, 437
    postpartum treatment, 653–654
    See also Anorexia nervosa; Bulimia
        nervosa; Infertility; Postpartum
        depression, eating disorders and
Prevention, **457–461**
    primary, 458
    secondary, 458
    See also Prevention programs, eating
        disorder
Prevention programs, eating disorder
    family-based, 460–461
    history of, 139–140, 459
    Internet-based, 460
    lack of, 458–459
    limitations, 460
    most effective, 459–460

need for male, 460
psychoeducation-based, 140
risk reduction, 140
school-based, 460
See also Cognitive dissonance
interventions; Healthy Buddies;
Full of Ourselves; Off the C.U.F.F.;
Prevention; Student Bodies
Pro-ana, websites/online communities,
105, 287, 298–299, 336, **462–463**,
640, 641, 644
body dissatisfaction, 641
content, 462–463
dangers and impact, 463
parent education, 463
self-presentation theory and, 518
social contagion theory and, 527
See also Pro-eating disorder websites,
treatment and; Pro-mia, websites/
online communities; Wannarexia;
Wannarexic
Pro-eating disorder websites, treatment
and, 640–645
cons, 642, 644–645
pros, 641–642
See also Pro-ana, websites/online
communities; Pro-mia, websites/
online communities
Pro-mia, websites/online communities, 287,
298, 299, 462, 640, 641, 644, 670
social contagion theory and, 527
See also Pro-ana, websites/online
communities; Pro-eating disorder
websites, treatment and
Prognosis, **464–465**, 670
anorexia nervosa, 464
bulimia nervosa, 464–465
See also Recovery; Relapse
Project HEAL, 15, 558, 560, 670
Protective factors, **465–468**
authoritative parenting style, 468
close family and friends, 466, 467–468
connectedness with parent(s), 467
good emotional regulation, 466
high self-esteem, 466
limited media exposure, 466
non-abusive childhood, 466
physical health, 466, 467
positive home environment, 467

positive role models, 468
positive spirituality, 466, 467
problem solving ability and coping
skills, 466
psychosocial functioning, 466–467
resiliency, 466, 495–500
social connections and skills, 467
social support, 467
stress management skills, 466
Pseudo-Bartter's syndrome, 179, 339
Psychodrama, **468–471**
anorexia nervosa therapy, 471
bulimia nervosa therapy, 471
eating disorder therapy, 470
Psychodynamic psychotherapy, **472–474**
eating disorders, 473–474
effectiveness, 473
elements, 472–473
Psychotherapy, traditional talk, 293
adolescents with eating disorders, 128
rumination disorder and, 506
See also Client-centered therapy
Puberty, 4–5, **474–476**
adrenarche, 4–5
changes and body image, 475
early maturing females, 475
early maturing males, 476
female body dissatisfaction, 475
female sexual development, 5
gonadarche, 5
late maturing males, 476
male body dissatisfaction, 476
male sexual development, 5
menarche, 5, 474
obesity, 475
precocious, 475
spermarche, 5
Purging, **476–478**
anorexia nervosa, 477
bulimia nervosa, 477
disordered eating, 477
diuretic and laxative abuse prevalence,
477
health consequences, 477
methods, 476
prevalence, 477
prevention, 477–478
See also specific sports; Anorexia nervosa;
Bulimia nervosa; Cutting weight

Quaid, Dennis, 120
Quetelet, Adolphe, 99, 628
Quetelet Index, 99, 628

Rabe, Bahne, 35
Raisin meditation, 292
Ramos, Eliana, 356, 358, 359
Ramos, Luisel, 356, 358, 359
Rational Emotive Behavior Therapy, 133
Recovery, **479**, 646–651
  anorexia nervosa, 647
  binge eating disorder, 648
  bulimia nervosa, 647, 648
  hope and, 651
  medical model, 646, 647, 648, 650, 651
  multiple paths, 651
  partial, 479, 646
  recovery-oriented approach, 650–651
  SAMHSA definition, 650
  twelve-step model, 648–649
  See also names of specific eating disorders;
    Relapse; Self-Care; Treatment
Recreational therapy, 493
Refeeding syndrome, 338–339, 391,
  480–483
  anorexia nervosa and, 34
  complications, 480
  edema, 194
  electrolyte imbalance, 199
  management of at-risk clients, 482–483
  post-WWII POWs and concentration
    camp survivors, 481
  prevalence, 482
  refeeding guidelines, 482
  risk factors, 481
  signs/symptoms of complications,
    481–482
  thiamine deficiency, 482
  See also Hypokalemia; Hypomagnesemia;
    Hypophosphatemia; Minnesota
    Starvation Experiment
Referring someone for eating disorder
  treatment, **483–485**
  strategies, 484
  victim denial, 484
  voluntary versus involuntary, 484–485
Reflections, **485–486**
Relapse, **486–489**
  anorexia nervosa, 489

body image and, 487–489
bulimia nervosa, 489
eating disorders rate, 649
exercise in treatment and, 620
guilt and, 488
patient prognosis and, 465
predictors for eating disorders, 486, 489
prevention, 489
pro-eating disorder website exposure
  and, 645
treatment experience dissatisfaction and,
  489
Relational therapy, 572
Religion, **490–491**
  negative influence on body image and
    eating disorders, 491
  no influence on body image, 491
  positive influence on body image and
    eating disorders, 490–491
Remuda Ranch treatment center, 573
Renfrew Center, xxiv, 286, 388, 574
Resch, Elyse, 301
Residential treatment, 328, **492–495**, 571
  challenges, 494–495
  common therapies, 493
  continuous monitoring, 492
  cost, 494
  counseling focus, 492
  current trends, 492–493
  discharge planning, 492
  effectiveness, 493–494
  males, 494–495
  number of U.S. centers, 492–493
  supervised meals and snacks, 492
Resiliency, **495–500**
  belief in self-control over weight, 498
  body image satisfaction, 497
  conception of ideal body, 498
  coping strategies, 498, 499
  model for women, 498–499
  parental relationships, 498
  physical self-concept, 498, 499
  process view, 496–497
  sense of holistic balance and wellness,
    498, 499
  sex role satisfaction, 498–499
  strategies for promoting body image,
    499–500
  trait view, 496

view of beauty and, 498
See also Parents; Recovery
Reston, Ana, 356, 358–359
Restricting, food. *See* Anorexia nervosa;
  Avoidant/restrictive food intake
  disorder; Orthorexia nervosa; Picky
  eating; Selective eating disorder;
  Visceral sensitivity
Revised Restraint Scale, 173–174
Reward-sensitivity, 289
Rigby, Cathy, 276
Risk factors, **500–502**
  duration, 501
  examples, 501–502
  identification problems, 501
  intensity, 501
  timing, 501
Roberts, Julia, 26
Rogers Memorial Hospital, 574
Role playing
  family therapy and, 230
  See also Assertiveness training;
    Psychodrama; Reflections
Romberg, Luci, 117–118
Rooted Recovery, 11–13, 14
Rosas, Carlos, 384
Rosas, Debbie, 384
Rosewood Centers for Eating Disorders,
  567, 573
Rowing, **502–503**
  disordered eating and eating disorders
    in, 202, 275, 503
  endurance sport, 201
  females, 502–503
  lightweight, 623
  males, 502, 503
  weight pressures, 202
Rumination disorder, **504–506**
  developmental disabilities and autism,
    505
  DSM-5 criteria, 504–505
  frequency, 505
  health effects and risks, 504, 505
  infants and young children, 504–505
  pica and, 504, 505
  ROME Committee, 505
  secrecy as barrier to treatment, 502
  signs and symptoms, 505
  treatment, 506

See also names of specific treatments;
  Nissen fundoplication
Runners' high, 211
Running. *See* Distance running
Russell, Gerald, 165
Russell's sign, 347

Sanchez, Emanuel Jose, 311
Santé Center for Healing, 573–574
Schaeffer, Eric, 561
Schenk, Erica, 446, 447
Schwarzenegger, Arnold, 23, 100, 187
Second Sex, The (Simone de Beauvoir), 64
Selective eating disorder, 287, **509–510**
  autism spectrum disorder and, 509
  consequences, 509–510
  DSM-IV-TR omission, 191
  DSM-5, 287, 509
  versus picky eating, 287
  prevalence, 509
  symptoms, 509
Seles, Monica, 59
Self, development of, 8–9
Self-awareness, body image and, 78
Self-care, **510–511**
  eating disorders and, 511
Self-esteem, 74
  body image and, 78
  eating disorders and, 429–430
  emotional eating and, 200
  male body image programs, 97
Self Esteem Scale, Rosenberg's, 294
Self-evaluative perfectionism, 21
Self-help interventions, **511–514**
  anorexia nervosa and, 513–514
  benefits, 514
  binge eating disorder and, 513, 514
  bulimia nervosa and, 512–513, 514
  cognitive behavioral therapy guided self-
    help, 512–513
  drawbacks, 514
  guided, 512
  pure, 512
  results for eating disorders, 512–514
  versus traditional psychotherapy, 511
  web-based treatment and prevention
    programs, 298, 299–300
Self-injury, **515–516**
  anorexia nervosa and, 516

bulimia nervosa and, 516
child sexual abuse and, 547
cutting, 169, 229, 515, 546–547
eating disorders and, 515, 516
mental illness and, 515
suicide risk, 546–547
therapy, 169
Self-objectification, 402–403
media and, 403–404
men, 404
psychological consequences, 403
women, 403
Self-presentation theory, **517–519**
controversy about eating disorders, 519
See also Social anxiety disorder; Social
physique anxiety
Self-silencing, 8
Sensation-seeking tendencies, disordered-
eating behaviors and, 428
Separation-individuation theory, 7
Sexual abuse, child
body alienation and, 64
body dissatisfaction and, 565
eating disorders and, 501, 545, 564–565
impulsivity and, 565
late-onset eating disorders and, 318
perfectionism and, 565
self-injury and, 547
See also Post-traumatic stress disorder;
Trauma
Sexual assault, PTSD and, 449, 450
See also Sexual abuse, child
Sexual identity, case study of body image
and, 663–664
Sexual promiscuity, bulimia nervosa and,
109
Sexual trauma, bulimia nervosa and, 109
Sexualization messages, internalization of
body dissatisfaction and, 558
body dissatisfaction and male, 559
Shapiro, Francine, 217
Sialadenosis, 670
bulimia nervosa and, 157
Sibling with eating disorder, interview with
sister of, 227–229
Silverstein, Jamie, 248
Simmons, Richard, 16
Sizeism, 599, 670
Sizes, women's clothing

average American woman, 446, 447
fashion industry sizing, 446
See also Average American Woman
project; Plus-size models and clothing
Sjostrom, Lisa, 268
Ski jumping, **520**
anorexia athletica in, 30
anorexia nervosa in, 35
eating disorder risk in, 623
eating disorders in, 538
gravitational sport, 538, 623
weight pressures, 520
See also Anorexic rule
Skin tone, **521–522**
body dissatisfaction, 521
cultural influences, 521, 551
skin bleaching, 521–522
See also Africa, body image in; Japan,
body image in
Skinner, B. F., 132
Smith, Bob, 576
Snapchat, 528, 531
Soccer, 538, 553
Social anxiety, appearance-specific. *See*
Social physique anxiety
Social anxiety disorder
anorexia nervosa and, 517
bulimia nervosa and, 517
eating disorders and, 517–518
See also Self-presentation theory; Social
physique anxiety
Social comparison theory, **523–525**
Barbie and, 523–524
body dissatisfaction, 524–525
body dysmorphic disorder, 524
boys and men, 524–525
downward comparisons, 523, 530
girls and women, 523–524
media images, 523–525
muscle building behavior, 524
social media usage, 530–531
upward comparisons, 523, 530–531
Social contagion theory, **525–527**
eating disorders, 526–527
mental illness symptoms, 525–526
sense of community, 527
sorority binge eating behavior, 526
treatment implications, 527
versus self-selection, 526

Social media and eating disorders, **528–531**
  differences among platforms, 531
  prevalence of use, 528
  research, 529–530
  social comparison theory and, 530–531
  versus other media, 529
  See also Facebook; Instagram; Pinterest,
    body control/body shame and;
    Snapchat; Twitter
Social phobia, 37
Social physique anxiety, 37, 518, **532–533**
  assessment, 533
  self-presentation, 532
Social Physique Anxiety Scale, 533
Somatic experiencing, **534–535**
  See also Post-traumatic stress disorder;
    Trauma
Somatomorphic matrix, 185–186, 372
Sorenson, Jackie, 16
Sorority Body Image Program. *See*
    Reflections
Sorority women, **536**
  binge eating behavior, 526, 536
  dieting, 536
  social contagion theory and, 526
  See also Reflections
South America, body image in, 88
  cosmetic surgery and, 88
South Beach Diet, 221
Spears, Britney, 26
Speed skating, 201
Spelt, Jeanine, 287
Sport Fitness International, 16
Sportaerobics, 16
Sports, **537–541**
  disordered eating in lean versus nonlean,
    537–538
  prevalence of eating disorders, 537–539
  *See also names of specific sports, categories
    of sports, and athletes*; Athletes, eating
    disorder risk in; Athletes, eating
    disorders and; Weight manipulation;
    Weight pressures in sport
Sports, combat, 590–591
  See also Judo; Martial arts; Weight class
    sports; Weight manipulation
Sports, gravitational
  eating disorder risk, 622, 623–624
  eating disorders, 538

See also Cross-country skiing; Distance
    running; Ski jumping
Sports, lean
  disordered eating in nonlean versus,
    537–538
  See also Dancing; Distance running;
    Diving; Gymnastics; Wrestling
Sports, nonlean
  disordered eating in lean versus,
    537–538
  See also Basketball; Soccer; Swimming;
    Track and field
Sports Illustrated swimsuit edition, 553
Stages of Change model. *See* Motivational
    interviewing
Starving in Suburbia, 368
Steiner-Adair, Catherine, 268
Stepdaughter, The (Caroline Blackwood), 106
Street dancers, body satisfaction and, 153
Structured Clinical Interview, 42
Structured Interview for Anorexic and
    Bulimic Syndromes for *DSM-IV* and
    ICD-10, 42
Student Bodies, 460
Students Promoting Eating Disorder
    Awareness and Knowledge (SPEAK),
    542–543
  outreach projects, 542–543
  research efforts, 543
Stunkard, Albert, 247
  binge eating studies and report, 59
Substance abuse, **543–545**
  anorexia nervosa and, 544
  bulimia nervosa and, 109, 544, 545,
    564
  case study of eating disorder with
    alcohol abuse, 662–663
  comorbidity between eating disorders
    and, 544–545
  impulsivity and, 289, 362, 428
  neurotransmitters, 648
  risk factors for eating disorders and, 544
  self-injury and, 515
  sexual abuse history and, 545, 564
  treatment, 158, 364
  treatment for comorbid eating disorders
    and, 142, 169, 545
  weak visceral sensitivity and, 583
Sugar addiction, 256, 670

Suicide, **546–547**
adolescent, 546
anorexia nervosa and, 286, 362, 464, 547
body dysmorphic disorder and, 72, 73
bulimia nervosa and, 362, 547
causes, 546
prevalence, 546
veterans, 352
See also Relapse; Self-injury
Surviving an Eating Disorder (Michele Siegel, Judith Brisman, and Margot Weinshel), 106
Swansea Muscularity Attitudes Questionnaire, 372
Swimming and synchronized swimming, **548–549**
body image and disordered eating in, 202, 538, 548–549
endurance sport, 201, 548
nonlean sport, 538, 548
swim suits and weight pressure in, 595
synchronized swimming, 548
weight pressures, 202, 595

Talk therapy. *See* Client-centered therapy; Psychotherapy, traditional talk
Talking to Eating Disorders (Jeanne Albronda Heaton and Claudia Strauss), 106
Tanning behaviors and body image, **551–552**
gay males, 551
Tanorexia. *See* Tanning behaviors and body image
Tardive anorexia, 318
Target weight range, determining, 393–394
BMI, 393
Hamwi equation, 393
Metropolitan Life Insurance weight charts, 393–394
Team sports, **552–555**
anorexia nervosa in, 553
benefits of participation, 554–555
bulimia nervosa in, 553
eating disorders in individual sports versus, 553
peer influence and eating disorders, 554
team subculture and eating disorders, 554

team subculture and uniforms, 554
weight pressures, 553–554
See also specific team sports; Athletes, eating disorder risk and; Athletes, eating disorders and
Teasing, 112–113, **555–556**
adolescent, 556
BMI report cards and, 632
disordered eating and eating disorders and, 112–113, 556
family, 498
friends, 498
parents, 421, 424–425, 499
prevention, 556
PTSD and, 450
sex differences, 556
Television programs and eating disorders, 252–253, **557–562**
actors and actresses, 558–559
body image, 252, 253, 335
Degrassi, 558, 560
eating disorder as subject, 558
Glee, 558, 559–560
Gossip Girl, 558
masculine body ideal, 559
Starved, 560–561
Starving Secrets, 561
See also Fiji study; Media; Thin ideal; Ultrathin ideal
Therapeutic massage/touch therapy, 292–293
Therapeutic recreation, **563**
Therapies, eating disorder. *See specific eating disorders, therapies, and treatment approaches*; Referring someone for eating disorder treatment; Treatment
Thin (HBO), 367
Thin ideal, 83, 113, 121
aging and, 23–24
anorexia nervosa and, 93
body image disturbances and internalization of, 245
bulimia nervosa and, 93
diet industry, 233
disordered eating behaviors and internalization of, 245
female athlete triad and, 240
internalization of, 245, 366, 558
media and, 233, 245, 403, 466
Mexico, 89

social comparison theory and, 523–524

television and internalization of, 558

television programs and, 233, 558

See also Ultrathin ideal

Thinking self, 2

Thinspirations, 299, 336, 368, 462, 641

Thintervention, 233

Thornton, Billy Bob, 120

Thought Field Therapy, 293

Three Factor Eating Questionnaire, 174

Thyroid hormone, 344–345, 670

Toddlers and Tiaras, 79

Toronto Alexithymia Scale, 28

Track and field, 538

Transcendental meditation, 292

Trauma, **564–565**

  adult sexual victimization, 565

  anorexia nervosa, 34, 564

  bulimia nervosa, 564

  child emotional abuse, 126, 228, 450, 564, 565

  child physical abuse, 223, 439, 450, 564, 565

  child sexual abuse, 64, 318, 501, 545, 547, 564–565

  exposure to violence, 565

  late-onset, 318

  POW experiences, 565

  See also Post-traumatic stress disorder; Trauma-focused therapies

Trauma-focused therapies

  residential treatment centers, 493

  somatic experiencing, 534–535

Treating Bodies Across the Globe, 543

Treatment, **566–575**

  adult women, 574

  athletes, 573

  behavioral health department state-licensed, 568

  children, 440

  cost and financial concerns, 425, 574–575

  counseling approaches, 572

  family and couples counseling, 570

  family involvement in child's, 568

  group counseling, 570

  health insurance coverage, 569, 574–575

  individual therapy, 566, 570

  Joint Commission accredited, 568

  late-onset, 568

  levels of care, 328, 492, 570–571

  low-cost alternatives, 575

  males, 573–574

  multidisciplinary team approach, 568, 573

  new mothers, 569

  parents, 569

  recognizing symptoms, 569

  when to seek, 567–568

  See also names of specific eating disorders, therapies, and level of treatment; Hospitalization; Nutrition treatment approaches; Referring someone for eating disorder treatment; Twelve-step programs

Treatment, outpatient, 328, 492, 570–571

  bulimia nervosa, 571

  intensive, 571

Tribole, Evelyn, 301

Trigger foods, emotional eating and, 200

Truth in Advertising Act of 2014, 323

Turlington, Christy, 26

Turner, Chevese, 63

Twelve-step programs, 575, **576–577**

  benefits, 577

  "in recovery" model, 648–649

  See also Anorexics and Bulimics Anonymous; Eating Disorders Anonymous; Overeaters Anonymous

21st Century Cures Act, 323, 324

Twiggy, 244, 335

Twitter, 231

UConn Rudd Center on Food Policy and Obesity, 233, 237

Ultrathin ideal

  America's Next Top Model, 244

  ballet, 55

  body image, 245

  disordered eating, 245

  eating disorders and internalization of, 528

  See also Thin ideal

Universal Dance Association, 183

Universal Dance Camps, 183

Valued living, 3

Veale, de Coverley, 211

Vegetarianism, 221, **579–580**
  anorexics, 33, 397
  eating disorder treatment implications, 579–580
  eating disorders, 579
  India, 86
  vitamin and mineral deficiencies, 397, 579
Virtual reality (VR), **580–581**
  body image therapy, 581
  eating disorder treatment, 581
  exposure therapy, 580
  relapse prevention skills and, 580
Visceral sensitivity, **582–585**
  binge eating and, 582
  body dissatisfaction and, 582
  bulimia nervosa and, 582–583
  children, 582, 583
  high BMI scores and, 583
  intuitive eating, 582
  problems studying, 582–583
  restrictive dieting and, 582, 583
  stages, 582
  strengthening strategies, 584
Vitamin deficiencies. *See* Nutritional deficiencies
Volleyball, 553, 554

Walsh, Nancy, 368, 561
Wannarexia, **587**
  See also Wannarexic
Wannarexic, 518, 527, 645
Wasted (Marya Hornbacher), 104, 105
Wasting disease, 285
Water polo, 201
Watson, John, 132
Wayne, John, 187
Websites, pro-eating disorder. *See* Pro-ana, websites/online communities; Pro-eating disorder websites, treatment and; Pro-mia, websites/online communities
Weight class sports, **588–589**
  anorexia nervosa, 35
  coaches, 589
  disordered eating behaviors, 589
  eating disorder risk, 622, 623
  eating disorders, 538
  pathogenic weight control methods, 589
  teammates, 589

  training for weight, 588
  See also Bodybuilding; Boxing; Martial arts; Rowing; Weight lifting; Wrestling
Weight Implicit Associations Test, 236
Weight lifting, 588, 623
Weight manipulation, **589–592**
  combat sports, 590
  deaths, 590
  methods, 589, 590
  obesity post-sports career, 592
  physical and psychological consequences, 591
  wrestling, 590
Weight pressures in sport, **592–598**
  coaches, 592, 593, 594–595
  eating disorder prevalence, 592–593
  family, 592, 593
  judges, 592, 593, 595
  media, 592, 593
  peers, 592
  perceived performance advantage, 595, 596
  self-pressure, 593
  sport subculture norms, 592, 593
  teammates, 592, 593, 595
  uniforms, 592, 593, 595–596
  weight requirements, 596
  See also specific sports and types of sports
Weight restoration techniques, 394
  osteoporosis and, 416
  See also Refeeding syndrome
Weight stigma, 63, **598–602**
  adolescents, 601
  adults, 601
  anxiety and depression, 598
  binge eating disorder, 63
  causes, 601–602
  children, 601
  coping strategies, 600
  effects, 602
  health promotion efforts, 600
  media, 599, 600
  medical settings, 601
  parents, 600
  underweight bias, 602
  work environment, 600–601
  See also Fat bias/fat discrimination; Weight teasing, weight-related
Wernicke's encephalopathy, 396, 482

Wilson, Bill, 576
Wilson, Rebel, 367
Winfrey, Oprah, 119
Winslet, Kate, 26
Wisdom eating, 301
Women's Sports Foundation, 554
World Health Organization, 99, 233, 357,
    674
Wrestling, **603–604**
    anorexia nervosa in, 35
    bulimia nervosa in, 604
    cutting weight, 590, 596, 623
    disordered eating and eating disorders
        in, 275, 538, 604
    lean sport, 537
    rapid weight loss strategies, 603, 604, 623
    weight class sport, 538, 588, 589, 623
    weight-loss related deaths, 604, 623
    weight requirements pressure, 596

Yoga, **607–609**
    adolescents with eating disorders, 128
    benefits for eating disorder treatments,
        608

eating-disorder knowledgeable
    instructors, 609
eating disorder patients, 208–209, 210
family therapy, 230
mirror checking, 608
neurotransmitter effects, 607
residential treatment centers, 493
self-care stress reduction strategy, 510,
    664
treatment challenges, 608
visceral sensitivity training, 584
Yoyo weight cycling, emotional eating and,
    200, 665

Zinc, **611–612**
    anorexia nervosa and deficiency of,
        397
    bulimia nervosa and deficiency of, 397
    supplementation as eating disorder
        treatment, 611–612
    taste test, 611
Zucker, Nancy, 410
Zumba, eating disorder patients and, 208,
    209, 210